Mahakavi K. V. Simon

Mahakavi K. V. Simon

The Milton of the East

Varghese Mathai

BLOOMSBURY ACADEMIC
NEW YORK • LONDON • OXFORD • NEW DELHI • SYDNEY

BLOOMSBURY ACADEMIC
Bloomsbury Publishing Inc, 1385 Broadway, New York, NY 10018, USA
Bloomsbury Publishing Plc, 50 Bedford Square, London, WC1B 3DP, UK
Bloomsbury Publishing Ireland, 29 Earlsfort Terrace, Dublin 2, D02 AY28, Ireland

BLOOMSBURY, BLOOMSBURY ACADEMIC and the Diana logo
are trademarks of Bloomsbury Publishing Plc

First published in the United States of America 2024
Paperback edition published 2025

Copyright © Varghese Mathai, 2024

For legal purposes the List of Figures and Acknowledgments on pp. ix and xviii–xx
constitute an extension of this copyright page.

Cover design: Eleanor Rose
Cover image: Noah releasing the dove. Detail from a mosaic in
Basilica di San Marco, Venice, Italy, 12th-13th century
© CPA Media Pte Ltd / Alamy

All rights reserved. No part of this publication may be: i) reproduced or transmitted in any form, electronic or mechanical, including photocopying, recording or by means of any information storage or retrieval system without prior permission in writing from the publishers; or ii) used or reproduced in any way for the training, development or operation of artificial intelligence (AI) technologies, including generative AI technologies. The rights holders expressly reserve this publication from the text and data mining exception as per Article 4(3) of the Digital Single Market Directive (EU) 2019/790.

Bloomsbury Publishing Inc does not have any control over, or responsibility for, any third-party websites referred to or in this book. All internet addresses given in this book were correct at the time of going to press. The author and publisher regret any inconvenience caused if addresses have changed or sites have ceased to exist, but can accept no responsibility for any such changes.

Library of Congress Cataloging-in-Publication Data
Names: Mattāyi, Vargīs, 1953- author. | Saimaṇ, Ke. Vi., 1883–1944.
Vēdavihāraṃ. English.
Title: Mahakavi K.V. Simon : the Milton of the East / Varghese Mathai.
Description: New York : Bloomsbury Academic, 2023. | Includes
bibliographical references and index. | Summary: "The first English
study of poet K. V. Simon (1883–1944), with sample translations,
including his 12,000-line epic Vedaviharam, and a critical
biography"– Provided by publisher.
Identifiers: LCCN 2023009991 (print) | LCCN 2023009992 (ebook) |
ISBN 9781501388491 (hardback) | ISBN 9781501388538 (paperback) | ISBN
9781501388507 (ebook) | ISBN 9781501388514 (pdf) | ISBN
9781501388521 (ebook other)
Subjects: LCSH: Saimaṇ, Ke. Vi., 1883–1944–Criticism and interpretation.
| Saimaṇ, Ke. Vi., 1883–1944–Translations into English. | Malayalam
poetry–20th century–Translations into English.
Classification: LCC PL4718.9.S313337 Z795 2023 (print) | LCC
PL4718.9.S313337 (ebook) | DDC 894.8/121–dc23/eng/20230510
LC record available at https://lccn.loc.gov/2023009991
LC ebook record available at https://lccn.loc.gov/2023009992

ISBN:	HB:	978-1-5013-8849-1
	PB:	978-1-5013-8853-8
	ePDF:	978-1-5013-8851-4
	eBook:	978-1-5013-8850-7

Typeset by Integra Software Services Pvt. Ltd.

For product safety related questions contact productsafety@bloomsbury.com.

To find out more about our authors and books visit www.bloomsbury.com
and sign up for our newsletters.

Dedicated to
Raj & Ash
Two lights to whom much is lent

Contents

List of Figures	ix
Foreword—Mahakavi K. V. Simon: Kerala's Reformer Laureate	
A. J. Thomas	x
Acknowledgments	xviii
Timeline	xxi
Introduction—Mahakavi K. V. Simon: A Prophetic Legacy	
Reverend Valson Thampu	1

1	The Life and Times of K. V. Simon	9
	An Overview	9
	Simon's Childhood	24
	A Lay Launch of Reform	40
	Debates and Disputations	51
	The Viyojitha Sabha [The Separatists]	73
	Vedaviharam, Simon's Epic Poem	81
	No Good Deed Goes Unpunished	86
	The Last Lap	95
	Resting Where the Cradle Rocked	97
2	Malayalam: K. V. Simon's Language	99
	A Brief History	99
3	Simon's Verse: Selected Pieces	111
	Songs and Hymns	111
	Pahimam Deva Deva [Entreat thee I]	111
	Manuvel Manujasutha [Manuvel, ManSon]	112
	Paadum Ninakku Nityavum [I will sing unto thee all days]	113
	Thenilum Madhuram [Sweeter than honey]	114
	Devajana Samajame [The Gathered Elect]	115
	Amba Yerusalem	116

Poorna Hridaya Seva Venam [Wholly given to serve]	117
Thunga Prathaapamaarnna Sri Yesu [Of glory utmost]	118
Paramaathmaav Ura Cheyyum ["Listen to what the Spirit has to say"]	119
Ariya Babylon Nadikkarike [Exiles on Babel's banks]	120
Nallarin Sundari [Starlet Virgin!]	121
Aadyantamillatha Nityante [Eternal One, to this comely pair]	122
Vandaname Deva! [Honor to thee, Lord]	123
Paadum Paramanu Parichodu [The Song of Moses]	124
Yeshunayaka Sreesha Namo [Jesu, Lord, hail to thee]	125
Salomiye Varikente Priye [Come away, my beloved]	126
Smarna Sabha Doothu [Letter to Smyrna]	126
Sardis Sabha Doothu [Letter to Sardis]	127
Paramadeva Vandana [To the God of gods]	128
Portions from Simon's Epic, *Vedaviharam*	128
Invocation	128
The House of Abraham	153
Jacob's Years in Paddan Aram	164
Wit and Wisdom from *Vedaviharam*	175

4   K. V. Simon and John Milton: Epic Stars of the East and of the West   179
    The Times and Home Grounds of Simon and Milton   184
    Vedaviharam and *Paradise Lost*: Concordant Contents   193
    The Songs of Simon   211
    Simon, a Lover of Peace   230
    A Sage of Letters   232

Appendix   234
Bibliography   239
Index of Key Names and Terms   243

Figures

1.1 Aranmula Vallamkali. The Annual Boat Race of Aranmula. Photograph by Arun Sinha, courtesy of Wikimedia Commons, Creative Commons Attribution 2.0 License. https://commons.wikimedia.org/wiki/Category:Aranmula_Boat_Race#/media/File:Aranmula-boat_race-_Kerala-India-1.jpg   11

1.2 The Puthuppally Orthodox Church. Photograph by Vijayanrajapuram, courtesy of Wikimedia Commons, Creative Commons Attribution-ShareAlike 4.0 International License. https://commons.wikimedia.org/wiki/Category:St._George_Orthodox_Church,_Puthuppally#/media/File:St._George_Orthodox_Church,_Puthuppally_fron_-_side_view.jpg   22

1.3 Tamil David Sketch. From *The San Francisco Call*. [volume], July 10, 1897. Public Domain. Image provided by University of California, Riverside, courtesy of Library of Congress, *Chronicling America: Historic American Newspapers* Collection. https://chroniclingamerica.loc.gov/lccn/sn85066387/1897-07-10/ed-1/seq-3/   30

2.1 Hortus Malabaricus Page. *Hortus Indicus Malabaricus* Volume 1 by Henrik van Reede tot Drakestein, 1678. Public Domain. Image courtesy of Archive.org. https://archive.org/details/Hortus_Indicus_Malabaricus_Volume1/page/n9/mode/2up   104–105

4.1 Banyan Tree. Photography by Delonix, courtesy of Wikimedia Commons, Creative Commons Attribution-Share Alike 3.0 Unported License. Image reproduced without modification. https://commons.wikimedia.org/wiki/File:Banyan_Tree_at_The_Valley_School_,_Bangalore.JPG   182

Foreword
Mahakavi K. V. Simon:
Kerala's Reformer Laureate

A. J. Thomas

Epoch-making visionary poets, polemicists, apologists, and philosophers rise in certain cultural milieux at specific historical junctures. They potentially set in motion a restructuring process of existing belief systems, marking a clear departure from long-established, outdated, or ossified ones. The towering figure of John Milton is an example of this truth with little contest. At the height of his poetic and political career, Milton was the guiding light for the Puritans who wanted stricter discipline in life through the scriptures than what the English Protestants (members of the Church of England who had broken away from the Catholic Church under King Henry VIII)[1] were inclined to settle for.

The early Puritans had advocated Presbyterianism, and non-Episcopal congregations thrived as an expression of the spirit of nonconformity, and independence from an overarching structure. Milton idealized the individual's liberty. His political, social, and religious writings paved the way for the upholding of the ideals of individualism and liberalism which became the cornerstones of British, and gradually, Western culture.

Professor Varghese Mathai's book, *K. V. Simon: The Milton of the East*, introduces to the world another revolutionary poet–reformist who came up in Kerala's Christianity during the period between the late nineteenth century and the first half of the twentieth. He was a Mahakavi (translated as "the Great Poet") in Malayalam, the language of Kerala, the southernmost Indian state. Simon was

---

[1] To illuminate this historical context, allow me a little digression. The Head of the Church of England was the English Crown. From the reign of Elizabeth I who presided over the flowering of the arts and literature during the English Renaissance, her successor James I took up her enlightened policies that brought in the humanistic loosening up of society; the next one in line, Charles I, despite being more authoritarian, had pursued the loose-rein-on-social-life policy of his predecessors. The Puritans were highly critical of the moral and ethical decline in high society, including that of royalty and the courtiers. Even the commoners were no exception. The Puritans believed that the dynamics of the Reformation had been derailed in England under the royals. They grew in so much strength as to stage the Puritan Revolution, execute King Charles I, and set up a republic. Milton took their side after his initial neutral stand.

by all means a Miltonic figure, both in his poetic achievements and his reformist impact. Born in a land half the way around the globe from England, exactly 275 years after the birth of John Milton (1608), his English counterpart, the trajectory of Simon's life was also filled with struggles in nonconformity to the orthodoxy of the Syrian Christian denominations of Kerala.

When considering the revolutionary restructuring of belief systems, what comes to my mind first in the historical context of Indian spiritual traditions are movements such as Jainism and Buddhism in the *Śramaṇa* tradition that made a clean break from the existing Vedic religion of about two and a half millennia ago.[2] The *Śramaṇas* initiated a changeover from Vedic Sanskrit scriptures to vernaculars like the Prākrits and Pāli. This fact is to be specially taken note of, to see how the reformatory action was carried out through the translation or writing of scriptures in people's tongues. Later, the Bhakti (devotional) movements of India—beginning with the Shaivite spiritual revival in Thamizhakam (the present-day state of Tamil Nadu forms a major part of it, with the adjoining Telugu-speaking regions included) between the seventh and ninth centuries—reinvented the ways in which one sought a relationship with the Self, bypassing the structured religion.[3] At the same time, the Sufi movement, which infused spiritual content (through devotional songs and dance leading to trance) into the mostly ritualistic Islam of that period, swept across India. Both the Bhakti and Sufi movements were complementary in many aspects. These movements restructured and reformed the religious aggregations of each era, transcending the existing value systems and social mores.

---

[2] As would be commonly known, Vedic religion was predominantly ritualistic and in the exclusive control of the priestly Brahmins who were at the apex of the *chāturvarṇya*, or the Four Castes. They conducted *yāgās* and anointed kings, establishing their permanent sway over the ruling class, and, power-drunk, had eventually sunk to evil practices. A millennium later, as Buddhism and Jainism began to decline, the Brahminical religion, revived by Adi Shankaracharya, regained sway, and over the next few centuries, it became oppressive through its caste system and marginalization of women and socioeconomically oppressed sections, as evidenced in the *Manusmriti*.

[3] This movement spread to the adjoining Kannada-speaking regions (which now include some of the Telugu-speaking regions as well), as manifested in the Vachana movement (writing of verses that cut through straight to the spirit) of the eleventh century. From there, the Bhakti movement traveled to the neighboring Marathi-speaking regions in Western India, with Jnaneswar and his sister Muktabai, Namdev, and Janabai in the thirteenth century; Chokkamela, in the fourteenth century; Kanhopatra in the fifteenth century; Eknath in the sixteenth century; Tukkaram in the seventeenth century; and others keeping the trail ablaze. The Bhakti movement in the Vraj regions across the Gangetic plains of North India found expression in the mystic poet Sant Kabir, Sarala Dasa of Odisha, and Sant Ravi Das in the fifteenth century and the latter's disciple, the celebrated saint poetess Meerabai, a Rajput princess in the sixteenth century. There are many more saint-poets in this stream, such as Jayadeva of Odisha writing in Sanskrit in the twelfth century), Guru Nanak of Punjab and Sankara Dev of Assam in the fifteenth century, Ezhuthachchan and Poonthanam Namboodiri writing in Malayalam, the language of Kerala, in the sixteenth century.

The most important feature of the Bhakti and Sufi movements and the related religious renaissance was that the scriptures were translated into vernaculars, and in the process, contributed to the development of modern Indian languages such as Malayalam, Tamil, Kannada, Telugu, Marathi, Gujarati, Rajasthani, Punjabi, Odia, Assamese, Bengali, and Urdu. Amir Khusrau's devotional compositions were instrumental in developing Urdu, which was the main language of Indian Sufi literature. He mixed words and phrases of Persian, the grand language of the court and literature, and Arabic and Turkic (the languages which were strongly in use in the region), with the proto-Hindustani known as Dehlavi/Khari Boli, in creating Urdu, also known as Hindustani and Rekhta (written both in Devanagari and Nastaliq scripts). In other words, religious revolutions were set in motion through translation and writing of scriptures in common peoples' languages.

Dante Alighieri, who shaped the modern Italian language from the synthesis of Tuscan and other existing vernaculars in direct challenge to Latin—the language of Papacy, the state and of high literature of the time through his poetry—could be the first one to be reckoned in this line in the Western world. The sixteenth-century Protestants such as John Bale and John Foxe had termed Dante as a proto-Protestant because of his opposition to the Pope.

The popularization of the Bible, hitherto existing only in Latin and Greek, made available in German by Martin Luther's translation and followed by other European languages, sufficed to propel reformation in Western Christianity. Gutenberg's printing press ensured the mechanized production of the Bible in large numbers, which laypeople could now have access to without clerical mediation.

The translation of the Bible, however, did not happen in Kerala until the nineteenth century, when, as Professor Mathai points out, Claudius Buchanan (1766–1815), the author of *Asian Researches*, visited Malabar as a state guest twice during 1806–08 and urged the Patriarch of the Syrian Christians, Dionysius I, to have the *Estrangelo* (early Syriac) version of the whole Bible translated into Malayalam. The patriarch arranged the translation through his clergy, starting with the gospels printed at the Courier Press of Mumbai, followed by the translation of the Syriac–Malayalam Bible in England by 1823. Within another two decades, Benjamin Bailey and his Anglican colleagues in Travancore brought forth the historic translation of the whole Bible. Now, Malayalee Syrian Christians could read the Bible in their own language and get into its soul and see for themselves what the scriptures really said.

At the beginning of Chapter 1, Professor Mathai gives a rather detailed historical background of Kerala around two millennia ago. That was the time of the supposed arrival of St. Thomas the Apostle on the Malabar Coast (the ancient name of Kerala), the beginnings of the formation of the St. Thomas Christians, and the eventual development of the Syrian Christian community of this land. He sheds light on this community's standing among the predominantly upper caste Hindu society of the times, how they enjoyed exclusivity and privileges almost on par with the higher castes, how their ritual worship and outward ceremonies reflected their sharing of the elitist Hindu practices, and how all this had cast them in a tight cell, resistant to change and evolution.

Professor Mathai devotes the major portion of this chapter to a biographical narrative, tracing Simon's childhood, education, and the eventual development of his genius. A poetic prodigy who proved his mettle in versification at the tender age of seven to nine, Simon who grew up into a deeply erudite young man had captured the admiration of almost all the leading literary figures of his time, including the great scholar poet Mahakavi Ulloor S. Parameshwara Iyer, Sarasakavi Mooloor S. Padmanabha Panicker, and a whole array of creative writers, scholars, and academicians.

Simon studied the scriptures in their source versions of Greek, Hebrew, Aramaic, and Latin, in each of which he had gained proficiency by personal study. Being the autodidact that he was, Simon composed the grammars of these languages first in his own verse. Added to these was his reading of the Bible in the Malayalam translation, which aided him in leading the laity who also had by now begun the widespread practice of Bible reading, inspired by reformist leaders visiting from the neighboring Tamil Nadu in the preceding decades.

Christianity, which is believed to have taken roots in Kerala two millennia ago, had remained by and large a faith-based monolithic belief system hardly amenable to timely change, as already seen. Simon, who belonged to the Mar Thoma (The Malankara Mar Thoma Syrian Church) denomination in Kerala, proposed a scripture-based approach to faith rather than a tradition-based one. For example, he argued that baptism should be administered to a volunteering, fully-grown individual by immersion in a waterbody, like Jesus Christ did in the river Jordan during the baptism-drive of John the Baptist, and not to an infant who is not able to make a conscious choice to join the church through this ritual. Simon took a second baptism as an adult, through immersion. He was also convinced that there was no place for an ecclesiastical hierarchy, as was instituted in episcopal Christianity. Simon saw, like the European Reformers, that a formal office of priesthood was not necessary in the church since it was a home of sacred equality. "All believers are priests of the Most High, Luther declared," notes Mathai; therefore, rather than considering priesthood an inherited or elected office, it was to be understood as universalized (Chapter 1).

Simon met with opposition from the Mar Thoma Church establishment regarding his convictions and his act of undergoing voluntary adult baptism. For this departure from the Church's traditional practice he was excommunicated in 1915 after a summary ecclesiastical trial. However, instead of stopping Simon in his tracks, this event only thrust Simon into a public career of Miltonic strengths. Native orthodoxy held the conviction that the Reformation in Europe was only a European matter with which Indians did not have to have any concern at all. Simon who knew what it was now chose to do for Kerala what Luther did for Germany, and even beyond. His affiliation with the Mar Thoma Church ceased with the aforesaid trial in 1915. Within the next three years, Simon founded a fully indigenous congregation called the "Viyojitha Sabha," which I would translate as "The Dissenters' Assembly." This movement merged with the Brethren Assembly in 1929. Though comparatively still small in numbers as a denomination, Simon's leadership turned it into a powerhouse of knowledge with its steady output of verse, prose, debate, oratory, and organized dissemination of historical and scriptural learning.

A born poet of high literary caliber, Simon established himself as a Mahakavi through his Mahākāvya titled *Vedaviharam* [A Sojourn through the Divine Scripture]. This title of honor is comparable to the "Poet Laureate" in the Western tradition, a close equivalent to the position of "Āsthāna Kavi" in the Sanskrit tradition. In Kerala, there are Mahakavis in all the prominent communities—Hindu, Christian, and Muslim. Other than Simon, the Mahakavis in the Christian communities are Kattakayam Cherian Mappilai, Pravithanam P. M. Devasia, Puthencavu Mathen Tharakan, Edayaranmula K. M. Varghese, and Mary John Thottam (Reverend Sister Mary Benigna the celebrated devotional poet), and a few lesser-known ones as well. All of them lived in the twentieth century. Kattakayam wrote *Sreeyeshu Vijayam Mahākāvyam* [The Triumph of the Exalted Jesus]. Devasia wrote five Mahākāvyams, of which *Israel Vamsham* [The Lineage of Israel] and *Rājākkanmār* [Kings] are rated as his best. All but two of these Christian Mahakavis followed the dogmatic line of the Catholic Church, which the majority of the Syrian Christians of Kerala subscribe to. There was nothing revolutionary or reformative about the works of these poets.

Simon stood apart even among the Mahakavis. Technically he was in the classical Protestant stream through his membership in the Mar Thoma Church, an episcopal entity far removed from Catholicism and leaning more toward Anglicanism. The *Gorgias Encyclopaedic Dictionary of the Syriac Heritage* describes the Mar Thoma Church as that section of "the non-Roman St. Thomas Christians, which has undertaken a degree of liturgical and doctrinal reform under the influence of Church of England missionaries in the nineteenth century." The "agenda" of its reform was very much determined by the issues that had dominated the English Reformation in the sixteenth century. Simon's revolt within this reformed Syrian Church corresponds to Milton's joining the Puritan Movement, disillusioned by the Church of England's policies that strayed from the spirit of reformation.

Simon's forte was epic and lyric poetry and bhajans or hymns, which he set to classical music of the Carnatic tradition. His epic, *Vedaviharam* (1931) came out as a masterly work of 12,000 lines in fourteen different Dravidian meters, offering his own interpretation of the scripture, further promoting the cause of reformation within the Kerala Syrian Church. Both *Vedaviharam* and Milton's *Paradise Lost* have their source story in the book of Genesis. At the release of *Vedaviharam*, *The Guardian* (Calcutta) hailed Simon the poet as "India's Veritable Milton." Dr. K. Raghavan Pillai, a leading Malayalam literary critic of yesteryears evaluates *Vedaviharam* as a Malayalam classic embedded in immense learning. He places Simon's poetic output in the tradition of the Bhakti poets of India, in general, and of Ezhuttachchan, in particular. He further analyzes the outward form of the epic and appraises the use of different meters, most of which were popular Dravidian ones (and wherever there was a Sanskrit meter used, it was one infused with Dravidian sentiments). Moreover, his selection of meters was very judicious because it was determined by the demand of the particular themes he was working on and in consonance with the content. Pillai concludes his essay making a thorough study of the inner structure of the epic—the way descriptive, narrative versification is used and how the various *Rasas* are deftly employed in the epic.[4] Several other eminent critics, scholars, and academics of Malayalam, such as K. Ayyappa Panicker, Sukumar Azhikode, Koduppunna, Mathew Ulakamthara, M. Leelavathi, B. C. Balakrishnan, T. Bhaskaran, K. M.

---

[4] "Vedavihaaratthile Rachanaathalangal" (Dimensions of Composition in *Vedaviharam*), *Mahakavi K. V. Simon Janma Shathābdi Smaranika* (Souvenir of Mahakavi K. V. Simon Birth Centenary).

Tharakan, and a few others have made insightful comments on *Vedaviharam*. There are also acclamations heaped on *Vedaviharam* by the leading figures of Malayalam literature of the time, the most important among them being Mahakavi Vallathol Narayana Menon, P. K. Narayana Pillai (Sahitya Panchanan), Punnassesri Nambi Neelakanta Sharma, Sarasakavi Mooloor S. Padmanabha Panicker, Chitramezhuthu K. M. Varghese.

Simon's creative prose contributed to the polemical literature of Malayalam to a great measure. It appears in a wide array of essays, pamphlets, treatises, histories, philosophical disputations, scripture commentaries and apologetic works. He also ran a journal called *Malankara Viyojithan* [The Malankara "Separatist" or Dissenter, 1919–35], which drew the attention of objective critical minds of all faith streams of Kerala in the early part of the twentieth century. Although we have thirty volumes of Simon's prose writings available or accessible, hundreds more of his articles and lectures of huge public interest await rediscovery, which if attempted can potentially be successful. A seven-part series on Renaissance scholar Erasmus or a series of literary lectures delivered on his Madras Tour or at the University of Kerala in Thiruvananthapuram would be quick examples of such.

In Chapter 3, through the translation samples of Simon's verse genres—lyric, ode, hymns, and excerpts from the epic *Vedaviharam*—Professor Mathai provides a glimpse into the oeuvre of this great poet. His translation is innovative and sensitive, making sensible coinages to correspond to specific Malayalam word-combinations. Let us consider a small assortment of examples: Simon's term "*manujasuthan*" meets a matching construct of "ManSon" in Mathai's rendition. It correctly recalls Jesus' own self-identification in Malayalam as "*Manushyaputhran*" or "Son of Man." Proper nouns of reverence like "*Po-ttie*" [Liege of life] and "*Sat-guru*" [the true Master], or Simon's profoundly theological Sanskritic kennings like "*Aadi veda nada*" [the sound of the primeval Vedic Syllable] appear as Christological synonyms that complement the meaning of the Word—become *ManSon*. Professor Mathai shows how retaining Simon's word sequences like "*vandan*" [laudation], "*chandan*" [the fragrant wood in presents of worship], *muni* [the revered one or Seer], *sani* [the destroyer of evil], *dwani* [the holy sound or echo], or *kani* [the fruit], in the place of their English equivalents produce greater elegance and radiate deeper allusive powers. In the rapid switches between languages, Professor Mathai valiantly keeps up with the beat-base of Dravidian meters.

In his overview of Simon's literary contributions in Chapter 4, the author begins with a comparison of Milton and Simon and their works *Paradise Lost* and *Vedaviharam*, respectively, with extensive passages from both works covering more than half the chapter. Further analysis of Simon's works and his mission shows the types and tropes he employed in his poetry, his versification of the Bible other than of the book of Genesis, his didactic and mystical poems, his occasional poems, the millennial songs and the pervasive dynamics of his music and metrics.

Professor Mathai sums up the life and work of Simon solidly, observing that he was a pioneer in all his contributions. Simon shaped for Kerala his own era of the native version of Europe's foregone Renaissance and Reformation. He came formidably equipped, like Milton, with every talent necessary in his calling as a revolutionary reformer, poet and prose writer, a polemicist and publisher, a scripture commentator and orator, a hymnodist and musician. If the Viyojithas or the Brethren had the practice of canonizing their apostles, we would be reading today of Simon as a doctor of the church. After all, he was a sage of letters with a massive following, a favorite peer to the likes of St. Augustine, St. Chrysostom, or St. Ambrose who addressed the whole world rather than a small eponymous village or town that took pride in him as its native son.

I heartily join the global readership that has the pleasure of hailing Mahakavi K. V. Simon, "the Milton of the East" into their midst.

Acknowledgments

"They are all good in themselves, and cannot fail to please but by the fault of the translator," said William Cowper about his own translation of John Milton's Latin poems of his college days. Cowper was no ordinary poet or translator. Within the first fifty-five years of the publication of the first volume of his verse, one hundred editions of Cowper's poems appeared in England. He was the foremost of the generation of poets between Alexander Pope and William Wordsworth, says Poetry Foundation. That said, the kind of respect he showed for Milton's verse applies in my case to Mahakavi K. V. Simon's. Let me be the first to say that there is no pretense of any translator talent in which to take pride here. Nonetheless, this is the first known effort to bring an assortment of specimens from Simon verse through translation in some form of English, as far as I know. The flaws the reader may notice would not be Simon's, but the translator's.

As would be true of Milton, it is impossible to exaggerate Simon's genius. His life was a massive movement of inspired acts in unison, producing historic outcomes. Like the teenager Blaise Pascal among the Parisian intellectuals was the early Simon among the literati of the Pampa Delta. In his autobiographical verse narrative *"Ente Grandhasala,"* Simon unwittingly seems to show that he let his childhood slip by, leaping into adulthood and the world of advanced letters. He mastered multiple languages like Milton or Herman Gundert and put them all to high practical use; he wrote a 12,000-line epic in metrical verse in record time of less than two years, in the midst of a heavy public life; he created and established a tasteful genre of native Christian hymnody, corresponding to Ezhuthachan's *bhakti* verse in the Hindu culture and religion; not only did he compose inspired *bhajans* and hymns by the hundreds but also sang them as a gifted musician; his "puissant prose," as Valson Thampu puts it, changed the thinking of his age; his debates trained the public to achieve intellectual independence as much as they enlightened them; the magazines he founded, co-founded, or contributed to, brought the "ample page of knowledge" within access to all; as a publisher and chief editor he was a Renaissance man of letters; there is no determined count of the scholars who lived in his home as his disciples or as seekers of help, but treated like sons; those "sons" in turn, taught an entire younger generation; his translations, both vocal and scripted, surpass and yet elevate their originals. Simon did for Kerala what Wycliffe, Calvin, or Wesley did in Europe; when Kerala had no knowledge of Europe's Reformation, Simon's teaching showed them what it was. He challenged people to examine their faith through the critical study of the scriptures as modeled by his own organization of the Viyojithas. As well-read as he was, he was also capable of delivering his knowledge with instant effectiveness.

Nonetheless, K. V. Simon's works still await greater scholarly labors than what present literature offers. The scholar and the lay person find equal hospitality in his writings. Interpretive studies and research on Simon remain a highly promising area for exploration. Simon is a goldmine for dozens of dissertations and critical books. What is commonly known of him today are only his epic, *Vedaviharam*, and a handful of songs, which comprise only a small portion of the corpus of his output. Though "hidden" by the limits of the language he mostly writes in, the polyglot Simon is richly poised to engage a global audience. Like the four lepers of Israel in 2 Kings 7 who found food and spoils in the deserted camp of the Syrian forces and reported the discovery to their starving compatriots, I stand compelled to direct my literary kindred to the epic gains from the Miltonic mind and career of K. V. Simon.

I sincerely appreciate Bloomsbury's warm response to my proposal for this book on Mahakavi K. V. Simon for a worldwide audience. It has been a pleasure to work with my commissioning editor Amy Martin and her assistant Hali Han every step of the way.

My good friend, poet and publisher Prabhu Guptara, had as much excitement with the idea of this book as I did. He has been a powerful resource with practical wisdom for me from start to finish. Prabhu tracked the progress of the manuscript making sure that I kept good pace with the timeline.

Author and educator Valson Thampu took strong interest in my work. He was quick as he was also kind enough to write an Introduction for the book. Professor Thampu knows Simon's native surroundings. I am honored to have his perceptive essay welcoming Simon readers worldwide.

Equally favored am I with the kindness of Dr. A. J. Thomas, the former chief editor of India's *Sahitya Akademi* journal, a leading scholar, poet and translator. May his support for my work be well justified, as it reaches a happy audience.

It was a joy to see the numerous names of Simon enthusiasts and lovers of Malayalam literature, especially in the Diasporic communities, welcoming this book. Leading that train was Mr. John Mathai Panikkamatt of Toronto, Canada, who had been longing to hold the very first available copy of this book. He even offered me financial support, should I need it, for this project. Much to my grief, this venerable elder suddenly passed on, despite his excellent health and active life. I use this moment to pay my respects to him and to thank his family, gratefully acknowledging their investment in Simon's legacy. The names that follow are of Professor Donald R. Davis, Chair of Asian Studies at the University of Texas at Austin; Professor Heiki Oberlin, Head of the Department of Indology, University of Tübingen; Professor Blesson Varghese, St. Andrews University, Scotland; Professor Stanley John Valayil of the Alliance Theological Seminary; Dr. James Kurichi of the Department of Malayalam at the University of Pennsylvania; and journalist–author Dr. Babu K. Verghese for their cordial offers of help whenever sought.

I acknowledge Ms. Tirza Habeeb, an outstanding Simon reader, for her service to his verse. Tirza came across the poetry of Simon four decades ago. A poet herself, she read the complete verse of Simon, more keenly the songs and hymns in his *Sangeetha Ratnavali*. Though possessing only extremely modest material means, Ms. Habeeb took it upon herself to find qualified musical talent to produce 250 of Simon's songs in five audio volumes, a sample set of which should be available on most media platforms. Broadcast journalist Koshy George Mylapra was co-producer and presenter of the project. Readers of this book will find Ms. Habeeb's audio collection a solid complement to the book. I thank Ms. Habeeb and Koshy George for their sacrificial labors of resource building in Simon studies.

I go on record as the grateful recipient of the round the clock support in all things I do, including the shaping of this book, from my wife, colleague, and consultant pro bono, Rani Mathai.

I hand this book over to the lovers of letters who would have the privilege of receiving Mahakavi Simon into houses of knowledge and faith all over the world.

Varghese Mathai
Judson University

Timeline

Feb 7, 1883	K. V. Simon is born in Edayaranmula, in the Pampa Delta of Kerala, India, as the youngest in a family of ten children.
1894	Simon's father dies at age fifty-seven.
1895	Attends the globally traveling revivalist Tamil David's evangelistic meetings and elects to follow Christ; Simon's older brother and revered "guru" K. V. Cherian also attends the meetings with much interest.
	K. V. Thomas, a brother employed, and engaged in English studies, dies of an abdominal illness.
1896	Simon completes formal schooling as a twelve-year old, earns a teaching license at the age of thirteen and starts teaching at the Mar Thoma School, under K. V. Cherian, the school's headmaster.
1898–99	Simon trains in music under D. James, a Tamil maestro; the Brethren mission commences its work in Central Travancore.
1900	K. V. Cherian dies of a sudden, undiagnosed internal ailment. After a period of intense grieving, a thoroughly shaken Simon steps forward to fill the position that his venerable brother left vacant, as the new headmaster; later in the year Simon marries Pantholil Rahelamma.
1902	Takes "Believer's Baptism" under the hand of lay preacher Varkey Upadeshi; the Mar Thoma Bishop Titus I, who controls the denomination's schools, dismisses Simon from employment. Nonetheless, the bishop hires him back with the help of mediators within a few weeks because no one wanted to assume Simon's place.
1905–10	Simon opens *Sahitya Darshini* [The Literary Forum]; a free academy of lay scholars of all faiths, its active membership goes over 100.
1907	Polemical writings and debates between Simon and *Sabha Tharaka* editor K. N. Daniel of the Mar Thoma Church run for a decade hence.

1913	Thalappil Narayana Pillai, a disciple of Simon and a leading member of his Sahitya Darshini, dies of a sudden illness. Deeply saddened, Simon writes a hundred-stanza elegy titled *Nishakalam* [The Spell of the Night].
1915	Rev. Iype Thoma Kovoor, the Vicar General of the Mar Thoma Church puts Simon on what turns out to be an aborted trial. The resulting "Circular #83" of Metropolitan Titus II excommunicates Simon from the Mar Thoma Church.
1916	Revives P. E. Mammen's *Suvisesha Kodi* [The Gospel Banner] with a new name, *Suvisesha Deepika* [The Gospel Beacon], Simon himself contributing the majority of its future articles.
1918	Simon launches the *Viyojitha* [Separatist or Nonconformist] movement. Resigns from school employment.
1919	Simon starts the *Malankara Viyojithan*, the official magazine of the Viyojitha movement. The publication runs till 1935. First World War ends.
1921	Volbrecht Nagel, a German missionary and co-worker of Simon who joined the Brethren in Kerala, mastered the Malayalam language, and wrote 120 popular hymns in the language, dies of a stroke. Nagel's wife Harriet Nagel carries on Nagel's work in Northern Kerala.
1925	*Sangeetha Ratnavali* (first edition), a collection of the first two hundred of Simon's songs and hymns, is published. Other collections and editions of his verse follow, over the years.
1926	Simon debates P. Krishnan Nambiathiri in multiple towns around Aranmula which result in the latter's withdrawal from the campaign against Christians. The transcript of a select set of these debates is published under the title *Satyaprakashini* [The Illuminator].
1927	Daughter Chinnamma (Simon's only child) is born.
1929	The Viyojitha congregations merge with the Brethren assemblies.
1930	Writes the 12,000-line *Vedaviharam* in one year. Poet Ulloor S. Parameswar Iyer invites its presentation at the annual *Sahitya Parishad* [Literary Conference]. Simon reads chapter 19 of the poem at the urging of I. C. Chacko. The work is placed first among the presented entries.

1931	*Vedaviharam* is published. The Pan Denominational Christian community of Kozhenchery East presents him with a citation. The Plenary Conference of the Christava Samiti awards Simon a celebratory gold medal.
	Simon's close friend and mentor Mooloor S. Padmanabha Panicker dies of smallpox. Simon had visited Mooloor ignoring the deadly risk of this much feared pandemic of that period. He also presided over the ensuing memorial gathering.
1932	Simon delivers a two-hour public lecture on religion and literature at Kottayam. The audience included K. C. Mammen Mappilai, newspaper owner and great literary patron.
1933	Travels to Madras to deliver a series of literary addresses at Madras Christian College, Women's Christian College, Memorial Hall, Wesley College, and Broadway Hall. Additional literary gatherings and poetry readings occur at Keralaya where Simon is the guest of philosopher Nataraja Guru of the Advaita Vedantic school and the founder of Sri Narayana Gurukula. Simon also visits the tomb of Apostle St. Thomas who was martyred in this city in the first century. *Vedaviharam* enters the Travancore school curriculum.
1934	*Nalla Samaryan* [The Good Samaritan], a canto, is published; delivers a series of literary talks in Trivandrum.
1935	Publishes *The History of Christian Churches*.
Nov 12, 1936	The Maharajah of Travancore issues the Temple Entry Proclamation which abolishes the caste restriction that had traditionally prohibited the lower caste Hindus from entering the temple grounds, even to the roads leading to the temples.
1937	Simon speaks opposing salaried ministerial work. Many of his co-workers are unhappy and part ways with him.
1939	*The History of Brethren Assemblies* is published.
1941	Simon's only daughter Chinnamma is married to Kochumuriyil Mathew George of Simon's own town.
1942	Simon's faithful associates organize their own annual conference in Arattupuzha, which runs until the year of Simon's passing.

1943	Bishops Abraham Mar Thoma and Yuhanon Mar Timotheus, both of the Mar Thoma Church that excommunicated him, visit Simon during his last days. Simon preaches his final sermon at the Arattupuzha Convention.
1944	Simon dies on February 20, the closing day of the Arattupuzha Convention. The Mar Thoma Church has been continually requesting Simon's family to accept their parish cemetery as Simon's final resting place. Simon had instructed his wife and daughter to bury him only at the designated site adjacent to his home, and it was so done.
1947	India secures independence from Britain. Native rajahs [kings] surrender their power to the Indian union of states. Simon lived his entire life in colonial India.
1952	T. A. Kurien publishes Simon's biography, first edition.
1980	Simon's wife Rahelamma dies.
1983	The State of Kerala celebrates the centenary of Simon. The organizing committee publishes the *Janma Satabdi Smaranika* [*The Centenary Essays on Simon*].
2018	June 23, Chinnamma, Simon's daughter, dies at 92 years of age.
2020	As of this date, the Brethren movement that Simon led has 600 congregations in Kerala and 2,200 assemblies nationwide in India, and a hundred more abroad. Organizations like the Indian Pentecostal Church with thousands of congregations (10,000 congregations) have also been demonstrably impacted by Mahakavi Simon.

Introduction
Mahakavi K. V. Simon: A Prophetic Legacy

Reverend Valson Thampu

Introductory articles can be of two kinds. The first kind seeks to motivate the reader to engage with the work in question with informed involvement. The second seeks to incentivize the reader vis-à-vis what the work points to beyond itself. Books too are of two kinds. Those that "passivate" as against those that "activate" their readers. Reading books of the latter kind does not end when the reader reaches their last pages. They impel readers to stay engaged by taking off from the springboards they are. Varghese Mathai's *K. V. Simon: The Milton of the East* belongs to that category. To me, such works make more rewarding reads.

What I propose to say here is envisaged accordingly. Ideally it should be read after, not before, the main text, paradoxical as this might sound. Despite the painstaking scholarship and protracted labor that the author has invested in this work, he effaces himself from it. It is rarely that the reader comes across a work of scholarship from which the author is so comprehensively absent as in this instance. So, knowledge does not have to "puff up," after all. The proof that the author carries his scholarship "self-denyingly" is that he trusts, indeed expects, his readers to take off from where he leaves, and to undertake their own investigations. Mathai rediscovers Simon, so that the readers may discover him after their own fashion. He trusts that others may want to and, further, that they can. This work is, it seems, envisaged as a Simon-revival catalyst.

The author's vignette of Simon reminds us of poet M. P. Appan's eulogy of this Christian literary genius of Kerala. The voice that resounded around the Pamba, says Appan's poem, crosses the oceans, even as we, here, continue to enjoy the nectar of its devotion. Appan attributes the greatness of Simon's poetic achievements to his rootedness in the spiritual–philosophical richness of *Arsha Bharat*, or India. He praises the *Vedaviharam* for its consummate polyphony of *rasas* (emotional states). To him, Simon would have merited literary immortality even if he had written only this epic poem, and nothing else. Mathai has rendered a stellar service to Kerala Christianity by offering the first comprehensive account of the life and works of one of its leading lights.

Mathai introduces the reader to the manifold expressions of Simon's genius: scholar, polyglot, preacher, pamphleteer, debater, poet, and so on. I am richer for reading this well-conceived, pioneering work. Till I did so, Mahakavi Simon was, for me, a vague presence in the oeuvre of Kerala Christianity. Through this work, Simon has become a present help for me, especially in understanding the larger reaches of my own calling as a follower of Jesus Christ at the present time.

Chapter 3 of this work deserves a special mention. It affords the reader an ensemble of Simon's works. The author offers us the Malayalam texts together with their English translations. The selections admittedly represent a critically limited range in comparison to Simon's vast and varied output, but they suffice to grant the global reader a taste of the spiritual–literary banquet that reading Simon could be. As one acquainted, somewhat, with the thorny path of translation, it is with trepidation that I read Mathai's renderings. It is a daunting task to translate poetry. Translating Simon compounds this inherent difficulty because of the Sanskritized and technically sophisticated character of his poems. The task becomes even more problematic when it is fitted into the straitjacket of the meter-and-rhyme schemata as contrasted to the easy-flowing fluidity of the blank verse. This problem would have been acute, had the author not provided the Malayalam texts in close proximity for ready reference and comparison. As regards the Diasporic reader, the order of difficulties could be reversed. The barriers of obscurity that occur in Simon's Sanskrit-heavy Malayalam in the Simon texts are thoughtfully foreseen in their translations by the author.

In relation to Simon's spiritual lyrics, however, it needs to be emphasized that lacunae remain that no translator can make up for. These intractable difficulties issue from the fact that lyrics are meant to be sung. The music of the original texts cannot be transported to *readers* in the target language. Reading can never be the same as listening when it comes to lyrics set to music. To the Malayalee reader, the Simon lyrics assume a life and vitality of their own when sung. It is apt to be missed when only read. The difference could be analogous to reading a play and seeing it performed.

There is a further, and even more complicated, issue. That issue pertains to translating the "indigenization" or "acculturation" markers that Simon allows into his more literary poems, *Veda Viharam* being the obvious example. Already

Simon is "translating" the Judaeo-Christian material into the warp and woof of the Malayalee-Hindu linguistic, literary, and philosophical apparatus. A language is the repository of a people's experiences and aspirations accumulated over the millennia. Literary Malayalam, as against *padre* Malayalam, is laden with Hinduisms, so to speak. How is this translated material to be translated, this time by Mathai, into English without losing the original sense and flavor, sparing the reader the strain that this aggravation of distance from the original entails? The author tries to overcome this formidable difficulty by retaining several of the key registers of the original text and offering, additionally, adequate footnotes. Perhaps that is as far as an author–translator could go.

A further issue emanates from this, which needs to be noted if only for the reason that it is taken for granted, which it should not be. Scholar and historian of Malayalam literature Sooranttu Kunjanpillai hailed Simon as a shining light of religio-cultural amalgamation. He likens Simon's *Veda Viharam* to Ezhuthachan's epic, the *Adhyatma Ramayanam Kilippattu*. He alludes, besides, to the skepticism that prevailed in Simon's days about whether Christian poets could write epics, even though a Christian epic—*Sreeyeshu Vijayam* by Kattakayam Cherian Mappilai—was already extant. To Kunjanpillai, Simon's characteristic strength comprised his being an ardent Christian and his felicitous at-home-ness in the linguistic, literary, cultural, and spiritual–philosophical heritage of Kerala. Kerala Christians, on their part, entertained the prejudice that it was impermissible to Christians to associate themselves with the Hindu cultural and literary heritage.

That prejudice survives to this day and it works to the impoverishment of Kerala Christians. It has bred the reciprocal prejudice that Christians are culturally passé and intellectually poor. This makes Christians feel uneasy, in sophisticated contexts, in upholding their religious identity in public. The last instances I can think of Christians who had wider appeals were Metropolitan Paulo Mar Gregorio (1924–97) of the Orthodox Church and Metropolitan Philipose Mar Chrysostom (1918–2021) of the Mar Thoma Church: the first for his erudition and philosophical genius, and the second, for his genial spirit and unmatched sense of humor. But none comparable to K. V. Simon has been seen on the landscape of Kerala Christianity in the last eight decades.

The issue that Simon adumbrates in his works, rather than pose rhetorically, will be understood better if we consider the notion entertained by many a Kerala Christian that Christianity is a Western religion. As sociologists of religion like Ernst Troeltsch and Max Weber maintain, Christianity poised itself so completely in the Western culture that it is impossible now to understand it in isolation from that process. If it was legitimate for the Asiatic biblical faith to be one with the European culture, why should the same be anathema vis-à-vis a religio-literary context of the Asiatic pedigree? Simon was, hence, not apologetic about being in an osmotic relationship—*aadan-pradhan*, or give-and-take—with the Kerala cultural matrix. It comes to us as no surprise that Simon is the only Christian evangelist–lyricist who is celebrated in Malayalam literature with a poem in his honor. Also, Simon's merits as a man of letters are better acknowledged by Hindu scholars.

This brings me to Simon's special significance for Kerala Christians in Diaspora. Mathai's painstaking, mnemonic sacrament of gratitude to Simon can cater to their need for spiritual renewal. Non-Malayalee readers, though, need to exercise greater degrees of perseverance in accessing the spirit of this work for the reason that they face the added burden of coping with the linguistic and cultural markers that cannot be excluded from a work of this kind. I have no doubt at all that, general and global readers who are willing to "walk this extra mile" with the author will benefit much from this book.

At the heart of all that Simon did was his fervent faith and his passionate sense of mission. He did not write an epic to carve out a niche for himself in the literary pantheon of Kerala. Nor did he write puissant and persuasive prose to leave his signature on Malayalam prose. Or, compose poems and lyrics to showcase his musical talent and poetic genius. He did these, and much else besides, as integral to his spiritual calling. He was, quintessentially, a disciple of Jesus Christ. To him, the lamp of his faith life had to shine on the lampstand of wider belonging; giving, as Jesus said, light to all in his homeland and beyond (Mt. 5:1–16).

That brings us to Simon the poet, whom our author likens, not without justice, to John Milton. Poetry is the mode in which the light of a language shines purest and brightest. Poets know language as light. That light is also the measure of their "authority." The authority of Jesus, keenly felt by all around him, was the authority of light, though in popular perception it might have been in his mighty deeds. Perhaps the greatest service that K. V. Simon has rendered to the Kerala Christian community is that he endeavored, as best he could, to reflect the light of Jesus to the soul of Kerala during a significant phase of its evolution.

The author acquaints us with that context, the details of which need not be duplicated here. Suffice it to say that Simon lived at a time of literary, philosophical, and spiritual vibrancy. I need to add little to what Mathai provides except, perhaps, to note that Simon breathed a spiritual ambiance shared by Sree

Narayana Guru in Kerala and Ramana Maharshi—whom Carl Jung visited in his *ashram* and acknowledged as a rare spiritual light—in the adjoining state of Tamil Nadu. Simon was born twenty-seven years after Sree Narayana Guru, four years after Ramana Maharshi, and barely two years before the founding of the Indian National Congress that would, under Gandhi's spiritual leadership, liberate India from her colonial subjugation in 1947; that is, three years before Simon's demise. This is not the occasion to provide a detailed analysis of these conjunctions and coincidences. Even so, a point of contrast between Simon and Ramana Maharshi is apposite in the present context. While Simon perfected his genius to articulate the divine light, Ramana Maharshi sought to evoke the divine presence by perfecting silence. If the word was Simon's medium, silence was Ramana's. They represent two great traditions and the reader might want to pursue them further and their reciprocal illuminations.

This was also a period of intense religious polemic in Kerala. The dissemination and growth of Christianity, the umbrella of patronage it presumably enjoyed under the British Raj, increasing responsiveness to missionary enterprises; all these combined to aggravate insecurity among the custodians of other religions. So we have a Hindu stalwart like Chattambi Swami writing hostile pamphlets like *Kristhumata Khandanam* and a Muslim scholar, Makti Thangal, lobbing polemical grenades like *Katora Kutaram*. Simon could not remain indifferent to these external threats on the one hand, and the distortion of the teachings of Jesus prevalent in churches, on the other. He countered both with energy and competence through an array of pamphlets. I wonder how Simon, if alive today, would view those efforts. Does a religion have to be *defended*, especially from its external detractors? Ramana Maharshi would say, hold aloft the light; darkness will flee! A religion can be defended, if at all, only by living it.

Though silence was his forte, Ramana Maharshi, like K. V. Simon, composed bhajans and poems. This raises a question of much significance. *What is the role of emotion in spiritual experiences?* Music is the soul of poetry. Music is emotion in motion. In this respect Simon was better equipped than Narayana Guru and Ramana Maharshi. Unlike them, he had been trained for seven years in Karnatic classical music. Here too the parallel that Mathai argues between Simon and Milton comes to the fore. Milton excelled as an epic poet. He was also the "organ voice of England." The same is true of Simon. His poems shorn of their music are like body sans soul.

What about the role of emotion in the ministry of the Word? Ask a hundred people exposed to it routinely. Almost every one of them is apt to say that the bane of contemporary preaching is the over-abundance of emotions. No! It is, instead, the poverty of emotions. The contrary impression stems from confusing sentimentality with emotions. Emotions stir the depth of life, whereas sentimentality flutters on the surface. What characterizes great works is the power and uniqueness of the emotions that inspired their composition. Ideas and insights weren't alien to them. Nothing great in art and literature can be farmed in colonies of extinct emotions. What powers the will and sustains it are not ideas, but emotions. Emotions are germane more to the poetic, than to the prosaic, mode. Those in the throes of overpowering emotions tend, for example, to lapse into the poetic and the musical. I have seen illiterate women singing out their sorrows in rhythmic strains: sorrows too deep for words.

Emotions do not spring from a vacuum. They emanate from the depth of significant experiences. Simon's contemporary, Sadhu Kochukunju Upadesi, was a classic example of this. His lyrics are powerful precisely for their spiritual–emotional sincerity. It is like the spell that the Ancient Mariner casts on his listeners. His power stems from the hypnotic spell of his mysterious suffering (for that reason, he had to be "ancient"). Biblically we are reminded of the poor widow who put two copper coins, virtually all she had, into the temple treasury. Wherein lay the riveting power of her offering? Not in the coins, but in the emotions that empowered her sacrificial giving. She embodied a mystery: the mystery of being enhanced by the deprivation she embraced. Nothing moves as powerfully as this thing does! She must have been like the angel-stirred Bethesda pool at that moment. Her self-as-offering embodied, in that awesome moment of transcendence, a mystic state of poetry-in-motion.

A word or two may be in place regarding why religious lyrics of today have pitifully short shelf-life. They are not instinct with unique sensibilities and emotions issuing from experiences. They weave together the sentiments already experienced by others. Their inferior poetic quality and thematic depth correlate to the ascendancy of shallowness in religious life. What purports to be new is, in point of fact, no more than *a new arrangement of the old*. What adds nothing to the existing, and is merely repetitive, cannot endure. So, these "annual convention songs" fail to survive the season. The decision to compose comes first, and themes and sentiments thereafter. The Simon lyrics are of a different order altogether! While the seasonal convention songs do their best in appealing to our aesthetic sense, reinforced by the orchestra, the three hundred lyrics we have inherited from Simon impel our whole being.

Why should we remember Simon and revive his legacy? Well, he is of the cloud of great witnesses surrounding us, unbeknownst to us. The Spirit-inspired work done in the past by men and women of faith remains there as a source to draw from. Founders and reformers of religion, mystics and saints, unknown or forgotten heroes of moral life dot our pilgrim path on the earth. They are all there. We'll do well to be inspired and sustained by them. The author has single-handedly carried the pallet on which we are laid at present to a vibrant source of spiritual rejuvenation in the living waters that Jesus is.

Perhaps this work has a significance that far exceeds the immediate intentions of the author. A nodding acquaintance with the role that the Jewish–Christian Diaspora played in interpreting and spreading the message of Jesus Christ in the wake of the destruction, in 70 CE, of Jerusalem—Temple and City—could help us here. In that dreadful year, the Christian community centered in Jerusalem was nearly wiped out by Rome. The understanding of the person and message of Jesus underwent a radical change through the Greek-speaking Christian Diaspora, who became the principal means for the preservation and propagation of the faith. It was in this process—at its heart the shift, thanks to St Paul, from the Jesus of history to the Christ of faith, that the Christian faith acquired its cosmopolitan and universal character. Nearly the whole of the doctrinal and theological elaboration of Christianity as well as the formation of the scriptural canon took place in this process.

India now seems set inexorably to morph into a theocratic state—Hindu Rashtra—wherein Christians could become ineligible for citizenship. The trauma of this, and a host of consequential changes, could be nearly as traumatic to Indian Christians as the trauma that the Jews, including Jewish Christians, experienced through the Roman reprisal in 70 CE. The fundamental right enshrined in the Indian Constitution enjoyed hitherto by Christians under Article 25—to practice, preach, and propagate one's faith—could be compromised. It could, in that event, devolve on Diasporic Indian Christians, Kerala Christians in particular, to play a role analogous to the role played by Diasporic Christians—Hellenistic Christians—in the decades following the destruction of Jerusalem. Admittedly, this is the worst-case scenario; and it may not come to pass any time soon. But if and when it does, the value of Mathai's work could be doubled and redoubled as a "chronicle-by-other-means" of what Kerala Christianity was in its golden era. It could serve as a source of inspiration to Kerala Christians in Diaspora to an extent hard to fully anticipate at present.

As I have written elsewhere, what is not written down is as good as not having happened in relation to the posterity. Simon has happened; happened not just to the Brethren Assembly, but to Kerala Christianity as a whole. The significance of his work is so huge and its contemporary relevance so compelling that we cannot pretend as though such a man did not walk and witness the faith on the soil of Kerala. Simon has happened to all of us wondrously. So, this book deserves to be a household possession, and Simon a legacy that parents bequeath to children, generation after generation.

1

The Life and Times of K. V. Simon

An Overview

K. V. Simon (1883–1944) is a colonial-era poet of Malayalam, a 2,000-year-old language of the Dravidian family of South India. When his 12,000-line epic *Vedaviharam* [A Vedic Odyssey] appeared in 1931, *The Guardian* featured Simon as "India's veritable Milton."[1] With the release of this poem, the Travancore Sahitya Parishad [Council of Letters] conferred the title of Mahakavi, the highest honor in Indian poetry, on Simon. He had already written over three hundred poems in six volumes by then, which consisted of songs, hymns, lyrics, elegies, didactic verse, *khanda kavyas* (cantos or longer poems), theme-sequences, and translations. While all Indian poetic meters are elegantly singable, Simon, as a trained classical vocalist, also had them set to the Carnatic ragas. His *Vedaviharam*, which critics compare with Milton's *Paradise Lost*, is a Malayalam rendition of the whole book of Genesis in Dravidian metrics. Simon's prose comprises essays, pamphlets, treatises, histories, philosophical disputations, scripture commentaries, and apologetic and polemical works. He has contributed hundreds of articles to periodicals while running his own learned journal *Viyojithan* [The Separatist], which drew a passionate, reformist following from all faith traditions.

Simon was a native of Kerala on the Malabar Coast of South India, a relatively small Indian state of the size of Switzerland, with a population of 37 million, of which around 19 percent is Christian. The majority of this number belongs to the apostolic (first-century) Christian community. Syriac was their liturgical language, which gave them the cultural moniker, "Syrian Christians." The Syrian Christians in India needed their own era and experience of reformation in the way the Europeans did, but they were hardly aware of it. Like Luther, Calvin, or Knox, Simon urged the Syrian Church to examine itself

---

[1] *The Guardian* (Calcutta), August 13, 1931.

conscientiously in the light of the scriptures, but they did not have the Bible in their language until the nineteenth century. Simon's call for reform within the Syrian Church earned him a quick inquisitorial trial and excommunication from the ancient establishment. This hostile move of the church only catapulted Simon into public life as a reformer, apologist, and prophetic figure like John Wesley or George Whitefield, revered all over South India. Simon's poems and hymns captivated vast, responsive audiences. His home became a classical *gurukula* where scholars of all levels resided and learned, without any material obligation. His writings and daily discourses produced a growing movement of enlightenment, which took the name of *"Viyojithas"* [Separatists]. Simon, like John Milton in whose works he was well-read, examined the polities of all historical church governments and elected to follow the simple, non-clerical presbytery model of the Plymouth Brethren for his own faith. Henceforth, Simon and the Brethren-*Viyojitha* communities became synonymous, while also inspiring the rise of other germane movements in South India and beyond that involve thousands of congregations today.

Scholars place Simon's poetical work on par with the *bhakti* classics of Ezhuthachan, the Father of modern Malayalam, and of Poonthanam, a Hindu metaphysical poet, both household names in the land. However, Simon distinguishes himself in a much larger world by his contributions to numerous knowledge fields that bridge him to world literature, modern history, colonial studies, religion, apologetics, rhetorical studies, and more.

The Lay of the Land and Its Faiths

The twin villages of Aranmula and Edayaranmula lie among a cluster of other ancient towns on both sides of the river Pampa in Central Kerala. Because it runs through numerous sacred sites of Kerala's religious centers, the Pampa is fondly adored as the "Southern Ganges" of India. Situated on its banks is the famous Krishna Temple of Aranmula, the site of many religious and cultural events. The place is well known to all Keralites for its annual *"vallam kali"* or snakeboat race, held in conjunction with *Onam*, the age-old harvest festival of the Malayalam-speaking people. Legends drawn from the antiquity of the temple and the elaborate rituals of its high days place Aranmula in the prominent portions of the *Mahabharata*, India's ancient epic.

The Pampa delta of Aranmula was as rich in poetic fertility as it was in its richness of agriculture. A cultural tour will show sites of homes of poets, artists, and men and women of letters with the closeness of rosary beads. Author

Figure 1.1 The Annual Boat Race of Aranmula. Photograph by Arun Sinha, courtesy of Wikimedia Commons, Creative Commons Attribution 2.0 License. https://commons.wikimedia.org/wiki/Category:Aranmula_Boat_Race#/media/File:Aranmula-boat_race-_Kerala-India-1.jpg.
Over forty riverside villages along the course of Pampa put out their handcrafted, sleek racing boats, each a 100 ft long, with an upcurve prow 20 ft above the waterline, and a hundred men at the oars vie for the lead. This water fiesta is also considered to be an offering to Krishna, the local deity of the Aranmula temple.

and physician Malakkara Kochuraman Pillai, poet and biographer Madassery Narayana Pillai, social reformer Neelakantan Channar, the Christian ascetic Sadhu Kochukunju Upadesi, author and founder of Sri Krishna Ashram Sri Nishadananda, literary critic K. M. Daniel, science writer K. Srinivasan, award winning translator N. K. Damodaran, public intellectual and scholar K. M. George, literary critic Hridaya Kumari, novelist Hariharaputran, poet Sugathakumari, Mahakavi K. M. Varghese, Mahakavi Puthencavu Mathen Tharakan, and literary critic K. M. Tharakan, lived within 10 square miles of Aranmula. Add to these other nationally honored poets like Vennikulam Gopala Kurup, Mooloor Padmanabha Panicker, Vishnunarayan Namboodiri and more, the list will keep extending. All of them share the same wider neighborhood. Considering the density of literary productivity, Aranmula will exceed the numbers of literary names in England's Lake District or America's Concord, Massachusetts.

The Malabar Coast on the Southwest of India differed from any other part of Asia, culturally. Its 400 miles of coastline attracted the trade imprints of Sumerians, Babylonians, Assyrians, Egyptians, Greeks, and Romans. The monsoon-soaked terrain of Kerala produced massive amounts of pepper, cardamom, cinnamon, cloves, ginger, coriander, nutmeg, turmeric, and the like, for regular exports to the Middle East and to Europe. The port city of Muziris was an ancient maritime destination where, according to Sangam

Literature (third century BCE),² Roman ships laden with gold would arrive to return with spices. A pound of pepper, it is said, was priced high enough to secure the freedom of a slave in France. Alaric, king of the Visigoths, famously demanded 3,000 kilos of pepper besides the massive quantities of gold, silver, silks, and scarlet as settlement price from the Romans for lifting the siege of their city. Incidentally, there have also been immense holdings of gold in Kerala from ancient times. While Kerala's majority religious stream is Hindu—as is the case with the rest of India—Christianity and Islam have had their presence in Malabar right from the early days of their respective origins. Though not large in numbers, even the Jewish people have had their historic presence near the ancient port cities of the state. From the time of King Solomon, Kerala had well-established Jewish communities in Kochi and its surrounding districts. Fifteen hundred years before the first Westerner set foot in India, or five centuries before Pope Gregory sent St. Augustine of Canterbury as a missionary to King Æthelberht of Kent in pagan England, Orthodox Christianity had taken root in Malabar. An undivided, autonomous, native church flourished here under an archdeacon who held the title of "the Prince of Believers" with temporal powers over the church. Patristic and European sources from 200 CE onwards confirm its existence as the fruit of the labors of Apostle Thomas (the "Doubting Thomas"), one of the disciples of Christ. Evidence of Thomas' arrival in 52 CE, his founding of India's very first church, and his eventual martyrdom occur in numerous historical sources and artifacts, both native and foreign. Eusebius of Caesarea (260–339), Origen (185–253), Mar Ephrem of Edessa (306–73), St. Ambrose (339–97), Gregory of Nazianzus (329–90), St. Jerome (c. 347–420), Theodoret of Cyrrhus (393–457), Gregory of Tours (538–94), John of Saba (c. 690–780), Isidore of Seville (560–636), St. Bede the Venerable (673–735), King Alfred [in the Anglo-Saxon Chronicle] (848–99), the Syriac Codex of Vatican (1301), John Marignolli of Florence (1290–1360), and Vasco da Gama (1469–1524) are among the names that provide historically significant references to Thomas and his following in Malabar.³

---

² K. S. Mathew (ed.), *Imperial Rome, Indian Ocean Regions, and Muziris* (Abingdon: Routledge, 2017), 11, 28.

³ Pius Malekandathil, "A Commonwealth of Christians in the Indian Ocean: A Study on the Christians of St. Thomas Tradition in South-West India," in *Early Christian Communities of the St. Thomas Tradition in India*, ed Peter Kannampuzha (Kochi: LRC, 2017), 88–137, https://www.nasrani.net/, accessed June 13, 2022.

The Thomist Bridge from the Semitic West

Why did Doubting Thomas choose Malabar? The apostles of Christ sought out Jewish émigrés in other lands, traveling long distances, as one could see from the book of Acts or the New Testament epistles, and presumably so did Thomas, too. The history of sea travel of the early Christian era shows that ships could sail from Alexandria to Muziris in India in two weeks if the winds were favorable. The Jewish society of the first-century Malabar would have been a prominent destination for Thomas. The royal court of Crangannore with which the Jews had distinguished accreditation, accorded him warm hospitality. Thomas' early audiences were believed to have been Brahmin aristocrats, or if not Brahmins, at least privileged gentry with access to native royalty. They received Thomas warmly and supported his evangelistic work through land gifts and patronage to build "seven and a half" churches in the towns of Kodungallur, Kokkamangalam, Paravoor, Chayal (Nilakkal), Niranam, Kollam, Palayoor (modern Guruvayoor), and the "half church" at Chattukulangara. These congregations grew into a native faith stream known by a number of synonyms: the St. Thomas Church, Malankara Church, Malabar Christians, Eastern Orthodox, and others, depending on the context and the source. Periodical arrival of merchant clans from the Middle East to the Malabar Coast afterwards enlarged the ancient St. Thomas core. Most notable were at least two waves of immigrants from the Middle East, the fourth-century "Knanayites," so named after their leader Thomas of Cana, and an eighth-century Chaldean or Nestorian group. Ecclesiastical interactions between the St. Thomas Church and churches of Baghdad and Syria had existed from medieval times.

The social order of Malabar society was built on rock-fast traditions of caste and its attendant claims of racial privileges. The lower a caste rank, the less valued its people were. At the very bottom were the untouchables and the segregated, who were still indispensable across caste lines in their inherited roles of skilled or menial labor, with no upward mobility at all. Native rajahs ruled the land, where human rights or labor law mattered only where it favored the master or the landowner. The rajahs were essentially rulers of feudal territories, small or large, although a medieval Keralite "kingdom" could be crossed by a modern traveler in minutes. Places that are average towns today have been kingdoms or principalities before. Consider examples like Mavelikara, Kayamkulam, Edapally, Pandalam, Poonjar, Alamcode, Kodungallur, Valluvanad, Kolathunadu, and Venadu. They were all "kingdoms" once. In Malabar, Syrian Christians were generally respected as strong contributors to the economy. Traditionally, they owned farms, plantations, and businesses. Anthropologist Susan Viswanathan notes that the Hindu kings, pleased with the hardworking and prosperous Syrian Christians, gave them privileges and honors that distinguished them as high caste.[4] As a result, many of the social perils of caste and the vulnerabilities of feudal dependency on the upper social ranks were not a concern to them. Agriculture, commerce, civil, and military service were their primary occupational sectors.

Malabar, the Colonial Magnet

The arrival of Portuguese maritime explorer Vasco da Gama in 1498 on the Malabar coast marked the beginning of a double front invasion of India in its modern history. First, they targeted the highly strategic, geographical territory of Malabar and its riches. Their second target was ecclesial: they made a surprise discovery of the historically ancient Christian community in Malabar, of which they hitherto had no knowledge. They wasted no time in initiating efforts to forcibly bring the native church, i.e., the Syrian Church, under the Church of Rome. This mission had the mandate and support of the Portuguese crown. The native traditions and practices of St. Thomas Nazranis (another synonym for Kerala's ancient Christians, the term meaning, "followers of the Nazarene") were distasteful to the Portuguese. Though Syriac had the use and status of other *lingua francas* of the time such as Latin, Persian, or Greek, the Portuguese threw out the Syrian liturgy that Kerala's Nazranis had followed and replaced it with Latin. The literary works and archives of the Syrians were destroyed in public burnings. Only what could survive in oral form did, such as the *Margom Kali* (a round dance with songs on the apostles' lore), wedding songs, and the *Ramban Pattu* (folk songs attributed to the early followers of St. Thomas). Native attempts to draw support from sympathetic Orthodox patriarchs of the Middle East were consistently intercepted, even by ambush and murder. After enduring half a century of such alien control, the natives revolted. Twenty-five thousand Syrian Christians staged a massive protest against the Portuguese, culminating in "the Oath of the Coonan Cross." The Oath asserted the native Indian faith

---

[4] Susan Viswanathan, *The Christians of Kerala: History, Belief and Ritual among the Yakoba* (New Delhi: Oxford University Press 2001), 2–3.

and identity of the St. Thomas Christians, abjuring the imposed usages of the Portuguese. As a conciliatory move, Pope Alexander VII replaced the Catholic missionary leadership with the Carmelites, which helped to subdue the revolt. However, when it did, the hitherto single church of Malabar saw the largest schism in its history: the larger part of Malabar's Nazranis took the papal side, and the other chose the native heritage and allied itself to the West Syrian Patriarch of Antioch. The Catholic side now had a new name, "Syro-Malabar." The native wing came to be called "Jacobites," or more formally, the Syrian Orthodox. In the nineteenth century, the Anglicans entered Travancore, and the Basel Mission of Switzerland entered Malabar, with their respective service missions of literacy, education, employment, economic uplift, and evangelical work. Both the Portuguese and the Protestant missions, in the process, introduced printing and publishing, and built schools and colleges. In addition, the Basel Mission of Switzerland brought major industries such as tiles, textiles, printing, and crafts to Malabar.

Even though their once single family of faith became a nation of divided houses, each distinctive by some fine-tuned point of contention or affiliation, all Syrians fully agree on their heritage part in St. Thomas, and only on that part. "Every Syrian Christian," says Viswanathan, "even if comparatively passive, sees himself as an agent of history."[5] All of them still retain the descriptor "Syrian" because of the Syriac language used in their liturgy and the historical connections their church had with the Middle East. Proficiency in Syriac was an important criterion in the training of their clergy. The laity, at least in the earlier days, also were able to use the language in personal or business writing. The source text of the Bible that they use is the *Peshitta*, which the Orthodox Church affirms as the original Aramaic version received from the apostolic days, without change or revision.

"Pride in the high caste accorded to the Syrians in their Christianity was so great," says Julius Ritcher in his study of missions in India, "that they avoided all intercourse with the lower classes and discountenanced and sought to prevent the conversion of low castes to Christianity." As for sharing the Christian witness with their neighbors, he adds: "Within memory of man they had never carried on any kind of missionary activity. The Syrian Church was thus, as it were, 'a mind your own business Church,' wholly self-contained in the midst of the

---

[5] Viswanathan, *Christians of Kerala*, 41.

populace of Malabar, and for that very reason the more tenacious of its customs and traditions."⁶

The Caste Grid and the Curse of Touch

Both in Malabar and in the wider India, extremes of racism, untouchability, and bonded labor created a culture of exploitation of the vulnerable. The elaborate grid of Malabar's caste hierarchy was a social science altogether. As is universally known, in the broader fourfold division of Indian society, the Brahmin was at the top with a genius for manipulating everything to his advantage. He had priority in religion, government, education, and land ownership. He was prophet, priest, and pundit to the king and to the aristocracy. Next to him was the Kshatriya or in Kerala, the Nair, the warrior caste that took pride in its glorified identity. Most of the Kshatriyas were also rulers or kings to whom typically the Brahmin was the prime minister or chancellor. Still, as the practice went, the Nair should yield 15 feet of "respect space" for the Brahmin. On the unpaved country road which was the only thoroughfare there once was, the Brahmin passed with priority, but he also did so with all space around him cleared. A Vaishya should yield 25 feet of distance from the Brahmin, a Shanar thirty, and still lower classes, sixty. In many parts of India, even the shadow of a low caste person falling on an upper caste man or his dwelling was considered ceremonial pollution. As unfortunate as this legend of segregation might seem, even the segregated castes themselves considered castes lower than themselves untouchable!

As for their dwellings, the lower castes could live only in the outlying spaces that offered no sign of civic development. The lower caste homes had to stay low in looks and value alike. Tiled roofs, two-storey structures, and the larger *nalutkettu* [four-wing or quad style house] were forbidden to the non-elite. If the low caste folk wore jewelry, it would cost them a tax called *meniponnu*; the moustache was assessed per the norms of *meesa kazhcha*; Over a hundred such frivolous taxes were imposed upon Dalits or "avarnas." The lower castes could ride in a bullock cart, but not anything higher; if a Pulaya went to the open air market, he would have to wait on the outskirts of it and cry out for the article he needed, ensuring social distance of many yards; his money would be laid out for the vendor to pick up, he himself standing far from the spot of transaction;

---

⁶ Julius Ritcher, *A History of Missions in India* (New York: Fleming H. Revell, 1908), 78.

the lower caste man could tend a cow, but when it calved, the cow belonged to his master after its first ten days of ritual impurity. In their communications with the *savarnas* (the upper caste), the *avarna* (the low caste) had to speak in self-debasing language: instead of the first person "I," it had to be *adiyan* (the lowly slave); his home was only "*canaka kuntu*" or "*kuppappadu*" (the manure pit); if he took a bath or washed his body, it was *ceru nana* (a little wetting), and oiling his body was only a *thottu purattal* (finger smear).[7] Kerala was a place where, at least in retrospect now, a woman could yell out to the government, "Get out of my hair," or "My body, my business." Attire and appearance rights were tied to one's caste heritage. Women of higher castes wore their hair tied into a knot over their right ear as a status symbol, but the lower caste women were forbidden to style themselves that way. When a privileged upper caste woman went out, she would hold a palm leaf umbrella, somewhat like the large, shade hat a Western woman would don. A lower-class woman would have to settle for the long and wide banana leaf instead. Weaving was the traditional work of the Ezhava caste. They knit the *mundu* [the *dhotie* or waist cloth of common wear for men and women], but they were not permitted to wear it full length down to the ankles, only down to their knees. There were no blouses for the upper part of the body for lower caste Hindu women. Instead, they used a shawl-like breast cloth. However, Ezhava and Nadar women had to go about bare-breasted. For centuries, this had been a practice unquestioned and, therefore, a normal way of life for them. The Channar Revolts of 1813–59 demanded the abolition of this practice. John Munro, the Dewan of the king, ruled that Ezhava and Nadar women converts to the Christian faith could wear blouses like the Syrians, the Muslims, and the upper castes. The king overruled Munro under pressure from his council. Meanwhile, there appears to have been a solution of sorts introduced: the lower caste women could pay a tax, if they wished to cover their breasts. It was the duty of the state employees to go door to door, collecting the "breast tax." It went on this way until 1924 when Ezhavas rose en masse against the law as an outraged woman named Nangeli severed her breast and cast it in front of the tax collectors. The deed cost the woman her life, but her bloodshed did alter history. The details of this rule are too sordid for narration here.

The upper caste Hindus, including royalty, took their descent and ranks through matriliny. This extremely complex family order dictated that a male or female born in the family followed the line of descent and succession from the

---

[7] S. N. Sadasivan, *A Social History of India* (Delhi: APH Publishing, 2000), 88.

mother, not the father. The father of a Nair could be Brahmin but did not have to be. Who becomes a Nair woman's husband was a matter of her sexual autonomy. A Brahmin or Nair male could come to a Nair *taravad* or natal house of a Nair woman and give her a simple but symbolic *pudava* or raiment, and if she accepted it, he would be her legitimate lover or even her husband. That husband could be dismissed by the woman at will, with no damage to her status. She would not be dependent on any man because she had control of her portion of the family property. The *taravad* was her stronghold. Paternity in a *taravad* birth is ultimately determined or vouched for by the mother and none else because of the shifting male figures. Even kings have found themselves helpless in giving their status-appropriate patrimony to their sons because the king's nephew had greater rights to the royal wealth than his biological children did. It was only in the twentieth century that the law of succession was changed from matriliny to patriliny. As for the *taravad* women themselves, in spite of their position, they were not free from abuse of various kinds as one could see from the well-known writings of Kamala Das, a modern Nair woman, and Lalithambika Antharjanam, a modern Brahmin writer. Brahmin women had few of the liberties that the males in the house had. They were generally homebound and forbidden to have any contact with the world outside. When they went out on rare occasions, the aforementioned palm leaf umbrella had to shield them from public view. Between the Brahmin woman and the Nair woman, the latter had slightly greater liberties, but not even remotely close to a free society.

Castes still lower than Ezhavas and Nadars suffered abuse that showed the utmost of human depravity. They were Pulayas, Kuravas, Pariahs, Panars, Ulladars, Uralis, Vanian, Odan, and so many more. The state list of castes comprises more than a hundred subcastes.

In the 1850s, when the Travancore population was less than 1.3 million, over 13 percent were slaves who were considered part of the land where they lived under the absolute ownership of the higher caste Hindu or the Syrian Christian. Like the African–American slaves in the US, they could be bought or sold, their transaction papers showing the proviso, "you [i.e., the owner] may kill or you may sell"[8] as ethnographic scholar Sanal Mohan notes. Mohan retraces the history of Keralite slaves as a people group with no human rights of

---

[8] Sanal Mohan, "Creation of Social Space through Prayers among Dalits in Kerala," 40–57, https://www.tandfonline.com/doi/full/10.1080/20566093.2016.1085735, accessed October 19, 2021.

any kind at all, not even the right of open air space. They worked in the fields from dawn to dusk for no wages at all, seven days of the week, with no external contacts except through a field leader of their own caste. Neither the Syrians nor their peer castes did anything to reject caste or to remedy the ills by which it afflicted the poor. The missionaries of the Church Mission Society (CMS) in Travancore and the London Mission Society (LMS) in the southern regions of the state made their advocacy for them, only to be fiercely resisted, even by the Rajah's government because slave ownership was in the firm control of the upper castes, the temples, and the government. The missions started their schools for the Dalits and built modest community halls for prayer and learning, which also aggravated the slaveowners. To their credit, the Portuguese clergy, like all of the other missionaries, also opposed it firmly, which did not bode well for the Syrian Christians.

There were no other reasons at all for conflict between the Syrians and the Hindus. In fact, there were built-in traditions to privilege both Christians and Jews. Though a densely populous region, Kerala has historically enjoyed harmony among people of all its diverse faiths, but the Hindu culture generally permeated the entire society. Hindu and Christian worship places certainly had visible differences, yet they had mutually shared cultural celebrations in their festive events: the elephant procession, the *pancha-vadya* (the percussion pentad), *chenda melam* (the team-played rolling drum ensemble), performance arts, musical narratives, religious orations, and the closing fireworks—all found alike in the programs of the Hindu temple as well as the Syrian Church.[9] Accessories such as ornate umbrellas, censers, and ceremonial furniture moved as friendly loans between churches and temples. It was customary to arrange for a Christian to be living adjacent to a Hindu temple, as their beliefs held, to annul any ritual blemish in their observances by touching the Christian's compound wall. The churches and temples shared the native tastes in architecture and furnishings. The golden mast in front of the church, the large, hanging wick lamp inside the sanctuary, feasts and meal offerings, naming ceremony, presentation of the child for a first lesson, *dakshinas* (offerings or formal presents), and memorial feasts are sights of similarity between Malabar's Orthodox Christianity and its Brahminism.

---

[9] Paul Manavalan, *Kerala Samskaravum Christava Missionarimarum* [The Culture of Kerala and Christian Missionaries] (Kottayam, Kerala: DC Books, 1999), 27.

A Cambridge Guest to the Syrian Christians

Claudius Buchanan (1766–1815), the author of *Asian Researches*, visited Malabar as a state guest twice during 1806–08. He was the vice-provost of Fort William College, the institution that trained young Britons as civil service officials in India. He also held a colonial position as Chaplain of the Presidency that allowed him to travel, research, and write extensively in the British territories on their culture and religions. Buchanan was eager to learn about the Syrian Christians. That the Syrian Christian faith and Buchanan's Anglican faith shared common ground surprised his host, the Maharajah of Travancore. His subjects using the Syriac language in their religion intrigued the king all the more, we are told. The king readily offered protection and assistance for Buchanan to visit the churches of his kingdom and their venerable seventy-eight-year-old Patriarch, Dionysius I.

Buchanan was struck by the communal traits of the Syrians: he describes them as a people of evident nobility and intelligence. They knew of Western Christianity only through the Portuguese who had appeared to them practically as an "enemy," with whom therefore they desired no communion. Buchanan noticed that as a society, the Syrians were in a state of decline, representing a kind of "fallen glory." He told their patriarch Mar Dionysius the Great that the absence of the Word of God was the reason for their weakness as a church. The patriarch welcomed Buchanan's offer of help for education and spiritual ministries for the betterment of his people. Buchanan promised to urge the rulers to grant Syrians their due respect, as enjoyed by the British Anglicans; to provide the Bible in translation; to train a Syrian youth in England for ordination, and to establish affiliation between the two denominations.[10]

The patriarch was wise and astute: he quizzed Buchanan on the orthodoxy of the Anglican faith to test them against his own. Knowing that his own days were but few, the patriarch wanted the best for his people, once he was gone. Certainly, getting the Bible in the language of the people was a matter of high priority. The Syrian Church already had the Gospel of Matthew in Malayalam. The other three could likewise be produced by the *catanars* (priests) who had knowledge of both Syriac and Malayalam. "I have determined to superintend the work myself, and to call the most learned of my clergy to my aid,"[11] he said

---

[10] W. H. Foy, ed., *Buchanan's Christian Researches in India* (London and New York: Routledge, 1858), 32–33. Digital copy retrieved from https://books.google.com/, accessed June 13, 2022.
[11] Ibid., 29–30.

to Buchanan. The translation of the gospels was soon set in motion with a one-year timeline.

Ironically, the patriarch was at that very moment in possession of the priceless lone copy of the *Estrangelo* [early Syriac] version of the whole Bible, which had come down to his provenance by virtue of his office. It had been put together in Syria as a manuscript sometime between the ninth and the twelfth centuries and brought to Malankara (another name for Malabar) around that time period. K. R. N. Swamy, in his book *Moghuls, Maharajas and Mahatma*, states that this great work survived the Portuguese book-burning decree to the Syrians by a mere quirk of fate. The Portuguese were convinced that the native church and all its writings were heretical.[12] Accordingly, the autocratic Bishop Alexio de Menezes ordered the churches to bring all of their religious literature to the Synod of Diamper or Udayamperoor to correct the "errors" in them. Any church not complying with the order would be destroyed. The Syrians had no option but to obey. Entire libraries of churches and of prominent families were thus wiped out. The Estrangelo copy survived only because it was at some interior location that failed to receive the bishop's order. It was now ready to come to light through Buchanan's translation partnership. The manuscript of the gospels was chosen as the first portion to be completed under the leadership of Ramban Philippose.

At the appointed time, Buchanan returned to Travancore. That would be in 1807. He took the work to the Courier Press in Bombay for printing, and the Syrian Christian experts assisted in the process to the very end. Soon the Syrians had the gospels in their language. Mar Dionysius gave the *Estrangelo* copy of the whole Bible to Buchanan as a gift, with the understanding that its printed copies would be supplied back to Malayalee Syrians who would continue to use and appreciate it. By 1823, a printed edition of the Syriac Bible did come to India, as promised by Buchanan, eight years after his death. The original Indian gift copy is now in Cambridge University's Oriental collection.

Buchanan presented the Syrian community in strongly favorable terms in his *Researches* and his commencement address at Cambridge. Through his urging, Colonel John Munro, the chancellor to the Maharajah of Travancore, brought a team of learned missionaries of England's CMS to Travancore. Notably, three of them would make their home in Kottayam: Benjamin Bailey, Henry Baker, Sr., and Joseph Fenn. In just a few years they turned the small rural village of

---

[12] K. R. N. Swamy, *Moghuls, Maharajahs and the Mahatma* (Delhi: Harper Collins, 1997), 42.

Figure 1.2 The Puthuppally Orthodox Church. Photograph by Vijayanrajapuram, courtesy of Wikimedia Commons, Creative Commons Attribution-ShareAlike 4.0 International License. https://commons.wikimedia.org/wiki/Category:St._George_Orthodox_Church,_Puthuppally#/media/File:St._George_Orthodox_Church,_Puthuppally_fron_-_side_view.jpg

Tracing its local history to its initial erection in 1557, the St. George Church stands as a major landmark of Puthuppally, a suburb of Kottayam, famed also as a pilgrim destination. It is one of the prominent parishes of the Malankara Syrian Orthodox Church, which reports 1,200 member parishes in its denominational statistics. The shrine in front, the brass flag mast, the ornate steeples, and crosses are unique to the design of worship centers of the Orthodox churches of the St. Thomas tradition.

about three hundred people into a pioneer town of modern literacy, printing, publishing, and education. The missionaries received the support and the hospitality of the Syrian Church for the first two decades, but then discord set in, and they parted ways. During the friendly decades the church and state worked together and successfully built the first liberal arts college of India in Kottayam, with the generous support and ongoing advocacy of Colonel Munro. The institution was named "Cotym College." The curriculum consisted of mathematics, geography, history, English, Sanskrit, Greek, Latin, Syriac, and Malayalam. The non-Indian languages were included as components of a formal theological education for the Syrian clergy, which up to that point had been trained for their vocation in *malpan* residences. Benjamin Bailey was the first principal of the new college. He mastered the Malayalam language well enough to translate the entire Bible into it in twelve years. Bailey created his own hand press with craftsmen's help. Carpenters made the print assembly. Ironsmiths forged the fonts, which he improved upon while on furlough in England. The squarish Malayalam characters were aesthetically rounded off to be eye-friendly and elegant. In its historical significance, Bailey's Bible corresponds to the King James Version in English history. A gaping hole in Kerala's history of literacy may be noticed in the absence of any judicious recognition of Bailey's press and his translation of the whole Bible into the Malayalam language. Bailey is no less to India than is Johannes Gutenberg to Europe. Bailey's service prepared Malayalam literature for its own Renaissance. Its Romantic era was yet to begin. A little over two decades after Bailey, there came another missionary successor, the great German scholar, Herman Gundert.

Abraham Malpan and Native Reforms

One of the professors of theology at the "Cotym College" was Abraham Malpan (1795–1845) of the Palakkunnathu family of Travancore, which traces its roots to the first-century families that received the ministry of Apostle Thomas. Many distinguished clergy and prelates of the St. Thomas Church have been descendants of this house.

The Malpan (which means professor) was ordained a priest of the Syrian Orthodox Church in 1815. From his own study of the scriptures in Syriac and his open association with the CMS, he was convinced of the need to make faith in Christ personal rather than a cultural legacy. His Orthodox bishop had little theological sympathy for his position, and the majority of the laity saw no reason for excitement in the Malpan's zealous discoveries. Yet as a man of influence, the Malpan made two bold moves, challenging the Orthodox attitude: firstly, he abolished the annual festivities of a particular saint's day. This event used to attract a huge crowd, which brought much revenue to the church coffers. The Malpan threw the venerated image of the saint into a dry well and canceled the annual memorial procession, much to the outrage of the Syrian mainstream. Secondly, the Malpan, with a group of reformist clergymen, drew up a set of articles of faith as a memorandum to the British Resident, seeking the abolition of twenty-three corrupt practices in the old Syrian Church. The Resident, as advisor to the Rajah, apparently had control of the governance of the Church.

The liturgy of the Eucharist (Qurbana) was still central to corporate church life. Hitherto, the Qurbana was recited only in the Syriac language. Proficiency in Syriac was a criterion for priesthood. The Malpan and his associates saw the use of a foreign language in his church's liturgy unserviceable, if not absurd, given the poor literacy statistics of the century. Along with his colleague Kaithayil Geevarghese Malpan, he revised the prayer texts to make them more scriptural. The CMS had made the Anglican Book of Common Prayer a liturgical gold standard to the reformist congregations of Travancore. Abraham Malpan celebrated the Qurbana in Malayalam in his home church of Maramon. His peer clergy also did the same in solidarity with him, each in his own parish. Conservatives strongly resisted the move. They wanted the whole liturgy in Syriac only, whether they understood it or not.

Not surprisingly, the Malpan and his colleagues faced harsh retaliation from his traditionalist bishop. Candidates for priesthood trained under the Malpan were disqualified for ordination. The Malpan now looked to the church abroad for support. He sent his nephew, Mathew, a young seminarian, to the Syrian Patriarch in Mardin, Syria to seek consecration as bishop. The patriarch obliged, ordained him first as priest, and later as bishop, under the name Mathews Mar Athanasius. The new bishop returned to India in 1843, and assumed his charge tactfully, attempting to keep the old and new together. The general zeal for reform quickly waned, however. The Malpan died in 1845, only fifty years old, yet not without some notable success in what he had set out to do. The small number of congregations that followed his lead organized themselves as the Mar Thoma Church, a name that still held the appeal of tradition. The Malpan's work was important enough for Church historians to call him the "Wycklif of the Syrian Church in Malabar."[13] K. V. Simon's family belonged to Abraham Malpan's church. The Malpan's home, parish, and teaching sites were all within 10 miles of Simon's home.

Simon's Childhood

K. V. Simon was born on February 7, 1883 at the hilltop home that stood a half mile east of Aranmula's Parthasarathy Temple, on the banks of the Pampa. The "K" of his name stands for the house name, "Kunnumpurathu," meaning "hilltop," and the "V" for Varghese, his father's name. It has been common among South Indians to have their first name and middle name contracted to the initials, at

---

[13] William J. Richards, *The Indian Christians of St. Thomas, Otherwise Called the Syrian Christians of Malabar* (London: Bemrose & Sons, 1908), 30.

least since the days of the British, possibly for the practical advantages of shorter forms. Simon's ancestral family traces its past to the 1600s. As descendants of the first-century Namboodiri families that espoused Christianity, they had migrated from Northern Kerala to this region immediately after the historic Oath of the Coonan Cross, settling into agriculture. The traditional communities of the area, mostly of Hindus and Christians, lived in harmony, rarely with any signs of religious or sectarian tension.

Simon's parents were workers as much with the soil as they were with the scrolls. His father was respected widely for his expertise in Indian classical literature. Hindu households customarily recited the *Ramayana, Bhagavata,* and other sacred texts. It was quite common to find any Hindu child being capable of memorizing numerous portions of the great Indian epics. School curricula and civic performances of arts and drama predominantly had the same content, which made these great works familiar to the whole culture. Simon's parents held social hours in discourses in their home on the Indian classics. Neighbors would request help from the Kunnumpurathu family with commentary and interpretation of the epics and the puranic works. This was the British colonial era, which to the privileged, big-city residents provided the option of Western education; for the majority of the nation, however, the Western school was inaccessible and unaffordable. Broader native literacy depended on teachers who could teach multiple subjects and prepare scholars according to the traditional expectations. Pupils would live with the master until their training time was completed. They were more like "sons" to the teacher and his wife than boarders under contractual terms for tuition, housing, and food. The teacher's wife would have the role of a mother to the resident scholars, who would share all the facilities of the house with the members of the family. About this period, Simon says in his (lost) autobiography:

> In the *gurukula*, the teacher had greater authority on a child than even his parents did. Even a child self-willed and rebellious at home assumed that the guru's word was not negotiable. The difference is huge between the bygone golden age of *gurubhakti* (devotion to the teacher) and the modern era of learning where teachers are not regarded in any great awe. Western ways have shifted the paradigm of the guru and disciple into trader and customer. The pupil now comes bidding for the best market value.[14]

---

[14] T. A. Kurien, *Mahakavi K. V. Simon: A Biography,* 2nd ed. (Angamally, Kerala: Premier Press, 1990), 49.

Signs of precociousness were very pronounced in Simon as a little lad. His older brother, the headmaster of the Mar Thoma School on the family property adjoining the home, was his teacher—"preceptor" might be a better term. The man's name was K. V. Cherian, a polyglot, a mathematics enthusiast, and a composer of verse. Simon was enrolled in the school, but real learning resulted from Simon's own self-driven readings and the inspirational dialogues with Cherian. Like all gifted autodidacts, Simon resented rigid, formal learning. As a seven-year-old, Simon had been composing verse and completing allusive riddles (from contextual lines given for instant completion, matching matter and meter alike). Between 1889 and 1891, aged seven to nine years, Simon had two vacation stays at his sister's residence in Mavelikara, a town about 15 miles west of his family home. Arrangements were made at both times for him to attend the school close by temporarily where his brother-in-law was a master, but Simon was a school unto himself, helping himself to the private library of his host, instead. One of his older brothers also had secured employment in the same town as a plantation manager and language tutor. Although only a visitor and a pre-teen then, Simon had drawn the curious attention of the townspeople right from his first visit. During the second visit, Simon was spending a good part of his time with his brother's literary friends. One of them, Mr. Sankara Pillai, asked him if he could compose a descriptive poem on the house in which Simon was staying. The poem was ready with no delay, to the delight of the solicitant. The news traveled fast, and tasteful friends of Mr. Pillai came to seek more and more of "on demand" verse from the composer lad. Others entertained themselves hearing him recite large blocks of memorized lines from various classics. The city registrar, one of the prominent visitors of the family whose estates Simon's brother managed, asked Simon to recite a portion of Kunchan Nambiar's *Kalyalana Sougandhikam Ottan Thullal*. Simon delivered the poem in its entirety (for comparable length, consider Pope's *Dunciad* or *The Rape of the Lock*). Next came a physician (these are Ayurvedic physicians, who are also masters of classical Sanskrit verse) with seventeen *samasyas* for Simon to complete. The *samasya* is a verse riddle—an ancient creative exercise starting with a puzzling line or an allusive clue, which must be completed like a repartee, or like an instant poem of startling immediacy in content and connotations. Here is an example:

Why build an idol if you must its head spare?

Let us say, the "clue" could apply to the Tower of Babel. People of Shinar are building a city to hold the world's population in one place. The city tower must rise high enough to pierce the clouds, says a leader. If not, why bother?

So, a contestant could complete the *samasya* as follows:

> Shinar's splendor should its tower declare,
> And in eminence high its heraldry fly;
> Else, should Babel's pride in dry dust lie?
> Why build an idol if you must its head spare?

Simon's *samasyas* could have been longer. Witnesses have affirmed that he completed the seventeen *samasyas* of this vacation period before his stay was interrupted.

How his stay was "interrupted" is another story. The mild-mannered Simon somehow managed to annoy his in-law's brother, who, in turn, gave the little poet a little drubbing. The matter, even in those times of unquestioning submission to authority and quiet suffering of wrong, was grave enough to end up in court. Simon the nine-year old plaintiff was given his turn to testify before the magistrate. Mr. Sankara Pillai, who took pleasure in anything Simon said or did, urged him to present his complaint to the magistrate in the form of a poem. He did. It was immediately evident that the magistrate was greatly pleased with the little boy and his poetic gift. The defendant quickly appealed for reconciliation, and the case thus closed. Simon went back home.

Within a short period of his return, the press carried the story of a political tussle between Peshkar [Regional Officer of the IRS] Govinda Pillai and Magistrate Prakkulam Padmanabha Pillai of Tiruvalla. Once again, the pre-teen Simon covered the whole chronicle in verse, yes, indeed, at the proud urging of his goodly mentor, Mr. Sankara Pillai.

Mooloor S. Padmanabha Panicker: A Lifelong Mentor

Poet Mooloor Padmanabha Panicker (1869–1931), fourteen years Simon's senior, was the first to document the marvel of what he saw in Simon. Mooloor enjoyed widespread recognition in the princely state as a state legislator, a social reformer, the first chief editor of *Kerala Kaumudi*, an educator and a close associate of Sree Narayana Guru, the philosopher–reformer among Hindus. The latter half of the nineteenth century was a fecund period of revival in classics in Malayalam poetry. Conversing and corresponding in instant verse was a popular pastime among poets. Mooloor had made a name for himself in swift verse, and he saw the tender Simon being exceptional at it. Kerala Varma, Prince Consort to the Queen and literary patron, conferred the title of "Sarasakavi" [laureate] on him. Mooloor, who was a resident of Simon's neighboring town of Elavumthitta, introduced the younger poet to his literary friends, all of whom expressed gratitude for their connection with him. Mahakavi Ulloor in his commendation of Simon's *Vedaviharam* states that it was Mooloor who turned his mere acquaintance with Simon into deeper friendship. We shall see more about Mooloor in the upcoming pages. For a verse portrait of Simon by Mooloor, please see Section III.

Tamil David's Travancore Visits

In 1894, a team of two Sri Lankan men, one called "Tamil David" and the other, L. M. Wordsworth, arrived in Travancore as guests of the CMS on a four-month revival preaching circuit. The spotlight was largely on David, who was of Tamil heritage, although he had been a permanent resident of Sri Lanka. They came without any letters of commendation, nor any formal credentials, but in the utter simplicity of the power of the Spirit. David was a well-known name in the US, UK, Australia, and all over the Indian subcontinent at that time. This was their first visit to Kerala coming to the Syrian Christian community. They had no preset itinerary, but requests came from all over Travancore for them to speak. David preached in unprecedented gatherings all over Kerala from 1894 to 1907 in three successive visits to which the Syrian Christians responded with great respect. For the sake of comparison, it may be said that Tamil David did for South Indian Christianity what John Wesley did for the Church of England or what George Whitefield did for the American colonies. Volbrecht Nagel, a German eyewitness, writes of the second round of David's meetings thus:

> Large crowds gathered day by day, and on Sunday the audience numbered 15,000. There was a special cause which drew these crowds—Tamil David, the well-known evangelist, had come. About twelve years ago he had a special mission amongst the Syrians in Travancore, when many places were mightily shaken and thousands were really converted …. Oh, what a shaking there was of the depths of hearts when, before many thousands, he humbled himself in dust and ashes and compared himself with the meanest dog who was not worthy to

live on His Master's earth! Hundreds began to sob and weep with him and were utterly melted and broken down before the Lord.[15]

The meetings, according to Mr. Edwin S. Bowden, an Englishman, "continued for seven days, three meetings daily, occupying about seven hours"—and this was at one location. Many other towns in Travancore were also in David's itinerary.[16] E. H. Noel, a colleague of Nagel and one of the attendees, estimates that at least 30,000 conversions resulted from David's preaching, among them many clergy and deacons of the Syrian Church. Simon and his brother Cherian attended one of David's meetings in Puthencauvu. The messages were in English, translated into Malayalam. The brothers were pricked to their heart at what they heard. With no hesitation, both of them dedicated their lives to God, convicted of the need for personal internal change and forgiveness of sins rather than inherited religious traditions. It also stirred them to study the scriptures for spiritual growth. Decades later, himself a highly visible public figure and a widely sought-after speaker, Simon said of Tamil David:

> The anointed utterance of the man and the inspirational power of his messages are unforgettable for me, even now. In my life of forty-two years I am yet to see another speaker, European or native, who could speak on the topic of one's need for personal conviction about salvation. Mr. David's speeches are clear and impactful, even as they are fresh with illustrations of good humor. He never loses his audience. They sit absorbed, listening to him. Mr. David had the extraordinary ability to seize the hearts of the people, like a horseman bridling his dashing horse to a still stop .... Boldness, as found in no other preacher, was evident in him. From David I learned that forgiveness of sins and salvation were instantly achievable.[17]

A studious man like Cherian was impressed by David so much as to have taken astute notes of all his addresses and to acquire booklet volumes of his London messages.

Tamil David gave the people of Travancore the irresistible call for scripture study and personal devotional life. Lay prayer gatherings began to crop up across Travancore. Wherever one turned, one could see signs of a widespread spiritual move. What began as a cottage gathering birthed the Maramon Convention, which

---

[15] *Echoes of Service: A Record of Labor in the Lord's Name in Many Lands* (London and Bath: 1899–1935), 1908.
[16] Ibid.
[17] K. V. Simon, *History of the Malankara Separatist Churches* (Tiruvalla: Satyam Publications, 1999), 59–60.

TAMIL EVANGELIST DAVID.

Figure 1.3 Tamil David Sketch. From The San Francisco Call. [volume], July 10, 1897. Public Domain. Image provided by University of California, Riverside, courtesy of Library of Congress, *Chronicling America: Historic American Newspapers* Collection. https://chroniclingamerica.loc.gov/lccn/sn85066387/1897-07-10/ed-1/seq-3/
"V. D. David" or "Tamil David" (1853–1923), born a Tamil in Tirunalveli in South India, grew up in Sri Lanka with little formal education, but was diversely skilled. Somewhat like the young John Bunyan in his early life, David, by his own admission, was a profligate. The story of his dramatic conversion and his compelling ability to communicate the essence of his faith drew massive crowds to his revival addresses in the US, Europe, Asia, and Australia. He was highly commended by D. L. Moody, E. Stanley Jones, and George Grub, among others. Tamil David's US itinerary appears in the archives of *The New York Daily*, *The New York Tribune*, *The San Francisco Call*, *the Roanoke Times*, *The Morning Oregonian* and other such publications. https://chroniclingamerica.loc.gov/lccn/sn85066387/1897-07-10/ed-1/seq-3/.

since then has become the largest annual gathering of Christians in Asia. Over 100,000 people gather for a whole week of meetings every summer on the Pampa riverbed. David was the keynote speaker of the very first convention in 1895.[18]

Simon's brother Thomas, who was the estate manager mentioned earlier, also attended the Tamil David convention. He too was led toward spiritual convictions similar to his siblings'. At this time, Thomas was in the process of securing his credentials as an English tutor, at the urging of Mr. Sankara Pillai, the family's well-wisher. Unfortunately, Thomas was soon beset by the aggravation of a chronic abdominal ailment that cut short his promising life, at the age of nineteen—in 1895, exactly one year after the death of their father.

Moving on to 1895, Simon is now twelve. His formal education would last only for one more year, if at all. Even if he were to continue in that school for a few more years, the duration would make little difference, given its limited facilities. Promoted students and failing returnees were, as a rule, enrolled together in the new year in the same class space, under the same teacher. Even formal schools of the time operated like *gurukulas*, the same teacher for all, all students learning together, the weak and strong alike. Thanks to Cherian's farsighted training, Simon had already begun advanced readings in Sanskrit, on his own. He had been reading *Sri Ramodantam*, Kalidasa's *Raghuvamsa*, and Sukumara's *SriKrishna Vilasam*, all of them epics prescribed for higher-level certification.

A derivative effect of his Sanskrit studies was the natural movement from grammar and rhetoric toward "*sadaachara*"—principles of good conduct and practical spirituality. Here, one is apt to recall Benjamin Franklin's autobiographical account of electing and practicing the seven ethical virtues in his personal conduct. Simon was reading Vedic works, the *Puranas*, and philosophies of Hindu traditions, side by side with biblical literature. His readings were judicious. There was no pressure from anywhere to lean to one way of thinking or another. The life of "good works" became instinctive for him, but the deeper yearnings for something beyond himself seemed unrealized.

The Teen Schoolmaster

By the time Simon was thirteen years of age, his formal schooling was either past or had become irrelevant. Cherian urged him to take the state test for teaching

---

[18] Ibid., 67.

certification, which Simon did. He passed the exam with a 96 percent score, the 4 percent missed only because of being held back at the main entrance for identity verification. After all, this was a test for qualified adults, rather than a middle school kid.

With the test results in hand, Simon entered his career as a school teacher. Cherian was the school administrator. A period of active learning followed. In a few short years Simon acquired superior skills in Sanskrit, Tamil, Telugu, Kannada, Hindustani, English, Latin, Hebrew, and Syriac. He felt the need to read the scriptures in their original texts and hence the studies in Hebrew, Greek, and Latin. Like Milton in his post-Cambridge period at his Horton Estate, during this period, Simon devoured the great masterpieces of Asia and Europe. Incessant reading filled every free hour of his life. He could seldom be found without an open book in hand. His memory was formidable, capable of easy retrieval of large passages after a single reading.

Hindu homes and temples all over the Indian subcontinent sing *bhajans* for their devotionals. A temple town like Aranmula and its surroundings evidently would have far greater appreciation and use for them. Great medieval Malayalam poets Ezhuthachan, Poonthanam Nambuthiri, and Cerusseri are Kerala's exemplars of sublime *bhakti* verse. The *bhajans* are the prime gift of the Bhakti movement to Indian literature in general. All Indian languages have individual representation of Bhakti writings, both as native works and as translations. The Bhakti song is appealing in musical quality, with deeply allusive scriptural or puranic content, addressing gods in the form of a prayer or praise. It could be sung solo, by a whole family during its devotional time in the morning and evening, or by a community at a "*satsung*," which is a choir, to the accompaniment of instruments for any occasion chosen. The hymns could range from folk tunes to classical ragas. Their literary quality is tasteful and their inspirational effect immediate. Simon admired the Hindu *bhajans* greatly; he knew hundreds of them by heart, which was no surprise to anyone. He suggested to his brother that Christians could attempt their own *bhajans* as a new devotional option.

Bhajans for Syrians

The Syrians of Kerala only had the hymns and chants from their liturgies as devotional music. The compositions of St. Ephrem (fourth century), Mar Addai and Mar Mari (with arrival date set at seventh century in Kerala) continue to be used in the Syrian Qurbana or the Eucharist. Ephrem's songs are heard in all Syriac churches in their annual cycle of worship. Cultural ballads of *Margom Kali* [The Song of the Way], *Thoma Pattu* [The Song of Thomas] and the classical wedding songs have their unique ethnic voice of the remote past. However, they still lacked the topical range of a congregational hymnal that an Anglican or Wesleyan sanctuary offered. By the time of Simon, Western Protestant hymns or their Indian versions were only beginning to get noticed among Keralites. The Bohemian Brethren inaugurated the still-thriving practice of hymn-singing in European churches even before Luther wrote or sang his own songs. The Pietist movement which grew from the Bohemians and the Moravians rapidly had become a recognized force in German poetic literature. Count Nicholas Ludwig Zinzendorf who preached "the heart religion" applied his Moravian piety to create oneness among believers of all persuasions. The Wesleys of England admired Zinzendorf and did for England and America what Zinzendorf and his community did for the German-speaking world. Charles Wesley wrote nearly 9,000 hymns, fifty-three volumes in fifty-three years, each with its own music and message. The Anglicans and the German Pietists arrived in Travancore and the Lutherans in Malabar with large-scale educational programs that had a rich poetic component in the form of hymns and songs. Some of these foreigners learned the Malayalam language as well as the other vernaculars and wrote original hymns in them. Volbrecht Nagel, a German Pietist, learned Malayalam well enough to be considered a mainstream hymnist with his 120 widely anthologized songs. A handful of talented native writers produced volumes of excellent hymns as original compositions and as works of translations from the East and the West. Chief among them were Rama Iyer, a highly gifted Brahmin, also known as Yustus Joseph or Vidwankutty (more about him below) and Moshe Valsalom of the Nadar community. Without losing any time, Simon and his brother K. V. Cherian jointly produced the maiden collection of their Christian *bhajans* in Carnatic melodies.

An influential layman by name Muripurackal Yohannan seemed respectful of Simon and his brother. He helped facilitate a cottage meeting of lay attendance for them. When the people arrived, Simon and his brother turned out to be the only possible speakers, though they themselves were still only two young seekers of direction for their own lives. At this point Simon knew only of practical virtues such as righteousness, charity, forgiveness, and the general notion of divine love. Their first task was to move their audience from staid orthodoxy to the rudiments of applied faith. The early reflections were on what could make a primer of reformist glossary with terms such as "sin," "repentance," "internal change," "forgiveness," "rebirth," or "sanctification," which were all faint notions at best to the people. Simon and Cherian were aware how Reformation Protestantism had its message encapsulated in these terms, how Luther had forced a scrutiny of beliefs and practices in the late medieval church, how Calvin had become both the political and the religious oracle for Geneva, and how the Wesley brothers moved the English nation toward experiential religion that welcomed the conviction of sin and the desire for sanctified living. Simon's later writings show that he had studied the impact of the Wesleyan holiness on Europe and the US, resulting in the Great Awakening and the rise of new evangelical missions and churches. Those churches adopted reformist faith statements consonant with the New Testament accounts, and the apostolic models of applied faith, personal or congregational. The Nazarenes, the Pentecostals, the Baptists, and the Brethren were among the numerous organizations that appeared on the revival map, nearly all of them by now in India too, though not in large numbers or in any specifically organized pattern.

Lessons from European Reformation

Tamil David's visits made thousands of Syrian Christians rethink their spirituality. In a matter of weeks of David's visit, the newly translated Malayalam Bibles registered blockbuster sales. Bailey's translation was the prevailing favorite for the Malayalam reader. The publishing company could not print or ship out the Bibles fast enough to keep pace with the demand. Simon and Cherian began their in-depth reading of the scriptures and related literature. Simon studied the scriptures in their source versions, in each of which he had gained adequate knowledge. In studying these languages, Simon first composed their rules of grammar in verse. The ongoing studies systematically deepened many of his already formed convictions about faith. As did the European Reformers, Simon also believed that neither a formal office of priesthood nor its hierarchy was necessary in the church since it was a home of sacred equality. All believers are priests of the Most High, Luther declared; therefore, rather than considering priesthood abolished, it was to be understood as universalized. This would mean an existential threat to the mainline episcopal denominations, including Simon's own Mar Thoma Church. For about ten years Simon had to live by the light he received from personal study and prayer, while he was by degrees coming across kindred spirits here and there. He studied the scriptures on baptism in depth as a point of doctrine in the same manner the "Radical Reformists"[19] of the Reformation did in Europe. Approaches to baptism varied from one denomination to another, where options of aspersion (sprinkling), affusion (pouring), and immersion exist. Luther retained baptism as a sacrament for which an infant could be a presented candidate. This is practiced without disagreement in the Catholic, Orthodox, and the episcopalian churches. However, the reform groups such as the Anabaptists, Baptists, Pentecostals, Brethren, and an increasing number of modern evangelicals consider baptism by immersion, also called the "believer's baptism," more supportably scriptural. They argue that an infant could not take a major personal decision of this kind voluntarily, nor could it legitimately be taken for the child by proxy. The Moravian Brethren and the Baptists in Europe emphasized this position in their teachings. Simon's own reasoning was in agreement with theirs, and he even wrote a book on baptism along the same line of thinking. At the age of nineteen (1902) he took baptism by immersion, an act of outright dissent in the Syrian Christian denominations at that time. Like any other Marthomite, he was baptized as a child, but here he was making a personal statement of rejecting the infant baptism in which he had no volitional part. To the mainstream churches, infant baptism is the very first of sacraments and the symbolic beginning of ecclesial life. The news of Simon's baptism traveled fast through all surrounding towns. The Mar Thoma bishop Titus I dismissed Simon from his service of school teaching and administration, with instructions to hand over charge to his successor the very next day. With no resistance, Simon quit his position, thus stripped of his only means of living.

Bishop Titus' impetuous action against Simon backfired. There was no countermove from Simon. The new man who replaced Simon reported that he neither had the ability nor the desire to be in the place of a man much loved and capable. For many weeks, the position remained vacant, with the impending risk of the school losing its government grants. Friends had come around to help Simon pursue higher tracks in teaching with formal training in the capital. Meanwhile, the bishop was advised to call Simon back to the school. Several contacts occurred through intermediaries, but Simon declined the invitations for a meeting. A final mediating party that included a clergy relative made a successful plea with the assurance that the bishop would discuss only school business in the meeting. Accordingly, Simon met with the bishop at his

---

[19] Michael G. Baylor, ed., *The Radical Reformation: Cambridge Texts in the History of Political Thought* (Cambridge: Cambridge University Press, 1991), xvii.

residence. Simon agreed to return to his position as headmaster. As he was about to take leave, the bishop tried a verbal stroke designed to echo a hint of control: "So, now," said the prelate, "is it understood that you will be fully in step with us?" Simon quipped back: "Yes, but only as far as it concerns the business of the school." The bishop managed not to show his embarrassment at Simon's firmness, leaving him speechless. Those that knew both Simon and the bishop say that this was the final meeting between the two men.

The Great Awakening in Travancore

A decade before Tamil David's first Kerala tour, a period of great awakening had already begun among Syrian Christians in Kerala. The Arulappan revivals in the neighboring state of Tamil Nadu had helped create a new spiritual landscape in Travancore. A prodigy that seized the essence of that movement was Rama Iyer (1835–87) or Yustus [also spelt as Justus] Joseph, a.k.a Vidwankutty (mentioned above), son of a Brahmin family that migrated from Tanjavur to Mavelikara. Temple singers by profession, they lived in a number of South Indian temple cities before arriving in Sasthamkottai, where he would marry his ten-year-old child spouse Sita, as was common Brahmin practice. A case of healing of Rama's mother from chronic illness through churchmen's prayer brought the entire family into the Mar Thoma Church, eventually affiliated with the CMS. Thanks to his Brahminical upbringing, Rama was well-grounded in the religious *sastras* and literature. In particular, he was trained in astrology and the *Vedas* at *gurukulas*. One of his gurus, Azhakathu Karunakara Kuruppu, allowed him access to his family archives of ancient *granthas*, which Rama took to, like a duck to water. This is said to be the time the young fellow earned the nickname "Vidwankutty," meaning "the bright lad," rather than a proper name. A contesting story attributes the name as a compliment of the maharajah who had an accidental chat with the little boy at the temple, with his whip-smart wit. As a growing adult, Vidwankutty was a scholar, writer, poet, musician, orator, and natural leader. His five brothers were of the same mold. Two of them, in particular, were adoringly styled "Sons of Thunder." Vidwankutty and his brothers became a united force of unprecedented religious awakening in Travancore as inspirational speakers and organizers, well-received into the Syrian Christian denominations. They had come in contact with the revival movement of Arulappan's leading in Tirunalveli and had spontaneously become catalysts of its revival message in Kerala. As a result of his teaching and preaching, there was a dramatic surge in scriptural and theological inquiry in the kingdom of

Travancore. Every believer's home had a copy of the vernacular Bible, which was a new phenomenon. Along with it came the volumes of hymns by Vidwankutty. He wrote over three hundred hymns of devotional ardor and mystical depth, all of them in Carnatic style. The entire family of Vidwankutty was musically gifted, and they made sacred music a substantial part of their faith's expression as at one time they did in the temples. These hymns marked a new phase in the history of Christian spirituality in Malayalam songs. Other talented composers began to rise all over Travancore and Malabar: Rasalam Ulyam, P. V. Thommy, T. J. Varkey, T. J. Andrews, T. Koshy, T. D. George, M. J. Kochukunju, David Isaac, and many others. Vidwankutty's short life of fifty-two years ended with the tragic doom of espousing what was widely shunned as a millennial heresy. He claimed to have a visionary understanding of the return of Christ in October of 1881, which evidently did not take place. As a result, his following rapidly dwindled to a handful of local churches, which also faded away soon, bringing them to merely vestigial levels.

Simon was only four years old when Vidwankutty died. Simon's compositional and vocal abilities in music showed great promise. At the age of thirteen, he wrote and presented three Tamil songs (not his native language). He also had a self-acquired proficiency in its literature, which would grow in great measure in the years following. Providentially, as it were, a Tamil maestro of Carnatic music arrived in Edayaranmula as a new resident when Simon was fifteen years old. Besides being a man of sound learning, James was an expert musicologist and instrumentalist. A phase of musical studies and training immediately followed for Simon. The hymns of Vedanayaka Sastriyar (who was among generations of court poets of Tamil monarchs), *Chokkanathar Kauthuvam* (music of the Chokkanathar Temple), *Paadal* (songs or *bhajans*), *Guruswami Keerthanangal*, and Tamil Christian Hymns were among the key streams that Simon studied and practiced with James. Training sessions were provided by Malayalee masters too, in the renditions of *Ramayana Natakam*, *Nathan Charitam* (in the form of *Kadha kaalakshepam*, a very elaborate musical narrative with instrumental accompaniments), the *kirtanas* (hymns and sacred songs) of Moshe Valsalom, Vidwankutty, the compositions of Swati Tirunal the Travancore Rajah, *Vaathilthura pattukal* (wedding songs, folk style), songs of *Kathakali* (classical dance-drama of stylized gestures and music, performed outdoors on temple grounds as all-night performance), among others. These titles comprise a typical curriculum for a young adult artist preparing for a career in performance, but let us not forget that Simon's goal was different and that he was still in his mid-teens at this time.

Losing a Brother and Guru

Simon received a series of rotational postings in his multicampus school system in the first five years in the nearby towns of Maramon, Kalarikkal, and Poovathoor, before he returned in 1900 to Edayaranmula. This was the year in which Simon was the ranking "assistant" to Cherian for six months. Tragedy was to strike the household once again. Some ailment, suspiciously similar to what claimed their brother Thomas' life, struck Cherian too. Doctors ruled its condition too far gone for any viable treatment. After three weeks of rapid decline, he succumbed to the illness. The family was in inconsolable grief at the loss of the father and the two sons, all three widely respected in the society, three deaths within the space of five years.

Marriage and Family

The death of Cherian was a major communal loss. His mourning peers and the school's management unanimously agreed to have Simon succeed his guru and brother as head of the school. Thus within four years of the start of his teaching career, still only seventeen years old, Simon became the headmaster of the school, the same year he also entered married life. His bride was Rahelamma, a member of the Pantholil Peedikayil family of Airoor, a neighboring town. The groom had the pleasure of his bride being found for him by the family, as the way of the society went in the early twentieth century of Kerala. Marriages were arranged between families, which is still the most common mode there of finding life partners. A middleman or a mutual well-wisher of the two families might act as a go-between. This was also a time the dowry from the bride's family to the groom was a strong expectation, as one in the Western world would see in Robert Browning's "My Last Duchess" or the stories of Oscar Wilde or Dostoevsky. Conversations—negotiations, rather—on the dowry part can make or break a deal. A hefty dowry fed the vanity of the giver and taker alike while it put a tragic burden on people of modest means. Of course, this was a cultural curse that bound all races and societies of India, across the board, and it does not show any signs of fading at all even in this digital age. Anyway, there is hardly any mention of bridal money or even a courtship period preceding Simon's wedding, the latter being utterly unlikely, given the expectations of the time. Like Simon, Rahelamma was of Syrian Christian heritage, from the parish of Rev. C. T. Philipose, a clergyman of some prominence in the Mar Thoma

Church. This priest appears at many places and times in Simon's career, in positions of institutional advocacy. He officiated Simon's wedding. The bride was fourteen years old, coming into a joint-family homestead. As for the marriage itself, Simon and Rahelamma lived in steadfast mutual love throughout their days, with the deeply tacit understanding that they were both parents as well as servants to multitudes. With the steady concourse of visitors and residents, all things were considered common in Simon's home, where Rahelamma was known as "Airoor Amma," whom Simon in his allusively romantic manner called "the Shunemite."[20] The great learning and the skills that her husband possessed were matched, say those who knew her, by the humanity of Rahelamma. Looking for displays or stories of sweet delicacies of spousal affection in their life might yield few results. Simon traveled frequently, most of the time on foot. Taking his wife along those strenuous journeys would not be practical. When he was home, they were mostly with guests. Airoor Amma had no resentment that her husband belonged more to the wider world than to the home or to her. Records show that she did travel with Simon occasionally, however. Rahelamma lived to be ninety-four, after a widowhood of thirty-six years.

It took twenty-seven years before Simon would see his progeny. He and Rahelamma had only one child, a girl, Chinnamma, born in 1927. Chinnamma had an older sibling born in 1925, but that was a stillbirth. Chinnamma was the object of great parental affection, but here again, a great man's only daughter had only a basic education, far less than any of the many scholars living under his roof. Of course, in the 1930s, education beyond the basic level was not particularly crucial for practical living in rural India, and for that reason, opportunities for formal education for women were also very limited. Even aristocratic women such as the daughters of chieftains and rajahs, as Kamala Das writes in her autobiography, had no formal education. Das mentions the life of an aunt of hers who attained puberty at the age of nine, and according to the status the family enjoyed, was then given a ceremonial elephant ride to the temple, an event designed to get the attention of a prospective young man to be her spouse.[21] Chinnamma had slightly better luck than that. She did get her elementary education and was married in 1941 to Mr. M. George Kochumuriyil, a police officer of the same town.

---

[20] Joy Pampady, Interview with Rahelamma in *Simon Biography*, Appendix III.
[21] Kamala Das, *My Story* (New Delhi: Sterling Publishers, 1976), 126. Retrieved from https://archive.org/stream/in.ernet.dli.2015.220167/2015.220167.My-Story_djvu.txt, accessed June 14, 2022.

A Lay Launch of Reform

If Simon were merely a literary man, an educator, or a musician, he would have faced little resistance in the society. One might say that it could have been true of Wycliffe, Luther, Melanchthon, Calvin, or Wesley, because these were university men with profound cultural influence. They experienced conflict with their understanding of faith and their convictions about reform. We do know that institutional teachings on doctrines, though seemingly simple or almost immaterial, have caused revolutions, hostilities, and even wars among religions. In Europe, the doctrines of baptism, transubstantiation, purgatory, justification by faith, priesthood or episcopacy in general, or teachings about indulgences, beliefs on faith and work, veneration of saints, and a whole catalog of such matters stirred numerous winds of doctrine. Simon's understanding of the scriptures had considerable intellectual independence; yet, as an avid reader, he acquainted himself well with the entire church history, both of the East and the West, and wrote articles and books on both. He knew that Kerala's Orthodox Church was at least three hundred years behind the Reformation timeline of Europe. The Kerala Church was essentially oblivious to the revivals or the holiness movements of Europe and America from the time of John Wesley and Jonathan Edwards. A few small islands of evangelical activity were appearing in certain towns of Kerala, such as the Basel Mission in Calicut, the CMS in Central Travancore, the LMS in Southern Travancore, along with the still smaller individual missions of the Baptists or the Pentecostals. The Syriac-using laity of the mainstream faiths, though socially privileged, generally had little critical knowledge of doctrines or of the scriptures. That is the first place Simon saw as the launching site of his mission. He also organized the youth of the whole region through the YMCA, the YMEF (Young Men's Evangelical Fellowship), and intra-denominational retreats.

Ecclesiastical Trial and Excommunication

The Mar Thoma Church wasted no time in setting up a trial for Simon regarding his baptism. The church had gained its identity as a denomination following the reforms of Abraham Malpan, but it found Simon's spirituality heretical. For the sake of comparison, Simon merely sought to read and to follow the scriptures in the manner Luther or Wesley did in their times and places. In 1915, he was summoned for trial by the ecclesiastical court set up at the headquarters of the church in Tiruvalla. Vicar General Abraham Kovoor was the inquisitor, ready with his own handpicked witnesses. A good-sized audience gathered to watch the proceedings. Simon was seated on a bench. Curious observers filled the available space. With minimal procedural courtesies, Kovoor took over the scene. He asked Simon:

> "Your parish?"
> "The parish of Llaka," answered Simon.
> "Write Llaka," Kovoor instructed the scribe and turned to Simon again:
> "And where do you live?"
> By now, Simon had a counter question:
> "Sounds like I am on trial. Am I?"
> "Yes," answered the Vicar General.
> "By what law, if I may ask?" demanded Simon.
> "You have no right to question us," came the reply.

"I should think I'm the one under interrogation. If so, I believe I do have the right to know by what law I am being interrogated. Is this a civil court or a Church court? Unless I know which, I cannot proceed."

"We have tried people here according to our own established tradition. It still holds."

"I beg to differ. You can only move by a law, civil or canonical. If you spare the canon, try the Bible instead. Whichever option you take, a law of some kind should be our common ground."

> "Do you know of any Church that holds trial by canon?"
> "The Roman Catholics, Jacobites, Anglicans and such others do."
> "It will be long before we can create a canon similar to theirs."
> "Call me back when you have it ready, and I shall be happy to return for a deposition at that time."[22]

The attempt ended as a mistrial. Regardless, the Vicar General ordered that the proceedings state that the defendant refused to answer his questions. The court secretary prepared the documents accordingly and only witnesses of the church party signed them. As he left the premises, Simon asked Kovoor,

---

[22] Kurien, *A Biography of K. V. Simon*, 2nd ed. (Angamally, Kerala: Premier Press, 1990), 144–45.

"There would be no objection to a report of these proceedings in our publications, I suppose."

"You may leave," answered the prelate.

Two months later, the bishop sent out the now infamous "Circular 83" to all of his churches, proscribing any ministry by Simon or association of the church with Simon. The language of the circular was intended to hurt and insult. A spate of further vocal and written attacks from the church followed. Ironically, all of it only thrust Simon to the forefront as a rising public figure. Writing about the event years later, Governor M. M. Thomas commented that Simon was the giver of the verdict on the church in the "case," rather than the other way around. Marxist historian and literary critic P. Govinda Pillai comments on the event in these terse lines: "The trial did not take place. Documents were not signed. The court disbanded. That great prophet was shoved out. He asked them: 'You preach Christ, and do this to me?' 'Such things happen,' they responded, coldly."[23]

Simon was not the first notable Marthomite to draw the denomination's ire on questions of doctrine. A few years earlier, Itty Varghese, better known as Sadhu Kochukunju, a fellow townsman and parishioner, was arraigned by the same Vicar General Kovoor. Kochukunju was a *bhakti* poet and a saintly lay preacher who chose an ascetic way of life while still young. He traveled widely in South India and in Ceylon, preaching and providing ministries of charity to the afflicted. The Sadhu [meaning, ascetic] felt that he should take voluntary baptism by immersion and did so with the help of non-Marthomite ministers. Vicar General Kovoor had a provincial reputation for ready wit, and he was confident of its disarming power. His family was of landed gentry and of societal influence in Tiruvalla. However, while his armor served him little as Simon's inquisitor, he was able to rattle the peaceable Sadhu with little resistance in a "hearing" to which he was summoned. Utterly humiliated by Kovoor's taunts and snide remarks, the Sadhu was served an excommunication letter from the bishop. The Sadhu's easy capitulation and the subsequent defense of it were discussed in many magazine articles and pamphlets, some even in Simon's own periodicals.

The Mar Thoma Church had an official magazine called *Sabha Tharaka*, meaning, "The Star of the Church." A theological writer named K. N. Daniel

---

[23] P. Govinda Pillai, *Selected Treatises*, ed. R. Gopalakrishnan (Thrissur: Kerala Sahitya Akademi, 2012), 533–34.

was its editor. Daniel in the next few decades became Simon's chief adversary. The magazine was a ready platform for Daniel as a denominational spokesman. Daniel published polemics regularly against Simon. They were further aired by face-to-face debates too, with Simon. Attendance at these gatherings, without any major publicity, was invariably large, and people of all faiths and social ranks attended them. Here arose a need for Simon himself to start his own publications. In 1914, a periodical run by P. E. Mammen, a reformist priest of the Mar Thoma Church, had shut down because of budget strain. Simon encouraged Mammen to revive the magazine. Mammen agreed on condition that Simon himself become the editor. Money would not be as big a concern as a steady supply of good quality articles would be, Mammen added. Simon promised Mammen all the help with content and let the latter stay on as editor. Thus in 1916 the *Suvisesha Deepika* [The Gospel Light] came out. Its ongoing volumes regularly carried Simon's articles.

Around this time, Daniel wrote a polemic called *Infant Baptism*. Simon refuted Daniel through a series entitled *Howitzer*, the choice of the title itself allusive of the Hussite Wars in Czechoslovakia. It was followed by another series on *Nicolovite Religion*, its theme being the rejection of episcopacy, in dual allusion to the apostasy condemned in Revelation 2, and the anti-episcopal tracts of John Milton.

The early loss of his brothers and his father deepened Simon's personal spirituality; questions of life, death, and eternity occupied him profoundly. He saw no difference between his own family and the many who had always surrounded him for the privilege of learning from him. His home had become the *gurukula* in the fullest sense: *sishyas* (disciples) joined his household as sons and scholars, eating at his table, learning under his roof, sleeping wherever space was found. The house itself was not large, but that never was a concern to the hosts or to visiting scholars. Some of them were candidates preparing for advanced professional examinations. Academic positions in public institutions were filled by qualifying examinations by the state. Content knowledge was the prime consideration in screening assessments. Large volumes of readings across disciplines were covered in a single or a series of proctored examinations. The texts were from the centralized syllabus of the state. In schools and colleges, the faculty would teach and prepare students for the diploma-granting exams. For the advanced titles of Vidwan, Visharad, Mahopadhyaya, Sastri, or college degrees involving research, learned guides would be necessary. Scholars flocked to Simon for help and guidance. His services or even a small gift of his time would have fetched a decent fee, but there was no expectation of money in anything Simon did, nor was any money taken.

Wherever Simon moved about, a throng of active learners accompanied him. Of them, some helped as note takers of his speeches, which often lasted two to three hours. Others were "repeaters" who took turns to repeat the words of his speeches; in the absence of a PA system, a person of strong, articulate voice would stand next to a speaker and repeat every word in the right tone and power to the audience. Among them were also singers, trained in composition, skilled in the use of instruments, and of course, talented in the classical delivery.

According to his biographer Kurien, Simon, for a twelve-year period from 1894 had been studying the scriptures and their related literature intensely. This was a solitary period in his growth. The episcopal establishments of the time offered little scope of any formative strengths for a seeker. A few European-influenced "Separatists" or Nonconformists appeared spottily in the state. Kerala's wider laity was far from being ready to welcome any new ecclesiastical movement. For them, the St. Thomas heritage as reflected in the land from the patristic era was sufficient. The Reformation was a movement that only Europe needed to concern itself with—the Indians did not need it—at least that was the conviction of the native orthodoxy. Now was the time for Simon to do for Kerala what Luther did for Germany, and even beyond. His affiliation with the Mar Thoma ceased with the aforesaid trial in 1915. Within the next three years, Simon founded a fully indigenous congregation called the Viyojitha Sabha [The Separatist].

Sahitya Darshini, Simon's Literary Academy

In 1909, Simon organized a literary arm called Sahitya Darshini to the local YMCA. Let it be said that in colonial India the YMCA was the gathering place for significant civic events. The purpose was to stimulate active reading habits in the local population and to immerse them in the steady reading of the classics as well as to encourage original writing. Many of the members were people of advanced levels of literary knowledge and abilities. Over fifty men of the area formally joined the study group. However, attendance ranged from one hundred to two hundred, the attendee ages varying from young to older adults of diverse religious backgrounds, but mostly Nairs and Christians. Good public standing was a requirement for membership. Admitted members were to demonstrate the highest standards of ethical conduct. Incidents of disciplinary correction and occasional dismissals by communal consent have also been reported. Great works of philosophy and literature from the Vedic stream, among others, were taken for study, the *Bhagavat Gita* and Solomon's Ecclesiastes being one set of paired texts. This was a successful attempt to acquaint Hindus and Christians with each other's scriptural heritage. Opportunities for poetry or topical presentations was one notable part of the program. The renown of Pampa delta for its literary figures, the critical tastes of its people, and their interest in dialectics have in one way or another come from this group, Simon once said. One of the members was Simon's own academic colleague and his former student, Mr. T. K. Narayana Pillai. This lifelong student later had some illness of the intestine, which claimed his life. Simon's *Nishakalam* (1913), an elegy of a hundred stanzas, laments his friend's death, an event that deeply affected Simon. This work has since been lost, except for a fragment of ten stanzas.

This organization ran well for five full years. By the end of this period, Simon had a crowded itinerary involving regular distance travel.

Glimpses of Simon's Home as a *Gurukula*

Simon's home as a family residence and as a place of learning looked the same. Among the many residents there was the future award-winning writer and translator N. K. Damodaran who was brought to Simon for Sanskrit studies, following his change of career direction from medicine. Damodaran lived in the house for only one year—a period he regrets having been too brief. About the constant learning happening in the home, he says:

> Learners were of diverse levels. The Sanskrit scholars work on *Amarakosa, Siddharoopa, Balaprabodham, Sriramodantam*—these are for beginners. The advanced ones read *Krishnavilasam, Raghuvamsam, Magham, Naishadham,* and such other heavier works of verse; yet another set would read *Ashatanga Hridaya, Horah, Manushyalaya Chandrika*; he does not seem to need a book to read from: all is in his memory. Not only does he recall each line, but even breaks the compound terms, parses them, translates and paraphrases them, leaving no room for ambiguity. When not directly speaking with the pupils, he is reading a new book as is his wont. This he does pacing along the narrow verandah of

the house, every now and then entering the southern room to pick up the slate on his bed to scribble the fresh lines of verse that flow into his mind. The slate version will be copied into the book later.[24]

Mahopadhyaya Daniel

Mahopadhyaya [Sanskrit term for *professor*] Daniel was one of Simon's well-known disciples, an outstanding Sanskrit scholar, educator, and future editor of his poetical works. In his recollections of Simon, he says that the poet could grasp learned texts of any level of density in a single reading. Whatever he read would also be securely stored in his memory "with the firmness of a rock carving."[25] His recall was exact to the chapter, paragraph, and page numbers. He always had a book in hand, no matter what he was doing or where: while brushing his teeth, while at the table, or in bed. His catnap mode of sleep might interrupt his reading for a half hour. He would wake up after each half hour and keep on reading. In the morning, he would be ready with an organized and thorough synopsis of the complete work. While reading, he had no discomfort in talking with visitors.[26]

The Mahopadhyaya describes one of his consultations with Simon, which happened to be on a passage from Mahakavi Dandi's *Dasakumaara Charita*. This was the first time Simon had seen this book. He read the first *sloka* with exact enunciation and put the book aside, then recited it instantly:

ബ്രഹ്മാണ്ഡച്ഛത്രദണ്ഡ: ശതധൃതി ഭവനാം	[bhrahmaantascha thra dantda: shata dhriti
ഭോരുഹോ നാളദണ്ഡ:	bhavanaambho ruho naaladantda:
ക്ഷോണീ നൗകൂപ ദണ്ഡക്ഷരദമര	Kshonee noukoopa dandta: ksharadamara
സരിദ്പട്ടികാ കേതുദണ്ഡ:	sarit pattikaa kethu dantda:
ജ്യോതിശ്ചക്രാ ക്ഷദണ്ഡസ്ത്രീ ഭുവന	Jyotitschakraksha dantdas thribhuvana
വിജയസ്താംഭ ദണ്ഡോംഘ്രീ ദണ്ഡ:	vijaya sthambha dantdomghri dantda:
ശ്രേയത്രയ് വിക്രമസ്തേ വിതരതു	Shreya sthrai vikramastheh vitharathu
വിബുധദ്വേഷിണാം കാലദണ്ഡ:	vibhutadveh dveshinaam kaaladantda:]

Note: Simon frequently writes original lines in Sanskrit as he does in *Vedaviharam*, or cites Sanskrit texts in his other works or speeches where their

---

[24] N. K. Damodaran, "Ente Gurnadhan" [My Great Master] in *Mahakavi K. V. Simon Satabdi* [Centenary].
[25] Mahopadhyaya P. M. Daniel, "The Multifaceted Mahakavi" in *Satabdi* (Kottayam, Kerala: National Book Stall, 1984), 171.
[26] Ibid., 171.

use is necessary. Though Sanskrit is written in Devanagari script, common practice allows Sanskrit matter to be written in vernacular characters of other Indian languages like Malayalam, Kannada, Telugu, Bengali, Gujarati, and so on. This passage here and similar ones hereafter provided within square brackets in Roman characters transliterate the Sanskrit original in Malayalam, accordingly. They are not textual interpretations.

In yet another meeting with Simon, Daniel sought his help on Sankaracharya's commentary on Badrayana Muni's work. There, Sankaracharya compresses a large portion of profound but difficult content. The initial *sutras* that describe the "*Adhyasa Vichar*" not only elude the grasp of even thorough readers, but they also presuppose a rather comfortable knowledge of *Vedanta*, says Daniel. He marked out certain portions that were too challenging for him, which included the following precept:

സൂത്രാർത്ഥോ വർണ്യതേയത്ര	[Sutrartdho varnyatheh yathra
പദൈ: സൂത്രാനുസാരിഭി:	padaii: sutraanu saribhi:
പദാനിച വർണ്യന്തേ ഭാഷ്യം	Swa padaani cha varnyantheh bhashyam
ഭാഷ്യ വിദോ വിദു:	bhashya vidovidu]

"As soon as I started reciting the lines," says the Mahopadhyaya, "my Master [Simon] completed the rest and proceeded to explain it in very accessible language."[27] That was a moment for Daniel to see how well he had mastered Vedic literature and philosophy. He had committed the *Chaturvedas*, *Brahmanas*, *Upanishads*, and the *Smritis* to memory. His exceptional skills in rhetoric, logic, and dialectics, without a doubt, made him an impeccable critic and dialectician. Any text, no matter how complex or puzzling, all of his students and associates alike say, he could grasp in the first reading itself; there was no question of what he commits to memory ever fading from it.

Once while Simon was dictating the matter for his book, *The Tabernacle*, referring at the same time to a number of open English texts, a visitor engaged him in conversation. The scribe felt that verbal activity on an entirely different matter in the middle of writing about such detailed, symbolic material would be disruptive, but Simon told him that the dictation could go on. It was normal for him to give simultaneous dictations or explanations to three or more.

---

[27] Ibid., 170.

The Malankara Viyojithan, a Model Magazine

Simon says he had noticed as early as 1914 that good inspirational writings were a major need for the people he had been addressing. Accordingly, he and Mr. Thomas Kunnath visited Mr. P. E. Mammen, a former Marthomite priest who had shut down his evangelical magazine, *Suvisesha Kodi* [The Gospel Banner]. The magazine was discontinued not for want of funding, but of quality articles. Simon offered to supply that part, which Mammen welcomed, but he wanted Simon to be the editor as well, which he declined. Nonetheless, *Suvisesha Kodi* resumed its publication in 1916 with a new name, *Suvisesha Deepika* [the Gospel Light]. Simon's contributions were the mainstay of the magazine. His presence also drew polemical questions from its growing audience. Among the lead topics featured were controversies on infant baptism and priesthood. The depth of issues debated sufficed to produce collected articles that soon appeared as a series of books. *The Howitzer* series of polemical essays responding to K. N. Daniel, as noted earlier, were magazine articles at first. Likewise, the exchanges with the same man on priesthood resulted in another title, *The Nicolatian Religion*, the title alluding to Revelation 2:6, 14–15. The readership engagement was so vigorous that a new magazine as the print organ of the *Viyojitha* movement seemed timely. Thus, within three years of the inception of the *Deepika*, a new bimonthly publication called *Malankara Viyojithan* (alternately titled, "*The Malabar Separatist*"), was started in 1919, with himself as its chief editor. The opening issue contained the biography of William Carey, the Great Prophecies—Daniel and Revelation, and Book IV of *Sabha Subodhini*, a timeline of the history of the world from Creation to the time of Christ. The idea of "separation" as a principle of holy living was a steadily maintained theme in the magazine. The marketplace had no other publication with similar content. The study of biblical prophecies in the manner that Puritan scholars or learned exegetes had studied and written about was completely unknown in Malayalam until then. The magazine quickly gained popular respect as an outstanding publication with its exegetical serials, polemical articles, poems, creative features such as dialogues in the manner of Plato between a master and disciple, allegorical illustrations, book reviews, formal debates, responses, or rebuttals to issues of controversy, letters to the editor, and diverse topics of reader interest and edifying value. Priced at just one rupee for a whole year, this publication ran until 1928. Reviews say that Kerala history has not had a journal of religious knowledge of its quality before or since. Here is an excerpt from a comment by artist and literary critic Chitramezhuth K. M. Varghese:

> I am boundlessly pleased to see you launch this publication with its masterly strengths. Your work as the nurturing parent of the young "*Viyojithan*" answers the call of the times when Christian publications, even their academic journals of theology, tend to be filled with uninspiring subject matter, not to speak of their pedestrian [provincial] Malayalam. *Viyojithan* sets the bar so high for the industry that our people need no more fear embarrassment from the poor writing normally seen.
>
> Your editorial delighted me. It shows how to shape a sharp editorial. Every sentence spells sweetness while it also is profound .... The exposition of Revelation was edifying ... things only Simon could expound with such power ... the diction is so fresh: I commend you on the title of "bhashyam" [exposition] rather than "Interpretation."[28]

P. J. Thomas of Madras University, one of the foremost Christian literary historians of India, says:

> I wonder how many Keralites there could be like Mr. Simon who have acquired so much learning by sheer personal interest and ability, yet using it all unselfishly as a vocation of *dharma* [one's duty in life in harmony with the cosmic order or the divine law]. The language of your journal is immaculate and the matter under each head of high seriousness.[29]

Poet Mooloor S. Padmanabha Panicker wrote a laudatory sloka on the magazine, along with a prose introduction, commending it to the global audience thus: "So remarkable is the wisdom Simon presents in his *hithopadesa* [rendition of the great teachings] that he is received as a Hindu among Hindus and as a Christian among Christians. Only a person of Simon's abilities could bring out such a learned journal on literary and religious ideas so warmly welcomed by all."[30]

---

[28] T. A. Kurien, *A Biography of K. V. Simon* (Angamally, Kerala: Premier Press, 1990), 205–06.
[29] Ibid., 206.
[30] Ibid., 206–07.

In his *History of the Brethren Churches*, Simon writes of William Kelly (1821–1906), a classicist of Trinity College, and the sequential editor of two magazines, *The Prospectus* (1849–50) and *The Bible Treasury* [Dublin] (1857–1906). The latter was widely acclaimed as the most outstanding religious magazine of its times. Kelly was a close associate of John N. Darby and Samuel P. Tregelles, scholarly authors and Bible commentators of the nineteenth century. What Simon says of Kelly's magazine aptly describes the *Viyojithan* on the Indian subcontinent.

The *Viyojithan* was a necessary and effective voice for Simon. The density of his arguments required study before an opponent would counter it. His writing and speech had the finest tastes of rhetoric as one would find in Augustine's *City of God*, the Apologies of Justin Martyr, or tracts and speeches of Milton. The magazine served as the platform for Simon to respond formally to the Mar Thoma bishop how indefensible his Circular was. Incidentally, in this society, these communiqués of bans and prohibitions from religious hierarchy could hurt a victim in more or less the same way the Nonconformists of England could be hurt in the days of Anglican hegemony.

From his early days onwards, Simon had earned the trust and respect of society, enough to justify poet Mooloor's comment that he could be looked upon as a "Hindu among Hindus and as a Christian among Christians"—this without any trace of disingenuousness in his life. The people of his neighborhood felt happy to join him at 5:30 in his morning prayer at home, where *bhajans* of Christ would be sung, the scriptures read, a brief teaching delivered, and prayer for the day offered. Simon also rendered scripture verses into Sanskrit as their learning texts of added value. This teaching strategy alone distinguished his disciples, young and old alike, as correct and skilled users of language. The morning *vacana-dhyan* or Word meditation was an inherited way of life for him, rather than invented, because his parents used to do the very same thing in their day.

The Viyojitha movement had a powerful literary role, eclipsing most of the religious or social organizations of its period in Kerala history. The *Malankara Viyojithan*, which started out as a bimonthly, became a monthly in short order. Nearly a dozen works of Simon came out during the 1919–28 years, initially as serialized portions, and subsequently as full volumes. These include *Kristheeya Subodhini* (1919), a treatise on baptism; *Sammarjani* [The Cleanser], a refutation of one of the debates with K. N. Daniel; *Sishu Snana Kutaram* [Voiding Infant Baptism], again, another debate with K. N. Daniel; *Sathya Veda Mukuram* [the Mirror of the True Word], a refutation of Thomas

Menachery's *The Protestant Religion and the Bible*; and *Who Turned Catholic?* answering an article in *Satya Deepam*, which Simon mentions also as a door opener in Mallappally, a town deeply entrenched in traditionalism. Many attempts to organize a public event here had resulted only in cold response. All of a sudden, there occurred a mass exodus from the city's Jacobites toward Catholicism. The Jacobites and Marthomites seemed to need someone to shore up their strength, or at least to stem the tide of their loss. An opportunity was suggested to Simon for a public address, which he accepted, delivering a talk on "The Real Catholic Religion." W. O. Oommen, a distinguished Anglican clergyman and educator, provided public support and participation. The event was impactful enough for the city to become the home of a new Viyojitha congregation.

Within its first decade and a half, says Simon's biographer, hardly a town was unaware of the marvel of Simon's orations, the grandeur of his compositions and the sweetness of his music. Literary societies and the religious communities were stirred alike by his skilled writings. In 1928, the Marthomites hosted a literary conference in Pulikeezh at their school grounds, with Father Kuriakose, a priest and university man, presiding. Simon was the chief guest, speaking by request, on Christianity and literature. Around the same time, he gave a civic address to the city of Niranam at the request of its leadership. On a northern trip in 1932, he spoke in a multi-day series on the press grounds of C. Krishnan's newspaper, *Mithavadi* [The Moderate].

Debates and Disputations

As time went on, debates became a recurring need in Simon's mass communications. Debates were part of the culture of Simon's day. An audience that could sit glued to an *Attakadha* presentation, or pick up the allusions of a puranic tale in *Thullal* or folklore, could also listen to a bristling argument of two contested sides of an issue of immediate consequence. Simon seldom initiated them, personally. He was either approached or pressured into giving a response. Of course, he would consent only to causes that agreed with his beliefs and values. However, invariably in all of them, Simon had enormous success and support. In an age when electricity had not reached Aranmula or Kozhenchery, and when the first radio station had not even been set up in the state's capital until after Simon had passed on, print or the spoken word would be the only means of reaching larger audiences. There was no lack, however, of questions for dialogue, or controversies to resolve.

Some of the early issues disputed had to do with fine-spun distinctions of abstract concepts in the phrasings of creeds, questions of eternal security, questions on how the Holy Spirit operates in this age vis-à-vis in the first century, or issues of doctrine that might always remain unresolved. In Maramon, a group arose that preached "sinless perfectionism." The people of Poovathoor, a neighboring town, requested that Simon address this teaching. A public gathering was arranged, granting open time for opponents to respond. Not one did. Similar events occurred in the Ranni debates on the Sikh faith, in Mallappally on the Adventists, and in Kottarakara on Trinitarian controversy. These were mostly spotty wildfires rather easily put out. However, there were two that became long range and historic. The first was with K. N. Daniel, who has already been mentioned, the Marthomite lay leader who was appointed the editor of the church's official magazine called *Sabha Tharaka* [The Star of the Church]. The second was a Krishnan Nambiathiri, latterly known as Swami Agamananda, a Hindutva monk about whom we shall see more below. Daniel was a religious historian, a liturgiologist, and the spokesman for the Marthomite establishment. Ironically, within a short time after the passing of Simon, Daniel became a founding leader of a newer breakaway, yet reformist faction of the Marthomites known as the St. Thomas Evangelical Church of India, which sought to be slightly more pietistic than its source church that he had been defending for the greater part of his life.

The Face off with K. N. Daniel

The Marthomite *Tharaka* had a break in operations for a certain period. When it resumed circulation in 1907, editor K. N. Daniel announced a Q&A feature to involve the audience a little more than it did before. Simon put together a handful of questions on infant baptism and the modus of it. Additionally, he asked what immediate sacramental privileges would be given to the infant to partake of the Holy Communion. Daniel was not heard from for a whole year. Then Simon made a repeat contact with the offer to send the same old questions in case the mail had been lost or misplaced. Simon maintained copies of his correspondence even in those days when there were no mechanical devices of storage and retrieval easily available in the entire country. Daniel had no excuse now. Here is Daniel's reply (notice the absence of any correspondence courtesies):

> I am in receipt of your recent letter. I am not sure where your previous letter is. I will need much time to locate it. I am not sure what the point of your letter is. If my opinion [on the topic of baptism] is of much interest to you, I suggest that you schedule a visit to my office. In fact, I desire to see you and converse with you. Normally I should be in my office from 1–15 of every month. If your purpose is argument, I welcome that too. Let us have a public debate. Feel free to bring as many questions as you might like …. If not, let us write a book together [on these issues] with the arguments of both sides. We can split the publishing costs. Answering your questions by mail, I'm afraid, yields little benefit to the public. Unless the questions sent to me are for the benefit of the public, I cannot set apart the time for it.
>
> K. N. Daniel[31]

Fresh correspondence ensued. Daniel's tone was still acerbic, not much different in tone from the specimen provided above. Daniel had opened another polemic on baptism in *Tharaka* in 1916. Simon answered it exhaustively in thirteen points of refutation. Public opinion had it that Daniel was caving in to Simon. Then, Daniel made a crafty move: he announced in *Tharaka* that Simon had requested (he had not) a debate with him on a series of doctrinal topics. Simon had his own announcement in *Suvisesha Deepika* (The Gospel Light), stating exactly how the call for a debate came about.

On April 22, 1916, the debate started in a *pandal* erected on the grounds of Kochu Koshy Vaidyan of Arattupuzha, with C. T. Varkey of Eraviperoor presiding. Mr. Varkey was a Marthomite, trusted and respected as an educated man, but in his role as a moderator, he proved to be of regrettable ethic. In the ground rules, he stated that he would not comment on the content or the merit of the arguments of either side, nor would there be a verdict of any kind from him as moderator. Simon rose next to ask that the tedious history of the Daniel–Simon correspondence be bypassed for the sake of focusing more intently on the topic of the debate. The correspondence history could only lead to predictable personal attacks or ridicule of his opponent early on,

---

[31] Kurien, *A Biography of K. V. Simon*, 176.

given the tone of Daniel's correspondence in general. Daniel insisted that the background correspondence and each letter should be covered in the debate, which even the moderator felt would be distracting. Daniel had his way. Simon took eight points of flawed reasoning from Daniel's letters, refuting each. At each step, Daniel's lackeys booed, hooted, and made mocking gestures, still losing ground rapidly. Even Daniel himself, instead of addressing the topics, mocked Simon, speaking of his lowly occupation (school teacher), his stature and looks, to tickle the mirth of the groundlings. Simon commented on the rabble thus in this ready epigram:

അലക്ഷ്യം ലജ്ജയില്ലായ്മ യജ്ഞത എന്നിവ എതിരാളിയിൽ	Spite, snub, scorn and catcall the rival;
അട്ടഹാസം പ്രഭൂതോത്രം	The ally, hail: for these
ജയോപായങ്ങളഞ്ചിവ.	five moves the boorish fall.[32]

By his claims and contradictions, Daniel made himself a laughing stock on the very first night. At the end of what seemed like a rain of folly from Daniel, Mr. K. G. Cherian commented in his concluding remarks that Daniel had caused disorder in the meeting by his faulty conduct and frivolous behavior. "He is not going to forget this day, you watch!" Daniel had declared before the debate, but he darted back to his lodge, avoiding any possible contact with the audience at the end. "All I need is a clown's stick, I could do better than Daniel, I swear!" cried out a Hindu guest in the audience.[33]

Then there was the afternoon session, the same day. Simon announced that if the Marthomites were planning to distract the proceedings, the event would have to be canceled. The public sentiments showed great respect for Simon. Daniel's party returned, this time in seriousness. Daniel appeared to flag as the debate progressed. On the day following, it was reported that he had to have medical attention for an upset stomach and vomiting. People joked that the illness could have been out of his anxiety over the debate's outcome. Another Hindu attendee cautioned the gathering that Daniel could slip out before the day was out, and even set a bet on it. Later on, Daniel claimed that he left the debate site because Simon did not answer his questions. The truth was "not that I did not answer, but that the answers were not what Daniel wanted to hear,"[34] said Simon. Incidentally, Simon's photographic memory and his disciples' astute

---

[32] Kurien, *A Biography of K. V. Simon*, 178.
[33] Ibid., 179.
[34] Kurien, *A Biography of K. V. Simon*, 180.

note-taking make any false charges difficult to defend. The complete, attested script of the debate, along with the background correspondence from both sides, appears in Simon's *Sammarjani* [The Cleanser] or the *Job Description for a Marthomite Editor* (1917). This was Simon's response, though gentle, to Daniel's lampoon of Simon, "*A Brethren Leader's Competencies*." By then, Simon also had a following of independent thinkers who were insisting on scriptural support or other such reasons for them to accept a belief or a religious practice. Daniel resumed his attacks, once he had the "*Sammarjani*" in hand. Simon responded promptly through his *Malankara Viyojithan*. These exchanges continued for a decade.

Since Simon's refutations were exhaustively analytical, closing all gaps for a backfire, it was easy to see the audience making clear judgment calls as his reasoning advanced and the flaws of the opponent appeared too large to hide. These debates also give a compelling description of the society's vigorous interest in philosophical and theological questions, regardless of their faith traditions. One is reminded here of the great debates of Augustine in his day against the Manichaeans, Pelagians, Semi Pelagians, Arians, Donatists, and others.

As public discourse was part of his daily routine, be it teaching, preaching, colloquies, or debates, the respect Simon would accord to the opponent reflected the model practices of classical rhetoric, be it Indian, Greek, or Roman. In Simon's day, this virtue was exemplified in no one else, says Chitramezhuth:

> For me to say anything about Simon's literary brilliance will be redundant. More importantly than with writing, I see Simon as a model debater who extends unaffected respect for the opponent. Debates among religious groups, as a rule, tend to be rudely combative, to say the least. The market value of a debate is rated by the degree of insults and injury inflicted on the other party. To speak of an opponent by disparaging terms like "lunatic," "oaf," "muckhead," "cheat," "scavenger," or whatever else, is no etiquette violation at all. "I am solid, he a featherweight," "I am learned, he a bonehead," "I am highborn, he a streetling," and other such claims resound in the debate hall. Some would bluntly decline to engage an opponent on the haughty claim that the opponent lacks the status or is not worthy of their time. Regrettably, the content worth of an argument mattered little. A prominent South Indian denomination uses the "*mooron*" [Syriac term known to most people in Kerala] or the holy anointing oil in their sacraments. Mocking dissenters debating doctrines deride it as "fish oil" used as "barge grease." All that we have known in Christian debating until [Simon's time] have only been expressions of such brutish hatred, utterly disregarding

the dialectical value of a public discussion. There was only one respectable exception to this fact among all debaters, besides Simon: Chief Editor K. C. Mammen Mappilai of Malayala Manorama. Since his work was with political audiences, Simon remains the lone example in religion for civility in debates.[35]

Chitramezhuth says this much about Simon's debate in some measure of indignation about K. N. Daniel at his uncharitable portrayal of Simon even in his autobiography, *Athmavrittha kadhanam* [A Narrative of My Life]. He reminds Daniel that at least after a decade of interactions with Simon, he ought to have known that Kerala has thousands of enlightened individuals who know that Daniel's vilifying tongue and pen can only affirm Simon's nobility.[36]

It was common practice to deliver a formal note of "Intent to Dispute [question]" when there was a concern or controversy voiced by a public figure. The date, time, and the format of a desired response would also be settled upon by mutual agreement. People, regardless of religion, were generally very interested in all of Simon's speeches and debates. The presentation materials were often ready for distribution by overnight printing. Note-taking in all meetings of all parties was a keen journalistic art. Simon had as many writers as were needed because his home was as much a literary place as it was a house of faith, but his opponents were not entirely helpless. They too would be ready for public meetings or counter debates as quickly as they needed to be.

Simon, despite his confident resourcefulness and understated manner with his argumentative abilities, never took pleasure in them. He reminded his disciples that Christ and his apostles conversed with adversarial listeners and even magistrates and rulers in modes of argument, but only to declare the truth and not to hurt others. Simon also believed that while a person may be disarmed in argument, he can never be won by it. Also, rather than choose a learned manner in his discourse, Simon chose deliberately simple speech and showed unaffected courtesy to his opponent.

Hindutva Monk P. Krishnan Nambiathiri: A New Adversary

In the mid-1920s, Simon found a new challenger in P. Krishnan Nambiathiri, later on known as Swami Agamananda (1896–1961), a militant champion

---

[35] Chitramezhuth K. M. Varghese, "Abhiprayam" [Preface] in T. A. Kurien, *Mahakavi K. V. Simon: A Biography*, 2nd ed. (Angamally, Kerala: Premier Printers, 1990), 17–23.
[36] Ibid.

of *Vedantism* and the classical *Hindutva*. Nambiathiri started his vocation as a teacher at a Hindu mission school in Chengannur where he eventually established a religious center as well. He traveled the country as an itinerant Hindu monk of the *Advaita* School, preaching and teaching the philosophies of Sankaracharya, Ramakrishna Paramahamsa, and Vivekananda with the professed goal of creating a unanimous religion based on the *Vedic* or *Brahminic* tradition. As his mission expanded, he relocated to Kalady in central Kerala, which became its headquarters. The swami was among the civic leaders who campaigned for equal rights and Temple Entry through the historic protests of Vaikom and Guruvayoor. Until the 1930s, the *Avarnas* or the *untouchables* were prohibited entry in temples even though they were counted among the Hindus. The swami's support of the cause of the disenfranchised brought him in touch with other nationalist movements and Marxist leaders such as A. K. Gopalan and P. Govinda Pillai. Agamananda founded a Sanskrit high school in Kalady in 1938, which, over the years, grew into a university. His calls for promotion of the knowledge of the *Vedas*, the *Upanishads*, and the *Puranas*, and for the establishment of an egalitarian society, won him the support of India's statesmen like President and philosopher S. Radhakrishnan, President Rajendra Prasad, and the Maharajah of Travancore. His lectures were put together in an anthology entitled *Viravani* in four volumes.

Though Agamananda's vision of life celebrated egalitarian values, his missional agenda through writings, lectures, and debates were adversarial to Christianity. In a widely read tract that he wrote, entitled *Did Christ Die on the Cross*? [Yeshu Kristhu Kroosil Marichuvo?], he attempted to discredit the gospel account of the crucifixion and resurrection of Christ. Simon answered this topic through a response tract titled "The Crucified Christ," which by its content weight and popularity attained the status of a book. The swami would not rest his case, however. He moved on to other fights through a series of public gatherings in different towns where similar provocative claims or questions would be put forth as presentation topics. Here is a short list of topics that the swami spoke on:

- The statement that Eve was created from Adam's rib does not stand to reason. The Vedantic religion accepts only what is rational.
- The Christian religion is a product of whoring. It is devoid of paternity. [The Swami's word choice is too coarse for exact translation.]
- Christian missionaries lack knowledge of *tatvas* [philosophy].

- The Bible and the Koran are vulgar. Nonetheless, both of them or all such works contain the way of salvation. I believe [in] the Bible. The Gospels of Matthew, Mark, and Luke contain great principles. They have helped my formation.
- The Christian religion is not worthy of the name of religion. Hindutva is widespread and teaches *sanatana* [eternal principles]. The Christian religion has no importance among religions.
- It is true that animals were brought for sacrifice [in *vedic* rituals], but sacrifice is not done by slaughter of animals. *Ajamedham* only means to "tie the goat," not kill. The sacrifice of *jnana* surpasses all other sacrifices.
- In Edayaranmula or so, a fellow [Simon] using some nonsense book of Hindus has been heard saying that Siva [the divine being in the Hindu trinity] lusted. Siva is worthy of no higher a position than of ordinary, wayward men like Govinda Pillai, Raman Nair, or others.
- A certain writer [implying Simon] has argued that *yajna* and *yaga* are the same. *Amarakosa* uses the terms as synonyms, but incorrectly. *Amarakosa* has many errors.[37]

The onus of giving a response to Nambiathiri was on all Christian denominations—Catholics, Orthodox, Marthomites, Anglicans, and the fledgling nonconformists like the Brethren and the Pentecostals. The mainline churches that had tens of thousands of laity and titled clergy had none to come forward as a voice of defense against such a challenger. An enlightened minority attempted to dissuade Nambiathiri from his campaign. A collective response was determined to be necessary, but who would be capable of delivering it? Simon did not seek to be that voice, but it was unanimously agreed that Simon should be the person for that role. A two-day meeting with multiple debate sessions was arranged. People from many surrounding towns of Chengannur gathered. Here Simon specifically refuted Nambiathiri's tract, "*The Padre Vs Myself.*"

A month later, an even greater Nambiathiri campaign was initiated. Nambiathiri was the lead speaker again, but he had two other national figures, Messers Rishi Ram and R. C. Das, to assist. All three shared their oneness in goals. An appeal to change the harsh mode of Nambiathiri's mockery and attack went

---

[37] K. V. Simon, *Satyaprakashini: A Response to Three Speeches of P. Krishnan Nambiathiri*, 2nd Impression (Angamally: A. P. Paily Satyaprakashini Depot, 1927), 46.

unheeded. The Christian groups arranged a response event, this time a course of refutations lasting seven days. The venue was a place called Komatt Mattu on the banks of the Pampa. Simon's team examined the speeches of Nambiathiri's side each night with their meticulous notes, confirmed by third-party witnesses before Simon's response. Even then, the Nambiathiri camp would try to cause hindrances by refusing to acknowledge the review. "Hereafter, do not bother us for scrutiny; we have other things to do here," replied Nambiathiri to one of the submissions. Nonetheless, Simon always made sure that the process he elected was above reproach, giving no occasion to the opponent to level false charges later.

Let us take the least abstract of Nambiathiri's topics, an invective directed against the virgin birth of Christ: "The Christian religion is the product of whoring. It is a religion of bastardy."

Here is a portion of Simon's answer in translation:

It is necessary to know that the birth of Christ without participation of the human male fulfills the scriptural prophecy: Even as sin entered the world through woman [without the participation of *purusha* or man], the removal of sin also was to happen without the help of man. Notice the emphasis on Christ's name being the "seed of the woman" [but not of man].

If my opponent thinks Christ's birth rationally absurd, what might he say about the multiple [Hindu] deities that took birth without the participation or the presence of man *or* woman? What does the Vaishnavite work of *Bhagatamala* say about the birth of Kabir? When his mother was a virgin, yet in widowhood, this man [Kabir] was born by the blessing of Ramanand. Likewise, is not Buddha's birth claimed as from Queen Maya as a virgin? (*Pracheen Arya Vrittam* 131). Or, what does Vyasa say about the birth of Karna? While Kunti was yet a virgin, she was conceived of Surya [the Sun]. See a few more yet: From a long list of miraculous births in *Manu Smriti*, consider merely a few:

ഹസ്തിന്യാ മചലോ ജാത: ഉലൂക്യാം കേശ പിംഗല:	[Hastinyaam achalo jaatha ulookyam kesa pingala
അഗസ്ത്യോഗസ്തി പുഷ്പാച്ച കൗശിക:	Agasthyo gasthi pushapaacha kaushika
കുശസംഭവ:	kusha sambhava
ജാംബുകാജ്ജംബു ബുകാഖ്യാശ്ച"	jambukajjambukakhyashcha]

According to this passage, Muni Achala was born of a she-elephant, Kashapingala from an owl, Kaushika from the kusha grass, Marishi Jambu from a fox, the great

Dronacharya came out of an earthen pitcher [kooja], Madhu and Kaitab from Vishnu's earwax, and Sagra's sixty thousand sons from the seeds of a pumpkin gourd. These fabulous accounts offer no rational issue to my honorable opponent, but the Christ story doesn't have a chance, apparently. I wonder why he must single out Christ's virgin birth alone as a case of misandry to slander his followers?

Now, here is another point in the debate, disputing the meaning of the Sanskrit term "*Ajamedham*," which means "sacrifice of a goat." Nambiathiri likes for people to think that Simon either misunderstands or attempts to misrepresent the term. He says:

> A certain writer [Simon] has argued that *yajna* and *yaga* are the same. *Amarakosa* uses the terms as synonyms, but incorrectly. *Amarakosa* has many errors.

Simon's answer:

> The speaker contends that the root meaning of "medha" is "to bind," and that the term "aswamedha" means "to bind the horse." He argues that it only means that a sacrificial animal is bound to the altar, but not slain. Is this rational? If gods require the sacrifice, would they be appeased by merely binding the animal, when the intent of their "coming" is to partake of its sacrificial meat? If the speaker is invited to have coffee, would coffee seeds and sugar brought before the guest be considered coffee?

> We know [from *Vedic* texts] that gods partake only of meat roasted in fire. That fire is also called *havirvahi*. *Havis* is the object dedicated in fire. It is the office of fire to convey the roasted meat to the gods. If fire abandons its duty, gods will die of food deprivation. If *ajamedha* [sacrifice of the goat] and *ashwamedha* [sacrifice of the horse] were to conclude by the mere binding of those animals and followed by their release, the ritual would make no sense. Now consider the utensils of a *vedic* ritual:

> "Yupa," or the stake to which to tie the sacrificial animal
> Water basins
> Vessels to cook meat
> Knives to cleave, carve and bone
> Grill forks to turn the steaks
> Wooden ladles
> Cup to serve *soma rasa*
> Wooden sword to mark altar borders

These utensils signify the handling of a slain animal, not one merely bound. The sacrificial bovine is called *upaakritham*, which indicates ritual slaughter. *Manusmriti* also addresses this requirement thus:

യജ്ഞാർത്ഥം ബ്രാഹ്മണൈർ വധ്യാ:	[Yajnaartham brahmanair vadhya
പ്രശസ്താ മൃഗപക്ഷിണ:	Prasastha mrugapakshina
ഭൃത്യാ നാഞ്ചയ്വ വൃത്യർത്ഥം	Bhrithyananchaiva vrutthyarttham
അഗസ്തോഹ്യാചാരൽ പൂരാ:	Agasthyohyacharal poorah].

Meaning: Brahmins must kill beasts and fowls free of any blemish for sacrifice. For the sake of his servants, Agastya himself slew animals. *Manu Smriti* 8:22.

Another part of the same work firmly justifies animal killing for sacrifice:

യജ്ഞാർത്ഥം പശവ: സൃഷ്ടാ സ്വയമേവ സ്വയംഭുവ	[Yajnaarthham pasava srishta swayameva swayambhuva
യജ്ഞസ്യ ഭൂതൈ സർവസ്യ തസ്മാദ് യജ്ഞേ വധോവധ:	Yajnasya bhoothyei sarvsysa thasmad yajne vadho vadha].

Meaning: Bovines are created for sacrifice, as the main ingredient of every sacrifice. Therefore, killing them is not killing. *Manu Smriti* 5:39.

You would agree that the author of *Manu Smriti* must know more about *Vedas* and its rituals than my opponent does. Nowhere does it say that one may bring a goat, bind it to the altar, and then lead it back home; nor is there any admission that the sacrifice of bovines is a gradual error developed from the misunderstanding of *ajamedham*. The esoteric knowledge that my opponent claims to possess on this matter appears to have bypassed even Sankaracharya. After all, Sankara's *Laghu Dharma Prakashika* says thus:

ക്രത്വാർത്ഥഃ പശവ: പൂർവം വിസൃഷ്ടാ: പരമേഷ്ഠിനാ	[Krthwaattham pasa poorvam vsrushta parameshtina
ക്രതു ഭൂത്യയ്ഹി നിർദിഷ്ടാ: തസ്മാദ്വധോവധ:	Krathu bhoothyihi nirdishta krthou thasmadwtho]

Meaning: Brahma created bovines for sacrifice. Therefore, *himsa* [taking the lives] of them is not forbidden.

വേദേന വിഹിത ഹിംസാ യജ്ഞകർമണ്യനുഗ്രഹാൽ	[Vedena vihitaa himsaa yajna karmanya anugrahaal
ജ്ഞാതവ്യാസാ ത്വ ഹിംസേതി വേദോ ധർമ്മ പ്രവർത്തകഃ	Jnaatha vyaasaa twa himsethi vedo dharma pravartaka]

Meaning: *Veda* activates *dharma*. Cow-slaying is a *vedic* ordinance. For this reason, condemn it not as *himsa*[killing].

Let me add a few more observations on animal sacrifice:

The sacrificial animals mainly were sheep, cow, ox, buffalo, deer and, at times, horse. On occasion, the numbers were in multitudes, an instance of a sacrifice for Indra being made with three hundred buffalo. The historical shift in the venerable regard for the cow in modern Hinduism is at variance with the practice of the Aryan predecessors, who had it for meat. Not only do the Vedas make numerous references to cow sacrifice, but they also offer detailed instructions for the ritual. Yajurveda's *Taitariya Brahmana* is even rather amusing: for Indra, a cow of hefty shank; for Vishnu and Varuna, a barren cow; a black cow to Pushav; to Vayu, a cow of a single calving; to Mitra and Varuna, a single cow of two colors; to Rudra, a red cow; to Surya, a white, barren one.

Every five years they [the Aryans] held a great sacrifice called *pancha sama diyasavam*. Seventeen cows of a tender age were slain in this event, about which *Taitariya Brahmana* states: "He that seeks greatness, let him offer worship with *Pancha sama diyam*, for he shall indeed become great."

Bulls too were deemed suitable as well as cows for sacrifice.

In another portion of *Taitariya Brahmana*, it says:

For Vishnu, a lowline bull; for Indra, a cow of down-curve horns; for Savitri, a dappled one; for Mitra, one of milky white. This was the manner of the offering of the cows: After the recitation of the mantras of presentation, the animal would be tied to a stake tightly. Then, on a spread sheet, it is laid, head westward, legs northward, and killed. Afterwards, the priest announces, *adhwaryu samjnapu*, declaring that the animal indeed has been killed. Dr. Mithra says thus of the dividing of the meat of the sacrificed animals: remove the whole skin in one piece; split the rib cage of the animal to appear similar to an eagle of spread wings; sever the shoulders; sever the twenty-six ribs in proper order; dig a pit to dump the dung and other refuse; pour away the blood for *rakshasas*. O, killer of the cow, O, Agihu, fulfill your charge. Perform it true to the letter.

Gopatha Brahmana of *Atharva Veda* assigns the sacrificial portions to the partaking ministers: two jawbones and the tongue must go to the *Prasthatha* [the leader]; the *Prathihartha* [the chaser] gets the neck and the heel; the *Ulgatha* [the chanter] gets the portion that resembles the spread wing; the *Nestav* gets the right arm. To him in the audience [respondent] the left arm. The Master [the sponsor, offerer], the right leg. His wife, both the left legs. Portions to some were very small, but all could drink plenty of soma juice. Many malisons are pronounced on non-observants.[38]

---

[38] Simon, *Satyaprakashini: A Response to Three Speeches of P. Krishnan Nambiathiri*, 80–89.

Now let us compare for a moment Simon's responses to a similar context of adversarial challenge that St. Augustine handles. Pagan Rome charged that the fall of their empire was caused by the Christian faith when Rome by its own professed faith had the empire in the hands of a multitude of gods whom they appear to have not trusted, after all. In *The City of God*, Book 4.8 Augustine raises a question of logic in Rome's position with a huge array of examples:

> Therefore they set Proserpina over the germinating seeds; over the joints and knots of the stems, the god Nodotus; over the sheaths enfolding the ears, the goddess Volutina; when the sheaths opened that the spike might shoot forth, it was ascribed to the goddess Patelana; when the stems stood all equal with new ears, because the ancients described this equalizing by the term *hostire*, it was ascribed to the goddess Hostilina; when the grain was in flower, it was dedicated to the goddess Flora; when full of milk, to the god Lacturnus; when maturing, to the goddess Matuta; when the crop was runcated,—that is, removed from the soil,—to the goddess Runcina. Nor do I yet recount them all, for I am sick of all this, though it gives them no shame. Only, I have said these very few things, in order that it may be understood they dare by no means say that the Roman empire has been established, increased, and preserved by their deities, who had all their own functions assigned to them in such a way, that no general oversight was entrusted to any one of them.[39]

The sheer weight of Augustine's examples alone suffices to neutralize the argument, which, presumably would have happened in Simon's answers to Agamananda also. Simon is careful to use no personal information or opinions as his ammunition. The complete argument is text-based. He allows the language of the opponent's own resources to silence him.

Now back to the Nambiathiri debate site again. One night Rishi Ram, Nambiathiri's assisting panelist, surprised Simon who was resting in the riverside pandal by showing up there. He wanted a private meeting with Simon to discuss certain questions, he said. This was Ram's designed prelude for his own show with Simon. Simon had no hesitation, but politely asked Mr. Ram if he did not need the time to prepare. He was as prepared as he needed to be, Ram replied, and a debate followed the next day, as desired. Ram took the first turn, starting with a digest of the creed of the Arya Samaj and went on to argue that

---

[39] St. Augustine of Hippo, *The City of God*, Bk IV, ch. 8, https://www.newadvent.org/fathers/120104.htm, accessed June 11, 2022.

humankind would be saved through good deeds and that a provider of salvation was not necessary. He argued that Christ, Krishna, Rama, and the other avatars are not divine beings, and that God does not incarnate. Therefore, believing in beings professedly incarnate or worshipping them would be of no profit, Ram concluded.

As soon as Rishi Ram took his seat, Simon rose, and refuted each of Rishi Ram's points. Simon argued that incarnation, though singular in the Christian story, and numerous in Hinduism, was a common factor between the two religions. Rishi Ram denied both, thus unwittingly blowing the whole argument in the face of his own sponsors. Furthermore, Nambiathiri had his friends wager "one thousand British rupees and one thousand Hindus" to anyone who could prove that idol worship is ineffectual. Simon pointed out that Mr. Ram had done just that very service for him by wrecking the premises of his own claims instead of defending them as intended.

There were other questions also taken up and refuted during the rest of the week. This seven-nighter seemed to bring all of the fuming controversies to an end. Simon said that Nambiathiri could have served his people beneficently by helping them see the knowledge and values in the great works of his own people. In spite of the advantages of a university education, Nambiathiri made claims that were indefensible. As seen already, he would, at one point assert that Christ was not crucified at all; at another he would argue that there never was a person called Christ. Yet he would praise the Christ of the gospels and say that he admired him as an important influence in his formation. Two books came out of Simon's debates, the first a set of selections responding to Nambiathiri, and the other addressing the Arya Samaj. Kurien notes that with this particular debate, the Nambiathiri mission ceased to be a combative force against Christians in Central Travancore.

Rather than assert victory over his opponents, Simon always gave them respect and directed the attention of the audience to the issues in question. In his introduction to *Sathyaprakashini* [The Beacon of Truth], Simon calls the reader's attention to the questions raised, rather than to personalities. "I was only catching the missiles aimed at your house of faith, and sending them back to their source," he tells his readers. The benefit he desires for them is that "Perhaps this task will have helped in acquainting some of you with the writings from which proofs have been drawn." The writings chosen include *Ajnanakutaram, Athyathmaramayanam, Athmapuranam, Athmavidya, Rig Veda Samhita, Katopanishad, Kalisantaranopanishad, Kaveri Mahatmyam, Kumara*

Sambhavam, Krishna Gatha, Krishanarjana Vijayam, Kristhumatha Khandanam (Arya Samaj), Garuda Puranam, Geethartha Deepika, Gopatha Brahmanam, Panchathantra, Brahma Sutra, Brahma Subhashyam, Bhagavat Gita, Manu Smriti, Mandukyakarika, Magha Kavyam, Mundakopanishad, Vivekachudamani, Sivapuranam, and *Skanda Puranam*—at least sixty-five volumes, the majority of them in Sanskrit.[40]

Effective reasoning was at the core of everything Simon did. The articles in *Viyojithan* had regular features of polemical issues deeply studied, refuted, or defended as needed. The painstaking labor in providing authoritative matter in defense is common in every piece, written or oral. Even many of Simon's songs are composed as crystallized arguments and expostulations that serve well to inspire, instruct, convict, or to exhort. In this regard, Simon single-handedly took Malayalam to Mars Hill and prevailed every time he answered an argument.

An Academic Debate that Turned Public

An early episode of a linguistic question that evolved into an engaging public debate is another good instance of Simon's habitual confidence in what he says. Here is what happened. On July 28, 1913, Mr. Kesavan Jolsyar of Edasserimala gave an explication of a poetry portion in Simon's literary club, *Sahitya Darshini*. Jolsyar stated that the term "neela sara" meant "neela thaamara" or blue lotus. T. K. Narayana Pillai, a Simon colleague, politely disagreed, suggesting that the exact meaning should be "karim-koovalam" rather than "neela thaamara." Simon affirmed Narayana Pillai. Jolsyar protested. The matter went beyond the premises of Darshini. With wider scholarly support, three months of public correspondence ensued. Jolsyar claimed that the lotus does exist as a blue flower, and hence the name. Simon offered, as was his manner, a range of proofs supporting his original position and invited Jolsyar to do likewise. At the suggestion of community referees, a settlement debate was announced, appointing a prominent citizen as moderator. Simon produced ample evidence for his claim from *Amarakosam, Collins Dictionary, Siva Rama Apte's English Sanskrit Kosam, Sivarama Gole's Amarasahyan, Akbar Bhashyam,* and a dozen other such works. Jolsyar provided nothing but still kept asking for yet another date, which was declined. On the final day set, as the debate had barely ended,

---

[40] Simon, *Satyaprakashini: A Response to Three Speeches of P. Krishnan Nambiathiri*, 15.

Jolsyar was nowhere to be seen. The debate notes confirmed Simon's argument carried, and it was further attested to by the great grammarian, A. R. Rajaraja Varma at the state university.

Other important debates also occurred over the years, though their texts are missing in the archives. Formal disputations in far-away places such as Ochira were held with Mohemmadans and Nairs. A Hindu teachers' organization requested Simon to speak on the "Principles of Religion," which he did in a two-hour talk. "Hindus are generally well-disposed toward us," says a note by K. T. Mathai on March 3, 1923. In 1925, Simon spoke with visual graphics, in the somewhat distant coastal town of Karunagapally, which was an altogether new thing for the people. They were greatly intrigued, says the report of the event. In February of 1927, Simon and his party came to Pakalur in South Travancore to speak to a gathering of over a thousand; presentation time was also allowed to Mr. P. K. Madhavan Pillai, who "spoke reverently of Christ's incarnation, but castigated Christians and the priestly religion." Madhavan Pillai appears on later dates in other places too as a speaker with Simon at conventions. We are not certain who Pillai is, except that he was a man with university degrees.

Debates with a Former Disciple

Among Simon's early disciples was Pastor K. E. Abraham (1899–1974), the founder of today's Indian Pentecostal Church, which has nearly 10,000 congregations globally. Like Simon, Abraham also was on his career path as a school teacher in his neighboring town of Mulakuzha. His foundational spiritual formation was under the tutelage of Simon. However, the disciple's spiritual journey led him to interactions with Pentecostal missions, which had begun to appear in Kerala in the early decades of the twentieth century. Abraham's ministry as a Pentecostal grew rapidly with congregations forming all over the state and beyond. By 1935, his organization was registered as the South Indian Pentecostal Church, later changing the name to the Indian Pentecostal Church (IPC). Both the Brethren and the Pentecostals find common ground in the scriptures, which they assert as the prime source of their doctrine, but they differ on how the supernatural gifts or charisms of tongues, healing, prophecy, visions, miracles, and so on—as found in Acts 2, 1 Corinthians 12, 14, and other parts of the New Testament—are to be understood or pursued. Many denominations that do not necessarily use the term "Pentecostal" in their profile do exercise the charisms in their faith life all over the world. A joint publication of Nimi Wariboko and L. William Oliveri states that Pentecostalism overlays all denominations including the Catholic and the Orthodox and that their worldwide numbers are well beyond 640 million today.[41] Pentecostal scholar Stanley John Valayil places the number above 700 million, also pointing out that in the 1800s when the Brethren revivalist movements started out in India, the Brethren, the Viyojithas, the Pentecostals, and even the Marthomites had encouraged the experience of the spiritual gifts of the early church in their own practice of faith.[42] The Brethren now tend to believe that such gifts existed in the first century but have since ceased, having served their early purpose of demonstrating the supernatural in their faith. The Pentecostals contend that spiritual gifts are necessary signs of the active work of God, which do not "cease," because they are needed as much today as they were in the beginning. This issue also ended up as a polemical topic in Simon's writings and live debates. According to Abraham's autobiography, there have been ongoing responses to Simon from the Pentecostal camp.

Simon's role as an apologist began to be increasingly affirmed even by denominations that were least likely to recognize his position, much less to solicit his services. His audiences showed representation from all demographics. Nambiathiri and Rishi Ram had riled up the Travancore towns harshly enough even for the Syrian Orthodox Church to begin acting in cooperation with the Viyojitha. The Orthodox platforms tended to be restricted to invitees of their own tradition. A reformist like Simon speaking at one of their events would be a headline story. We have records of the Jacobite lay leader Mallieth Valliakunju scheduling Simon to speak at his denomination's Plenary Convention in Arattupuzha as the keynoter for three nights, Bishop Philexenos' father presiding. Likewise, at a trans-denominational response to Nambiathiri in Kozhenchery, Rev. K. N. Mathew of the Marthomite faith presided. Where communal tensions existed, Simon was escorted, though not at his request, to and from all meeting venues by the Jacobites or Marthomites.

---

[41] Nimi Wariboko and L. William Oliveri. "Society for Pentecostal Studies at 50 Years," in https://brill.com/view/journals/pneu/42/3-4/article-p327_1.xml?language=en *Penuma* (42), Dec 9, 2020, pp. 327–33. Pdf, p. 2.

[42] Stanley John Valayil, "The Rise of New Generation Churches in Kerala Christianity" in *World Christianity* (Boston: Brill, 2020), 273.

Simon's Oratory

Simon has delivered thousands of addresses—literary, cultural, and theological. Some of them would last at least three hours. In religious and philosophical talks, his language was deliberately simple. Such gatherings were generally large, from a few hundred to thousands. Expositions or interpretations of the scriptures as were never done before in the land were his teaching topics. People would come from great distances, say, as far as 20 miles of foot travel, to hear Simon. There was no fatigue at all to the audience in listening to him. An unforgettable anecdote of Simon speaking at a place called Pullad might underscore how keen people were to hear him. A meeting with a large gathering was in progress. A number of guests on the stage were given "courtesy minutes" to greet the audience. As they took their brief speaking turns, one man took a bit too long, with no sign of him coming soon to his much desired closing. Up rose a man then from the crowd, shouting: "Sir, would you be so kind as to yield the precious little time left to Mr. Simon? We have come from our far away homes hoping to hear him, if you don't mind!" Needless to say, the man's expressed impatience embarrassed the organizers, and the political fallout was nothing that could be ignored.

Hardly ever was Simon seen with notes and outlines when he spoke. Yet, his rich and learned thought showed integral build, regardless of the volume of matter delivered. His eloquence was steady from start to finish, reinforced with illustrations, fables, and maxims, recalls Mahopadhyaya Daniel. Lines of wisdom drawn from Sankaracharya, Bhartruhari, Kalidasa, Vyasa, and Valmiki glow like jewels in the body of each address. One should see how Simon brings proof texts from the suktas of the likes of Tayu Manavar and Thiruvalluvar as he clinches an argument, not to speak of the easy humor that laces it all together, says Daniel, who also points to Simon's presentations of science that readily intrigue any mind that has a research bent.

We read about the debating traditions of the church Fathers, the Greek Schools, the Roman Schools, and in later times, of the universities of Europe such as Paris and Oxford. In all of these, the audiences were trained in rhetoric and had expectations of classical merit in their delivery. We also know of the powerful oratory of Duns Scotus, Milton, Luther, and Calvin. Simon's audiences were more diverse. As far as possible, respectable citizens of the hosting city or organization, known for their character and education, would preside. His speeches magnetized the people of all faiths and walks of life. The K. N. Daniel debates had Christians and Hindus attending them, the latter finding full freedom to express their views. So were the other great debates such as those with Krishnan Asan, Rishi Ram, and Nambiathiri.

Dr. W. L. Ferguson, an American auditor, gave this personal account of Simon at the podium (not a debate, but a regular address) in these words:

> The meetings went on in growing audience size from February 10 to 14. The final day brought overflow numbers, covering even the surrounding grounds of the *pandal*, everyone fully absorbed in what they were hearing. Since I did not know the Malayalam language, my speech was in English. Pastor Simon and another speaker like him served as translators, which to me seemed efficient and as quick as the well fed and swelling fire. When Simon himself spoke, there was no need of a translator, obviously. He spoke eloquently, but he needed a "loud speaker." Because there was no PA system, one of his young disciples provided that service. That young man stood right by the speaker's side, repeating every word exactly as heard, in loud voice and clear articulation. How accurate even the tonal shifts were is a striking fact. Pastor Simon seldom spoke for less than an hour. An hour and a half or two was normal. He possesses extreme thoroughness about matters of faith. He does not become nervous before opponents or contrarians. He has a natural gift of humor. He can easily stir his audience and make them think. On the final day, I noticed three of Simon's young "loud speakers" rotating off, exhausted. While each of them lost his voice, Simon who usually suffers a cold, went on, unaffected to the end. Immediately after the closing of the speech, he went to the river with twenty-five of the attendees who were professing candidates for baptism. At the very least, this was an unforgettable event.[43]

The Twelve

As an independent thinker and seeker Simon was essentially "an army of one," in his early days. There were similar seekers, though not in large numbers, in the surrounding towns, however. Moothampakkal Kochukunju Upadeshi, a kindred spirit, organized the Kristheeya Bhrat Sammelanam [the Christian Brotherhood]. Simon was invited to join, and he did, and was soon made president of it. Simon taught topical classes of the Bible and led prayer gatherings on weekdays and open air addresses on Sundays. Good conduct of its members and holy living were important criteria for fellowship status in the Brotherhood. This group

---

[43] K. V. Simon, *The History of the Malankara Separatist Churches* (Tiruvalla: Satyam Publications, 1999), 210–11.

published the *Sangeetha Sathakam* [A Century of Songs] that Simon had composed during this period. They were given the symbolic appellation of "The Twelve" as close associates of Simon, but their headcount was larger. The most visible ones, thanks to their roles of service, were K. M. Varghese, who was with Simon until his last breath; C. I. Kunjikka, signatory and keeper of all records and chronicles, who also was with Simon unto the very end; K. T. Mathai, a faithful assistant and manager of publications; P. I. Oonnoonni, a much loved disciple who in latter days cast a dark cloud of grief over Simon's life; talented helpers such as K. T. Thomas (who also was with Simon, taking care of all matters); Poriyikkal Chacko, and Mathai Bhagavatar (a concert artist). In the history of Reformation spirituality, one sees this group of like-minded souls much similar to the Oxford "Holy Club" of the Wesleys. The label of "Holy Club" was a title of mockery from fellow collegians who found the "methodical" conduct of Wesley and his friends amusing. The "Club" had no more than twenty-five members in it, but all of its members turned out to be influential persons later on, like George Whitefield who led the Great Awakening in America, George Gambolt the Moravian bishop, and James Harvey the writer. Wesley's group set time apart for private prayer in fasting, communion, study of the scriptures and the classics. As an evolving spiritual community, "The Twelve" of Simon's inner circle did no less. They formulated their own lifestyle "rules" by consensus about which we shall say more a bit later. Simon was not keen on all of the proposed rules, but he was prepared to study them since the persons involved in all of them were seeking truth and were willing to formulate a biblical creed that would make sense for all.

The Viyojithas and the Brethren were completely independent congregations without a hierarchy or organizational structure. K. E. Abraham's IPC congregations did create a corporate structure, but nothing resembling episcopal governance. The doctrines of all three were articulated as outcomes of scripture studies. The experience of divine healing, for instance, was emphatically taught in all three, but it was relaxed in practice gradually. Some, like Simon associates Charipurath Scariah and K. C. Cherian, held on to the doctrine of healing more than others did. Skariah was Simon's brother-in-law, too. There were impassioned exchanges between Skariah and the less zealous fellow believers on this topic. However, Skariah himself died of cholera, which was another epidemic of the era.

Two Reports of the Miraculous

Simon appeared to be keenly cautious about the pursuit of "signs and wonders" in faith life, although the Bible supports their manifestation as an authentic part of experiential spirituality. A great many of the stories in the Old and New Testaments narrate the miraculous, most commonly of physical healings. Simon himself came to a point of need to ponder the teaching of healing personally. For a long period of time, he had suffered from a chronic infection on his face. A swelling would develop over a certain number of days, and cause much pain and end up as an open, bleeding sore. It would heal up briefly, only to reappear days or weeks later. The swelling seemed to follow when he was sitting down to write for longer periods, had lack of sleep, or was exposed to the cold wind at night. Many treatments were tried, but all were unsuccessful. The physicians had strongly forbidden stream or immersion baths, which residents of riverside towns habitually enjoyed. Simon turned to prayer, rather privately. Here is his personal account of it:

> The merciful Lord gave me both the guidance and the faith to seek his healing touch. As it states in James 5, I felt that I should be anointed with oil and prayed for. The medically refined oil I had at home would still be "medicine," which has been failing me; I arranged for a brother in the fellowship to anoint me with plain oil and to pray. According to the text, the anointing is to be done by the hand of the elder. I was unsure if the official elder or priest of my then church was a qualified elder [possibly a Marthomite elder who lacked the knowledge of this scripture]. The brother in whom I confided [Skariah Charipurathu] agreed to help and together we went to the riverbank. We knelt and prayed together. The brother then anointed me with oil and I received the promised healing. I then stepped into the river and had a full, immersive bath in its waters. Even though the gift of healing has [historically] ceased in the Church, prayers by divine promptings could still result in instant healing. I am a real-life witness to this truth.[44]

Simon goes on to say that this undeniable experience encouraged him to pray for many sick persons and to have had numerous healings resulting, in fact, to such an extent that there was a general feeling in the Viyojitha community that with such divine provision readily afforded, seeking medical treatment was both unnecessary and even wrong. Some in the fellowship refused to pray for those

---

[44] Kurien, *A Biography of K. V. Simon*, 101.

seeking medical help. Such a position gradually caused difficulties. After further studies, Simon concluded that prayer and medical care work without conflict and that it is not advisable to rule out either of them.

There was yet another incident involving the supernatural that appears in Simon's biography. C. I. Kunjikka has given a clear account of it as an eyewitness in Simon's company. Here is what he says:

> There was a certain Mr. Abraham in Nellikala [a neighboring town within ten miles of Simon's home] who had been under demonic oppression for a long time. The victim said that he could see an apparition dressed like a Brahmin woman approaching him on Tuesday and Friday nights. Once the evil spirit touched the man, he would have the ability to reveal the past of anyone after a mere glance. Many exorcists attempted to free the man of this scary ability. The Marthomites said to him that their bishop could free him from this evil spirit. The demon hissed in response as if to say, "Suit yourself!" and added, "The shepherd is the man who carries the weak sheep, but with your bishop, it's the other way around," mocking the inability of the clergy to engage in spiritual warfare. Another man said that Kochukunju Upadesi, the well-known saintly ascetic, could deliver the man through prayer. The demon replied, "perhaps in the past, but not anymore." Then it was Simon's turn. He came to the house with his disciples C. S. Skariah and C. I. Kunjikka. Simon asked the spirit if it recognized him. The answer was a ready "yes." Asked from where, it said, on the beach of Arattupuzha where Simon was preaching. At this point Simon cleared the crowd and secured the privacy of the family. The possessed man looked out to escape but was ordered to sit still in Christ's name. Simon demanded the demon's immediate departure, once for all. The spirit kept begging for a slight extension of time. Of course, in casting out demons, one does not entertain negotiations with them. Finally, it did leave, though not without some convulsive force exerted on Abraham, in a manner reminiscent of the Mark 9 demoniac.[45]

A number of New Testament portions show similar accounts of people afflicted by demonic spirits being set free. Kunjikka's story would demonstrate its scriptural agreement in the gospel stories found in Mark 5:1–20, Mark 9:14–29, and Acts 19:11–20.

Viyojitha narratives show that the deliverance story broadcast itself and promoted Simon's work in the area. However, Simon gives only a very small number of events that show the evidence of charisms. Instead, he appears to

---

[45] Kurien, *K. V. Simon: A Biography*, 214.

have drawn a line separating the Viyojitha from the Pentecostals on this point of spiritual gifts having "ceased," as he states in the story of his own healing from the facial infection. His debates, speeches, and articles on the subject only made the faultline between the Viyojithas and the Pentecostals even wider. To cap it all off, he even wrote a small booklet called *"Marubhashanishakam"* or a Refutation of the Gift of Unknown Tongues, which has proven to be of less critical value, when compared with his other writings.

The Viyojitha Sabha [The Separatists]

Simon had an active public life from his early twenties onward. His public discourses and teaching had created a following in all of the towns surrounding Edayaranmula. Over a five-year period, he could identify many random individuals with interest in spiritual life. He sent a general invitation to such persons to see if they felt the need for local fellowships. They answered yes. Simon had the option of affiliating them to the Baptist missions or the Brethren assemblies, both of which were small in size and of foreign origin. However, their beliefs were compatible with his own, though still evolving. The general sentiment among the people was to continue independently, with the name of "Viyojitha Sabha" [The Separatist Congregation]. On June 26, 1918, a gathering of delegates from fifteen surrounding towns met at Edasserimala (another riverside village on Pampa's banks). Although this was the first formal move toward organization, the attendees had been active in fellowship at least for five years prior, as kindred spirits of Simon. The fellowship immediately decided that each member ought to be his brother's keeper, as it were, and so, if any among them had been missing or absent for a while, they should be contacted, and if they were sick or had needs, they should be provided with all the support possible. A council of seven, like the seven deacons of Acts 6, was elected, Simon himself being one of them. This was a time of the plague of smallpox in Kerala, which claimed the lives of many households in every town. In Viyojitha's first meeting minutes, an entry appears on one Mr. Kulangara Abraham who died of the epidemic, only to be followed in death soon by his wife. Their two children became orphans, for whom the fellowship appears to have arranged provision for care.

With this initial formal meeting, Viyojitha congregations began to function as autonomous local bodies. Confession of personal faith, followed by baptism by immersion, was the primary step of membership. Participation in Holy Communion required general approval of open testimony. A guest desiring communion must produce a letter of commendation from his or her home church. A self-examination was to precede the partaking of communion. Involvement in litigation, use of intoxicants or tobacco, and the practice of "tying the knot" in wedding were shunned. The communion itself, though allowable in day services, was generally preferred for evenings as the atmosphere then was more suitable for meditation and reflection.

Persecution of the Viyojithas

Persecution from mainline Christian denominations was a common experience for the Viyojithas and the Brethren. Their professed pacifism made them an easy target for cowardly assailants. Reports of harassment and attacks occurred in distressing abundance. The Puthencavu Brethren congregation organized a three-day conference with Simon as the keynote speaker. Rev. Madakathil, a senior Jacobite clergyman, recruited the college youth and teachers of his denomination to disrupt the meetings from the first day to the last. He succeeded in blocking off the Friday night meeting. On Sunday the riot turned wilder as Simon opened his morning speech with the statement, "Christianity is not inherited, but experienced in regeneration." The hecklers told the Brethren to forget about the scheduled evening session, threatening to cut off all access to the place. As a cautionary move, the Brethren organizers abandoned their prepared tent and held the meeting in the prayer hall instead. By then, the Marthomites also joined the Jacobite rioters with gongs, bells, and drums, thus to drown out the speaker. However, since the speaker stood at a good elevation, the sound of his voice still served the audience, to the sheer fury of the howlers. They then sent notes into the meeting hall with topical "questions" as a mere ruse to disrupt Simon's address. Simon's promise to answer the questions in another session for questions alone, or even a debate, would not satisfy them. Many in the larger community of Marthomites and Jacobites, however, were not happy with this menacing behavior of their own disorderly people.

In 1925, the Viyojithas met for their tenth annual conference. The bullying denominational gangs of the previous year reappeared with greater energy. A Marthomite squad from the parish of Rev. C. T. Philipose of Airoor, surrounded the *pandal* on the final night. After the meeting, they approached the European guest speakers, attempting to harass them, but the Europeans ignored the rabble.

Feeling slighted, they made their way, as if in a battle, toward the home where Simon was staying. They were stopped for trespassing by a property owner on the way; "Forget the guy, cut right through," yelled out someone from behind; "No, let us sit out the night here," said others; "He lucked out, for sure. Where I'm from, this guy's home would be waste pile now," bragged another. The pandemonium went on till 1:00 a.m. The rioters decided on a counter meeting right next to [Simon's] *pandal* the following day, and put up signs for their program all over the town.

The next morning, Thottavallil Asan, an honorable citizen and owner of Simon's *pandal* site, posted his own signs to the effect that the place in use by the Viyojitha must remain fully free of any distracting activity. The signs sternly warned the would-be troublers against any disturbance. It helped until noon of Sunday, but in the afternoon, the opponents speedily organized another meeting with Rev. C. P. Abraham of Airoor presiding. Once again, after a deafening round of gongs, a line of speakers took their turns, including a pair of Jacobite youth. Rev. Abraham was unwell physically, but he performed his charge here quite well to please the miscreants. The leaders of this group, as it turned out, were all students and teachers. The news was received with righteous indignation by regional media. *Yuvakesari* [Young Lion], a regional paper from Tiruvalla, wrote on February 25, 1925:

> We have received a lengthy report here on how the Jacobite–Marthomite groups have conspired and carried out plans to obstruct the Viyojitha public conference under the pandal set up near the Kuriannoor Market. In the past there was a similar commotion created at a Hindu convention at the same location. Are we on a religious war here? We urge the religious leaders to rein in their respective followings for the general good of the society.[46]

The protesters could not be dismissed easily. They arranged another gathering with two lay speakers of their own ranks: one, Mr. Mulakuzha Varghese, and the other, a Jacobite catechist who delivered counter-speeches. One of the many college students in the crowd spiced up the challenge speeches with his own fits of loathing, while the mob threw rocks into the Brethren gathering.

In an earlier episode found in multiple sources, a band of opponents sought to waylay and to kill Lonappen, a lay catechist who worked with Volbrecht Nagel in Trichur District. The scheme failed. A tragedy in the Lonappen household that

---

[46] Kurien, *A Biography of K. V. Simon*, 238–39.

soon followed gave an alternative opportunity to the would-be ambushers. In February of 1919, Lonappen's ten-month-old infant twins fell ill by an epidemic. One of them died and was buried in the mission cemetery. Early next morning, Lonappen and his wife found the buried child's body with the coffin dug up and set out near their dwelling. "The people's hatred was at such a high pitch," wrote Nagel's wife Harriet, that the inspector of police advised them to bury the child close to the mission bungalow itself, which was so done. The very next day (March 27, 1919), the other child also died.[47]

Regardless of great persecution, the public image of the Brethren groups, which worked in tandem with the Viyojithas, was impeccable, even to the most reproving eye. There was a major criminal incident from the local Catholics of Trichur against the Brethren. They vandalized the Brethren farms for their crops and their homes for scriptures and gospel materials. The literature that they grabbed was burned in public bonfires. Caste-based services such as those of the barber, the washerman, or the domestics, all traditionally provided by the Dalits, were banned to the Brethren by Catholic threats. Lonappen and Thaiparambil Joseph, a fellow worker of Lonappen, were repeatedly targeted for attack.

A Court Judgment

The Brethren position was to suffer violence for the glory of the gospel rather than to sue the assailants. However, there was enough evil publicly done to them in Angamally that the government itself pressed charges against their local miscreants. In the written judgment, the court documented the beliefs of the victimized Brethren, their biblical values, and the differences between the traditionalists and them. Their refusal to go to court to secure protection was also underscored. What was done against these men and their families, noted the judge, was entirely out of religious hatred and that it was a mere replay of the Christian history of the first century. Fourteen of the mob leaders were convicted for violence and aggression in this case. In his *History of the Malankara Separatist Churches* Simon cites a portion of the court's judgment:

> October 16, 1922, Case #19, P5, ¶2
>
> This is a case of religious hatred. The Brethren believe that all Christians are equal as brothers and sisters, none higher nor lower than another, and therefore,

---

[47] Varghese Mathai, *The Malabar Mandate*, 2nd ed. (Zurich: ICHE, 2015), 69.

only Jesus Christ the Son of God has the power to forgive sins, not priests. This is contrary to the Roman Catholic teachings.

The animosities rose to the highest pitch during the week of 1097 Thulam 19–21. The able-bodied defendants assaulted Witnesses 1–4 of the Brethren by slapping, kicking, and battery. Defendants 5–7 forcefully entered the homes of the plaintiffs. They seized Bibles, books, and other literature, and led Witnesses 6, 7, and 8 by force all the way to the Jacobite Church, with the din of drums, trumpets, and the waving of palm fronds in mock procession, and forced them to worship by the Jacobite liturgy. The defendants burned the books they had seized, in a bonfire in the Angamally market square. Some of the others broke into the mission bungalow in Angamally. Witness #1 Lonappan's tapioca patches were thrashed and laid waste, the books, mats, clothes, and personal effects taken away. Rocks were thrown at the mission house and at the people in worship, harming them. The public were turned away from purchasing merchandise from Brethren businesses in Angamally.

Pages 9–11, ¶¶5–6: The Catholic displeasure against the Brethren is evident by the account in section B of the latter's petition. It describes the unearthing of the buried body of the child of Witness #1 with the coffin and placing it within sight from the mission bungalow. The police inspector of Alwaye has investigated and confirmed the report. The Catholic vicar of Angamally had prohibited his parishioners from attending any Brethren meeting, as he has testified. The Brethren consider Father Vettikapally, the curate of Angamally, a man of integrity, even by their testimony. Mr. Davies, an English Missionary and Witness #8 of the Brethren, was assured by the priest that "within 12 hours, he would make sure that all hostilities from his flock have ended." The court regrets that Father Vettikapally did little to assuage this distressing situation.

The Brethren seem disposed to forgive the offenses suffered and to decline their right to press charges. They appear to believe that it is a privilege to endure harm for the sake of their faith. When Witness #1 was manhandled, he knelt down and prayed, at which time the defendants hit and kicked him, shouting swear words at him. His appeal shows the man praying for them to be blessed. Likewise, when Witness #3 was stricken, he glorified Jesus. When they are robbed of their property or physically harmed, they refuse to take legal recourse.[48]

These are not rare events. It is not surprising at all that rioters can take the law into their own hands and do what they will. Both the aggressors and their victims belong to the same larger house of faith with separate labels. One can't help recall the lines of Milton, which Simon was well versed in:

---

[48] Simon, *The History of the Malankara Separatist Churches*, 312–15.

> O shame to men! Devil with devil damned
> Firm concord holds; men only disagree
> Of creatures rational, though under hope
> Of heavenly grace, and, God proclaiming peace,
> Yet live in hatred, enmity, and strife
> Among themselves, and levy cruel wars
> Wasting the earth, each other to destroy:
> As if (which might induce us to accord)
> Man had not hellish foes enough besides,
> That day and night for his destruction wait![49]

The Viyojitha Sabha continued until 1929, that is, until they merged with the Brethren. By this date, thirty-four congregations had become members of the Viyojitha general conference. As a denomination, the Brethren are of European origin. Their work in India began with the arrival of Anthony Groves from Ireland to India in the early 1830s, but carried on largely by very gifted natives, the chief of whom was John C. Arulappan. In numbers, the Brethren were very small and in polity they were independent assemblies with no organizational network. The merger was smooth for the most part. There were no material assets on either side to require transactional concerns. One sees no glaring differences between the Brethren and the Viyojitha except that the latter had a total native flair and passion to it. K. A. Philip's comment on this merger couldn't be improved: "It was so perfect a union that it was difficult to say who joined who, i.e., whether the Viyojithas joined the Brethren or the other way around."[50]

The Viyojitha Lifestyle

Among the Viyojithas were rigorous purists as with any other such movement. They held the view that their organization would take no name at all. The situation brings to mind an imaginary contest of medieval European monks that John Donne presents in one of his sermons. Here is the situation in paraphrase: a large community of monks pursues the practice of utmost humility in their vocation. Accordingly, they call themselves *Ignorantes*, meaning, ignorant men, professing to know nothing. Another order follows them with the humbler

---

[49] *John Milton, Paradise Lost*, 2, 497–505. http://knarf.english.upenn.edu/Milton. All subsequent quotations from *Paradise Lost* will appear with the title abbreviation of "PL" and line numbers.

[50] K. A. Philip, "A Short Biography of K. V. Simon," in *Kristheeya Sangeetha Ratnavali*, ed. P. M. Daniel (Mylapra, Kerala: Gospel Tract Society, 1983), p. xix.

name of *Minorites*, meaning, less than anyone else; however, they are soon outdone by the *Minims*, who claim to be less than small; yet another group goes still lower with the name *Nullani*, meaning, "nothing at all," all in good intent and in aggressive degrees of fervor.[51] Now, for Simon's people, the names "Viyojitha" and "Brethren" were in synonymous use. Their lifestyle was evolved by gradual emulation from culture, the scripture, and a kind of ongoing radical reasoning. All active members decided that they would keep themselves away from stimulants and intoxicants. A cultural habit of chewing tobacco with a mouth-reddening roll of green betal leaf, arec nut, and lime was condemned. The Viyojithas had little controversy among themselves in renouncing it. They began to be noticed in white garments, as Charles Lamb noted of the Quakers, whose gatherings looked like a field of white lilies. Eventually the simple, clean, white attire became the norm. For employment, although the choices were extremely limited in the early twentieth century, there was a general indifference toward the entertainment industry, alcohol manufacture and marketing, commercial careers of a shady nature, and even investment programs that used promotional gimmicks. A certain Puritan plainness moved them toward renouncing jewelry altogether. All of these lifestyle practices were, without any difference of opinion, adopted by the much larger Pentecostal churches too. As a result, at least in the Indian context, it became easy to spot a Pentecostal or Brethren individual by what she or he did not have on their person.

Culturally, the practice of forgoing jewelry did have some impact. In Indian wedding ceremonies of both Hindus and Christians, there is a traditional practice of the groom tying the proverbial "knot" of the *tali* around his bride's neck. The *tali* is a gold pendant on silk strands drawn from the bride's *mantrakodi*, or bridal gown. The word "gown" might signify something completely different in the West. The Indian bride generally has her special *saree* as the equivalent of a gown, with which she will be hooded after the tying of the knot. The word *minnu* is used as the synonym of *tali* among Kerala's Christians. So the *tali* or the *minnu* is a string necklace, one might say; the pendant on it for Christians is adorned with the goldsmith's craftwork of the figure of the cross over the shape of the heart. With the pendant on the string, the groom stands behind the bride and ties the silk thread knot to symbolize their union by marriage. After the "tying" (and after the whole ceremony), the pendant is transferred to a gold necklace to stay on it permanently. In the West, a ring takes the place of the *tali*. However,

---

[51] John Donne, "Sermon LXXII," in *Eighty Sermons*, ed. Evelyn Simpson and Reuben Potter, https://contentdm.lib.byu.edu/digital/collection/JohnDonne/id/3493/rec/2, 11–12, accessed June 14, 2022.

the Keralite Brethren and Pentecostals whose faith's origin is in the West, take exception even to the ring. There will be no exchange of rings at the wedding of a Keralite Pentecostal or Brethren believer even in the West, but young people have plenty of ways of getting around it. Either they will arrange the wedding in an English setting with an English-speaking minister or have compromises set in place with the desired changes accommodated. Historically, one can see marks of such avowed plainness of personal grooming in the Wesleyan and eventual holiness movements, but the Viyojithas of Kerala improved upon it further and made it a cultural signature. Decades earlier, Vidwankutty of the Yuyomite movement asked his followers to forgo ornaments, and they did. The practice prevailed and assumed the status of a doctrine since the mid-nineteenth century among Kerala's holiness revivalists.

In the 1920s the Viyojitha had a ministry wing called the *Prayer Samaj* which encouraged lay initiatives of faith-sharing. It gained considerable momentum, attracting new believers even from the distant provinces of Kochi and Malabar. Simon led the meetings as its principal teacher and speaker. Participants were at full liberty to share their knowledge and experiences to exhort others. It had many of the marks of a full-fledged revival movement. Prayers were spontaneous and fervent. Conversions occurred by the shared stories. At the close of the meetings, the hosting local *sangh* or home served a meal to all, even to the people who came as curious observers. Simon notes that private individuals gladly hosted the fellowship meals in their homes, spending as much as Rs 40.00 (a large sum for common folk in the Great Depression years). Lack of money seldom affected hospitality in Simon's home or ministry locations. A two-day meeting of two hundred representatives of the Prayer Samaj, says K. T. Mathai in his diary, "went well, the guests fed with 30 bushels of rice" alone. Another meeting with four hundred people, also notes Mathai, without details, closed, "all fed."[52]

The women's wing of the *Samaj* started in 1922, as a notable recognition of the gifts and leadership of women. The Youth Front held collective activities as much for intellectual development as they did for the spiritual. Affiliated to the YMCA, they practiced oratory, debating, literary review, and studies in comparative literatures. These activities produced a large number of speakers and writers in the Brethren community, despite their smaller population in comparison with the mainline denominations.

---

[52] K. T. Mathai, *The Beats of Time: The Diary of a Viyojitha*, ed. K. M. John and K. M. Philippose (Mumbai: Ebenezer Printing House, 2004), 96, 112, 123, 138.

Vedaviharam, Simon's Epic Poem[53]

In 1927, K. C. Mammen Mappilai, chief editor of *Malayala Manorama*, India's leading news daily, invited Simon for a personal meeting. Mammen Mappilai used the occasion to learn more about the nascent Viyojitha movement, Simon's responsibilities in it, the sources of support of the organization and even Simon's own, personally. The discussion then turned to Manorama's publications, particularly the literary magazine *Bhasha Poshini* and the daily in which Simon could have an effective role. Mammen Mappilai told Simon that his literary work ought to continue, even with the spiritual pursuits as a sacred priority because his gifts were far too great to be set aside. The great literary patron also had a request list for Simon: first, render individual books of the Bible [which at this time was a century old in its first native translation and awaiting a new rendition] in modern prose; second, compose the Bible in verse form, in the Kilippattu meter, in the way Ezhuthachan's *Ramayanam* is written; third, compose devotional songs and *bhajans* for common use in homes and for social events. All of these were long overdue in Malayalam literature, he said, but Simon was the man to begin the work. Mammen Mappilai promised the support of the entire Manorama establishment and of his own. He also asked Simon to relocate with family to Kottayam and to live close to Manorama, all costs borne by the company. Simon would have full liberty to set his own schedule for work or ministry.

Correspondence and occasional meetings between Simon and Mammen Mappilai continued. Simon was immersed in his public life as speaker and writer and kept on begging off the requests for formally associating himself with *Manorama*. However, Simon had fulfilled many of Mammen Mappilai's

---

[53] The title of the epic, "*Vedaviharam*" [Veda Viharam] would mean "movements through the sacred script," "A journey through the Vedic Vistas," or "Visions of the Veda." I choose the phrase "A Vedic Odyssey." To the Indian mind, the term "Vedas" primarily denotes the four Vedas or *samhitas* that are foundational to Hindu scriptures: *Rg*, *Yajur*, *Sama*, and *Atharva*, written in Vedic Sanskrit. They are considered "*sruti*" of what is "heard" from the great *rishis* or sages. Some believe that Brahma himself is the author of the Vedas. The knowledge received by the hearing has been inscribed on palm leaves dating back to 500 BCE. They contain teachings, hymns, rituals, and poems. Literally, the word means "sacred knowledge," which makes it a term applicable without conflict to the scriptures of other religions as well. When the Bible was fully translated into Malayalam, scholars like Bailey, Chattoo Menon, and Gundert called it "*Christu Vedam*" or "*Satya Veda Pusthakam*," i.e., the *Veda* of Christ or the Book of the True Veda of Christ. "Vedic" is the adjectival form of the word. The first printed and published book in Malayalam, *Samkshepa Vedartham* (1772) by Clement Peaneus, may be translated as *The Essentials of Veda* or the Quintessential *Veda*.

suggestions. Hundreds of songs and hymns were written; many scripture portions were rendered in performance quality verse, in Carnatic ragas. The Christ story and scripture texts appeared in *khanda kavyas* or longer poems. Even the largest project in Mammen Mappilai's list, the Bible in Kilippattu verse, was soon to start. He had the desire to do this even from his early youth. About this, Simon would say later:

> Christians of Kerala receive criticism, not unfairly, I should say, for their alleged disinterest in Literature. The consequent absence of appealing literary works is not easily defensible. Hindu children are fortunate to be born into the milieu of great literary works and devotional music that modulate their language. On the other hand, the Christian child has few of such writings to draw from. The *Biblia* that the Christian reads is written cryptically, with its emphasis on the narrative matter. Therefore, even as a child, I had felt that if the Christian story were written in the narrative vastness and the poetic beauty of the *Ramayana* and *Mahabharata*, the results would have been hugely different. A *gaatha* (the epic song) composed metrically, moves the heart and lifts the soul. In the process, the language of both writing and speech receive refinement. There is no greater theme more suitable for poetry than devotion to God. All nations and religions that possess great literature have found their source in God and in what is said about God. *The Rg Veda* and the Bible bear out this truth as the most ancient of literary works.
>
> From childhood onwards I had desired to see the Bible in verse, at least as an alternate form. I did little about it until I received the strong promptings from a literary man and dear friend, Artist K. M. Varghese, and Mr. K. C. Mammen Mappilai. An added incentive was an article by Mooloor in *Manorama* written in commendation of Kattakayam Cherian Mappilai's epic, *Seeyeshu Vijayam*. I started the work in 1929, rendering the book of Genesis in the native meter rather than in Sanskrit. The whole project took one year, but practical difficulties delayed the release of its first edition until 1931.[54]

Knowing that Simon had the full manuscript of the poem ready, some close friends like K. G. Thomas of Ranni and K. T. Mathai urged Simon to present a portion of it at the annual Parishad [conference] of the state literary society in the capital city. Although invited, Simon was hesitant to go, but agreed at the last minute. Mathai accompanied Simon, with a letter from Mooloor for Ulloor S. Parameswar Iyer, the president of the conference, recommending Simon for

---

[54] Simon, Introduction to *Vedaviharam*, 20–21.

inclusion in the program. For some reason, perhaps the lateness of Simon's request or the tightness of the program, Ulloor said that it would be difficult. More importantly, he did not want to be disturbed during his *murajapam* (a devotional exercise), which seems to have been going on according to the religious calendar. Ulloor was a very orthodox Brahmin, observant of all religious rituals and cycles of devotion. He seems to have been splitting his time between the devotionals and the literary conference. The request moved to I. C. Chacko, the state geologist and a great scholar who was to chair the gathering on Day Two. Mr. Chacko had heard select portions of the poem in a private recital by Simon himself and directed that its invocation be the presentation piece in the Parishad on Day Three. Though the opening lines of Simon invite startling comparison with the opening of Milton's *Paradise Lost*, Simon chose "The Burning of Sodom" from chapter 19 of his poem on the dreadful judgment of sin. Simon's musical delivery magnetized the gathering, a great ovation and spontaneous praises ensuing. His work *Vedaviharam* was adjudged the best in poetry in the Parishad of 1930, with commendable press coverage. It was still a private, lone copy manuscript.

The Madras Lecture Tour

The release and the reviews of *Vedaviharam* in 1931 brought numerous invitations from within and outside the state. The city of Madras had a significant Simon following, both academic and religious. In November, 1933 he traveled to the city for a packed circuit of literary addresses. On November 20, he spoke at the Madras Christian College. Lawyer, judge, and historian K. P. Padmanabha Menon presided. Simon gave a signed copy of *Vedaviharam* to Menon.

On November 24, he spoke at the Broadway Hall, on religion. The following day, he was scheduled to address the Women's Christian College on literature, hosted by Munshi Kuttikrishna Menon and Professor P. O. Oommen. Two days later, there was a public gathering at the YMCA, hosted by Dr. P. K. Koshy of Madras Medical College. November 28 was set apart for a formal recital of Simon verse, specifically, *Vedaviharam*. The audience was very large, all with equal interest in the dual value of poetry and music in Simon's renditions. He rested at Keralaya where Nataraja Guru, the Sorbonne-educated son of Dr. P. Palpu, the founder of SNDP, the Hindu egalitarian movement, visited Simon. The guru himself presided over another literary gathering in Simon's honor, where Simon spoke again. Sree Narayana Guru was the greatest of Hindu social reformers of Kerala. His caste of Ezhavas was the largest subcaste, deprived of many of the rights of mainstream Hindus, including the right to worship and the right for women to cover their breasts. Both Dr. Palpu and his son Dr. Natrarajan, despite their degrees from Oxford, Cambridge, and the Sorbonne, were denied employment and the deserved recognition by Kerala's royal government. They thus had to migrate to the neighboring state, which offered them places of honor that their home state chose not to give them. The significance of these individuals, not only as contemporaries but also as hosts of Simon, is worthy of historical study. On his final day of the Madras tour, Madras University's Malayalam Reader (professor) Chelanat Achutha Menon organized a session for university scholars, with a high tea following. K. N. Sankaran Unni, K. V. Sankaran Nair, Vidwan A. V. Kuttikrishna Menon, and Vidwan K. Govinda Pisharadi were among the distinguished guests.

The Madras visit, though brief, was packed with celebratory presentations of *Vedaviharam*. The majority of scholars providing leadership to the activities were Hindus. The time was used most economically, with hardly any gaps or waste. For his private pleasure, Simon spent time at the Madras Public Library, looking closely at the stacks of medicine, religion, history, and literature. Another stop was the tomb of Apostle Thomas, also located in the city. The visit brought financial relief to Simon who would not seek it voluntarily: Dr. P. K. Koshy inquired keenly of Simon's literary work and discovered that Simon owed Rs. 400 to the CMS Press, needless to say, an extremely large amount in the Depression decade, toward the publishing cost of *Vedaviharam*. Dr. Koshy took care of that burden then and there, entirely. Professor Chelatt Achutha Menon on his part recommended "The Loss of Paradise" section of *Vedaviharam* as part of the poetry syllabus for Travancore schools—in Indian education it takes great political leverage to make such things happen—but here the request came directly from a Travancore state official himself.

"Sons of Simon"

Simon had no son of his own, said his widow Rahelamma who outlived him by nearly four decades, but had many sons, in the sense we speak of the "Sons of Ben," or "Sons of the Prophet." While labels like Johnsonians, neo-Aristotelians, Pre-Raphaelites, Augustans, the Bloomsbury group, and others from age to age describe common traits or practices among them or perhaps the overarching influence of one person over the rest, with Simon, the impact was different. Simon personally nurtured a large number of scholars in his home itself or not too far from it. Easily recognized in the twentieth-century world of letters are Edayaranmula K. M. Varghese, Simon's nephew, educator, encyclopedist, and poet; Mahakavi and Professor Puthencavu Mathen Tharakan; Professor K. M. Daniel, a literary critic as well as another nephew of Simon; Padmabhushan K. M. George, author, literary historian, and chief editor of the Malayalam Encyclopedia; hymnodist, writer, and editor M. E. Cherian; artist, hymnist, poet, and orator T. K. Samuel; K. E. Abraham, author and founder of the 1-million strong Indian Pentecostal movement; K. G. Thomas, Brethren leader and writer; educator and Sanskrit scholar P. M. Daniel; and J. C. Dev, journalist, author, and scholar; add to these an undetermined number of *sishyas* of diverse talents in music, oratory, journalism, and what not, all of unselfish dedication.

In a review of the accomplishments of the Viyojitha movement, Simon said that nearly all of the well-known speakers of Kerala of his time either belong to it or have followed the mode of communications training received from it. He was not claiming that these included all social and political categories, but the hundreds of trainees enrolled in his Sahitya Darshini do underscore wide representation. Every Viyojitha, even the elderly, has the ability to question or debate a heresy and stand his ground, he noted. The practice of citing proof texts, even from poetry, is easily traced to Viyojitha influence. Women, who culturally had always been behind the scenes, found their own visible roles of service. Instead of blindly following set rituals, inquiry and analysis became the default steps of purposeful activity. Young men turned to studies of classics and the Sanskrit language, needless to say, emulating the "Sons of Simon," and found themselves well rewarded for their labors. The degree of "Sastri" or licentiate in language opened doors in education. Literary studies helped them appreciate Hindu religious texts and to engage in discourses with those that enjoyed them.[55]

In their publishing work, Simon's teams of helpers were as good as or better than professionals. They prepared copies of new manuscripts with speed that duly met the demand. In the days when printing was all manual and strenuous, all literature from Simon appeared clean and flawless, with glossaries and footnotes as needed. *Pashandta Matha Mardanam* [On Heresies], a book of

---

[55] Simon, *History of Malankara Separatist Churches*, 217.

150 pages, was written in merely two weeks and readied for marketing within another two. Not only were Simon's disciples scribes for their master, but they were also authors in their own right. Many of them wrote good poetry. Others wrote hymns. All of them wrote powerful prose and ran periodicals and publishing firms. In the biography column of *Viyojithan*, Simon once introduced the Venerable Bede, the scholar-monk of Jarrow, England to his readers. Bede wrote forty-five scholarly books, all of them without using anybody's assistance. He said of himself, "I am my own secretary; I dictate, I compose, I copy all myself."[56] This was so until his last illness at the age of sixty-two. For his final task, he had to use the help of a young scribe called Wilbert. Bede's dictation of John's Gospel in translation went on all day. In the evening Wilbert said to Bede, "Dear Master, there is one more sentence that we need to finish." "Write it down fast," said Bede. He did so and told Bede, "Master, it is finished." Bede responded: "Good. You have spoken the truth. It is finished."[57] Bede was literally in a race against the hour of his death, which was on May 24, 735. Simon's life was not dissimilar. He was shaping generations of people of letters through the school of the Spirit.

No Good Deed Goes Unpunished

It is difficult to see how Simon could have adversaries. While he had a multitude of "sons" of reverential affection as disciples, some turned against him, still firmly holding on to their places among the Brethren. From the early days on, his idealism antagonized some people. Simon opposed the practice of professionalizing the clergy with titles, salary, and a central administration. Affiliation with a large native organization or a foreign mission would ensure workers a livable income or better. Living with no contracted income was a much greater challenge for a nondenominational minister in India in the early twentieth century than it would be in a Western nation. Yet that is what Simon chose. Not many of his disciples favored this manner of living entirely by faith.

A designed plan of snubbing Simon played out, much to the dismay of the multitude, at an annual convention where all of the Brethren congregations and the public came together. From the early years on, Western missionaries would

---

[56] https://celticsaints.org/2014/0526a.html (accessed June 14, 2022).
[57] Ibid.

be the featured speakers at this large gathering. In due course, Simon was added to the panel, and soon it became clear that the entire crowd was coming mainly to hear Simon. This particular year, Simon as the speaker was seated on the stage as expected. A regional representative stepped up to announce that there was a change in the program with regards to the speaker for the day, who would be Simon. The man said that Simon was unwell and needed rest, and so one of the Westerners present would step in for him. Mr. George Mattackal, a leader sympathetic to Simon, then rose and demanded to know how a man seated in plain view of all in his normal health could all of a sudden be so indisposed as to need rest. Being put on the spot, the organizer had to explain his statement. The question went to Simon who said that as far as he knew, there was nothing wrong with his health and that he came prepared to speak. Nevertheless, since the organizers had arranged for the missionary guest, Simon gladly yielded the time to that person. Again, at another time, still in the same place, the usual keynote was taken away from Simon and the closing slot was assigned instead. That spot was only a space-filler of the last day when people prepare to leave early for their long journey back home on foot. They would not be able to stay back long enough to hear Simon completely and still make it home before it was late into the night. That was the result intended, however. Simon did speak, and the text he chose was double-edged: 2 Samuel 2:14, "And Abner said to Joab, let the young men now arise and play before us." Simon handled the moment with such witty mastery that makes one recall Hamlet's staging of the "play within the play" that helps convict his uncle Claudius for the murder of his father. Let it be said that Simon thought nothing ill of the political slighting in this episode.

Once, Simon arrived at the town of Anicatt to speak. Opponents denied him access to the building. The public intervened with their help. Simon spoke out of courtesy to those who had invited him and returned home on foot, in the rain. Likewise, a meeting at Edasserimala became impossible as planned when one of the men with him broke ranks, and his son took hold of the keys to the meeting hall to prevent Simon's entry. Instead of resisting, Simon walked over to the public grounds and delivered his talk.

Kurien states how the Kallissery Brethren church took keen pride in never letting Simon enter its premises. How a man whose presence was a rare honor anywhere in the world would be shut out of the fellowship of some is quite a mystery. A reasonable cause could only have been the question of money, however little there was of it, or envy, some say. Staying with Simon for monetary benefits would be a disappointing strategy if money were one's end goal. At the same time, someone envying Simon is no more to be minded than the wick lamp grudging the midday sun.

Closest to home, an inner circle disciple whose name has not been stated publicly, took complete control of the Edayaranmula congregational site, the Noel Memorial School, which was built on the property Simon had donated. This man managed to close access to the building in order to deprive Simon of his place of worship in his final years. Alternatively, an arrangement was worked out by some men to hold a "house church" at Simon's residence. It ended up being nothing more than Simon and his small household staying homebound, after all.

Speaking of rewards earned, Simon's priceless library, the prime piece of his estate, disappeared as quickly as could be imagined, no sooner than he drew his last breath. Simon had written his autobiography, which was ready for print and would have been a classic, without question. It is heard that a close associate "borrowed" the manuscript copy, but it never made its way back to the house. Some of Simon's disciples who knew the man inquired of him as to where it could be. He asserted that he indeed returned the sole copy to the house, but the house offers no trace of it. The work is presumed lost, but it is cited in parts of Kurien's biography. Reports further say that the same person who borrowed the manuscript also hauled away a large number of books from Simon's library in a bullock cart. In the 1930s, Simon had a money investment of $3,000 in the collection of the many major titles that he had acquired. In the 2020s, its corresponding value would approximate $50,000. His poem "My Library," written at the request of Malayala Manorama Special Edition, gives a partial glimpse of his favorite titles collected from across the globe:

Ente Grandhasala [My Library]
Selected Portions [The Malayalam original in whole is provided in Appendix]

My five-year-old eyes caught a luring sight:
Sikshamanjari, the primer pair, glowing tight,
In treasure wraps of ruby on sapphire.
And I the boy sobbed for them. My brother,
In haste, bought me a set, kindly his manner.
In my clutch by night and day,
The early aids of the lettering way,
Those fond gifts with me did stay.
Since then, if my home ever stood in want

Of a desired book, the sadness of that old infant
Would return to hurt me with its haunting pain.
In tight bonds with books, I somehow shunned
The skippy sports of the neighborly band.
Lost in reading, sitting stooped
My spine, in constant crimp, sculpted
A figure stifled, which I styled "a gradual gift,"
In the elite tongue of Sanskrit.
All my substance I forsook,
Caring little for penury's look,
Content with the recompense
A goodly book is bound to dispense.
Ages foregone through books I traverse,
Watching the wise in knowledge immerse;
Deeds of the well-worn word or the sword,
Of the lofty who shunned all sign of stain;
From Victoria's palace to the place of pain
Of Booker T, my journeys in letters
Spanned the globe, my mind never in fetters.
Kalidas, Bhavbhuti, Shakespeare, mighty Milton
Ravinder, Oh bards in their spheres, each a sun:
Spells in philosophy of Socrates
Plato, Spencer and Kant likewise;
Bacon and Newton of advancing worlds
A convivium thick, my home holds!
Caste-carved world is smoke-choke night:
Books alone unveil the vistas of light:
"Devan" and "Thevan" they equals make
For to ride as equals seats they take,
Foes no more, but souls in noble converse.
My tomes and scrolls have shown the way
How from the mire the Pariah[58] may
Rise as *dwijah*.[59] In proof, on my shelf sits

---

[58] "Pariah" is one of the lowest of the Indian castes, socially distanced as "untouchable." The word is now in the English lexicon as an adoption from Tamil. The term is shared by Malayalam as well.

[59] "Devan" in Malayalam means "god," or a divine being. In Sanskrit and Hindi, the term with the same meaning is "dev," like "Deo" in Latin. Many popular Indian names have the "Dev" component in them such as "Devraj," "Devkumar," "Devanand," "Sahdev," "Mahadev," and so on. Now, "Thevan" only slightly switches the first syllable of the "d" in "Devan" to "T," which is the way the caste tradition wanted the Dalit's name pronounced, though the meaning is still the same. Simon makes it clear that he is no respector of such racial usage of people. He sees all people as equals.

Valluvar's *Kural*,[60] and fast as it fits
With the ancient *Ramayan*, no caste row there.
In like manner, *Rg Veda* shares its sacral space
With the Koran, no rank contest for which to brace.
The bans of touch the Great Gandhi spurned,
Laudable deed, but ages ago my books forbade
Harming the image that God's hands made.

"Where your treasure is, there your heart also shall be," said Jesus in his teaching on things of eternal value. Next to the Kingdom of God, what Simon valued most was knowledge.

The Centenary

In 1983, the State of Kerala celebrated the Simon Centenary, which of course was a deserved honor for the poet. The media offered its unavoidable tribute to Simon, says Marxist scholar and journalist P. Govinda Pillai, "but conveniently ignoring any discussion of what his life and career was all about." The muses dance in Simon's Dravidian verses, which are rich in meaning and tone, Pillai adds. Although Mahakavi Vallathol, Sahitya Panchanan P. K. Narayana Pillai, and others shower compliments on Simon's work as a political courtesy, their patronizing manner of doing it is difficult to mask. Even Ulloor's own words of praise about *Vedaviharam* in the book and in what he says in the *History of Malayalam Literature* show different attitudes, Pillai states.[61] Pillai is indignant to note that small-time poets like Thamarassery Krishnan Bhattathiri, Kalady Raman Nambiar, Ponkunnam Sayd Muhammad, and such others enjoy generous coverage in Sahitya Akademi essays; yet the ten-volume *Encyclopedia of Malayalam Literature*, which contains needlessly elaborate matter on minor authors, has no mention of Simon. In Sahitya Akademi's 568-page *Poetic Literature of Malayalam*, Simon gets a total of four short sentences, in two parts of the book, like accidental trickles. In that short an entry, they misprint the date of Simon's passing as 1943 instead of 1944. Such examples are in no short

---

[60] "Valluva" is a highly revered Tamil poet and philosopher who is believed to have lived circa the fifth century BCE. His only known work *Kural* is a celebrated collection of aphoristic teachings of 1330 short couplets or "kurals" of seven words each.
[61] P. Govinda Pillai, *Theranjedutha Prabandangal* [Selected Treatises], ed. R. Gopalakrishnan (Trichur: Kerala Sahitya Akademi, 2012), 538.

supply. "It is undeniable that this remarkable literary man has been victimized by religious hostility, bigotry, casteism and such endemic evils," states Pillai with other supporting observations, adding also that "I have been told that there are threats against any attempt at new impressions or releases of Simon's works which have been out of print."[62]

Simon the Apostle of Humility and Charity

Simon was generous with everything he had. Once, a visitor gave him a cash gift in the form of a traditional "kizhi" or a cash pouch. He accepted it with thanks and set it on the ledge. Within minutes, while the guest was still with Simon, a neighbor arrived with the story of some pressing need. Simon took the pouch and gave it to the man, without having opened at all. Even the rarest of his books would be at the disposal of a visitor or a student. In conjunction with the release of *Vedaviharam* and the conferral of the Mahakavi title, the city of Kozhenchery had given him a gold medal and a plaque. The medal soon became a victim of its material value. Someone took it and sold it. When it was known later on who did it, Simon forgave the deed and forbade any further conversation by others about the matter.

It would not be incorrect to say that the greatest resources robbed from Simon were his time and the much needed rest. Night after night was spent in mediating one issue or another with people from near and far. Some were questions about doctrine, some about the conduct of people, and some about betrayals, of which there were many. There were splits and partings, writings and debates, yet Simon never lost his calm. Even in the midst of such distractions, as the K. T. Mathai diaries show, there was hardly a day without a scheduled public event for Simon.

These were the days before electricity, paved roads, motorized water transport, or even the modestly adequate bus lines.

Simon's life was set deep in unaffected humility. A little child was as important a visitor to his home as would be a dignitary. As his manner was, he would rise to welcome the child and give him or her all the time necessary. Children of his friends loved to stay in Simon's home for extended periods of study and joyful company. A story has been heard of Simon showing a little

---

[62] Ibid.

boy to his bed and the kid falling fast asleep in minutes. The great master then threw a grass mat on the floor next to that bed and went to sleep, which the little kid, to his shock, noticed in the morning as he woke up. In another instance, a poor farm worker came to Simon's door when the poet was talking with three or four VIPs, one of them a bishop. The poor man had saved the stub of his country roll of tobacco stuck away behind his ear. Simon greeted him in with the same respect he had for his other guests, but the man excused himself from the scene in an awkward hurry. Simon could be anyone's guest, even of the poorest man dwelling in a peasant's hamlet. He had no expectations or requirements for food or where he would sit or sleep. He ate what he was served. All his life he was a vegetarian.

Simon was as comfortable with little children as learners as he would be with an audience of great scholars or a public gathering. Consider this eyewitness account (1923) of C. I. Kunjikka, which shows how easily Simon could be comfortable with the expectations of surprising situations: Simon was the keynoter at the Eighth Convention of Mallappally Separatists, organized with the support of diverse groups. On the closing day, he led twenty-seven baptismal candidates in a procession to the Manimala River, for a public baptism. Over three thousand spectators stood on the banks of the river, mainly out of curiosity or for entertainment from the strange sight. Simon gave a gentle word of invitation for them to be seated in order on the river banks. The whole crowd of strangers readily obliged. Simon then gave them an in-depth talk on baptism: the necessity of it; the modus of it in the apostolic times; the practice of it in the patristic era; the practices of Eastern and Western churches over the centuries; opinions of scripture experts, and the etymological interpretations of it, altogether for two full hours.[63]

It is doubtful if Simon had more than two sets of formal clothes, though travels and public appearances filled his days. In this regard, he was like the medieval monks who used their only spare set while the other was in the wash. One day, a guest showed up at Simon's house with signs of a little displeasure on his face. The man had come from a place where Simon had a speaking engagement. It was obvious that he was late. Simon apologized to his guest for his seeming oversight and the consequent inconvenience to the program host. He set out with the man immediately, not even taking the time to change. He did not tell his guest that he had been waiting for fresh laundry to be readied. On the way,

---

[63] Kurien, *A Biography of K. V. Simon*, 218–19.

the man noticed the unfresh clothes on Simon. He slapped himself for rushing the poor man out of his home. He then stopped at the first store on the way and bought the clothes Simon needed, and then moved on. There were times when his disciples had likewise noticed his need for clean clothes while on the way. They would then break journey to wash and dry them at a wayside creek or so, which has happened time and again.

Simon and Money

If there is one thing conspicuous by its absence in Simon's life, that is money. It could be said with no risk of truth-twisting that Simon's financial net worth on the day of his passing was no more than what it was at the start of his career as a village schoolmaster. Simon hardly ever touched money physically. Kurien writes about an instance where Simon once happened to count up the penny-value copper coins as change for a rupee. He attempted it a few times, lost track each time, and handed the whole clump of Travancore coins over to one of the men standing by. In the days following his resignation from school teaching, Simon suffered such want as not to have enough to eat or to afford oil for a little hand lamp. At the same time, lucrative offers of better employment than school teaching came from prominent persons such as Mammen Mappilai, media magnate and literary patron, or even influential Hindu leaders like Swami Sadananda and Swami Mahaprasad. C. R. Vedanta Achary, a Hindu scholar-turned-Christian preacher, became a close friend of Simon. One night Mr. Achary saw Mr. Simon in a dream, shivering in the cold, without a blanket. The very next day, Achary bought and shipped the best possible blanket he could for Mr. Simon. Moneys mentioned in Simon's expenses were mostly for the publication of his writings, which were ongoing. The largest amount of money mentioned in his biography is a single gift of Rs 400 he received from Dr. Chacko of Madras to clear his outstanding debt of the publishing cost of *Vedaviharam*. In 1926, having readied the book on *Infant Baptism* for printing, K. T. Mathai borrowed Rs 20 on interest and against the security of a gold band. He paid back Rs 10 in fifteen days and another Rs 4 the following week, but the band was still with the lender. Whose gold band it was is a question that even Mathai's own sons are unable to answer, although as a family they have been curious about it for the last seventy years. This fact is curious for more than one reason: first, Mathai was an evangelist and a volunteer for Simon. No salary there. The second is the greater reason: the Kerala Brethren, like the Pentecostals after them in

Kerala, as we have seen already, are not users of jewelry. Records of 1937 show a debt burden of Rs 330 owed to a printer in Kumbanad. This amount resulted from arrears accumulated over the years and was renegotiated to Rs 350 with interest by promissory note, according to K. T. Mathai.

The *Viyojithan* magazine, as widely respected as it was, charged only a single rupee for twelve issues of high quality readings, provided largely by Simon himself. Any donations that came in were generally in extremely tiny amounts. A whole rupee seems to have been a respectable sum in those days. The larger contributions came up to five rupees, or occasionally, ten. Even with such ongoing stringency, his organization seems to have ignored the need for a fundraising arm to it.

Once Simon read a report on a Methodist construction project of a church in New York. The work had been in progress for the past thirty years. Massive amounts of money were spent on it, but the project was still not finished. Another 15 million dollars was needed to complete the work (again, in the early twentieth century). Simon commented: "Spending so much money on a lifeless building, how sad! Those funds could have helped far greater purposes, instead!"[64]

Neither the Viyojitha movement that Simon started nor the Brethren organization that it merged with had any material assets except a few simple meeting halls, no larger than a village house. No one held a paid position in their organization. Eventually, there were schools, and broadcasting or other communications, but those stood on their own as free enterprises.

A Man of Peace

Simon did not like war or violence. Samuel Chandanapally points out how Simon was spared the great grief of hearing of or witnessing the nuclear disasters of Hiroshima and Nagasaki by his passing the year before. A modern reader is apt to strike an easy chord with Simon's pacifism and abhorrence for violence and war. *Sangeetha Ratnavali* has prayer songs in it which seek God's move against Western powers that are poised for war and destruction. Had Simon been living today when the opposition to wars is getting stronger by the day, he might well have been the voice against war. We shall touch upon this a little more in Part IV of this book.

---

[64] Kurien, *A Biography of K. V. Simon*, 243.

The Last Lap

Simon was overall in good health except for his frequent spells of fever. In early 1941, his mobility was challenged by a stroke that caused a slight twist in the nose to the right and numbness in his tongue. Physician Madolil John provided treatment for two months resulting in a respite that would let him resume his travel itinerary to some degree. By the end of the following year, the numbness returned to his tongue. It affected the clarity of his speech. The physical strength began waning from that point on. Even then, books of diverse languages were arranged on two sides of his bed for whatever reading possible. The Malayalam Bible stayed inches away from his reach, on his bed. Visitors streamed in continually, with all of whom he conversed as well as he could. In February of 1943, Bishop Abraham and Bishop Titus II of the Mar Thoma Church visited Simon and prayed for him as the man who served all God's people. Dr. R. S. Churchward saw signs of high blood pressure and forbade reading and any attempt to speak or teach. Vayaskara Tirumeni (Brahmin physician, Ayurvedic) said that a certain nerve to the brain had been ruptured from decades of unabated stress and advised complete rest. Other physicians concurred.

February (1943) was the month of the annual convention of Aarattupuzha. This would be the one gathering where all of the people that Simon had led over the years would gather. Customarily, Simon would keynote the week-long convocation, but now he was not able to walk or even stand on his feet. Nonetheless, he was brought to the meeting pavilion and seated by the pulpit in a recliner. Once the scheduled speakers had finished their turns, Simon called K. M. Varghese (not the nephew), one of his disciples who was in constant attendance, to read out 2 Corinthians 4:7–18:

> But we have this treasure in jars of clay to show that this all-surpassing power is from God and not from us. We are hard pressed on every side, but not crushed; perplexed, but not in despair; persecuted, but not abandoned; struck down, but not destroyed. We always carry around in our body the death of Jesus, so that the life of Jesus may also be revealed in our body. For we who are alive are always being given over to death for Jesus' sake, so that his life may also be revealed in our mortal body. So then, death is at work in us, but life is at work in you .... Therefore, we do not lose heart. Though outwardly we are wasting away, yet inwardly we are being renewed day by day.

He spoke in his frail voice for a few minutes. The listeners inevitably recalled the times when Simon's speech, interspersed with the charming lines of verse melodiously sung, was the great draw of the Brethren meetings. When he described his own state through the words of Apostle Paul, the entire gathering was seen sobbing. Equally poignant was another line he asked to have read, the words of Apostle Paul from the book of Acts where he tells the Ephesians: "And indeed, now I know that you all, among whom I have gone preaching the kingdom of God, will see my face no more" (Acts 20:25).

The verses he requested read were such that they required no interpretation or commentary. It seemed as though the scripture and Simon were describing each other. With that message ended the convention of 1943.

In the months that followed, Simon's physical frailty persisted. Simon used to tell his guests not to pray for his healing, but only for him to be kept ready for his meeting with Christ. Physician M. C. John administered every possible treatment, regardless of the discouraging results in his patient. A new team of physicians, still with M. C. John leading, decided on a new course of Ayurvedic physiotherapy. The effort did produce relief, another respite again, for a good six more months. Though his body was frail, Simon's memory and recall stayed intact, even until thirteen days prior to his passing, when he could follow and comment on a study discussion carried out by some of his disciples in the house.

By now we are in 1944, in the month of February. It was twelve months ago that he had made his farewell speech at the Arattupuzha Convention. Simon is languishing in bed most of the time but is able to rise and take a few slow steps along the veranda. February 9, 1944 was the last date he stood on his feet. On this day, while in struggling motion, he collapsed all of a sudden into a nearby bed. His wife ran to the spot and so did his disciples, who carried him to the inner room. He lay unconscious for a full ten days, which also overlapped the whole week of the current year's convention which was apace, though in the sullen air of his absence. Updates on his condition were going out to the gathering every hour. By early afternoon, February 20, signs of his body yielding became noticeable. By 4:20 p.m., he passed on, surrounded by a tearful crowd of family, disciples, and friends. At that moment, his disciples offered a hymn of praise from one of Simon's own songs for their master to God:

Praise constant, unto thee my Sovereign,
Ring exalted thy glory's lore.

The great prophetic voice was stilled. The news of his passing cast a leaden pall of grief that only turned heavier in the days following, all over the whole land. Simon was called home.

Funerals were high stress affairs in those days. The burial of the dead had to happen within a day, considering the difficulties of preserving the body in tropical weather. Leaders of his mother church, the Mar Thoma denomination, had been in contact with Simon's wife and his daughter Chinnamma about burying Simon in the Mar Thoma cemetery. Yes, it was the same denomination that had excommunicated him a little over four decades earlier. The request was gratefully acknowledged by the family, but Simon had instructed that he should be buried in his own tiny parcel of land, and the preparations were made for burial there the next day. Despite the hardships of distance travel in those days, Simon's great family of friends and followers arrived from all over Travancore and beyond. The services lasted four hours, which would have been much longer, except for the rigorous time limits set. Public figures and heads of various denominations, civic societies, and organizations paid their respects in most endearing words. Kerala Varma of Aranmula Palace voiced the sentiments of many when he described Simon as the Martin Luther of Kerala.

Resting Where the Cradle Rocked

The gravesite had been prepared as determined before, in the small, terraced space hemmed in between the Brethren school building and the outer wall of his own home. There was no ornate work of masonry or artwork. The spot, as the house name in his initials says, is "Kunnumpurathu." It means "the hilltop." It stood at a fifteen-foot natural elevation from the house grounds. The tombstone shows this inscription from the book of Daniel, chapter 12: 3–4:

> And those who are wise shall shine like the brightness of the sky above; and those who turn many to righteousness, like the stars forever and ever.

In all that Simon has done, he was a pioneer. India did not have a Renaissance or a Reformation on the scale that Europe had, until the birth century of Simon. It was Simon who had to introduce those two great upheavals of history to Kerala's world of letters. He was a Renaissance man like Erasmus, Spenser, Milton, Bacon, or Donne. He was a Reformer like Calvin, John Owen, Richard

Baxter, or Daniel Williams as much as he was a major Malayalam poet of the new millennium. Simon is the inaugurator of critical biblical exposition in Kerala, as evidenced by his interpretive readings of the book of Revelation, the tabernacle, and the Song of Songs. J. C. Dev and Chandanapally note how Simon was the first to write books of history according to the principles of historiography. Chitramezhuth praises Simon for modeling elite journalism and editorial talents. Simon is arguably the first in Kerala to make effective use of formal democratic debate, which had not been found even in the legislative or the parliamentary bodies of the time. Just as he popularized library groups, literary clubs, and Bible study cells, Simon introduced the debate as a public means of community dialogue in ways easily comparable to what the Greek, Roman, or Antiochene schools did. The public had taken on to them with addictive pleasure, regardless of their religious beliefs.

Simon did on the knowledge front in South India what the church Fathers in Cappadocia, Carthage, Egypt, or Syria did in the early centuries. Origen, Jerome, Augustine, Basil, Gregory of Nyssa, Chrysostom, and Ambrose are among the most easily recognized among them. Nearly all of them ran schools of the classical tradition. Their institutions were forerunners to modern universities. Simon's home and movement resembled the patristic learning place and the Indian *gurukula*. Call it the School of Simon, the Viyojithas or by any other possible name, it was an idyllic place of learning and living. The only difference between the Western school of rhetoric and Simon's was that he excluded the mechanism for revenue from it. Rev P. J. Philip, Chief Overseer of the Church of God denomination, said in his eulogy: "Simon was such a luminary, well known all over Kerala and beyond; if there was one person who did not know it, it was Simon himself."[65]

---

[65] Kurien, *A Biography of Simon*, 367.

2

Malayalam: K. V. Simon's Language

A Brief History

Mother tongue to 37 million people of the Malabar coast, Malayalam is formally recognized as a *sreshtabhasha* or language of classical antiquity by the Government of India. Malayalam descends from its nearly three-millennia-old Proto-Dravidian parent as the youngest in that family. Historians trace Malayalam to its roots in the Sanghom period (fifth century BCE) when today's Kerala belonged to Tamilakom, the common name applied to the three Dravidian kingdoms of the South—Chera, Chola, and Pandya.

The alphabet of Malayalam has evolved through a long history of body changes before being stabilized by German philologist Hermann Gundert in the nineteenth century. Until around the 1980s, the total number of glyphs and symbols needed for writing Malayalam stood at around 900. New initiatives have brought the mammoth character body down to less than 90, which is also digitally compatible.

The Pattu Era

The literature of Malayalam arose from its oral tradition of the "Pattu age," which is found entirely as a corpus of musical compositions. Vast enough to cover the entire depth and diversity of their primitive agrarian culture, these "songs" range from the simple, pre-dawn "wake up" calls to ballads and longer narratives of heroic deeds. Festive occasions of harvests, weddings, temple celebrations, and major social ceremonies are contexts that typically inspired "pattu" creativity. The earliest written work of this genre is the twelfth-century *Ramacaritam* that tells the Pan-Indic story of the legendary king Rama. A contemporary work titled *Vaisikatantram* is the ideal model of the Pattu genre, according to the medieval rhetorical manual, *Lilatilakom*. Incidentally, *Vaisikatantram* has established its notoriety as a mother's counsel to her daughter, commending to her the career of courtesanship. The text uses the Dravidian graphology (script) of Vatteluthu.

Manipravala

From the eleventh to the fifteenth century, a hybrid language called "Manipravalam" was in vogue in Kerala for literary writing. It combined prose and verse in an admixture of Sanskrit and medieval Malayalam. The upper class Brahmins or Nambiars of Kerala preferred the Aryan language of Sanskrit, which served their hegemony in religion, philosophy, literature, and the sastras. Malayalam with a blend of Tamil was the language of common use.

The Manipravala era produced a spate of narratives of the genre called the *champoo*. The *champoos* were mostly of doubtful literary value with redundant feudal tales of debauchery, describing pursuits of courtesans and temple prostitutes. The *champoo* had a poetic kin called the *sandesa kavya*, or the "message poem," which also had its own prolific imitations, but without the sensual excesses of the *champoo*. The "message" in it was about the agony of a lonely man's longing for his sweetheart, separated by some misfortune. A trusted messenger from nature such as a bee, a peacock, a swan, the moon, or whatever that fits the narrator's fancy, is charged with the delivery of it. These poems follow the formula of Sanskrit poet Kalidasa's *Meghdoot* ["The Cloud Messenger"] in which the cloud is employed to take the tale of a Yaksha's love and laments to his beloved in the Himalayas.

The glut of *champoo* sensuality gave way to the vision of *bhakti* when Cerusseri, a fifteenth-century poet, introduced his *Krishnagatha* [the Song of Krishna] in the easy *manjari* meter that even the unschooled could sing and enjoy. Cerusseri leads a train of poets who show that Indian poetics and Indian spirituality are mutually integral. Three famed men of the Kannassa family of Niranam—Madhava Panicker, Sankara Panicker, and Rama Panicker (1350–1450)—demonstrate this reality. They successfully took on the monumental task of rendering the great Indian mythical works in Malayalam. Their writing makes a complete break with Tamil, thus giving modern Malayalam its own independent voice.

Ezhuthachan, the Father of Malayalam

Within an arm's reach from the Kannassas is the great bard Ezhuthachan (sixteenth century) in whom Kerala saw literacy, racial liberty, and transformative spirituality come together as a confluent force. Ezhuthachan was a non-Brahmin, which meant that he would have no access to learning. Nonetheless, he mastered the sacred texts on his own, both in the native tongue and Sanskrit. *Adhyathma Ramayanam* or the Story of Rama is the most widely read of all his works. Like Cerusseri, Ezhuthachan also invented a singing meter of his own called Kilippattu or the "Bird Song," employing a bird (a parrot, to be exact) as the teller of the story. He reduced the quarter-million-stanza epic of *Mahabharata* to one tenth of it in a marvelous show of narrative brevity. Ezhuthachan's language became the norm for later writers. While the priestly Brahmins reinforced the rigors of religion, Ezhuthachan spoke to the Hindu soul. All of his writings are devotional. However, neither Ezhuthachan nor his writings were kindly looked upon initially. A mocking Brahmin, punning on Ezhuthachan's caste-assigned trade of oil-milling, is said to have asked him, "How many measures could ply in your [oil] press?" and he answered, "Four and six do, for sure," meaning, the four Vedas and the six Sastras, which had been the monopoly of Brahmins alone. Ezhuthachan's *Harinama Keerthanam* as a popular devotional firmed up the Malayalam alphabet at fifty-one characters, for which history calls him the Father of modern Malayalam.

Kathakali[1] and *Thullal*, Two Kinds of Musical Drama

The century that followed was notable for temple arts literature, specifically the generic pioneer *Kathakali*, an operatic performance of stories from the *Puranas*. It was staged successfully on temple grounds and in royal courts. *Kathakali* audiences were well versed in mythology and could interpret the lines and gestures with a keen sense of performance nuances. The kings of Kozhikode and Kottarakara were renowned patrons of this art.

An inventive humorist by name, Kunchan Nambiar created "*Thullal*" as a kindred art form to *Kathakali*. "*Thullal*" means dance, but it was musical dance by a single actor with orchestral support, narrating very engaging, legendary tales. *Thullal* was largely for popular entertainment, laced with social satire.

---

[1] "Katha" is spelt alternatively as "kadha," commonly in interlingual contexts.

Development of Prose

Prose in Malayalam developed only slowly. The earliest work of prose, except for the *sasanas* and inscriptions, is *Bhasha Kautilyam*, a commentary on Kautilya's *Artasastra*, which is a treatise on economics and statecraft. Other prose compositions took shape in the form of manuals and instructions known as *kramadeepikas* and *attaprakarams* for performance arts like *Koothu* and *Kathakali*.

All of the Indian languages were developed by Western missionaries over a four-hundred-year period from 1500 to 1900. The Portuguese were the first European power to enter India. They needed language to interact with the people, but few learning tools existed in the language until then, and few to train learners beyond the rudimentary levels. When the renowned Patiri Arnos [Ernestus Hanxleden (1681–1732)] who came from Hungary sought out language experts to teach him Sanskrit and Malayalam, the native Brahmin pundits outright refused to help. Nonetheless, the Patiri mastered the language by other means and wrote original works, grammars, and dictionaries for Malayalam. Francis De Angelos, Bishop of Varapuzha, wrote the earliest work of grammar for the language, leading the way for a succession of peer works that would be known as Varapuzha grammars and dictionaries.

Clement Peaneus' *Samkshepa Vedartham* [The Essentials of the Christian Doctrine, 1772] is the first ever printed book in Malayalam. It was printed in Rome, obviously because such a task could not be carried out in India at that time. The twenty-four works of Peaneus' contemporary, Patiri Paulinus [John Phillip Wesdin], which include *Koodasa Pustakam*, *Divya Jnanam*, *Ettu Divasathe Dhyanam*, and *Adagia Malabaricum*, show the earlier prose in missional use.

The Portuguese were followed by the Dutch who had only smaller regions of India under their influence. They had no religious interest whatsoever, but they did a great honor to Malayalam through a twelve-volume treatise of medical botany that was produced in Kerala. Hendrik van Rheede, the Dutch governor, compiled the names of 742 medicinal plants and flowers of Malabar under the title *Hortus Malabaricus*, assisted, among others, by Itty Achuten, an Ezhava physician. The book contains one full page of Malayalam in longhand. Published over the years 1678–93, this work had the distinction of bringing the language, though in small measure but important, to Europe.[2]

---

[2] https://www.dropbox.com/home/KV%20Simon%20Images?preview=Page+14.png.

Then we have two native clergy writing Malayalam books of enduring fame: Bishop Joseph Kariattil, the author of *Vedatarkam*, a work of apologetics, and Paremakkal Thoma Kathanar, the author of *Varthamanappusthakam* [The Journey to Rome], the first ever travelog in an Indian language. Kariattil had eleven years of higher education in Rome, starting at the age of thirteen. He returned to Kerala as an ordained clergyman with a doctoral degree. Paremakkal had his clerical training in Kerala but had good knowledge of languages of India and Europe, through seminaries of Western founding. Kariattil returned to Rome again, this time with Paremakkal, to petition the Pope concerning the repressive policies of the Portuguese clergy in Kerala. The voyage took seven years to complete. *Varthamanappusthakam* is the record of the perilous journey of these two men in the eighteenth century. The work is a document of nationalism where the Kathanar boldly states that *Indians* should govern Indians, not foreigners.

Anglican Grammars and Dictionaries

The Anglican missionaries who had arrived in Kottayam in the early 1800s also wrote numerous grammars and dictionaries. Robert Drummond, Joseph Peet, A. J. Arbuthnot, F. Spring, R. Collins, Benjamin Bailey, and native clergyman George Mathen were the prominent grammar writers. While Bailey and his colleagues were progressing with their projects of infrastructure building, education, translation, and publishing, the Basel Mission of Malabar was establishing their own operational base in Thalassery. Here the indefatigable Hermann Gundert wrote his first ever scientific dictionary of Malayalam and the Malayalam grammar, which still are unsurpassed. He wrote over twenty books which speak authoritatively of Kerala's culture, traditions, proverbs, language, linguistics, and so on.

Translation of the Bible

Both Bailey and Gundert made their monumental mark on Malayalam prose through their separate translations of the Bible about thirty years apart. Bailey took twelve years to complete translating the New Testament, and another twelve to complete the Old Testament, bringing out the complete Bible in 1841. Chattoo Menon, a Nair civil servant, helped Bailey in the translation, in the

HOC EST.

EGo ITTI ACHUDEM Doctor Malabaricus Natione *Chego*, gentilis & naturalis in *Carrapuràm*, seu terra dicta *Codda Carapalli*, habitator ædium dictarum *Coladda*, qui proavis, avis & parentibus Medicis seu Doctoribus natus sum, testor me per mandatum D. Commendatoris HENRICI à RHEEDE, venisse in Civitatem *Cochinensem* & per EMANUELEM CARNEIRO Nobilis Societatis Indicæ interpretem dixisse & dictâsse nomina, virtutes medicas & proprietates arborum, plantarum, herbarum &

★★★★ con-

convolvulorum tum fcriptas & explicatas in libro noftro, tum quas diuturna experientia & exercitio obfervaveram ; quod verò hæc explicatio & dictatio abfque ullo dubio præterierit, nec ullus Doctorum Malabaricorum fit qui de veritate eorum quæ dixi dubitet, feci præfentes quas propria manu mea fcripfi & fubfcripfi. Datum in Civit. *Cochin.* 20. Aprilis 1675.

ITTI-ACHUDEM, Doctor Malabaricus.

Traductum ex lingua Malabarica *in* Lufitanicam *per*
MANUELEM CARNEIRO,

Et *ex* Lufitanica *in* Latinam *per me*
CHRISTIANUM HERMAN de DONEP,
Secretarium Civilem Civitatis *Cochinenfis.*

HOC

Figure 2.1 Hortus Malabaricus Page. *Hortus Indicus Malabaricus* Volume 1 by Henrik van Reede tot Drakestein, 1678. Public Domain. Image courtesy of Archive.org. https://archive.org/details/Hortus_Indicus_Malabaricus_Volume1/page/n9/mode/2up
The signed, longhand testimonial of Ayurvedic physician Itty Achuten in Malayalam Kolezhuthu.

process of which the man also espoused the Christian faith. The government promptly stripped him of his position as tahsildar since the prevailing law proscribed non-Hindus from holding such mid-level or higher administrative positions.

What Bailey and Gundert did in Bible translation has to be understood at no less a level of importance than what William Tyndale or Miles Coverdale did with their versions of the English Bible and what impact they had on the English language. England had a thriving prose by the fifteenth century or even a little earlier, but by comparison, Malayalam had hardly taken its baby steps in prose until the Bailey–Gundert translations came into being. Unlike in England or the wider Europe, the majority of the population of Kerala or of India had hardly any interest in the Bible, translated or otherwise. Nonetheless, the translations established a standardized prose style for the church, state, and business.

Bailey had never worked in a press, nor had he any knowledge of its technology. He read some basic materials on printing and had his press built on site and the typeface manufactured with the hired help of a carpenter and a blacksmith. Bailey took the square characters of Malayalam and rounded them into the eye-friendly font resembling the Calibri. Gundert created vowel symbols and punctuation marks for the language. Professor M. G. S. Narayanan said, "If Ezhuthachen is the father of Malayalam, Gundert is no less than its foster-father."[3] It was Gundert who christened the language as "Malayalam," which until then had been known by various names like "Malayanma," "Keralabhasha," or even some form of "Tamil."

Among the groundbreaking contributions of Gundert were the first ever newspaper in Malayalam, *Rajyasamacharam* (1847), followed by two more, *Paschimodyam* and *Paschimataraka*, intended for different tiers of readers. For the next forty years newspaper journalism was entirely the work of missionaries and missional institutions.

Translations of European Works

Printing and publishing produced a tidal flow of translations of European works in Malayalam. Oommen Philipose, a teacher turned news publisher,

---

[3] M. G. S. Narayanan, "Gundert was foster father of Malayalam, says MGS," *The Hindu*, February 3, 2016.

translated Shakespeare's *Comedy of Errors* with the title *Aalmaraattom* (1866); Kandathil Varghese Mappilai translated *Shakespeare's Taming of the Shrew* and a large portion of *Othello*. The Shakespeare spell continued with Chidambara Vadhyar's translation of *As You Like It* and *The Winter's Tale*. Around forty more translations of Shakespeare alone are known to have taken place by the early twentieth century. Archdeacon Koshy (1825–90), author of ten major works, translated two great classics of John Bunyan: *The Pilgrim's Progress* (1845) with the charming title, *Paradesi Mokshayatra* (1845), so consonant with the Indian instinct for mystical thinking, and *Tiruporattam*, the one-word title for Bunyan's *Holy War* (1870). To Koshy goes the credit also of writing the first novel in Malayalam, *Pullelikuncu* (1882). Chandu Menon's *Indulekha* (1889) follows Koshy by many years.

Journalism in Kerala

A rising number of journals and periodicals made standard prose and essay writing ubiquitous. Rev. George Mathen led the way as Kerala's first essayist. Mathen's *Satyavadakhedam* and *Vedasamyukti* are essays of sound critical thinking. As the first Keralite to be ordained as an Anglican clergyman, Mathen had a successful university education and the ability to address diverse fields of knowledge. He wrote and lectured on topics of science, economics, health, ethics, astronomy, history, social issues like women's status, and matrilineal traditions. Mathen's *Satyavadakhedam* (a work of apologetics) was the 1863 Royal Award winner as a model of prose. Ironically, the government blocked its publication because of references to religion in the book. He was asked to purge them, but Mathen saw no reason to do so, and published the work at his own expense, the same way his *Grammar of Malayanma* saw daylight, although religion was not an issue there. Aymanam P. John's translation of Morris' *The History of India* showed the use of prose in larger works as did Ityera Eapen's original work of *Panakarya Varnana* (1871) as the first book on Economics in Malayalam.

Nidhirikal Mani Kathanar, an influential visionary, founded *Deepika*, a Catholic daily. Father Gerard, who wrote *Alankarasastra*, the first comprehensive work of rhetoric in the language combining the Greek, Latin, and Sanskritic illustrations and thus making it a great classic on style, was *Deepika*'s manager. Soon to outpace *Deepika* appeared the nationally leading *Malayala Manorama*, under the leadership of Kandathil Varghese Mappilai. Both Mani Kathanar and Varghese Mappilai were men of letters and highly visible social figures.

Promotion of literacy was a missional goal of *Manorama*. A whole page of the then bifold daily was set apart for original literary contributions consisting largely of poetry, riddles, translations, questions, and letters received from readers. The paper, besides running the prestigious *Bhasha Poshini* literary magazine and later on the *Vidyavinodini* magazine of like fame, also sponsored conferences of writers and poets. A constellation of writers including Mahakavi Ulloor, Kerala Varma Valia Koi Thampuran, Swadeshabhimani Ramakrishna Pillai, Mulloor Govinda Pillai, Sardar K. M. Panicker, C. Anthapai, I. C. Chacko, and Mahakavi Kattakayam would suffice to show the caliber of writers in these publications.

The Modern Era

In the period following the 1880s, Malayalam falls in three phases of expanding growth. The first fifty years take the label of Neoclassic. It is followed by an impactful Romantic era from 1930 to 1947, and the third is the sequential era of the Progressives, the Moderns, and the Post-Moderns. In the Neoclassic era, Malayalam capitalizes on the classical Sanskritic models with weighty results. Alakathu Padmanabha Kurup and K. C. Kesava Pillai are the early lights of this movement. Their successful contemporaries that included K. V. Simon, Sister Beninja, and Kattakayam Cheriyan Mappilai, swelled the mahakavya hall of fame. The Romantic era rightly centered on Asan, Ulloor, and Vallathol, three outstanding contemporaries whose thought and writings permeated the culture. Among these three, Ulloor and Vallathol also wrote epics while Asan chose to write shorter length poems called *khanda kavyas* or cantos. Asan was learned and deeply reflective. He was the voice of reform tempered by Buddhist philosophy and the teachings of his preceptor Sree Narayana Guru in a caste-plagued society of which his own race was a victim. Vallathol's verse was all sweetness and light, his verse naturally musical and vibrant, pulling in a range of themes, the strongest of which was nationalism. Ulloor, though clubbed with the Romantics, was anchored in the ancient Indian lore. As a scholar and historian, his writing had a dragnet effect and was pedantic in taste and tone, but his services to Malayalam are of great excellence.

Many literary schools and movements in the subsequent decades have gratefully acknowledged the great trio of Romantics in their philosophy of composition. Changampuzha and Edapally, two influential lyricists that immediately succeeded them, are called the Late Romantics of Malayalam. Their careers are reminiscent of English Romantics Keats and Shelley. Among those who followed these two short-lived poets eventually were schools and movements, and even movements within movements. For instance, popular poets P. Bhaskaran, Vayalar Rama Varma, and O. N. V. Kurup wrote revolutionary songs, which nearly everyone in the land knows by heart; as Progressives with leftist or Marxian ideologies they gave their call for revolution, thoroughly using their talent within that movement; Vallathol-inspired poets make up another influential school that includes Nalappatt, Kuttipurathu, Vennikulam, Nalankal, M. P. Appan, G. Sankara Kurup, and Balamani Amma, to name another cohort.

Malayalam fiction in general is now easily on par with world literature, as Ayyappa Panicker has pointed out.[4] The short story has had its fastest and steadiest growth, with not thousands, but tens of thousands of selections available, as the studies of Professor Krishna Pillai[5] and D. Benjamin state.[6] The novel is the most popular form of narrative in Malayalam with social realism taking the lead. We then see names of exceptional writers who cannot be forced tightly into any single class because of the variety of their works as poets, prose writers, fiction writers, and successful experimenters: the most visible of such are authors like K. Satchitanandan or Ayyappa Panicker, who write in Malayalam as well as English and translate from other languages.

Western influence has swelled Malayalam literary canon with growing additions of world classics. From Homer to Shakespeare, and from them to a global range of moderns like Chekov, Ibsen, Maupassant, Gorky, Hesse, Hugo, Steinbeck, Dostoevsky, Gabriel Marques, Neruda, Gibran, and so on, Malayalam has received and returned enough enrichment to set new trends among writers and critics. New titles in contemporary Malayalam show a tenfold increase from its preceding phase, says Padma Shri K. M. George. Its current body is, without question, amply rich to engage a global readership.

---

[4] Ayyappa Panicker, *A Short History of Malayalam Literature*, 6th ed. (Thiruvananthapuram: Information and Public Relations Department, 2006), 120. Retrieved from Archive.org, August 22, 2022.
[5] N. Krishna Pillai, *Kairaliyude Kadha* [The Story of Malayalam], Kottayam: DC Books, 2018, 370–71.
[6] D. Benjamin, "Cherukadha" in *Adhunika Malayala Sahitya Charitram Prasthanangaliloode* [Modern Malayalam through Literary Movements], ge. ed. K. M. George (Kottayam: DC Books, 4th impression, 2011), 414.

3

Simon's Verse: Selected Pieces

The variety of genres of Simon's verse is large, ranging from epigrams and maxims to cantos and a full-length epic. This section assembles samples of Simon's songs and hymns as well as key portions of *Vedaviharam*. Simon's reputation as a songwriter was firmly established in his youth itself, as early as in his twenties. The hymns included in this section come from his 1925 edition of *Sangeetha Ratanavali*, which consisted of 210 compositions. Other editions with more songs or contributions from Simon continued over the later decades of his life.

Songs and Hymns

Pahimam Devadeva [Entreat thee I]

About half of Simon's poems are composed as *bhajans*. Simple and sweet, and yet profound in its impact, the *bhajan* is very singable as solo, in teams of small numbers, or as a choir or even a whole congregation. Meaning, music, and mood produce their harmoniously unified effect in a *bhajan*. Besides its prosody and lyrical content, the *bhajan* follows *a raga*, which is its melodic framework. The *ragas* have their spiritual attributes and are assigned to *bhajans* according to the context intended. "Pahimam Devadeva" is a model *bhajan*.

പാഹിമാം ദേവദേവാ പാവനരൂപാ!	Entreat I thy staying arm, Adonai of holy form,
പാഹിമാം ദേവദേവാ!	Entreat I thy saving arm.
മോഹവാരിധി തന്നിൽ കേവലം വലയുന്ന	Souls myriad in *moha's*[1] whirls, hapless on its tides they ride;
ദേഹികൾക്കൊരു രക്ഷാ നൗകയായ് പരമേശാ!	Rescue's Ark! Oh, most High One, who with them abide.
ക്ഷാമ സങ്കടം നീക്കി പ്രാണികൾക്കനുവേലം	Creatures thine fare free from want, by thine unspent favors flown,
ക്ഷേമജീവിതം നൽകും പ്രേമഹാർദ്യമേ! ദേവാ!	Content by thy hands provident, housed in thee, Love's Lord, lone.

---

[1] "*Moha*" is a Sanskrit term meaning "insatiable desire," which causes all human unrest.

പാപമാം വലയിൽ ഞാനാപതിച്ചുഴലായ്‌വാൻ	Lest in luring lust I fall and lose myself in depths of rue,
താപനാശനാ നിൻകൈ ഏകിടേണമേ നിത്യം	Grief-ridder, hold me in thy mercy's view.
ധർമ്മരക്ഷണം ചെയ്‌വാൻ ഊഴിയിലവതാര	For dharma's sake on earth incarnate,
കർമ്മമേന്തിയ സർവ ശർമദാ നമസ്‌കാരം!	Blesser serene, adore we thee prostrate.
നീതിയെൻ ഗളത്തിന്മേൽ ഓങ്ങിയ കരവാളം	The blade of the Law at my neck swayed;
വീതമാക്കിയ ജഗത് ത്രാതാവേ ശരണം നീ	Oh, World-wielder, thou had it stayed!
ജീർണമാംവസനത്താൽ ഛാദിതനായൊരെന്നെ	Wrapp'd in rags was how I stood,
പൂർണ ശുഭ്രമാങ്കി തൂർണം ധരിപ്പിച്ചോനേ!	Before in glory thou didst me hood.
നിത്യജീവനെന്നുള്ളിൽ സത്യമായുളവാക്കാൻ	For thy lauded life in me to spring
സ്തൃത്യത്യമാം പുതുജന്മം ദത്തം ചെയ്‌തൊരു നാഥാ!	The new birth's gift, Lord, thou didst bring
ദീനരിൽ കനിവേറും പ്രാണനായകാ പോറ്റീ![2]	Bounteous *Pottie!* By thy mercy's nards
താണു ഞാൻ തിരുമുമ്പിൽ വീണിതാ വണങ്ങുന്നേ	The weak rejoice! Praise we thee, thy humble wards.

Manuvel Manujasutha [Manuvel, ManSon]

This is a song of adoration of "Manuvel," which is a variant of "Emmanuel," a prophetic name for Christ, recounting the blessings received. There are anaphoric phrases at the end of couplets or stanzas that loop back to the refrain, enhancing the pleasing tension of the melody.

Simon frequently uses well chosen Sanskrit terms with highly functional effect. Their attraction is irresistible. For that reason I let words like *vandans* (obeisance), *chandan* (sandalwood, a fragrant tree), or *Chitpurush* (the Omnipresent Being), stay. "ManSon," is a phrase intended to mean "Son of Man" as Jesus spoke of himself.

മാനുവേൽ മനുജസുതാ!—നിന്റെ	Manuvel, ManSon! *vandans*[3] rise,
മാനമേറും തൃപ്പാദങ്ങൾ വണങ്ങി ഞങ്ങൾ	Magnus, to thee O, *vandans* rise,

---

[2] The word "പോറ്റി" [po-tee] is a nuanced term. Literally it means keeper or preserver; someone who has the trust and respect of people as their guide and leader; a Brahmin noble of social standing, the Brahmin caste notwithstanding; a priest in charge of temple duties; here the term addresses God, indeed, as worshipper's keeper and protector.

[3] "ManSon" is the exact literal meaning of "manuja-sutha." It should be taken as a synonym for "Son of Man," that Jesus uses in self-reference. *Vandan* is a Sanskrit term for greeting or reverential salutation. As mentioned in other spots too, many of Simon's Sanskrit terms would be more effective, if used unchanged.

മംഗളമോതിടുന്നിതാ—നിത്യം	With thy footstool's courtly strains,
മഹിമയുണ്ടായിടട്ടെ നിനക്കുനാഥാ!	*Vandan* chants, in joyous cries.
ഏദനിലാദി മനുജർ—ചെയ്ത	Lovely vast thy labors' lore,
പാതകം പരിഹരിപ്പാൻ ഭൂതലേ വന്നു	For Eden's folk thine advent set,
ക്രൂശതിൽ മരിച്ചുയർത്ത- നിന്റെ	The slaying cross, and the rising yet,
പേശലമാം ചരിതമെന്തി വിപുലം	The bane of sin to sting no more.
അല്പമാമുപകരണം കൊണ്ടു നൽപ്പെഴുന്ന	By little tools do craftsmen make
മഹത്തായ വേലകൾ ചെയ്യും—	Works of marvel in their skill;
ശില്പികൾകുടയവനേ നീയേ	Of such too thou art Maker still—
ചില്പുരുഷൻ ചിരന്തന! നമസ്കാരമേ!	*Chitpurush*,[4] so due praises take!
നീചരായ് ഗണിച്ചിരുന്ന—പേത്ര	Esteem'd low were Peter's kind,
നാദിയായ ധീവരരെ ദിവ്യ കൃപയാൽ	Coastal men of fisher's trade;
ശേഷ്ഠികൊണ്ടലങ്കരിച്ചു—പരം	Such for th' world were Rabbis [*gurus*] made
പ്രേഷണം ചെയ്തവനിയിൽ ഗുരുക്കളായ് നീ	With thine unction unrestrain'd.
വന്ദനം പരമഗുരോ! നിന്റെ	*Vandans* to thee, O, Guru Great! Thy ways
നന്ദനീയമാംഗുണങ്ങളുരപ്പതാമോ	Comely, past any telling of man's device;
ചന്ദനം പുഴുകിവയെക്കാളും	Thy story savored, of accents sweeter
തോന്നിട്ടുന്നു നിൻചരിതം സുരഭിയായി	Than *chandan*,[5] spices, or any such matter.
സ്ഫീതമാം കരിമുകിലേ! സാധു	Laden cloud, thou moving flood!
ചാതകങ്ങളാണു ഞങ്ങൾ നീ തരുന്നൊരു	Fowls are we of parching broods,
ശീകരമനുഭവിച്ചു സർവ	Craving signs of breaking rain:
ശോകവും ശമിപ്പിക്കുവാൻ കൃപ ചെയ്യണേ!	Quench our griefs, O, sovereign.

Paadum Ninakku Nityavum [I will sing unto thee all days]

A song of thanksgiving not limited to a single moment, event or auspicious days, this song shows a grateful heart's quick ascent to God. The poem begins with an apostrophe addressed to "Paramesh," which means "ruler of all" or "God of all." That term of devotion runs through the entire poem.

പാടും നിനക്കു നിത്യവും പരമേശാ!	For ever I'll sing to thee, *Paramesh*,
കേടകറ്റുന്ന മമ നീടാർന്ന നായകാ!	O Mender of flaws, thou, in form perfect!

---

[4] *Chitpurush* is a term to refer to God as the true self, eternal and unaffected.
[5] *Chandan* is a tree of fragrance and of ritual use in Hindu religious ceremonies.

പാടും ഞാൻ ജീവനുള്ള നാളെന്നും നാവിനാൽ	All my days my tongue will bring
വാടാതെ നിന്നെ വാഴ്ത്തുമേ, പരമേശാ!	Notes unfading, thee adoring, *Paramesh!*
പാടവമുള്ള സ്തുതി പാഠകനെന്നപോൽ	Like the scribe with his courtly scroll
തേടും ഞാൻ നല്ല വാക്കുകൾ, പരമേശാ!	Seek I words that suit thy state, *Paramesh!*
പൂക്കുന്നു വാടിയൊരു പൂവല്ലി തൂമഴയാൽ	Yester shoots that seemed to wilt
ഓർക്കുന്നു നിന്റെ പാലനം, പരമേശാ!	Spring afresh in thy crowning care, *Paramesh!*
ഗന്ധം പരത്തിടുന്ന പുഷ്പങ്ങളെന്നുടെ	Spread their scents, lo, thy fields florid,
അന്തികം രമ്യമാക്കുന്നു, പരമേശാ!	Blossoms crowding hearts long torrid, *Paramesh!*
ശുദ്ധരിൽ വ്യാപരിക്കും സ്വർഗ്ഗീയ വായുവാൽ	The Breath of thine in earthly saints
ശുദ്ധമീ വ്യോമമണ്ഡലം, പരമേശാ!	Hallows realms we inhabit, *Paramesh!*
കഷ്ടത്തിലും കഠിന നഷ്ടത്തിലും തുടരെ	Lapses, losses, trail me long?
തുഷ്ടിപ്പെടുത്തിയെന്നെ നീ, പരമേശാ!	Feastly shall you keep me strong, *Paramesh!*
സ്നേഹക്കൊടിയെനിക്കു മീതേ വിരിച്ചു പ്രിയൻ	Flutters ov'r me thy love's banner,
ഞാനും സുഖേന വാഴുന്നു, പരമേശാ!	Live I in fear of no manner, *Paramesh!*
ആയവൻ തന്ന ഫലം ആകെ ഭുജിച്ചു മമ	Well fed of thy garden's pick,
ജീവൻ സമൃദ്ധിയാകുന്നു, പരമേശാ!	Surge I have of new life quick, *Paramesh!*
ദൈവപ്രഭാവമെന്റെ മുന്നിൽ വിളങ്ങിടുന്നു,	Heaven's splendor before me glows
ചൊല്ലാവതല്ല ഭാഗ്യമെൻ, പരമേശാ!	Past all telling my bliss flows, *Paramesh!*
എന്നുള്ളമാകും മഹാ ദേവാലയത്തിൽ നിന്നും	From my Templed-frame exude
പൊങ്ങും നിനക്കു വന്ദനം, പരമേശാ!	*Vandans* of love for thee, *Paramesh!*

Thenilum Madhuram [Sweeter than honey]

This song may be read as an apology (meaning, "defense," not a plea for forgiveness) for the study of the *Veda* or the Word of God, or as a dramatic monologue serving the same function. The sagacious persona with great experience of life reasons with a close friend (a "peer") as to why the truth of the scriptures has to be his life's foundation. The title has immediate allusion to the Word as "more precious than gold, sweeter than honey and the honeycomb" (Ps. 19:10).

തേനിലും മധുരം വേദമല്ലാതി-	Besting the tastes of nectars rare
ന്നേതുണ്ടു ചൊൽ തോഴാ!	Is *Veda's*[6] word, aught else, my peer?

---

[6] *Veda* originally referred to the Hindu scriptures, but now the term is used to speak of the sacred writings of other religions too. They embody inspired or revealed knowledge and utterances. Here Simon is speaking of the Old and the New Testaments.

നീ സശ്രദ്ധമതിലെ സത്യങ്ങൾ വായിച്ചു	Search and own its sacred spell
ധ്യാനിക്കുകെൻ തോഴാ!	And on its sounds you constant dwell.
മഞ്ഞു പോൽ ലോക മഹിമകൾ മുഴുവൻ	Like melting snow, world's glitters all
മാഞ്ഞിടുമെൻ തോഴാ! —ദിവ്യ	Shall give way, my peer!—the celestial
രഞ്ജിത വചനം ഭഞ്ജിതമാകാ	Word that quenches not, but conciliates—
ഫലം പൊഴിക്കും തോഴാ—	Its bounteous fruit none abates, my peer!
പൊന്നും വസ്ത്രങ്ങളും മിന്നും രഥങ്ങളു—	Gold and garbs and glowing gems—
മിതിനു സമമോ തോഴാ!—എന്നും	Dare they match its claims, my peer?—
പുതുബലമരുളും അതിശോഭ കലരും	New strength ordains, fresh light fetches,
ഗതിതരുമന്യൂനം	And steadfast this your course prospers.
തേനോടു തേൻ കൂടതിലെ നല്ലതെളിതേ—	Not finer drips nor purer drops
നിതിനിനു സമമോ തോഴാ! ദിവ്യ	Of pristine combs of honey, my peer!—this
തിരുവചനം നിൻ ദുരിതമകറ്റാൻ	Wisdom has your plagues purged,
വഴിപറയും തോഴാ!	Oh, hear my kin—see new paths forged!
ജീവനുണ്ടാക്കും ജഗതിയിൽ ജനങ്ങൾ	Life it gives for earth's mortals,
ക്കതിശുഭമരുളീടും—നിത്യ	And added goodness day by day—Grants them
ജീവാത്മ സൗഖ്യം ദേവാത്മാവരുളും	Weal, everlasting weal of the Holy One—
വഴിയിതുതാൻ നൂനം	The path to keep is this alone.
കാനനമതിൽ വച്ചാനന്ദരൂപൻ	The Fallen One in arid waste
വീണവനോടെതിർക്കേ—ഇതിൻ	Stood to test the Lord of Hosts—His Word
ജ്ഞാനത്തിൻ മൂർച്ച സ്ഥാനത്താലവനെ	Of Wisdom him repell'd,
ക്ഷീണിപ്പിച്ചതെന്നോർക്ക—	Its judging edge by none withheld.[7]
പാർത്തലമതിലെ ഭാഗ്യങ്ങളഖിലം	The gains of th' earth evolve and pass
പരിണമിച്ചൊഴിഞ്ഞീടിലും—നിത്യ	In turns and courses their entire mass—the Word Eternal
പരമേശവചനം പാപിക്കു ശരണം	—the fast abode for sinners still:
പരിചയിച്ചാൽ നൂനം.	Own it to see it by tractable will.

Devajana Samajame [The Gathered Elect]

As a song on the doctrines of the Old and New Testaments, the content of this poem is largely typological. The poet calls the congregation of "new-heart" people

---

[7] The reference in this stanza is to Satan's attempt to tempt Christ as described in the Gospels of Matthew 4:1–11 and Luke 4:1–13. Here Satan twists the scriptures to fit his schemes, but Jesus repels the foe by the power of the Word that he uses. This stanza also gives a nutshell account of the plot of Milton's *Paradise Regained*.

to reflect on how sin-ridden humans were adopted into the divine household; how the stone-writ law has been fulfilled to give them the life of grace instead; and how the picture of the tabernacle and the active priestly offices in it are played out in Christ's work for humanity.

ദേവജനസമാജമേ! നിങ്ങളശേഷം	Sacred throngs, in counts entire,
ജീവനാഥനെ സ്തുതിപ്പിൻ	Praises raise to the Lord of Life;
ജീവനരുളും ദിവ്യ ജീവാമൃതമാമേശു	Being's source, life's own substance,
ദേവൻ നമ്മുടെ മദ്ധ്യേ മേവുന്നതു നിമിത്തം—	Jesu Himself amidst us moves, hence.
ചാവിന്നവകാശത്തിൽ നി-ന്നതിദയയാൽ	From mortal clasps, by mercy great
ദേവൻ ദത്താക്കിനാൻ നമ്മെ	As the Lord's adoptees we rank;
ശാപമകന്ന പുതു ഭൂവാനങ്ങളിൽ സദാ	Heaven our homestead, space of state;
മേവുന്നതിനായ് നിത്യ ജീവൻ നൽകിനാനവൻ	Of sin, free; here our converse, and Him we thank.
കല്ലുകളിൽ വരച്ചതാം ചാവിൻ ശുശ്രൂഷ-	The stone-carved law of mortal script
യ്ക്കുുള്ളിലിരുന്ന യീനമ്മെ	Had each of us in rigid text;
അല്ലൽ കൂടാതെതന്റെ തുല്യമില്ലാത്ത കൃപ-	He, instead, through hearts renate
യ്ക്കുള്ളിൽ കടത്തിപ്പുതുവുള്ളം നൽകിനാനവൻ	And grace unmatch'd, gave us life unvex'd.
ഏകാത്മ സ്നാനം മൂലവും—അത്രയുമല്ല	Immers'd as one, rose we up,
ഏകാത്മപാനം വഴിയും	Drawing from His only cup;
ഏകശരീരമായിട്ടേകീഭവിച്ചതിനാൽ	One body of nations in Him merg'd,
ഏകപൂപാനുഭോഗ ഭാഗികളായിതുനാം	Break we together the selfsame Bread.
താനേ കഴിച്ചൊരേകമാം -	Lone he gave himself for slaughter,
ബലിയാൽ തന്റെസൂനുസമുദായങ്ങളെ	A filial fold, earned by blood-spilt altar;
ഊനമകറ്റി നിത്യവാനരാജ്യാവകാശ	Install'd he them in Kingdom rights
സ്ഥാനമതിങ്കലാ ക്കീട്ടാനന്ദാമൃതമേകി	Of celestial state of joy and might.
കർത്ത്യ നിർമ്മിതമായുള്ള പൊരുളാം	Abides He as Priest High glimps'd,
ദിവ്യ സത്യകൂടരമതിങ്കൽ	In the Tent of Truth of charge esteem'd,
ശുദ്ധ ശുശ്രൂഷകനാം നിത്യപുരോഹിതൻ താ—	Divine Workman, the pleading priest,
നത്യാദരം നമുക്കായദ്യാപി ജീവിക്കുന്നു	Alone suffic'd, yes, and for us offic'ed.

Amba Yerusalem

"Amba" is a Sanskrit term meaning "a woman of noble lineage," or the "queen mother." The poem draws its content from Revelation 21 in which a city of divine handiwork, personified as a beautiful bride, ready to be presented to her ruler groom, is seen descending from above. It is another vision of the kingdom of God on earth. The city that inspires such great awe is the New Jerusalem, the appearance of which also will mark the end of human history as we know it now.

അംബ യെരുശലേം അമ്പരിൻ കാഴ്ചയിൽ	Amba, Jerusalem! Vision on high!
അംബരേ വരുന്ന നാളെന്തു മനോഹരം	Great is thy advent's gladsome day!
തന്മണവാളനു വേണ്ടിയലങ്കരി-	For her groom so duly deck'd
ച്ചുള്ളോരു മണവാട്ടി തന്നെയിക്കന്യകാ—	Is this bride, his virgin chaste.
നല്ലപ്രവൃത്തികളായ സുചേലയെ	Vested in robes of virtue's deeds,
മല്ലമിഴി ധരിച്ചുകൊണ്ടഭിരാമയായ്	Arrayed grace from her proceeds.
നീളവും വീതിയും ഉയരവും സാമ്യമായ്	Equal run her width and height,
കാണുവതിവളി ലാണന്യമില്ലെല്ലതു	Length likewise for eye's delight.
ഇവളുടെ സൂര്യചന്ദ്രർ ഒരുവിധത്തിലും വാനം	Her sun and moon never quit their course
വിടുകയില്ലിവൾ ശോഭ അറുതിയില്ലാത്തതാം—	She herself their staying source.
രസമെഴും സംഗീതങ്ങൾ ഇവളുടെ കാതുകളിൽ	Melodies *rasa-rich* muses she;
സുഖമരുളീടുംഗീതം സ്വയമിവൾ പാടിടും—	In realms she moves of ecstasy.
കനകവും മുത്തു രത്നം ഇവയണികില്ലെങ്കിലും	Shuns she though gold and gems of glittery beam,
സുമുഖിയാം ഇവൾ കണ്ഠം ബഹുരമണീയമാം—	Comely-fac'd, her neck does carven seem.

Poorna Hridaya Seva Venam [Wholly given to serve]

The content of the poem is hortatory. A person of any religious faith would accept it without controversy because the matter taught is about purity of heart and ethical uprightness. The illustration of the sacrifices of Cain and Abel is employed as the central object lesson.

പൂർണഹൃദയ സേവവേണം ദേവജാതനു	Whole of heart must the God-born serve,
പരിപൂർണനാകുവാൻ ഇതു വേണ്ടതാണഹോ!	Perforce so, in wholeness to live—
പാതിമനസ്സോടേകിടുന്ന ദേവപൂജയെ	Shuns the Lord the split-serve heart
പരൻ സ്വീകരിച്ചിടാ	Nay, He does forbid all show of art:
പരമാശിസ്സായ് വരാ—	Of it comes His blessings none.
കയിൻ സേവ പല വിധത്തിൽ ന്യൂനമായിരു—	Begrudg'd set was Cain's gift
ന്നതു ദോഷഹേതുവായ്	In plural flaws of fatal fit:
പെരും ശാപമായത്—	Bane's byword a son thus he.

പാകമായ മനസ്സിൻ തീർച്ച ദൈവസേവയിൽ	Noble hearts heed God's behest,
സ്ഥിര ജീവനേകുമേ	Firm they rest in life full set:
പരനായതേൽക്കുമേ—	God Himself shall have it so.
നമ്മുടേതെന്നിവിടെയോതും സ്വമ്മിലൊക്കെയും	Goods that hold us, or hoards that seize us
വരധർമ്മമായതു	Must to Him first duly go,
പരനേകണം സദാ—	Solely to Him, them we owe.
കൊടുത്തശേഷം തിരിച്ചെടുക്കാൻ തുടങ്ങിടൊല്ല നാം	Vowed a gift and regret it? Kill the wish
ഫലമൊടുക്കമായ് വരും	To seize it back. Crooked holdings perish
ദൃഢമൊടുക്കമാമതു—	Soon: Void go their lusted weight.
സ്വർഗതാതനെന്നവണ്ണം പൂർണ്ണരാകുവാൻ	Bade the Lord that we be whole
പരനാജ്ഞ തന്നഹോ!	As the Father, so the child,
നിറവേറ്റണമതു—	In us this must show fulfill'd.

Thunga Prathaapamaarnna Sri Yesu [Of glory utmost]

The subject matter of this poem is the person and the sacrificial ministry of Christ.

തുംഗപ്രതാപമാർന്ന ശ്രീയേശു നായകനേ!	Glory-altus, reigning King,
ഞങ്ങൾക്കു നന്മചെയ്ത കാരുണ്യവാരിധിയേ!	Mercy's sea, Yeshu Lord, Doer of good
വണങ്ങിടുന്നടിയാർ—തവ പദങ്ങളാശ്രയമേ	Bow we down—at thy feet secure.
നിർമ്മലമായ രക്തം ശർമ്മദാ നീ ചൊരിഞ്ഞു	Unblemish'd blood, Joy-giver spill'd,
കന്മഷംപോക്കി ദുഷ്ട കർമ്മഫലത്തിൽ നിന്നു	Evil quell'd, its claims full null'ed
വിടുതൽ ചെയ്തതിതിനാൽ—ഞങ്ങൾ അടിവണങ്ങിടുന്നേ	Our freedom will'd, we prostrate fall!
ഗതസമേനയെന്ന തോട്ടത്തിലെത്തി ഭവാൻ	Grief-ground Garden, blood-sweat tale
രക്തം വിയർത്തധിക ദുഃഖമനുഭവിച്ച	Of crush-heart cries in Gath-semne,
ചരിതമോർത്തിടുമ്പോൾ മന—മുരുകിടുന്നു പരാ!	Rends our hearts, Christ the crown'd!
പേശിപുലമ്പി ദുഷ്ടർ ക്രൂശിച്ചിടും പൊഴുതും	Lash-tongue men on the rood thee laid;
വാശിക്കധീനമായി തീർന്നില്ല നിൻഹൃദയം	Harsh was not thy heart for it:
വിമലകാന്തി ചേർന്നു—മുഖം—വിളങ്ങി ശാന്തിയാർന്നു	Purity flush'd, and glory glow'd on thy face, instead.
നിൻസൗമ്യമാം സ്വഭാവം നന്നായ് പഠിച്ചെടിയാർ	Meek in manner, master mine, in thy minions
വൻപ്രാതികൂല്യ മദ്ധ്യേ മുമ്പോട്ടു യാത്രചെയ്വാൻ	Move in might, 'midst their strife of course adverse:
തിരുമുഖ പ്രകാശം ഞങ്ങൾ—ക്കരുൾക നീ സതതം	Face of thine, its shine our strength, constant grant!

ലോകൈക സത്ഗുരുവേ! സ്വർജീവനക്കരുവേ!	Sat-guru[8] to all the world! Tree of Heaven's Life!
ദാസർക്കഭീഷ്ടമേകും മന്ദാരമാം തരുവേ!	Desire-granting wood immortal! Thy feet's spot
തിരുവടി നിയതം ഞങ്ങൾ—ക്കരുളുണ മഭയം	To us ordain, refuge eternal.
തത്വ വിത്താം മുനിയേ! ദുഷ്ടലോക ശനിയേ!	Sage of science's whole substance! Foe to every force fierce!
സത്യവേദ ധ്വനിയേ! ജീവാഗമക്കനിയേ!	Sacred script's solely sound! Life-imparting fadeless fruit!
കരുണയിൻ ധ്വനിയേ! ഞങ്ങൾ വരുന്നിതാ തനിയേ	Mercy's voice! To thee we come in worship, Oh, Lord!

Note: I offer another possible version to the final stanza, choosing to keep the rhyming bisyllabic endings unchanged:

To all truth, thou, Great *Muni*,
To the odious, their fell *Sani*,
Of the holy word, its true *dwani*,
Of the life-giving tree, its unique *kani*!.[9]

Paramaathmaav Ura Cheyyum ["Listen to what the Spirit has to say"]

Simon has written seven poems as a sequence addressing the seven churches of Asia Minor. It is a verse rendition of the seven letters that Apostle John writes in the book of Revelation, chapters 2–3. The words heard in each piece are of Christ admonishing the first-century churches of Ephesus, Sardis, Pergamos, Smyrna, Thyatira, Philadelphia, and Laodicea individually. This poem is the message John was asked to send to the church of Laodicea, as an indictment of its show of religion without any power thereof at all in it.

പരമാത്മാവുര ചെയ്യും മൊഴിയെല്ലാ—	Ecclesial throngs, hear ye all!
സഭകളും ശ്രവിക്കേണം	The Sole Lord's voice on thine ears fall!
സ്ഥിരമാം സാക്ഷിയും വിശ്വസ്ഥനുമായി സൃഷ്ടിയിൻ—	Witness Enduring, Faithful One, the First
ആദ്യനില ലഭിച്ചൊരു വിമലനോതിന	And justly adored source of all that exist
മൊഴി ധരിക്കുകിൽ ശുഭമെഴും തവ—	His utterance grasp, and bide thou well.
ശീതമല്ലുഷ്ണവുമല്ല—തവ ഗുണം	Cold nor hot, thy virtue shifts;
ഏതെന്നു നിജവുമില്ല	To the tepid cup thou well compare;

---

[8] *Sat-guru* is Sanskrit for "the True Teacher."
[9] *Muni* means a saintly hermit or seer; *Sani* is the mythical Destroyer; *dwani* means echo; *kani* means fruit.

ഈവിധമിനിയും നീ വാടിയ ജലം പോലെ	Were thus thy days ahead to fare,
നാൾ കഴിക്കുകിൽ നിന്നെഞാൻ മമ	And none thy faith's fame serves or lifts,
വായിൽ നിന്നു പുറത്തുമഴ്ന്നിടും—	Spewn out shall thou go from my mouth.
ഞാനൊരു ധനി തന്നേ—എനിക്കില്ല	"Misery none, and substance much,
ദീനത ലവമിന്നേ	My days run with portions such,"
മാനമോടിദം ചൊല്ലി ഹീനനായ് കുരുടനായ്	Sayst thou, so self-deceiv'd, sight-impair'd:
നീയിരിപ്പതു കാൺക പരനുടെ	Which plight, confess, thy true state,
മുന്നിൽ വീണറിയിക്ക നീയതു—	Prostrate cast, rid fully of thy prideful boast.
സമ്പന്നനാവതിനുണ്ട്—തനിത്തങ്കം	Seek thou worth? Hold pure gold,
വെണ്വസത്രം ധരിപ്പാനുണ്ട്	In like manner, bright garbs too have;
നിൻ കണ്ണുതെളിയുവാൻ ലേപവും വിലയ്ക്കുണ്ട്	Of Me buy, eye's bright'ning salve,
വന്നു വാങ്ങുക ശിക്ഷയാൽ പ്രിയന്മാരേ	Darling soul! my stirrings heed!
ഞാണുർത്തുന്നിതറിക നീ—	
മാനസാന്തരപ്പെടുക—എരിവോടു നീ—	With quickening zeal return in haste:
മാനസം തുറന്നീടുക	By precious space of heart prove chaste;
വാതിലഹം നിന്നു മുട്ടുന്നായതു കേട്ടു	Hark, the knock that bodes thee well
യാതൊരു നരൻ തുറന്നു തരികില-	And seeks to raise thy state to mine
പ്പൂതനോടു ഞാൻ വിരുന്നു കഴിഞ്ഞിടും—	With you my host, as I sit to dine.
സത്യമായ് ജയം കൊള്ളും ഭടനുഞാ—	The striving knight of heroic quest,
നൊത്തിരുപ്പുരുളീടും	His lauded triumph as witness set,
കൃത്യമായ് അഹം മേവും ഭദ്രാസനമതിങ്കൽ	By my throne shall sit installed—
നിത്യമായവൻ വാഴും ലവുദിക്യ	A secure prince of fame that loathed
മദ്ധ്യതോ ജയിച്ചെന്ന വിരുതിനാൽ—	The loose living of Laodice.

Ariya Babylon Nadikkarike [Exiles on Babel's banks]

This song is a lament of Israel in their Babylonian captivity as narrated in Psalm 137. The forces of Nebuchadnezzar deported the whole of Judea to Babylon after sacking Jerusalem and burning down the temple that Solomon had built. They are homeless and spiritually desolate now. Jerusalem is the city with its temple toward which every Jew raises hands in worship and prayer. Every Jew, high and low, had the same sentiments about where they were and where they would rather be.

അരിയ ബാബിലോൻ നദിക്കരികെ ചെന്നിരുന്നെങ്ങൾ	Exile bands on Babel's banks, sat we all in long lament
തിരുസീയോൻ പുരമോർത്തോരള വേറ്റം	Of Seeyon's Mount our souls bereft, our bodies
കരഞ്ഞുപോയ്	under captors bent.

കരതാരിൽ ചെറുവീണ കരുതിയെങ്കിലും പാടാൻ	Harps on hand, but mute of song, on the wailing shores
അരുതാതങ്ങലരിമേലവതൂക്കി യുടനങ്ങൾ—	They hung, Babylon's ripples spelling our remorse.
ഉരു മോദമെഴുംസീയോൻ തിരു ഗാനങ്ങളിലൊന്നു	Famed for joy run Sion's notes, sweet and noble numbers sound;
പരിചിൽ പാടുവാൻ പ്രേരിച്ചുടമക്കാർ ചിലരന്നു	From wailing mouths our captors sought one such lay as service bound.
പരമദേവാ നിൻ ഗീതം പരദേശമതിലൊരു	Sovereign Lord, thy sacred hymn, could we waste on alien sands?
വിധവും പാടുവാൻ മേലാഞ്ഞെടിയാർ മൗനികളായി—	This we thought, and numb we sat, with no song on our lips or hands.
പുരികൾക്കൊക്കെയു മേറ്റം തലയാം ശ്രീ യെരുശലേം	Forbid it *Shri Yerusalem*,[10] crown of nations on earth known,
പുരമേ നിന്നെ മറക്കാനരുതേ യിങ്ങൊരുനാളും—	Bar the day that dares to mark my neglect of thy renown.
അമിതാനന്ദയായ് ഞാൻ ഭവതിയെ ഗണിക്കാഞ്ഞാൽ	Would I see thee, Mother Holy, less than at thy supreme state?
മമ നാവെന്നുടെ താലു ഫലകേ സംഘടിക്കട്ടെ—	Condemn'd may my tongue then cleave, fast to my palate's plate.
അടിയോളം ഭവതിയെ പൊടിയാക്കാൻ ശ്രമിച്ചേദോം	"Let's rise to rase her down!" Edom's charging forces yell'd:
കുടിലർ നിൻ ജയശ്രീ കണ്ടതിലജ്ജ കലരട്ടെ—	May they drown in their own shame, at thy glory's constant build.
അതിനാശമണഞ്ഞുള്ള ഹതബാബേൽസുതേ! നിന്റെ	Oh, Babel, *femme fatale!* Just deserts meet thy prideful deeds!
കൃതി പോൽ നൽ പ്രതികാരം തവ ചെയ്യുവോൻ പരം ധന്യൻ—	From avenging hands towards thee it surely speeds.
കുലടേ! ദുർഭഗേ! നിന്റെ ചെറിയ മക്കളെ തൂക്കി	Womb of sin and hell's horrors! Thy seed be slung on rocky slopes!
ശിലമേലാഞ്ഞെടിപ്പോനാരവനെന്നും മഹാധന്യൻ—	Requiter hail, whose charge of rage thy power of slaughter stops.

Nallarin Sundari [Starlet Virgin!]

This song is a dramatized dialogue based on Solomon's Song of Songs 5:9–16, in the melody and meter of "Omana thinkal kidavo," the famous royal lullaby of Travancore. A rustic maiden known only as the "Shulemite" has a dream in which she hears her lover knock on her door, but in a mere moment's delay, he vanishes. She looks for him frantically all over the city, but he is not seen. The

---

[10] Literally meaning, "Blessed Jerusalem," both the spiritual and political home of Israel.

sentinels stop and harass her. On her way further, she meets with the "Daughters of Jerusalem," of whom she inquires if they saw him. They, in turn, ask her, "What is your beloved more than any other"? The poem is her answer:

നല്ലാരിൻ സുന്ദരീ! നിന്റെ പ്രിയ- നെന്തു വിശേഷതയുള്ളു?	Starlet virgin, won't you tell How thy groom his peers excel
എന്റെ പ്രിയൻ ചുവേപ്പാടു —നല്ല വെണ്മ കലർന്നൊരു വീരൻ	Ruddy, glowing is my heart's prince Handsome hero for eye and heart!
ആയിരം പത്താളെ നോക്ക്-അതിൽ എന്നേശു മുഖ്യനായുണ്ട്	Stands he over thousands ten Who for them is sole captain
പ്രാക്കളിൻ കണ്ണുകൾ നോക്ക് —അതിൽ എന്നേശുവിൻ കൺകളുണ്ട്	Sparkle the eyes of the meekly dove; Their eyes tell of Yeshu's love.
നന്മണപ്പൂന്തടം നോക്ക്—അതിൽ എന്നേശുവിൽ കവിളുണ്ട്	Watch the fragrant blossom's peaks Tell they not of Yeshu's cheeks?
താമര പൂവിനെ നോക്ക്! അതിൽ എന്നേശുവിൻ ചുണ്ടുണ്ട്	Watch the lotus bloom unfold, Fruits of Yeshu's lips untold!
ദേവതാരമരം നോക്ക്—അതിൽ എന്നേശുവിൻ ഗാത്രമുണ്ടു്	View thee not the cedar tree? Long thee not his form to see?
സർവാംഗ സുന്ദരൻ തന്നെ—എന്നെ വീണ്ടെടുത്തൊരു കുമാരൻ	Head to foot he handsome shows, The Prince who me by ransom chose.
ശാലേമിലെ മങ്കമാരെ —ഇവൻ എന്റെ പ്രിയതമൻ നൂനം	Salem's maidens, hear my vows, He alone, I swear, is my spouse!.

Aadyantamillatha Nityante [Eternal One, to this comely pair]

This was a song Simon dictated on the spot at a verbal request for a disciple's daughter's wedding.

ആദ്യന്തമില്ലാത്ത നിത്യന്റെ കാന്ത്യാ പ്രദ്യോതനൻ പോൽ പ്രകാശിച്ചു നിൽക്കും സദ്യോഗമാർന്നുള്ള ദിവ്യാനനങ്ങൾ ഇദ്ദമ്പതിക്കേകെ ശ്രീയേശു നാഥാ!	Eternal One, to this comely pair Grant thou looks of radiance rare; Add to their faces the seemly grace Of thee flowing in unfailing pace.
താല്കാലികങ്ങളാം ഭോഗങ്ങളെല്ലാം ആത്മാനുഭൂതിയിൽ നിസ്സാരമായി	Help them see in value low Joys trivial of life's fleeting show,

കാണ്മാൻകരുത്തുള്ള സ്വർഗ്ഗീയ കണ്ണാൽ	As indeed, Lord, thy Spirit would
ശോഭിക്കുമാറാക ശ്രീയേശുനാഥാ!	When it fills an earthen mould.
ആനന്ദവാരാശി തന്നിൽപ്പെരുക്കും	Lend them ears for the choric tides,
വീചീ തരംഗങ്ങളാർക്കുന്ന ഗാനം	The clapping waves in joyous strides,
വേദോക്ത സീമാവിലെത്തി ശ്രവിപ്പാൻ	In glorious realms of the sacred Word,
ഏകീടു കർണ്ണങ്ങൾ ശ്രീയേശു നാഥാ!	Of thee secured, Jesus, our Lord.
മൂഢോപദേശ കൊടുങ്കാറ്റു ശീഘ്രം	Grant them the flaming tongues of zeal
പാടേ തകർത്തങ്ങു ഭസ്മീകരിപ്പാൻ	To mute the spells of the heretic's spiel;
ചൂടോടെ കത്തി ജ്വലിക്കുന്ന നാവും	In power enduring, thy fire proceed,
നീടാർന്നു നൽകീടു ശ്രീയേശു നാഥാ!	In the manner, Lord, thy provisions speed.
സാധുക്കളായുള്ള മർത്ത്യർക്കു വേണ്ടി	Let them aid by hands of skill
ചാതുര്യയത്നം കഴിച്ചേതു നാളും	The poor of the world whom they'll fill
മാധുര്യ ദാനം പൊഴിക്കുന്ന കൈകൾ	By sweetness, where needs reside,
ഇദ്ദമ്പതിക്കേക ശ്രീയേശുനാഥാ!	As rightly dost thou thy gifts divide.
സീയോൻമണാളന്റെ പ്രത്യാഗമത്താൽ	In that day when night must flee
മായതമസ്സോടി മാറുന്ന നാളിൽ	And in the duskless dawn we thee see,
ജായത്വമേന്തി കിരീടംധരിപ്പാൻ	Oh, Zion's groom, thy spousal crown
ആശിസ്സിവർക്കേക ശ്രീയേശു നാഥാ!	Grant to these, in Christ, both one.
നിത്യം ലഭിക്കട്ടെ സൂര്യപ്രകാശം	Shine the sun on them each day
അഭ്യുൽ പതിക്കട്ടെ ചന്ദ്രന്റെ കാന്തി	And the moon, likewise, we pray;
നാനാത്വമാർന്നുള്ള പുഷ്പങ്ങളെന്നും	Flowering fields thy fragrance send,
സൗരഭ്യമേകട്ടെ ശ്രീയേശു നാഥാ!	Reigning Lord, of no start, nor end.

Vandaname Deva! [Honor to thee, Lord]

Each stanza of this song comes in two swift movements, the second part in strong percussion when sung:

വന്ദനമേ ദേവാ! തവ വന്ദനമേ	Honor to thee! To thee great honor, Lord!
വന്നിങ്ങലമിന്നും കൃപ തന്നീടുക! മന്നാ തവ—	Come, High King, with springs of grace thine!
നിന്നുടെ സന്നിധി തന്നിലണയുമീ	Look kindly on these servants
മന്ദരാം ദാസരെ നോക്കി—കൃപ	Of wits low, yet mercy pour;
തന്നടിയാരുടെ ചിന്നതയാകവേ	Ills by thy grace erase; help endure;
തള്ളീടേണം സ്ഥിരരാക്കി	In accord lone, thine errants restore.
ചിന്നീട്ടിഹ നിൻ രുധിരം	Blood of thine hither spilt,
മന്നിച്ചു മഹാദുരിതം	Expiate are we of guilt;

വിണ്ണിൽ സ്ഥിരമാം നഗരം	Sky's city bestowed,
തന്നിങ്ങിതിലെന്തുപരം?	Content we, thus complete.
യിസ്രായേൽ മക്കളെ സീൻ മരുഭൂമിയിൽ	Israel in Zin's scorching sands
താങ്ങിനടത്തിയ ദേവാ! ദുഃഖ	Moved along in thy sheltering shade;
മിശ്രമാം ജീവിതം നീക്കിയെന്നെ കനാൻ	So keep my life from mixes foul
നാട്ടിലയയ്ക്കണേ യോവാ!	On this Canaan course, Yovah, my soul.
യോർദ്ദാൻ ജഡവൻനദിയെ	Jordan, of tides fleshly,
മാറ്റിടുക; സൽഗദിയെ	Repel; right course
ചേർത്തീട്ടഹ ദുർവിധിയെ	Press; discord's force
തീർത്തീടു സഭാപതിയേ!	Reverse, O, liege of mercy!.

Paadum Paramanu Parichodu [The Song of Moses]

"The Song of Moses" is so named for more reasons than one. First, it appears in Exodus 15, a famous portion in Moses' second book in the Pentateuch. Secondly, the song celebrates the miraculous parting of the Red Sea under the hand of Moses, opening a path of deliverance for the enslaved Israel. The pharaoh and his forces pursue them into the dry path of the parted sea only to be devoured by the closing waves. Thirdly, the song marks the new identity of Israel as a free nation. Fourthly, echoes of this song permeate all of their history. Fifthly, the Song of Moses and the Song of the Lamb in the book of Revelation together resonate a thematic fusion. It is a song of epic victory, suitable with its lofty diction, majestic action, and powerful musical movement, for a triumphal march. We limit the selected portion to only four of Simon's eleven stanzas.

പാടുംപരമനു പരിചൊടു ഞാൻ	Sing will I lays sublime,
വരുമവനു സതതംജയം—	To the most high, in victory—
ഓടുംവാജിയെസാദിയോടുകൂടവേ കട—	The speeding steed, with its rider proud
ലൂടെതള്ളിത്തൻ തേജസ്സോടെപ്രബലപ്പെട്ടാൻ	Into the seabed cast, His might He showed.
യുദ്ധമനുഷ്യനവൻ യാഹെന്നവന്റെ നാമം	Man of War is He, Yah is His name;
സത്വരം ഹറവോനിൻ സൈന്യം രഥങ്ങളേയും	An instant sea-sweep was His move of fame;
അണ്ണിയിൽ തള്ളിയിട്ടു യുദ്ധ നേതാക്കൾ മുങ്ങി	To the nether went the pharaoh's rider and horse
ഗുപ്തരായ് ചെങ്കടലിലത്തലോടവർ താണു—	In the sea-jaw ride of his proud concourse.
നിൻ കാറ്റു കൊണ്ടൂതി നീ; സിന്ധുവവരെ മൂടി	Thy winds blew; the Sindhu's haul, a gyring roll,
ചെങ്കടലിലീയം പോൽ ശങ്കയന്യേ താണവർ;	Sank them, like leaden lumps, a loathed toll.

നിന്നത്ഭുത ക്രിയകൾ, പങ്കഹീനസ്തുതികൾ	Marvels thy deeds unravel, displays of growing glory.
തങ്കലെത്രയും മാന്യൻ ശങ്കനീയൻ നിസ്തുല്യൻ—	Unvanquished is thy man chosen for any story.

നിൻഭുജ വല്ലഭത്വ സ്തംഭിതരായവർ നിൻ	Thy potent arm did freeze the foe; thy treasured
സമ്പാദിതജനം കടന്നുപോകും വരേയ്ക്കും	Tribes, the troops triumphant, onward marched.
കമ്പനമില്ലാതുള്ള കല്ലുകൾ പോലെതന്നെ	Like desolate rocks on death's still way,
കുംഭിനിനാഥനേ! നിൻ മുൻപിലിരിക്കുമവർ—	All-earth's Lord, before thee they lay.

Yeshunayaka Sreesha Namo [Jesu, Lord, hail to thee]

"Yeshunayaka shreesha" is an ode that is thickly allusive of the acts and attributes of Christ. Every line holds metaphoric capsules descriptive of who Christ is or what he does. Edayaranmula K. M. Varghese states that this poem was written at the request of Mammen Bhagavatar, a national honoree in music, for his own performance repertoire.

യേശുനായക! ശ്രീശാ! നമോ നമോ!	Jesu, Lord, hail to thee, hail to thee
നാശവാരണ! സ്വാമിൻ നമോ നമോ!	Ruin's ruiner, Swamin! Hail!
മോശിപൂജിതഃ രൂപാ നമോ നമോ! മഹീപാദാ!	Moses-shadowed incarnate! Hail!
	Ruler of Earth, this thy footstool!
മാനുവേലനെ പാഹി നമോ നമോ!	Thou our Shelter, Oh, Manuvel, Lord,
മാനവസുതവര്യാ നമോ നമോ!	Son of God and pure love's Lord, us uphold,
ദീനവത്സല ക്രിസ്തോ നമോ നമോ! ദിനമാകേ!	Compassion's fount, preserve us, do,
	All our days, even so do.
കുഷ്ഠരോഗവിനാശാ നമോ നമോ!	Repuls'd leper's cleanser, hail,
തുഷ്ടിനല്കുമെന്നീശാ നമോ നമോ!	Grantor of comfort, hail, hail,
ശിഷ്യപാലകവന്ദേ നമോ നമോ ദിവപീഠാ!	Innocents' stronghold, we adore and hail!
	O, Holiness-throned, on praises dwell!
പഞ്ചപൂപ പ്രദാനാ നമോ നമോ!	Host of the five-loaves feast, hail! hail!
സഞ്ചിതാധികപുണ്യാ നമോ നമോ!	Object divine of desire's utmost,
അഞ്ചിതാനനയുക്താ നമോ നമോ! പരമീഡേ!	Meeting place of all the good known,
	With praises unceasing I thee crown.
ആഴിമേൽനടന്നോനേ! നമോ നമോ!	Thou of feet o'er the waters, hail, hail,
ശേഷിയറ്റവർക്കീശാ! നമോ നമോ!	Refuge to the faint, O Lord, hail! hail!
ഊഴിമേൽ വരുംനാഥാ! നമോ! തൊഴുകൈയായ്.	Whose soles the Earth will touch again, hail!
	Worship receive, Lord, of hands of *pranam*!.[11]

---

[11] The term means "obeisance" or a hand-fold salute where the respectful gesture of the two hands closing and the head bowing, is the normal traditional practice.

Salomiye Varikente Priye [Come away, my beloved]

"Salomiyeh, Varikente Priye!" ["Salome, come away, my beloved"] has been labeled "the Manifesto Song of the Viyojitha" movement. The song celebrates the beauty of Salome and the attraction of the place to which her lover invites her, away from the mundane distractions that surround her. The call of the lover is intended to urge the audience to shun worldliness and to espouse holy living. The song is simple with its folk melody and clear spiritual message. We are taking only two out of its twelve stanzas here.

ശാലോമിയേ! വരികെന്റെ പ്രിയേ!	Salome, come away my beloved,
ചേലെഴും സ്വർലോക സുന്ദരിയേ!	Oh, Beauty of such celestial adorn!
മാലൊഴിക്കും നിന്റെ പ്രേമരസം വഴി—	Thy love's *rasa* that dispels gloom
ഞാലപിപ്പിക്കുന്നെൻ ചുണ്ടുകളെ മമ—	Loads my lips with lays on end.
ലോകവെയിലാറി തീർന്നിടുമ്പോൾ	The scorching sun now fades and sets;
മൂറിൻമലമേൽ ഞാൻ വിശ്രമിപ്പാൻ	The hills of myrrh bid us for rest;
സിംഹഗുഹകളും പുള്ളിപ്പുലികളിൻ	Come away, beloved, free from fears,
പർവ്വതവും വിട്ടു പോരിക നീ ശുദ്ധേ!	Of dens of lions and leopard's lairs.
കെട്ടിയടച്ചുള്ള തോട്ടമേയെൻ	A garden walled, my fountain sealed,
മുദ്രയിട്ടുള്ള ജലാശയമേ!	Undrying surges thy love's springs feed;
വറ്റിടാതുള്ള നിൻ പ്രേമവെള്ളങ്ങളിൽ	There I rebound in ecstasy,
മുത്തം ലയിച്ചു രമിപ്പെൻ സദാപിഞാൻ.	Rapturous is its constancy.

Smarna Sabha Doothu [Letter to Smyrna]

The letter to "Smarna" or Smyrna is the second in the sequence of Simon's Revelation poems. Please see the headnote of Song #9 above that introduces the poems and their context.

സ്മർണാവിൻ സഭാ ദൂതനേ! നിൻപേർക്കു	Smyrna's steward! To thee
ഞാൻ നൽകുന്നീ ലഘുവാം ലേഖം	I send this short scroll.
വൻമൃതിയിൽ വീണു പിന്നെയുമെഴുന്നേറ്റു	He that rose from the great descent, with his redrawn breath,
പുണ്യജീവനെയായണ്ട തുടസ്സമൊടുക്കമാം	Who the end as start begins,
വിദഗ്ദ്ധനുരയ്പിതു—	the all-endowed, thus speaketh:
പ്രത്യക്ഷം നീ ദരിദ്രൻ തന്നെ—എന്നാലും നീ	Poor in looks thou, yet art deeply rich:
സത്യത്തിൽ ധനികനത്രേ;	Behold, I am in constant watch of thy niche—

നിത്യം ഞാനറിയുന്നേൻ—മിഥ്യാ യൂദരായ് നിൽക്കും	As of the covens of false Jews I am—
സാത്താൻ പള്ളിയാർ നിന്മേൽ	Of calumnies cast on you, to bring harm.
ചുമത്തു മനവധി കടുത്ത ദുഷിമൊഴി—	
ഒട്ടും നീ ഭയപ്പെടേണ്ട—വന്നിടാനുള്ള	Fret not, nor by fear thy gains reverse
കഷ്ടം നീ സഹിക്കേ വേണ്ടു	Let run the sorrows set for their course;/
ദുഷ്ടനാം പിശാചിപ്പോൾ പത്തുനാൾ മതപീഢ	Endure those alone, none more.
സൃഷ്ടിക്കും പരീക്ഷിപ്പാൻ തടവിൽ ചിലർ കിട—	A mere ten days has Satan in design
ന്നുഴന്നു വലഞ്ഞിടും	To test thy faith with prison and pain.
വിശ്വസ്തനായിരിക്ക നീ മരണത്തോളം	Abide thou faithful to the hour of death;
വിത്രസ്തനാകരുതൊട്ടും;	Resist all fear: a crown of life is thine to don
പശ്ചാൽ ജീവകിരീടം—ദത്തം ചെയ്തിടുവേൻ ഞാൻ	As children to God's own high truth born;
സത്യസ്തർക്കഹോ! രണ്ടാം മരണമതിലൊരു	The second death and its baneful pit
വിനയും വരികില്ലാ—	Shall claim thee not, nor harm one bit.

Sardis Sabha Doothu [Letter to Sardis]

Sardis is the fifth of the seven addressees of the letters of Apostle John in the book of Revelation. Fabled for its wealth and impregnable defense, Sardis was also the capital of Lydia. The message condemns the deadness of the faith of its people, but still invites them to undefiled conduct of life, to be worthy of having their names written in the Book of Life (Rev. 3:1–6).

ഹാ! ഞാനിതറിയുന്നു ജീവപേർ മാത്രം	Alive, art thou, but in name alone
നീ താൻ ധരിക്കുന്നു	Sad truth for me, do take heed.
താതൻ സുരനാഥൻ ഏഴാവികളുള്ളോൻ	Father, heaven's High King, of Spirits Seven
താരകമേഴാർന്നോനോതുന്നീവണ്ണമായ്:	Wielder of Stars seven, says thus:
നിൻക്രിയകളാൽ നീയെൻ ജീവനറ്റുള്ള	Thy deeds declare the lifeless lump
മണ്ണെന്നറിയുന്നേ നിന്നുണരുക—ചാ	Of dirt thou art, alike thy look and life: stir up
വിന്നടുത്തവയെ താങ്ങിയുറപ്പിക്ക	Those fading parts that lie to death's door nigh;
നിന്നുടെ ക്രിയയെൻ പരനുമുൻ	The works of thine, see thee betray,
പൂർണതരമെന്നു കണ്ടതില്ലയി—	Much wanting in the Father's eye.
എങ്കിലുമുടുകൾ പങ്കിലമാക്കാത്തോ—	Yet remain of spotless garb a few,
രെൻകൂടെ നടക്കും വെണ്ണുടയുടുക്കും	Apace with ME, bright in view;
വിൺകുറിയീന്നവർ തൻപേർ മറയ്ക്കാഞ്ഞാൻ	Their names glow in celestial spell:
ശങ്കയില്ലവർ നാമം പിതൃ സുര—	For me to proclaim in the High Presence,
സംഘസവിധത്തിൽ താങ്ങിപ്പറയും ഞാൻ	To the Father's pleasure and to heaven's praise.

Paramadeva Vandana [To the God of gods]

This song is a *sthava* or an ode of adoration, expressing devotional pleasure and gratitude, in language that is easily accessible to all. It also provides an example of a meditation on the names of God through a series of synonyms, a genre of devotional verse popular in Indian spirituality.

മംഗളം ദേവദേവനു —	Blessings to the God of gods
പ്രതിദിനവും മംഗളം ദേവദേവനു	And lauds fresh to him each new day!
ഭംഗമില്ലാതെ പരമോന്നതനായുലകി—	To Him that all space in power does fill
ലെങ്ങും നിറഞ്ഞു മരുവും പരാപരന്നു	And acts likewise, the Supreme One
ജീവനില്ലാതിരുന്നോ രാദിജലമതിന്മേ—	Hovering, who, over the primeval floods
ലാവസിച്ചുയിർ കൊടുത്തപിതാമഹന്നു	Gave them life-stirring breath, the Great Father
ഏകജാതനാം തിരു സൂനുവേ ദയയോടു—	To the giver of the Holy Child to the world
ലോകരക്ഷയ്ക്കു നൽകിയ സുരാധിപന്നു	The gift of mercy in salvation's mould, the Ruler of *Suras*
നീതിയോടിഹ ലോക ജീവിതം കഴിപ്പതി—	To him that with His Spirit grants
ന്നാവിതന്നനുഗ്രഹിക്കും അഖിലേശന്നു	Days on earth and life lawful, Master to all!
ദേവനിവാസമാക്കി ബ്ഭൂവിനെ ശരിയാക്കി	To him who ordains grace to turn
മേവുവാൻ കൃപയരുളും സദാതനനു	This dreary earth into the home of God, God Eternal.

Portions from Simon's Epic, *Vedaviharam*

Invocation

The term "Vedaviharam" is a Sanskrit coinage, combining two words, *Veda* and *Viharam*. Veda means sacred knowledge of the scriptures. *Viharam* means exploration, survey, or abode. *Vedaviharam*, therefore, can be interpreted as "A journey through the Vedas," or "A survey of the Vedas." My preference is to call the work *A Vedic Odyssey*. Like Milton's *Paradise Lost*, it tells the story of human fall in the Garden of Eden and its aftermath, and the revealed plan of salvation through the Messiah, but Simon's epic covers the entire book of Genesis, which still has a range of ensuing Bible stories like those of Noah, Abraham, Isaac, Jacob, and Joseph. Like all verse in Dravidian meters, *Vedaviharam* with its rich metrical variety is a highly singable narrative. It is also the work of a poet quite well versed in literatures of many languages, native and foreign, modern and classical. A quick scan of the work shows that

Simon wrote with comfortable knowledge of astronomy, archaeology, biology, histories of various disciplines and of ancient to modern times. *Vedviharam* and *Paradise Lost* invite close comparative readings, especially because Simon was an admirer of Milton and was well acquainted with Milton. Consistent with the epic formula as much as for personal reasons, Simon opens the great song, as does Milton, with an invocation, first identifying whom he is invoking (1:1–34) and then offering a prayer for heavenly assistance in the telling or the singing of it:

യാതൊരു കാലത്തെയാണാദിയായ് നിർദേശിപ്പ	Whatever time can be as *aadi* eyed,
തായതിന്നരുതിയില്ലാതൊള്ള യുഗംമുൻപും	Aeons endless prior still, if surveyed,
വീതരൂപനായ് വിമലാഭനായ് നിന്നമഹാ	Formless and effulgent stood Truth Infinite,
നീതിനീരധിയെ ഞാനാദരാൽ വന്ദിക്കുന്നേൻ. (1:1–4)	Whom I worship, in His measureless state.
സകല ലോകങ്ങൾക്കു മാദികാരണനിവൻ	He it is to all worlds Cause very First;
സകലഭൂതങ്ങൾക്കുമാഹാര പ്രദനിവൻ	He to all beings the provider host;
സകല ദേവ വൃന്ദ വന്ദിത പദാംബുജൻ	He is who of all celestials duly worship'd,
സകല നിഷ്കലത്വം പേറുന്ന പെരിയവൻ. (1:5–8)	He the form of holiness, degreed utmost.
ആഗമകാരന്മാരിലാദിമൻ മോസസ്സു സർ	Of the Genesis train, Moses in knowledge prime,
വ്യാഗമപ്പൊരുളാകുമീപ്പരാശക്തിക്കത്രേ	Of origins, received, in revealment, the all-do syllable
"ഏലേ"ന്നൊരിബ്രീയമാം നാമമോതിയതു	Of Hebraic Fear, *El*, the all-ruling person'd name
മൂലവസ്തുവാം നാഥനുപദേശിച്ചതല്ലോ. (1:9–12)	Of the Oversoul—that potent parent of all that be.
ഇലോഹ, ഷദ്ദായി, യും എലോഹി, മദ്ദൊനായി	Eloha, Yahweh, Elohi, and Adonai,
വിലോപമന്യേ യാഹ്‌വെ, യഹോവ, യാഹെന്നെല്ലാം	The self-same as Jehovah, Yah, and Shaddai,
മോശീയ ഗ്രന്ഥങ്ങളിൽ പറഞ്ഞിട്ടുള്ള നാമ	Names from on high through Moses unveiled
മീശനാൽ പ്രകാശിതമായവ തന്നെയത്രേ. (1:13–16)	By the same Lord who to them all does title wield.
ഗൂഢവിഗ്രഹനായിട്ടെങ്ങുമേ വർത്തിക്കിലും	Unseen though He, of nothing unaware,
കൂടസ്ഥൻ നിജാശയമാത്മാവെന്നിവ രണ്ടും	Unhindered, His mind does declare
കാലാനുസാരം പ്രകടീകരിച്ചീടും പുഷ്പ	As times unfold, his deeds, set to match
കാലത്തു കളകണ്‌ഠം കളകൂജിതം പോലെ. (1:17–20)	New turns, like the peafowl's call on the vernal watch.
അല്ലായ്‌കിലധീശനേ മാനുഷ്യനറികെന്ന	Were it not so, Ruler of All, dwellest thou not
തില്ലൊരിക്കലുമവ നഗാധസ്ഥിതനല്ലോ. (1:21–22)	In the Being's Seat, for mortal reach far too remote?
പ്രപഞ്ചത്തിന്റെ മൂലകന്ദത്തെ കണ്ടെത്തുവാൻ	Earthlings strive in futile labor,
പ്രപഞ്ചവാസികൾക്കു കഴിവില്ലായ്ക മൂലം	In attempts to reach the cosmic core;
സ്രീയമാം മഹത് തത്ത്വബോധനം നടത്തുവാ—	In pitying presence thy helping spirit
നീയുലകിങ്കൽ ദൈവമയപ്പൂ നിജാത്മാനം. (1:23–26)	Lets them from thy knowledge in profit visit.

"കാരണംവിനാ കാര്യംനോൽപദ്യതേ" എന്നുള്ള
സാരമാം പ്രമാണത്തെ മറന്നിങ്ങനാസ്തികർ
പൂരിതപാപരായിച്ചരിക്കും പോതും തന്റെ
കാരുണ്യവർഷമീശൻ പൊഴിക്കുന്നവരിലും. (1:27-30)

ആശ്രിതമന്ദാരമാമിപ്പരൻ തന്റെ പാദ
മാശ്രിയിച്ചനുദിനം വസിക്കും ജനങ്ങൾക്കു
വിശ്രുത ദയാഹസ്ത പരിരംഭണം ദുഃഖ—
മിശ്രിമാമീഇജീവിതമാനന്ദമാക്കിത്തീർപ്പൂ (1:31-34)

യാതൊന്നിൽ നിന്നു സർവമുൽപ്പന്നമായിടുന്നു
യാതൊന്നിൻ സാഹായ്യത്താൽ നിലനിൽക്കുന്നു സർവം
യാതൊന്നിലെല്ലാമന്തേവിലയിക്കുന്നാ ദിവ്യ
"യാ" തന്റെ പാദാരവിന്ദങ്ങളേ മമാലംബം. (1:35-38)

നിന്തിരുവടിയുടെ മാഹാത്മ്യമുരയ് ക്കുവാൻ
അന്തരാ ചിന്തിച്ചൊരുങ്ങീടുന്നൊരു വാഗിയുണ്ടോ?
എന്നിരിക്കവേ വെറും മന്ദനാമിവൻ ജ്യോതിർ
മന്ദിരാ നിൻചരിതം എങ്ങനെ വർണ്ണിച്ചീടും? (1:43-46)

ദുഷ്കരതരമാകുമീ ക്രിയ നിർവഹിപ്പാൻ
പുഷ്കരം പൃഥ്വീ തലമെന്നിവ വാങ്മാത്രത്താൽ
സൃഷ്ടി ചെയ്തൊരു ഭവൽ കടാക്ഷമുണ്ടെന്നാകിൽ
നഷ്ട നൈപുണ്യനാമിബ്ബാലനും കഴിവുണ്ടാം. (1:47-50)

കാശിന്നു കൊള്ളാതുള്ള ഖരത്തിൻ താടിയെല്ലാൽ
നാസിരായോരു ശിംശോനായിരം ഫിലിസ്ത്യരെ
കാശിനി തന്നിൽ കൊന്നു വീഴ്ത്തുവാൻ കഴിഞ്ഞെങ്കി—
ലീശനേ! നിനക്കെന്നാൽ ദുശ്ശകമെന്തൊന്നുള്ളൂ? (1:51-54)

സപ്തവർണ്ണങ്ങളുടെ മിശ്രണമായുള്ളൊരു
സപ്തസപ്തിയിൻ കിരണങ്ങളാൽ കാർമേഘവും
ചിത്രവർണോജ്ജ്വലമാം ചാപമായ് തീരുമെങ്കി—
ലുത്തമാ! നിൻ ദീപ്തിയാലെൻ ബുദ്ധി ശോഭിക്കില്ലേ?
(1:55-58)

നമസ്തേ സർവേശ്വരാ! നമസ്തേ കൃപാർണവാ!

നമസ്തേ ദേവദേവാ! നമസ്തേ വിശ്വവന്ദ്യാ!

നമസ്തേ നതജനപാലനപാരായണ!

നമസ്തേ ഭക്തനേത്ര ബാഷ്പമാർജന! വിഭോ!
(1:59-62)

Effects and cause bespeak their tie
Reason's laws for how and why,
Bar to the mocker, in folly sloshing,
Though God's rain is him still washing.

For their shelter, the destitute flee
To His feet, their Life's very tree;
His ancient hand of famous might
Gives them joys, in a world so grief-beset.

That from which all beings source
That by which all feel one force
That which indwelt radiates all
That Yah's footstool, my strength I call.

Lives a rhetor, declaim-set,
By design in words of needed might?
How then would a slow wit wight,
Oh, Glory's Castle, of thee indite?

Mine to do, this daunting deed?
Of little strength, this lad must feed
On earth and sky's first shaping Word
Whose love-behest is power conferred.

A worthless jawbone Samson found
Yet it fit him in war-gear sound;
The Philistine mob, his swings felled;
Need then my hand with thee be shriveled?

The hue rich sun over the welkin's dark
Casts his bow, the glowing arc;
And so with me, O, Craftsman Great,
Wouldn't thy rays change my wits' dull state?

I bow to thee, Lord God of all, Namaste! Thou Merciful!

I bow to thee, Great Celestial! Namaste! Of all cosmos adored!

I bow to thee, Preserver of reverent souls! Namaste!

I bow to thee, Who in deserved praises dwell! Namaste!

മോശയിൻ നാവിനെ നീ പ്രവർത്തിക്ഷമമാക്കി	Moses' tongue thou empowered,
സ്വാശയം കഴുതയെ കൊണ്ടു നീ പറയിച്ചു	A braying beast thy counsel told:
ദാശരെ പ്രഭാഷണ പടുക്കളാക്കിത്തീർത്തു	Oarsmen coarse thy script revealed:
മോശമായൊന്നുമില്ല നിന്നുടെ കരം ചേർന്നാൽ.	Nothing dull, if by thy hand helped.
(1:63–66)	

ഊഴിക്കു നിർമ്മാതാവേ! ദൈവനിർണ്ണയമാകു-	Maker to this dusty orb, thy counsels wholly prevail,
മാഴവും ബഹുവിധ വ്യാഖ്യാനഭംഗങ്ങളും	Sense shadowed, substance sealed, scope of no scale;
ചുഴറ്റ് ഗഹനാർത്ഥ ശബ്ദമാം തിമികളു-	Who dares traverse the swelling tides
മേഴുന്ന വേദമാകു മാഴിയി ലാരിറങ്ങും? (1:67–70)	Of Veda's springs thy Spirit pervades?

എങ്കിലുമവിടുത്തെ സാഹ്യമായിട്ടിന്നൊരു	Nevertheless, secure in thy deep-sea ship
തുംഗമാം പ്ലവയന്ത്രാ തന്നിൽ ഞാനിരിക്കുകിൽ	Voyage-bound as thou wouldst equip,
വൻ കടലിതിൻ ചില ഭാഗങ്ങൾ വീക്ഷിക്കുവാൻ	Through tides massive of Vedic waves,
സങ്കടമെന്ന്യേ സാധിച്ചിടുമില്ലൊരു തർക്കം. (1:71–74)	Shall marvels unravel, my heart raves.

The Story of Origins

ആദിയിലാദി ദൈവമാകാശഭൂമികളെ	In the beginning of beginnings, planets and space
മേദുരഭാഗങ്ങളായി സൃഷ്ടി ചെയ്തനന്തരം	Emerged as realms of God's manifest grace.
മേദിനീ തലവാസമാർന്നുള്ളൊരാകാലത്തെ	Earth stood pristine, until the wasting touch
പാതകപുരിഷയിൻ ദണ്ഡനദ്വാരാ ലോകം	Of the treacherous host, rid this haunted patch,
നിർജ്ജനമായിത്തീർന്നു; പ്രളയതോയം കേറി	The world, of dwellers. Ground and elements
മജ്ജനം ചെയ്യിച്ചെല്ലാദിശയും നശിപ്പിച്ചു	Lay dead; floods filled the earth in deluge depth,
വായുവിൽ ചരിക്കുവാൻ പക്ഷികളില്ലാതായി	But with fishes none, and the air with no avian life.
തോയത്തിൽ മത്സ്യങ്ങളെങ്ങുമേ കാണ്മാനില്ല. (1:75–82)	

മഹത്താമന്ധകാരം വെള്ളത്തെ മുഴുവനും	Great was the darkness that settled on the water,
മറച്ചു വ്യാപിച്ചിതു കണ്ടിക്കാർനിര പോലെ.	Like ranging mountains of light-lorn matter.
ഇങ്ങനെ നൈമിത്തിക പ്രളയവെള്ളങ്ങളിൽ	Causes obscure and effects untraced,
തുംഗമാം ശിഥിലത പൂണ്ടലക്ഷണമായും	Besieged lay the world for ages ahead,
അവ്യപദേശ്യമായും മഞ്ഞയമായും ലോക—	So it seemed, of God ordained.
മവ്യയ നിയോഗത്താൽ കിടന്നു ബഹുകാലം. (1:83–88)	

എത്ര നാളിപ്രകാരമിരുന്ന വെള്ളങ്ങളിൽ	How long lay the earth submerged in this state
പ്രിഥ്വി നിർലീനമായിക്കിടന്നെന്നറിവില്ല	Also remains unknown. All the same, at its end
തദ്യുഗാന്ത്യത്തിലീശൻ പ്രളയോഗദകമധ്യ	The Lord's Spirit by desire stirred, moved to create
ത്തുദൃത്താം സിസൃക്ഷയോടവരോഹിച്ചു സ്വയം. (1:89–92)	An order afresh, Himself solely, Himself sufficient.

ഇമ്മഹാദേവനുടെ ജീവദായകശക്തി	The life-lending power of God's might
കർമ്മവൈഭവമോടു നിർജ്ജീവ ജലോപരി	While yet hovering over the watery waste,

സംഖ്യയില്ലാത്ത ജീവരാശികളുരുവാകാൻ	Filled its immense depths with species spate.
പ്രോഷണം ചെയ്തു കൊണ്ടങ്ങിരിക്കെ പരമേശൻ	Swift and certain of its position set, God spoke:
ദീപ്തിയുണ്ടാകെന്നുരച്ചീടിനാനപ്പോൾ ദിവ്യ—	"Light, Be!" And Light there was, with a quelling stroke
ദീപ്തി യൊന്നുണ്ടായ്‌വന്നു, പിരിഞ്ഞുകൂരിരുട്ടും. (1:93-98)	In the same instant to the reign of darkness and its duke.
അന്ധകാരത്തിൻ ചളിക്കുളത്തിൽ വികസിച്ചു	Lotuses white, golden, red or of more hues blossom
പന്തിയായ് നിൽക്കും സീതാംഭോജങ്ങൾ രക്താംബുജം	To shame the slime of their past lightless home;
ഹാടക നീല വർണ്ണ പഭമങ്ങളിവയ്ക്കുള്ള	Fair of face, each its neighbor's lovelier peer,
ധാടിയെക്കവിഞ്ഞുച്ചാവചമാം നിറങ്ങളിൽ	These mudlings draw the eyes that admire
ശോഭിക്കുമിദ്യുതിയാൽ ഗംഭീര ജലത്തിന്റെ	The deeply taking glory of God in them spread,
ശീഭരതമോമുഖം തെളിഞ്ഞിതെല്ലാടവും. (1:99-104)	Like the light that on this world His glory first shed.
തോയമദ്ധ്യത്തിലൊരു ശൂന്യമായിടമുണ്ടാ—	Amidst the wet vast was a region void
യായതുബഹുസൂക്ഷ്മ വാതമിശ്രിതമായ	Readied, for aery mixes and deployed,
വായുമണ്ഡലമായി തീരുകയെന്നു ദേവ	A construct verbed as the sphere of virgin air
നായകനുരച്ചപോതാഗിരം ഫലവത്തായ്. (1:105-08)	From the Craftsman's mind for creation's care.
ലോകമാംകിടക്കയ്ക്കു മേലതു ചേലിയന്ന	Over Nature's world its tasteful cast held
നീലമേലാപ്പെന്നപോൽ ലാലസിച്ചതിവേലം.	A cerulian robe of unaging weld.
പട്ടുകൾ സ്വർണം വെള്ളി രത്നങ്ങൾ വിദ്യുത്ദീപ-	Satins, gold, silver, gems, lights electric and resplendent
മൊട്ടുസ്സംഖ്യ മായേവം വിഷ്ഷപം തന്നിൽ കിട്ടും. (1:109-12)	Fill in bounteous range this brave new firmament.
പുഷ്ഷഭാസ്സെഴുന്നുള്ള സാധനമേതിനാലും	Objects of much effulgence endowed,
ത്വിട്ടിനുസമം കൂട്ടിചൊല്ലുവാനരുതാതെ	Equals wanting, stay uncompared,
സ്പഷ്ടമായായാനന്യാലങ്കാര വസ്തുത്തേന	And likened only to themselves stand
സൃഷ്ടിയിൽ തത്താദ്രുക്കെന്നുള്ളൊരു നിലയാർന്നു	*sui generis*, lofty-lone in glory,
പുഷ്കരതലം തന്നിൽവിളങ്ങിത്തിളങ്ങിയീ— നിഷ്കളതേജ:പുഞ്ജം സുഷമാവിശേഷത്താൽ. (1:113-18)	Called to flourish, in this house of glows.
വെള്ളങ്ങളൊരിടത്തു കൂടട്ടെ; ശുഷ്കഭൂമി	Let waters in one place gather; the barren earth
നല്ലപോൽതെളിയട്ടെയെന്നീശനുരയ്ക്കുമ്പോൾ	Vigor receive, so said the Maker,
അങ്ങനെസംഭവിച്ചു സർവസസ്യാദ്ധ്യായി	And so it became, all green clad,
മംഗലകാന്തിയേന്തിബ് ഭൂമിയുംപ്രകാശിച്ചു. (1:119-22)	Beauty flushing, all earth shone.
രാപ്പകൽ ദിനവത്സരാദികൾ കണക്കാവാ—	So for days and nights their courses to mark
നഭ്രവീഥിയിലെന്നും താരേന്ദു ദിവാകരർ	Let lights, said God, their stations embark:
സപ്രഭം സ്ഥിതി ചെയ്യട്ടെന്നുള്ള വാക്കിൻപടി—	Stars and the sun then their positions filled,
യപ്രഭാ മൂർത്തി വ്യൂഹം വാനത്തു നിരന്നതേ. (1:123-26)	Other stellar billions in ranks rallied.

The Solar Neighborhood

ജ്യോതിശ്ച്ചക്ര നിർമ്മാണവൈചിത്ര്യം വിചാരിക്കി—	See from the views of the astral spread
ലാദിനായക പാദമാരാലുമാരാധ്യമാം.	Its designer's adoration warranted;
മീതേയുള്ളോരുവാനമീശ്വര മഹിമയെ	"The heavens declare," said King David,
വേദിപ്പിക്കുന്നുവെന്നു ദാവീദനോതിടുന്നു. (1:127–30)	"God's great praises of the starry myriad."
ഭൂഗോളമിതിൻ വ്യാസം സഹസ്രാഷ്കം മയിൽ	Seven thousand miles is the earth in radius,
ആകവേ ഇരുപത്തയ്യായിരം പരിണാഹം	Five and twenty thousand its circumference;
ചന്ദിരൻ രണ്ടുലക്ഷം മുപ്പത്തെണ്ണായിരവു—	Out at two hundred thirty-eight thousand miles
മൊന്നുചേർന്നകലത്തിൽ നിന്നു ഭൂമിയെ മാസി	Moves the moon, circling the earth in monthly course,
ചുറ്റുന്നു; രണ്ടായിരം നൂറുമാണിതിന്റെ വ്യാസം	Twenty-one hundred is its radius, no, not wrong,
തെറ്റല്ല, സാമീപ്യത്താൽ വലുതായ് കാണ്മൂ ചന്ദ്രൻ. (1:131–36)	Closer it is, so we see it large.
ഒൻപതുകോടിയോടു മുപ്പതു ലക്ഷം മയി—	At a frightful ninety-three million miles
ലമ്പരക്കുമാറകലത്തി ലാണഹസ്കരൻ.	Situate is earth's day-ruler, his sphere
എട്ടുലക്ഷവുമാറു പത്തഞ്ചു സഹസ്രവു—	Crossable, a decimal shy, if ever,
മൊട്ടുമേ കുറയാതെ വ്യാസമുണ്ടിതിന്നഹോ! (1:137–40)	Of another million through its center.
ജ്വാല ജ്വാലയാലെങ്ങും സംവൃതമായുള്ളോരു	Surging mounts of fluid fire, cleaving, winding, and flying take
ഗോളമാമിതിൽ നിന്നു മേലോട്ടു രണ്ടു ലക്ഷം —	A quarter million miles in height, whirls of lightning course they make,
മൈലോളം പായുന്നുണ്ടു തീഗ്മാം ശിഖാസ്ത്രങ്ങൾ	Shooting tongues, a thousand thousand, fed and refed of zealous supplies–
മാലുണ്ടാമിതിൻ ചൂടു കേവലം ചിന്തിക്കിലും. (1:141–44)	The selfsame fire—mere thought of it one petrifies.
വിസ്തീർണ്ണതരമാമീ സൂര്യന്റെ യുൾഭാഗത്തു	Mammoth measure is this star's inside
സുസ്ഥമായ് കൊള്ളുംഭൂക്കൾ ദ്വാദശലക്ഷാധികം	For twice a million earths to reside.
അർക്കനു നേദിഷ്ടമാം നക്ഷത്രംപഞ്ചവിംശ	Not unique, but his proximal peer
ലക്ഷം കോടികൾമയിൽ ദൂരവേ നിലകൊൾവൂ. (1:145–48)	At Light years four is situate near.
പ്രേക്ഷകരെണ്ണിട്ടുള്ള നക്ഷത്രമാകമാനം	Observer counts of total stars
സൂക്ഷ്മായറുപതു കോടിയെന്നറിയേണം.	Stand now set at sixty crores.
ഭൂവിലുമായിരത്തിമുന്നൂറു മടങ്ങെഴും	Thirteen hundred times the greater is Brhspati
ഭാവുകൻ ബ്രഹുസ്പതിയെട്ടുചന്ദ്രന്മാരും	The wellborn astral moves, moons eight in his trail;
ദ്വാദശസാഹസ്രകഗുണവാൻ ശനിപത്തു	More eye-filling, times twelve thousand the larger Saturn (Sani)
മേദുരേന്ദുക്കളോടും ചേർന്നിഹനൃപതീന്ദ്രൻ	With attending ten of his own minions
പരിവാരങ്ങളോടുകൂടവേ നിൽക്കുംപോലെ	Move, as suits a king in his court's midst
പരിചിൽഗഗനത്തു വിലങ്ങുന്നതമിതാഭം. (1:149–56)	Stately in pace and positions of the firmament.

ശരത്താമൃതുവിലെ ജ്യോൽസ്നയിലേകചന്ദ്രൻ
പരത്തുംരശ്മി ഭൂമിക്കലങ്കാരകമെങ്കിൽ
ഇന്ദുക്കളെട്ടുംപത്തും ഒന്നുചേർന്നുദിക്കുന്ന
സുന്ദരഗ്രഹങ്ങളിൻ ചാരുതചൊല്ലേണമോ? (1:157-60)

കർമകൗശല്യമേറും സ്വർണകാരകനേറ്റം
ചെമ്മയായ് കേവണത്തിൽ കല്ലുകൾ പതിക്കുമ്പോൽ
നമ്മുടെ ദൈവമെത്ര ഭംഗിയിലംബരത്തീ—
നിർമലഗോളങ്ങളെ സംസ്ഥാപിച്ചിരിക്കുന്നു! (1:161-64)

The lonesome moon in the dead of winter,
Drapes the earth in its garb of glamor;
Starlet huddles that together rise
Eight or ten, how do we their glory appraise!

The skillful smith on the strip of gold
The precious stones fix in charming hold
How far beyond in effortless skill
God's jewels the skies all fill!.

Creation of Animal Life

"കൂട്ടമായ് ജനിക്കട്ടെ വെള്ളത്തിൽ ജന്തുവൃന്ദം
കൂട്ടമായ്പറക്കട്ടെ പക്ഷികളാകാശത്തിൽ"
ഈട്ടമേറിയ പരൻ തന്നുടെയീ നിദേശം
വാട്ടമെന്നിയേ ഫലിച്ചഞ്ചാകും ദിനത്തിങ്കൽ (1:165-68)

വന്യജീവികളുരോഗാമികൾ ഗ്രാമ്യജന്തു
വൃന്ദങ്ങളിവ മന്നിൽ നിന്നുംസംഭവിക്കട്ടെ;
എന്നീവിധത്തിൽ പരനോതവേയവയെല്ലാ—
മുന്നമിച്ചതുഭൂവിൽ നിന്നു താമസമെന്യേ. (1:169-72)

"Let creatures in the waters play or ply,
And fowls in flocks fill the air and fly";
Instant effect had that Word forthwith,
God's command of Day the Fifth

Beasts of the wild and of the friendlier woods
Cattle, rangers, reptiles, rovers, and critters,
Fit in purposed places, none sought as betters
Filled the earth's fresh, behooving sods.

Creation of Man and Woman

തദനന്തരം സൃഷ്ടി ജാലത്തിൻ മകുടമായ്
ത്രിദിവേശ്വരൻ നിജരൂപത്തിൽ മനുജനെ
ധരണിക്കധി ഭർത്തൃസ്ഥാന നിർവഹണാർത്ഥം
ധരണീതലേ നിർമ്മിക്കുവാനാരംഭിച്ചു. (1:173-76)

അന്തിമദിനസൃഷ്ടി കഴിഞ്ഞശേഷം ദേവൻ
തന്തിരു മനോരഥ പ്രേരണക്കനുസാരം

മണ്ണിന്റെ പൊടി കൊണ്ടു മർത്യനെ വിരചിച്ചു
തിണ്ണമായ് അവൻ മൂക്കിലൂതിനാൻ ജീവശ്വാസം.
ആയതിൻ ഫലമായിജീവനുള്ളൊരു ദേഹി—

യ്യായവൻ തീർന്നു കർമസ്വാതന്ത്ര്യ
ബുദ്ധിയോടും. (1:177-82)

തനിയേയിരിക്കുമീ യാദമിന്നൊരുതക്ക
തുണവേണ്ടീട്ടുദൈവം ഗാഢമാംസുഷുപ്തിയിൽ

Thereafter Elohim commenced the deed
Of creation's crowning with submission owed,
His own Image bearing, all earth to rule
With husbanding hands that heavens enable.

Creatures all in paired kinds homed
In their happy habitat. Astir still, Wisdom formed

From elemental dust, the sinless Adamus,
The Ruah's breath streaming, God's very opus.
More than flesh-man was Adamus, a thinking soul,

Free of will, and in reason's motions, none afoul.

Lone lived Adam in his mind and mould,
A soul mate wanting in so large a world.

അവനെനെയാക്കീട്ടവൻ പാർശ്വത്തിൽ നിന്നൊരസ്ഥി	A sleep that made all surroundings obscure
ഭവനാശകനെടുത്തായതുകൊണ്ടുതന്നെ	Yahweh brought on Adam to secure
വിശ്വാദിഭർത്രീയായും വിശ്വമോഹിനിയായും	A side-rib of his: from it came the meetly shape,
വിശ്വയ്കമാതാവുമായുള്ളൊരു വനിതയെ	As World's Queen whom all graces did drape,
നിർമ്മിച്ചുപ്രഥമ മർത്യന്നുടെ മുൻഭാഗത്തു	And came to the First Man that made him erupt
നിർമ്മലാനന്ദം വരുമാറങ്ങു നിർത്തീടിനാൻ. (1:183–90)	In ecstasy, over love incorrupt.

Adam Discovers His Soulmate

ഉറക്കമുണർന്നവൻ കണ്ണുകൾമന്ദംമന്ദം	In softly blinks his leaden eyes from repose freed
തുറക്കുന്ന നേരമൊരു ദിവ്യയാം നാരീരത്നം	When an angel-form before him stood; his senses seized,
തനിക്കുമുന്നിലായ് നില്ക്കുണു വിഭാതത്തിൽ	Like the dawning sun seemed she, on a clear morn,
കനല്ക്കുനേരായ് കിഴക്കുദിച്ചഭാനു പോലെ. (191–94)	In glory's glow, as fresh in the orient it shone.
എന്തു ഞാൻ കാണുന്നതീ ചന്തമേറിയ കാഴ്ച്ച!	Ravishing sight! this comely form!
ഹന്ത! മിന്നലീ ഭൂവിൽ പിണ്ഡിതാകൃതിയായോ?	What? Is lightning bodied for an earthen home?
ചന്ദ്രനെ വെടിഞ്ഞിങ്ങു ചന്ദ്രിക വരാവതോ?	Or, from the moon its goodly glow, now sever'd flow?
സാന്ദ്രസൗഭാഗ്യ മൂർത്തി യെന്തൊരു നവസൃഷ്ടി? (197–200)	Or, Delight dense, imaged as new creation show!
എന്നു മാത്രവുമല്ല മാമക ഹൃദയത്തെ	Furthermore, no celestial has heretofore entranced
മുന്നമീവിധം കവർന്നില്ലൊരു വാനവനും	My heart this way. The cascading tresses tumbled
കേശഭംഗിയും ദേഹകാന്തിയും മുഖാബ്ജത്തി—	Over her flawless body, caressed by the breeze;
ലാശുകൻപോലെ കളിയാടുന്ന പ്രസാദവും	The unfading smile of restraint that would mesmerize
പുഞ്ചിരി കൊണ്ടു തിര്യഗ് ജാതിയും വശപ്പെടു—	All the world; the teeth, like pearls in row;
മഞ്ചിതമായ ദന്തമുകുള പ്രഭയതും	The lotus hue and charm of her face's glow;
പാടലാധരം, മനോമോഹനം നാസികയും	Lips crimson; the nose of shapely nobility;
പേടമാനടിവണങ്ങിടുന്ന മിഴികളും. (1:203–10)	And the doe-eyes of innocence otherworldly.
ഉല്ലസൽകല്ലോലം പോലിളകുംചില്ലീയുഗം	Like the glimmer in the rippling waves, her eyebrows,
നല്ലൊരു ദാഡിമത്തെ വെല്ലുന്ന ഗണ്ഡങ്ങളും	And the pomegranate look of the cheeks, in each
ആകവേ ചിന്തിക്കുകിലത്ഭുതപരവശ—	Perfection exudes; even the gods at a sight such
രാകാതിരിക്കുകില്ല മൃതാശികൾപോലും. (1:211–14)	Would by envy be struck and blown away with awe.

കിടപ്പാനെനിക്കൊട്ടും കഴിവില്ലെഴുന്നേറ്റു	Hold still in gaze? No, how must I? Rather, dash
പൊടുക്കെന്നവളുടെ യടുക്കലോടിച്ചെന്നു	Would I, o'er to her celestial self, and have awash
തുടുത്ത കാന്തിചിന്നുമവൾ തന്നുടലിന്മേൽ	Her exuding loveliness in affection's showers
വെടുപ്പായ് പ്രേമമാല ചാർത്തണമാശ്ലേഷത്താൽ. (1:219–22)	And embraces like garbs of unearthly flowers.

ഇങ്ങനെ പറഞ്ഞവനംഗനാമണി നിൽക്കും	Musing thus he flew with restraint none
പിങ്ഗള കാന്തി പൂരം തിങ്ങിന ദിക്കിലെത്തി.	To the peerless form of the beauteous one
മംഗളകമലിന്യാം സംഗമ സുഖം തേടി-	Unveiled over the virgin lush. Unknown desire
ത്തുംഗമോദേന പായും ഭൃംഗമെന്നതു പോലെ	For her rose ablaze in him with a tyrant fire;
ഭംഗിയിലവളുടെ യംഗവല്ലരി സമാ-	As the bee and the blossom would mutually find
ലിംഗ്യ നിർവൃതനായാൻ ഭംഗമൽപവുമെന്യേ (1:223–28)	Did Adam and Eve in weaving love-wraps bind.

The Serpent Meets with Eve

ദേവനാം യഹോവയിൻ സൃഷ്ടികളെല്ലാറ്റിലും	Of all creatures of Jehovah's world,
കേവലം സരീസൃപം ഖലനായി തീർന്നു കഷ്ടം	The subtle Serpent was in Satan's wield.
ദാനവനായകന്റെ കൗശലച്ചുഴിയതിൽ	Suited in charms, the slithering beast
താണ സൽകോമരമായ് തീർന്നൊന്നരിയുരഗേന്ദ്രൻ	With deployed courtesies began a chat,
സ്ത്രീയുടെയടുത്തെത്തി ട്ടായവളോടുനിജ	A crafty converse of infernal spell:
മായികവിദ്യയെടുത്തീവിധം ചോദ്യം ചെയ്തു: (3:1–6)	

രമണീയക മന്യാദൃശ്യമാം വിവേകമെ—	Image of beauty and wisdom unequaled!
ന്നീവകഗുണങ്ങൾക്കു ധാമമേ! തോട്ടത്തിലെ	Could thou be under such restraint harsh
വൃക്ഷസഞ്ചയ ഫലമൊന്നുമേ ഭക്ഷിക്കായ്‌വാൻ	To taste not of the fruit so copious, so lush,
രൂക്ഷ്മമാമാജ്ഞ നിങ്ങൾക്കീശ്വരൻ നൽകീട്ടുണ്ടോ? (3:7–10)	Of the virgin groves that have thy grounds so filled?

നാരി ചൊന്നിതിനേവ: ഉദ്യാനദ്രുമങ്ങളിൽ	Said the woman in terms plain: of the garden's trees
ചാരുവാം ഫലം ഞങ്ങൾക്കശിക്കാമെന്നാകിലോ	All fruit may we pluck as might us serve or please,
ആരാമമദ്ധ്യ സ്ഥിതമായുള്ള ഗുണദോഷ	Though, situate in the midst is one that bears knowledge
ഭൂരുഹ ഫലം ഭക്ഷിക്കാവതല്ലൊരിക്കലും;	Of good and evil, to us barred; its taste, even the touch,
സ്പർശിക്ക പോലുമാകാ; ലംഘിക്കിൽ മൃതിയുണ്ടാം;	Imports instant death: so has the Lord as caution spoken.
കർശനമായിട്ടീശനിങ്ങനെയുദ്ഘോഷിച്ചാൻ. (3:11–16)	

സർപ്പമുത്തരമോതി: മറ്റുള്ള മരങ്ങളി	Said then the Serpent: the fruit of all other trees,
ലുത്ഭവിച്ചിടും ഫലമൊക്കെയുമശ്യമെങ്കിൽ	If edible and harms not, the greater yield
നൽപ്പെഴുമിതിലുള്ള കായ്കളുമശിക്കുകിൽ	Of this supreme tree should cause regret none
ഉൾപരിതാപം വരില്ലായിരും നഷ്ടപ്പെടാ. (3:17–20)	Nor shall it imperil life.
ഹൗവ്വാ ചൊന്നതിനേവ: മീഫലമശ്യമെങ്കിൽ	Howwah [Eve] then answered thus: so goodly
സർവപാലകനതു തടയാനിടയില്ല.	If this fruit be, the Great Ruler's ban of it is unlikely.
ക്ഷുദ്ര ജീവിയിൽ പോലും കൃപയുള്ളവൻ തന്റെ	Would He that in mercy pities the meanest pest
പുത്രരാം ഞങ്ങൾക്കിതു നൽകാതെയിരിക്കുമോ? (3:21–24)	Withhold for His children His garden's best?
ഓതിനാൻ വ്യാളം: നിങ്ങളെന്തെറിയുന്നു? ജഗ—	The Serpent said: What dost thou of motives know?
ന്നാഥനു തത്താദൃക്കെന്നുള്ള പേരുറപ്പാകാൻ	"Himself His own equal," the Lord did self-bestow
നന്മയുമുൽക്കർഷവുമന്യനുണ്ടാകും വഴി	The styling title. Strength and honor coming others' way,
കല്ലുവച്ചടച്ചുപോം; സ്വാർത്ഥമേ പുരുഷാർത്ഥം. (3:25–28)	Like selfish mortals, block with boulders, He may.
എന്തൊരു കുറവുണ്ടാമിപ്പലം ത്യജിച്ചെന്നാ-	"What can be lost leaving it as told
ലെന്തൊരു ഗുണമുണ്ടാമിതിനെയശിച്ചെന്നാൽ?	And what gain, eating it in folly bold?"
ഏവമത്തന്വീമണി ചോദിച്ച നിമിഷത്തി-	The Queen of Eden demanded quick,
ലാവിലേശയപാശ നുരച്ചാനശങ്കിതം: (3:29–32)	And the ropey rogue gave this answer slick:
നിങ്ങൾക്കു സത്യജ്ഞാനമരുളും നേത്രമയ്യോ	The eyes that grant you knowledge of truth, alas,
മങ്ങലാർന്നടങ്ങുപോയി, ക്കാഠിനാജ്ഞ മൂലം.	Are bedimmed by commands of severity;
നന്മയെന്നതു പോലെ തിന്മയുമറിയേണ്ട	As is virtue known, so should the mystery
മർമ്മമാണതുമൂലം ജ്ഞാനാഭിവൃദ്ധിയുണ്ടാം. (3:33–36)	Of evil be weighed, in knowledge ripening.
ജ്ഞാനത്തെ കവിഞ്ഞു നാം കാമിപ്പനെന്തൊന്നുള്ളൂ	What more to aspire than power in knowledge,
ജ്ഞാനിയായ് തീരുമ്പൊഴു തീശ്വരനായീ, ഭദ്രേ!	Which raises us as equals with God in peerage!
നിഷ്പ്രയാസേന ദൈവ നിലയിലെത്താമെന്നു-	One easy leap to God's very state! The Great Mother
ള്ളത്ഭുതവാർത്ത കാതിൽ തട്ടവേ ജഗന്മാതാ	Of all Earth took the bait, rising in rapture
സ്വർഗ്ഗത്തിൻവാതിൽ കണ്ട മട്ടിലങ്ങാനന്ദിച്ചാൾ. (3:37–40)	To the gates of heaven, in joy beyond measure.
ഭർഗനാം സർപ്പത്തിന്നു സ്വാഗതം ചൊല്ലീടിനാൾ	The deceiver received his designed welcome
തർക്കമൊന്നുണ്ടതിനും പ്രത്യുക്തി ലഭിക്കുകിൽ.	Though not without unease in Eve, some.

തർക്കം വേണ്ടിതു നല്ല മാർഗമെന്നുറച്ചവൾ	The queries go well, she thought, and answers convince;
ചോദിച്ചു: സഖേ! ഭവദ്ഗീരു പോൽ പ്രവർത്തിച്ചാൽ	She then asked: "Friend, were I to do as thou biddest,
ഭൂതവുമുദർക്കവു മില്ലെന്നായ് വന്നേക്കുമോ? (3:42–46)	Will I lose the good I own and future's promises withal?"
വാഗ്മിയാം ഭുജംഗേന്ദ്രൻ ചൊന്നു: ഞാനൊരു സർപ്പം	The fawning Bhujanga [serpent king] continued: A mute
വാഗ്മിതയെന്നല്ലറിയാട്ടവും ഞങ്ങൾക്കില്ല.	Reptile merely am I, of no gift of sound or speech.
എന്നുടെ സംഭാഷണശക്തിക്കു നിദാനമീ	The voice you hear of me is solely by the fruit
സുന്ദരദ്യമഹഫലഭോജനമൊന്നു മാത്രം. (3:47–50)	Of power thou fear, even at such touching reach.
തുര്യകാം എനിക്കിത്ര വൈശിഷ്ട്യം വരുത്തിയ	To me, a lowly crawler, has this celestial fruit
വീര്യവൽഫലം വ്യർത്ഥമാവില്ല നിങ്ങൾക്കൊട്ടും	Such excellence lent. Have no cause to dispute,
അതിനാൽ ഭയപ്പെടാതെടുത്തു ഭക്ഷിക്കുവിൻ	And therewith to ponder. Take the welcome relish;
മൃതിയുണ്ടാകയില്ലീ സൽഫല സമാസ്വാദാൽ. (3:51–54)	In no wise shall one by such great gifts perish.
ദൈവതുല്യരായി നിങ്ങൾ തീർന്നീടുമെന്നൊരീർഷ്യ	That you will turn godlike, and equals in divinity—
ദൈവചിത്തത്തിലുള്ള കാരണമാണിപ്ഫലം.	A discomfort in God's mind, is the sole cause
ഭക്ഷിച്ചു കൂടെന്നൊരു കല്പന നിഷ്കാരുണ്യം	Of this harsh command, void of lenity,
സൃഷ്ടിച്ചതെന്നറിഞ്ഞു ബുദ്ധിയായ് പ്രവർത്തിപ്പിൻ. (3:55–58)	Set in place. Discern this, and act in prudence.
സുരവിദ്വേഷിയുടെ വാഹനമാകും സർപ്പം	The sinister speech of heaven's foe,
പെരുതാം പ്രൗഢിയോടു ചൊന്നോരീഗിരം കേട്ടു	Fell on the ears of Eve in corrupt echo:
ശരിയാണവനുടെ വാണിയെന്നവൾക്കുള്ളിൽ	His tidings to her rang like settled law,
സ്ഥിരമാംബോധമുണ്ടായ് വളർന്നുനിർഭാഗ്യത്താൽ (3:59–62)	For contest any room she saw.
ഉടനെ മനസാക്ഷി തടയാനാരംഭിച്ചു	Anon conscience put up resistance
പിടിയായ് സർപ്പത്തിന്റെ വാണിയുമതും തമ്മിൽ	To the serpent's words of assurance
ചക്രി ചൊന്നുള്ള ഭാവി നന്മയുമതിലുള്ള	Concerning her possible future estate
കർക്കശ വിശ്വാസവും യോജിച്ചു വിപ്രകണ്ഡം	And the belief therein for none debate:
ഞെരിക്കും രണ്ടു ഘോര ചണ്ഡാളരെന്നപോലെ	Like two wild wrestlers in muscle lock,
ഞെരിച്ചു മനസാക്ഷി ഗ്രീവയെ ശകത്തി പൂർവ്വം. (3:63–68)	The Lie and Conscience vying, heels in chok.
തൽഫലമായി തളർന്നടിയിൽ വീണുപോയി	By and by fell Conscience, the sacred chest,
ചിദ്ധ്വനി കളിക്കുന്ന ശുദ്ധമാം മനോബോധം	That carrier of divine wisdom within;
ദേവോക്ത വികണനയാകിയ ധത്തൂരവും	Signs foreboding of God's spirit parting

Eve Reaches for the Fruit

ഭാവിനിയായ നാശാവസ്ഥ തൻ പിശുനമായ്
ഹാവ തന്നകക്കാമ്പാം പാഴ് പറമ്പിന്റെ മധ്യ—
ത്താവിനാഴിക മുളച്ചുയർന്നു പുഷ്ടിയോടും
ഇരുമ്പുചങ്ങലയ്ക്കും ബന്ധിപ്പാൻ വയ്യാ മട്ടിൽ. (3:69-75)

And doom looming, Havva ventured,
Impelled, with such driven strength
That no chains of iron could help restrain.

വരമ്പുകടന്നവളാശയാൽ പ്രേരിതയായ്
രോധത്തെ പുറംകാലാൽ തട്ടിയങ്ങെറിഞ്ഞിട്ടു
വ്യാധന്റെ വലയിലേക്കോടുന്ന മൃഗം പോലെ
പാഞ്ഞിതു വൃക്ഷത്തിന്റെ യരികിൽ നിസ്സന്ദേഹ-
മാഞ്ഞു തൻ കൈകളതിൽ കനിക്കായ് നീട്ടിടുമ്പോൾ
ദൃഷ്ടിരമ്യവും ഭക്ഷണാർഹവുമതുപോലെ
ബുദ്ധിനൽകുവാൻ ശക്തിയുള്ളതു മെന്നുകണ്ടു
നിഷിദ്ധ വൃക്ഷത്തി ന്റെ വിഷോത്പാദക ഫലം
മുഴുത്ത മോഹം മൂലം പറിച്ചു തിന്നീടിനാൾ. (3:76-84)

All caution thrown to the wind
Mere passion in control of the mind
Forward she sped, like the bounding beast
That blindly heads into the deadly net.
Her mind solely set on the prize plum,
The eye, palate and intellect said,
"Welcome, heaven's most Powering gift!"
Its lusted taste now served in haste,
Forbidden or no, she took its cursed bite.

സേറ്റനാം വഞ്ചകന്റെ വലയിൽപെട്ടി ഫല
മുറ്റ കൗതുകത്തോടു ഭുക്തി ചെയ്തപ്പോഴേതോ
വൈദ്യുതമായ ശക്തിയാപാദശിഖം വ്യാപി-
ച്ചുദ്ദാമഭയം ഭ്രമംവേദനയാദിയായ
ഭവിഷ്യൽഫലങ്ങളെ യുദ്ദീപിപ്പിച്ചപോലെ
യവൾക്കുതോന്നീ, മാറ്റമുണ്ടായി പ്രകൃതിക്കും. (3:85-90)

When by Satan the Deceiver's ploy,
Eve's wont manner of natural joy,
A tremor seized, and smarting pains
From head to foot were her immediate gains,
All Nature in alarm spinning rattled.

Eve Brings the Fruit to Adam

Words and Thoughts of Alarm

പെട്ടെന്നുവിരക്തിയുമുണ്ടായ് വന്നെങ്കിലും ത-
ന്നിഷ്ടനാം പ്രിയതമന്നാപ്പഴം കൊടുക്കുവാൻ

മുതിർന്നു കയ്യിലേതാനെടുത്തു കൊണ്ടുചെന്നു
പതുക്കെ പതിയുടെസമീപത്തിങ്കലപ്പോൾ

ആദമായതു കണ്ടുചോദിച്ചു: പ്രിയേ! നിന്റെ
ഭാസുര കരങ്ങളിൽ കാണുന്നതെന്താണാവോ?
നിരുദ്ധകവൃക്ഷത്തി ന്റെ ഫലങ്ങളല്ലേയതിൽ
വിരക്തിതോന്നാതവ പറിച്ചതെന്താണുന്നീ? (3:91-98)

Deathly regret gripped the woman. Filled with fright,
In unsteady steps she bore her pluck's share to her mate.

His anxious eyes sensed some great wrong done.
"Sweetheart!" he asked, "What do thy fair hands bear?"

Did we depart, without restraint or fear
From the command to touch not the forbidden fruit?

സർവേശ്വരാജ്ഞയെ നാം നിസ്സാരീകരിക്കുകിൽ	Were we to neglect the Sovereign's dictate,
ദുർവഹമായ ദുഃഖം വരുമെന്നറിവില്ലേ?	Ensue not sorrows, none to help abate?
ആജ്ഞാലംഘനമാകും തീവ്രപാപത്താലത്രേ	Wasn't it by sin of self will that angels of light
പ്രജ്ഞാവത്തുക്കളായ ദൂതന്മാർ ദ്യോവിൽനിന്നു	From the heavens to the Hades have been hurled?
വീണതിഭയാനകമായുള്ള നരകത്തിൽ	
താണിന്നു കിടപ്പതെന്നോർത്തുകൊള്ളേണ്ടൂ നമ്മൾ. (3:99–104)	
മത്തമാം ഗജത്തിനോടെതിർപ്പാൻ പിപീലിക	Would the miniscule ant fight the rutting elephant?
ശക്തമാകുമോ? തൃണം തരുവിന്നെതിരാമോ?	Or the grass shoot threaten the grand trunk tree?
പ്രചണ്ഡ വാതത്തോടു ഗുസ്തി വയ്ക്കുമോ തൂലം	Or can a cotton boll a hurricane stall?
രചിപ്പാൻ നമുക്കൊല്ല ദൈവവിദ്വേഷദുർഗ്ഗം. (3:105–08)	Note this: beyond our esteem rests the divine call.
അതിനാൽ ദർശനീയമെങ്കിലുമിപ്പഴത്തെ	Therefore, though worthy of sight this matchless fruit is,
കളക; ശോഭകണ്ടു തിന്നുമോ തീക്കട്ടയെ?	Cast it away; the live coal, though glows, could the lips kiss?
ഇത്തരമാദി മർത്യസത്ത മനുരചെയ്തോ-	At this word from the First Man by failure yet untouched,
രത്തവ്വിലമിതദുഃഖത്തോടോതിനാൾ ഹവ്വ: (3:109–12)	His sad half in much anguish said to her husband:
പ്രാണനായകാ! ഭവാനോതിന മൊഴിയെന്റെ	My Soul's Lord! What thou biddest me do
മാനസം ഭയശോക വിഹ്വലമാക്കിടുന്നു	Shakes up my inward with dismay and rue.
മോഷ്ടാവുപോയിപ്പട്ടി കുരച്ചാലെന്തു ഫലം?	What good is watchdog's bark when the thief has fled?
നഷ്ടമായ് ജലം പിന്നീടെന്തിനു സേതുബന്ധം? (3:113–16)	Or the levee when the river becomes a dry sandbed?
കല്പനാ വ്യതിക്രമ പ്രഹരിയിൽ ചാടിയിവൾ	A crashing fall this was from my steps errant
സർപ്പത്തിൻ ചതിവാക്കാം ബാഹുവിൻ തള്ളലിനാൽ	By the Deceiver led with my full assent,
വീഴ്ചയാൽ സുകൃതമാം ശിരസ്സു തകർന്നുപോയ്	All innocent thinking thrown in disarray
താഴ്ചയുമായി സർവ സൗഭാഗ്യ സൗഖ്യങ്ങൾക്കും. (3:117–20)	And the abundant well being gone awry.

Fear of Death, a New Horror

മരണഭീതിയെന്നെ പണ്ടില്ലാവിധമിപ്പോൾ	Fear of death, never felt before, no fancy or sport
ഭരണം ചെയ്തിടുന്നു, സന്ധികൾ തകരുന്നു.	Now seizes me, which the trembling joints report;
പശ്ചാത്താപ ജന്യമാം മൂർച്ചയാലെന്നാത്മാവു	Scourging remorse smarts my soul;
നിശ്ചയമഗാധമാമിരുളിൽ താഴുന്നു ഹാ! (3:121–24)	I stand on the mantle of the infernal sinkhole!

എന്നെന്നേക്കുമായിട്ടു വസിപ്പാൻ നമ്മൾ തമ്മിൽ	To live as one flesh in eternal vow
മുന്നമോതിയ കരാറെൻമൂലം ഭഗ്നമായി	Made we our bond, by me now undone,
ദുരിതപാത്രമാകുമീഞാനും സുകൃതിനാം	How might I, the birther of misery, and thou,
വര! നാമിരുവരു മെവ്വിധം ചേർന്നുവാഴും? (3:125-28)	Virtue's paragon! Continue in union?
ഇരുളും വെളിച്ചവുമൊരുമിച്ചിരിക്കുമോ?	Shall light and darkness share the same space?
കനലും ജലവുമായ് യോജിപ്പു സാധിക്കുമോ?	Or live coal in water remain unquenched?
ദൈവാജ്ഞ ലംഘിച്ചോരു പാപിനിയാകുമെന്നെ	God will remove thee, O Pure Self, from me,
പാവന! നിന്നിൽ നിന്നു വേർപിരിച്ചീടുമീശൻ. (3:129-32)	A sinner, and a first at that, the breaker of His command.
വയ്യൊട്ടും സഹിക്കുവാനക്കഥയോർത്തിടുമ്പോ—	Not a tale that I should live on to tell:
ഉയ്യയ്യോ കഷ്ടം! കഷ്ടം! ഞാനിതാഹതയായി!	Woe is me, I am of death smitten, of counsel fell,
എന്നുരച്ചവൾ നിജ ഭർത്തൃ മാനസത്തിന്റെ	Said she in rising lament, and crashed to the ground.
നിർണ്ണയഭിത്തിയോടു കൂടവേ താഴെവീണു. (3:133-36)	Her husband's wall of courage was imploded found.
നയാഗ്രാ നിർദ്ധരം പോൽ കണ്ണുനീർ വാർത്തു മുമ്പിൽ	Like the falls of Niagara had her tears been gushing,
മയങ്ങി വീണുള്ളൊാരീ വാത്സല്യഭാജനത്തെ	As she fell at his feet, the vessel of his love, brimming;
ഇയത്തിലില്ലാതുള്ള ദുഃഖത്താൽ വിയർത്തുതൻ	A grief not of this world, and so of power beyond this world,
മിനുത്ത കൈകൾ കൊണ്ടു താങ്ങിയോതിനാനാദം: (3:137-40)	Invaded Adam, who in beading sweat, said to her in arm's fold:.

Adam's Resolve to Stand with Eve

എന്താണെൻ പ്രിയേ! നീ താൻ ചൊൽവതു ചെവികളി-	Why do, my beloved, thy stated words strike
ലന്തരാ ലോഹമായനാരാചം തറയ്ക്കുന്നോ	Mine ears with ruinous dread of an iron spike?
ദൈവശാസന നിഷ്ഠനായിട്ടുമെന്നിൽനിന്നു	Wilt thou remove thyself from me to self-destruct
പാപത്താലകന്നുനീ നശിപ്പാനൊരുങ്ങുന്നോ? (3:141-44)	From me who moves solely under the Law of God?
കാമിനീമണേ! മമ മാനസഭൂവിൽ തഴ—	The Light of my life! the prime bloom
ച്ചായമെന്യേ പൂത്ത പ്രേമവല്ലരിയുടെ	Of my heart's arbor, no matter how great thy fall,
കോമളപ്രസൂനമേ! നിന്നുടെ വീഴ്ചയെത്ര	Parting from thee is far too grievous to me.
ഭീമമെന്നിരിക്കിലും നിന്നോടു വേറായ്നില്പാൻ	In pleasure or pain, want or plenty,
എനിക്കു കഴിവില്ല; സുഖദുഃഖങ്ങളിലും	Why, even through death, our lots run as one.

കനത്ത മൃതിയിലും നിന്നോടുകൂടിത്തന്നെ	Even death lacks the power
മമ ജീവിതം പോകുന്നുണ്ടുങ്ങാൻ; സ്നേഹചിത്രം	To undo love or its image to erase.
മരണത്തിനുകൂടി മായിപ്പാൻ കഴിവില്ല. (3:146–52)	
ഈദൃശമുരചെയ്തു ജായാസ്നേഹത്താൽ പരി	In forlorn oneness and compassion-impelled
ഭൂതചിത്തനായ്നാരീ ഹസ്തസംസ്ഥിതംഫലം	Adam took the remnant meal she held
പെട്ടെന്നുവാങ്ങിതിന്നു കട്ടത്തീനരകത്തിൻ	And made of it an instant eat, the formal seal
മട്ടലും താഴ്ചാരവും മക്കൾക്കു സമ്പാദിച്ചു. (3:153–56)	Of the estate infernal for his progeny's weal.
അത്ഭുതമല്ലീ പ്രേമമാർക്കുമുണ്ടാകാം നിത്യ-	Love works alike in all human race;
മിമ്പ്ഭുവനത്തിലേവമല്ലയോ കാണുന്നുനാം	This active world is its staging space;
ജഡസംബന്ധമായ ഹാർദ്ദത്തെപ്രമാണിച്ചു	In the stormy seizings of sensory bondings,
സ്പുടമായ്മറക്കുന്നു ദൈവശാസനം മർത്യർ. (3:157–60)	Roundly let go we of divine biddings.
ആദമൻ തന്റെ പത്നിയാകിയ ഹവ്വയെപ്പോ-	Adam too, like Eve his ensnared helpmate,
ലാദിദേവന്റെ ശിഷ്ടി ലംഘിച്ചോരാനന്തരം	By his breach of the Ancient of Days' plain command
പൂർവദേവരാം സേറ്റൻ താനും തൻ ഗണങ്ങളും	Doubled the joy for the heaven's expelled hosts
സർവാസുരസ്ഥാനമാം പാൻഡെമോണിയത്തിങ്കൽ	Who held a high day in Pandemonium; raised toasts
ഒന്നിച്ചുകൂടി നിജ തന്ത്രസാഫല്യത്തിന്റെ	To their chief for his skilled fetch of death's touch
വെന്നിയെ സ്മരിപ്പിക്കും പരമോത്സവമൊന്നു	To the new species. The whole nether world
നടത്തി സന്തോഷിച്ചു പാതാളലോകമാകെ	"Raised hell" with the din and the dust cloud
പൊടിപാറിടും വണ്ണം വിജയഘോഷം ചെയ്തു. (3:161–68)	Of demonic delirium, exulting in
	The gains of pride with yet a fresh edge.

The Almighty Arrives in Paradise

പുത്രന്റെ ശരീര യാഗാർപ്പണംമൂലം നാശ-	For to undo world's doom by His Son's sacrifice
പാത്രമാമിലോകത്തെ രക്ഷ ചെയ്‌വാനും തന്റെ	In atoning equity that heaven justifies
നീതിക്കു തൃപ്തി വരുത്തിടുവാനായും പരി-	The Great God saw fit to move the darling humans
ത്രാതാവു നിശ്ചയം ചെയ്തിട്ടു തൽക്കാലത്തേക്കു	For a time from Paradise as well to sentence
പരമാരാമമാകും പരദീസയിൽ നിന്നു	The disguised reptile, the foe of the high place;
നരരെ ബഹിഷ്‌ക്കരിച്ചിട്ടു ദേവാരിയാകും	Thus resolved, proceeded the Most High
ഉരഗപ്രവീരനെത്തരസാ ശിക്ഷിക്കുവാൻ	To His judgment's site.
കരുതിബ് ഭൂതലത്തേ ക്കെഴുന്നെള്ളിനാൻ ദേവൻ. (3:177–84)	

ഖെരൂബാഖ്യങ്ങളാകും ദിവ്യജീവികളുടെ	The wings of cherubs, those beings on holy watch
മരുത്തിന്നൊത്ത വേഗമുള്ള പക്ഷങ്ങളിന്മേൽ	Whose strength and speed serve in mutual match
വാഹനമേറുന്നൊരു സ്വർഗീയ രാജാവുതൻ	What heaven's King bids: Now to Paradise they sped;
മാഹാത്മ്യമമ്പും പാദപല്ലവം പറുദീസിൽ	His glowing feet touched Eden's luscious spread,
പതിച്ചപ്പോൾ പരമാത്മാനന്ദഭരിതമായ്	To the unstained joy of creatures great and small.
ഭവിച്ചുചരാചര ജീവികളശേഷവും. (3:185–90)	
വൃക്ഷങ്ങൾ പവനനാൽ കമ്പിതശാഖങ്ങളാ-	Waving winds danced in the fanning boughs
യക്ഷീണാദരം തല കുനിച്ചു വണങ്ങിതു.	Of trees untiring, their heads to the Lord in vernal bows.
പക്ഷികൾ കള കള നിസ്വന വ്യാജേനസ	Birds, of colorful flocks, for their part, in clucks and whistles
ദീക്ഷ്യനാ മീശന്നു നൽസ്വാഗതഗാനം പാടി. (3:191–94)	Sang notes of welcome to the Most High in his land of idylls.
മേഘത്തിൽ നിന്നു വർഷമുതിരുംപോലെപുഷ്പ	As do the clouds send their refreshing showers,
ശാഖികൾ സുമങ്ങളെ ച്ചൊരിഞ്ഞു ധാരാളമായ്	So strewed the groves their grounds in layering flowers.
ആറുകൾ തരംഗമാം കരങ്ങൾ കെട്ടിക്കൊണ്ടു	Rivers, festive, clapped their crystal hands
പാറയാം ബാറിൽകേറി മറിഞ്ഞു ചാടിപ്പാഞ്ഞു.	Over the impelling rapids with kindred bands,
നവപല്ലവങ്ങളാം ചെങ്കൊടിശാഖാഗ്രത്തി-	Merry at constant crashings on ravishing rocks.
ലവബന്ധനം ചെയ്തു, ശോഭിച്ചു തേന്മാവുകൾ. (3:195–200)	Filled with thickly, budding shoots of rich reddish hue
	Trees of honeying yield met their duty due.
പത്മരാഗത്തിനൊത്തോ രശോകപുഷ്പം, സ്വർണ	The sapphire shades of *ashoka*,[12] the firelit gold
വിദ്യുതി കലർന്നുള്ള കർണികാരകസൂനം	Of the *carnikar*, and the vying power in the *nochi*'s hold
മുത്തിന്നു നേരാം നൊച്ചിപ്പൂ വിവനിരന്നീടും	As purest peer to pearl: these in liquid blends imbue
വിസ്തൃത ശിലകളിൻ സുവ്യക്ത പൃഷ്ഠഭാഗം	The ranging lay of rocks of resplendent view:
ഇന്ദ്രനീലാശ് മദ്യുതി വഹിച്ചു വിക്രേയമാം	Facets of fresh gleam and glitter, like the lapidary
സാന്ദ്ര രത്നോച്ചയത്തിൽ സാമ്പിൾ പോലതു മിന്നി.	Work of *Indraneela* samples on display;
സ്ഥാവരജംഗമങ്ങളാകിയ സമസ്തവു-	Eden's glories, like adoring subjects drawn to hail

[12] *Asoka, carnikar, nochi, indraneela* are native flowers of Simon's world; by listing them among others that fill Eden's grounds Simon symbolically hints of the unity in creation.

മീവിധം നിർവ്യാളിക വിനയാദരപൂർവം	Their revered king on his triumph's trail
ഭംഗിയിൽ തയാറായി നിന്നിതു രാജാഗമം	Their wealth and stock for his pleasure set,
തുംഗമോദേന കാത്തു പൗരന്മാർ നിൽക്കും പോലെ. (3:201–10)	Arrayed stood in their civic best, for the crowning meet.
തദ്ദിനം വെയിലാറി ശീതമാരുത പോത-	That day in the cool breeze of the twilight hour,
മുദ്യാനമെങ്ങും പരി ക്രമണം ചെയ്യും വിധൗ	All garden pervading went forth the tremor
തോട്ടത്തിൽ സഞ്ചാരിക്കുംയാഹ്‌വെയിൻ സ്വരം കേട്ടു	Of Yahweh's movements and of his voice,
വാട്ടമോടൊളിച്ചാദ്യർ വൃക്ഷസഞ്ചയമധ്യേ. (3:211–14)	As the pair took the woodsy cover from omniscience.
പാപം ചെയ്തീശ്വരന്റെ വിദ്വേഷം സമ്പാദിച്ച	Sinners, those willful earners of the wrath of God,
പാപികൾ തിരുമുമ്പിൽ നിൽക്കാഞ്ഞതത്ഭുതമോ?	Should his presence flee, could that at all be odd?
മോഷണക്കാരൻ തൊണ്ടി സഹിതം പോലീസിന്റെ	A man caught in thieving act, and proof in hand, would he
ഭീഷണമായൊരശ്രേ നിൽക്കുമോ? ദ്രവിക്കില്ലേ? (3:215–18)	Meet the lawman readily? Wouldn't he his own peril see?

God Calls Adam

"ആദമേയെവിടെ നീ?" യെന്നു പൃശ്ചിച്ചുദൈവ	"Where art thou, Adam?," called out God,
മായതിനാദമാഖ്യൻ കൊടുത്തീ മറുപടി:	And the stripped prince this answer did accord:
നഗ്നനാകയാലഹം താവക ശബ്ദം കേട്ടു	"Naked was I, but at the sound of thy calling
വിഗ്നചിത്തനായ് ദ്രുമമധ്യത്തിലൊളിച്ചുപോയ്. (3:219–22)	Stricken in fear, I took to the woods in hiding."
ഭയത്താൽ മുഴുവനും പുറത്തുവരാതുള്ള	God's petrific voice had Adam churned,
രവത്തിലേവംചൊന്ന സമയംചോദിച്ചീശൻ	Required to tell how he naked had turned:
നഗ്നനെന്നാരുനിന്നോടുരച്ചു? വിരോധിച്ച	God asked: "Broke or burked thou my command that forbade,
വൃക്ഷത്തിൻകനി തിന്നുകല്പന മറുത്തുവോ? (3:223–26)	Tasting the fruit on which thine eyes were wrongly laid?"
ഉത്തരിച്ചുടനാദാം: എനിക്കുകൂട്ടായ് നിന്നാൽ	Said Adam, answering God: "the woman, that gift
ദത്തയായുള്ളനാരി തന്നുഞാൻ തിന്നക്കനി	Of thine as my mate, proffered it to me, and I ate."
പപ്രശ്ചമഹേശസ്താം "കിമിദം ത്വയാകാരി	The Lord to the woman: "And Why didst *thou* do this"?
സർപ്പത്തിൻചതിവാലെന്നവളും ചൊല്ലീടിനാൾ. (3:227–30)	"I fell for the tale that the serpent spun," was her response.

Curse of the Serpent

ഉദിച്ചകോപത്തോടു ദന്തശൂകത്തിൻ ശിക്ഷ	In blazing wrath the serpent's deserts just
വിധിച്ചു പരമേശൻ ഗദിച്ചാനുടനേവം. (3:231–32)	Pronounced the Almighty in that instant thus:
കർമ്മേദ മകരോ സ്ത്വം; തസ്മാദ് ഗാർഹികവന്യ—	This deed thou hast done; see thyself therefore found
പശൂനാം വൃന്ദാദ്ഭൃശം ശാപാഭി ഗ്രസ്തോ ഭൃത്വാ	Of creatures all, of the wild and the common ground
വക്ഷസാ ഗമിഷ്യസി; കിഞ്ച ത്വം യാവജ്ജീവം	Most curse-lain, on thy belly crawling,
ഭൂതലോ പരിസ്ഥിത ധൂളീ: സംഖാ ദിഷ്യസി	Eating the dust for thy meat, and groveling
യോഷിതസത് വാപി ച യുവയോർ വംശ്യാനാം ച	In disgrace. Between thine and the woman's progeny
വൈരിതാം പരസ്പരം ജനയിഷ്യാമി നൂനം.	Shalt exist, hear this, perpetual enmity;
ത്വ ഛരീര്ഷ്യം തസ്യാപത്യ മാഹനിഷ്യതി; തദ്വ-	From her seed thy kind shalt crush'd heads take
ദാഹ നിഷ്യസി തസ്യ പാദ ലേപി ത്വഞ്ച: (3:233–40)	Though on their heels thou might lesions make.

Curse of Eve

ചൊല്ലിനാൻ സ്ത്രീയോടീശൻ കള്ളനാമസുരന്റെ	Said God to the Woman in measure severe,
സൊള്ളിനു ചായ്ച്ച കർണ്ണം വിള്ളുമാറതേ ക്ഷണം	For she let the rogue spirit abuse her ear:
ത്വൽ സൂതി ദുഃഖമഹം വർദ്ധയിഷ്യാമി; തസ്മാത്	"Toward thy husband shall thy desire grow,
കഷ്ടതാ ബാഹുല്യേന സന്താനാൻ പ്രസോഷ്യസേ	To him shall thou defer and subservient go.
സ്വാമിനോ നിഘ്നീഭൂയഃ സ്ഥാസ്യസി; തവ ഭർത്താ	Thy motherhood shall much travail attend,
ശാസിഷ്യത്യനാരതം ത്വാമധീകാരമത്ത: (3:241–46)	Throes of pain shalt each birthing portend."

Curse of Adam

ഉച്ചമാം നിനാദത്തിലാദത്തോടുരച്ചീശൻ	God then spoke to Adam thus, lofty His voice:
യച്ച പാദപ ഫലം നൃഷേധ മാദൗ ഭോക്തും	"The tasting of this fruit was culpable and forbidden,
യോഷിത:കഥാം നിശമ്യമാ ഭുങ്കീഥാ: തൽഫലം ത്വം	Yet ye let prevail the scheme of the villain,
തേന ഹേതുനാ ഭൂമി രഭിശപ്താസ്തി മയാ. (3:247–50)	Casting thy native ground with curse by choice."
സംക്ലിശ്യ യാവജ്ജീവ മസ്യാ സ്ത്വം ഭക്ഷിഷ്യതേ.	"Much toil shall fill thy days in this soil
സംഭവിഷ്യന്തി തസ്യാം നാനാകണ്ടക ദ്രുമാഃ	Amidst plants of the field, where to foil
ക്ഷേത്രൗഷധീഭ്യസ്തവ ഭോജനം സംഗൃഹൃതാം	Thee shall grow thistles and thorns diverse
ഘർമ്മാക്ത മുഖതയാ ഭോക്ഷ്യസി ഭോജ്യവസ്തു	In manner. Labor's sweat shall drench thy face
മൃത്തികാഭവസിത്വം; മൃത്തികായാജായഥാ:	And beading brows show thy need for rest.

നിർല്ലീനോ ഭവിഷ്യസി മൃദി ത്വം പുനരപി. (3:251–56)

The bread of sorrows will for thee be broken,

For dust thou art, to it to be taken."

ഇത്തരം ഭീഷണത്തിലതി ഭീഷണമായ
കർതൃഭാഷണമാദംഹവ്വുമാർ കേട്ടനേരം
വിറച്ചുദാഹം കൈകാൽ തളർന്നു നേത്രദ്വയ-

മിരുണ്ടു മൂർഛിച്ചയ്യോ! തടിപോൽ താഴെ വീണു. (3:257–60)

God's words thundered in their ears,

Every pore spiked fresher fears;

Limbs flagging, their frames in dread tremor,

And dizzied blind, down they fell, void of vigor.

സഹിച്ചുകൂടാതുള്ള വേദന മൂലം വാവി-
ട്ടലച്ചു മുറവിളി ചൊഴുക്കി ബാഷ്പം പിന്നെ
ഉരുണ്ടും കൈകാലുകളടിച്ചും കുറ്റമോർത്തി-
ട്ടുരണ്ടും നെടുതായി വീർത്തുമത്യുഗ്രമാകും

In heart-rend cries of unearthly anguish,

Writhing and rolling their bodies they bash;

Flashes of loss feed their frenzied pangs

Like a demonic wrestle of strangling crushings.

നരകവേദനതന്നകാലാസ്വാദം പോലെ
ചെറിയ യാതനയിൽ വിരാമമന്യേയവർ
ഞെരിഞ്ഞുപുളയുന്ന കാഴ്ചകണ്ടപ്പോളീശ-

ന്നുരുകീ ഗരിഷ്ഠമാം ഹൃദയാം ദയാവേശാൽ. (3:261–68)

This seemed like a day to betimes taste

A trial run of hell, still of a lighter state,

Which beholding, God in mercy's motions moved.

ഉറച്ച തറയിൽ വീണുറക്കെ കരയുന്ന
വിറയ്ക്കും ശിശുവിനെ തെരിക്കെന്നെടുത്തുടൻ
കുറുക്കുപാലിനൊത്ത മിറുക്കുചൊല്ലിയതി-
ന്നുറക്കം വരുമാറു മുറയ്ക്കു തലോടിയും
പരുക്കു പലവുരു ശരിക്കു പരിശോധി-
ച്ചുരുസ്സിലെണ്ണ പൂശി ശിരസ്സിൽ മുകർന്നും ത-
ന്നുരുക്കു മനസ്സിനെ ചുരുക്കിപ്രദർശിപ്പി-
ച്ചിരിക്കും ജനനിയെജ്ജയിക്കും കരുണാബ്ദി: (3:269–76)

Consider a child that took the hard floor fall,

Whither flies the mother at the frantic call.

Scoops she the darling into her rescuing arms

With soothing vocables for easing balms,

And caresses her pearl to restful degrees,

Dabbing the salve at the spots of pain

And kissing the silken crown over and over,

Easing the sobs into signs serene, all by instincts

Of effectual speed. Angelic is this mother,

Yet the Lord, much more, like none other—

The Father of mercies in His ways usward.

Great Peril Met by Great Mercy

നിലത്തു നിന്നവരെ എഴുന്നേല്പിച്ച ശേഷം

മലപ്പും കലക്കവു മറുതിയില്ലാതുള്ള

വിലാപനാദങ്ങളും നീങ്ങുവാൻ നതജന—

മലാപഹാരി ദേവ നീവണ്ണമരുൾചെയ്തു: (3:277–80)

Raising them rise from the dust of abject grief,

Disposed kindly, the Lord granted them relief

From dismay, fright, and laments of no relent.

Thoughtfully, the sin-quelling One spoke in this wise:

അപ്രതീകാര്യമായ ലംഘനമത്രേ നിങ്ങ—	Indefensible stands your offense, willfully done,
ളുത്പ്രഗൽഭതയോടു ചെയ്തു നിരൂപിച്ചാൽ	The powers, endowed of me, of free thinking and reason,
സ്വാതന്ത്ര്യ ബുദ്ധിനിങ്ങൾ ക്കേകിയ കാരണത്താൽ	Run in abuse. The calls of intellect and duty could deter
നീതിയിൽ നിന്നു പിഴയുണ്ടാവാനരുതാഞ്ഞു. (3:281–284)	All harmful impulse that could tempt you to err.
താദൃശ കാരണത്താൽ നിങ്ങൾ ശിക്ഷാർഹരെന്നു-	With ample reason then, the cost of guilt
ള്ളാദൃതമൊഴിക്കുണ്ടോ വിപ്രതിപത്തിചെറ്റും?	Settles on you, no denying of that verdict;
നിങ്ങളിന്നസ്ഥിത്വവു മാഹാരം ശ്വസനവും	Your very being, sustenance and breath
മംഗളോത്പാതകങ്ങളാകിയ സമസ്തവും	And all things that comport with wellness are mine;
എന്നിൽനിന്നല്ലേ ലഭിച്ചീടുന്നതായതോർത്താൽ	Must you then not know why good faith should most shine?
നന്ദിതോന്നുവാൻ ന്യായമുണ്ടെന്നു ചൊല്ലേണമോ? (3:285–90)	
എങ്കിലും മമ വൈരി തന്നുടെ ഗിരം കേട്ടു	Instead to my foe's scheme you gave quick assent
ശങ്കയന്നിയേ പാപമാർജ്ജിച്ച നിങ്ങളെഞാൻ	And courted the foul spirit's ploy. Incumbent
അന്ധകൂപത്തിന്നടിത്തട്ടിലേ ക്കപ്പൊലിയോൻ	On thee thus is a lightless estate now to own—
ബന്ധുവായിട്ടും സ്ഥലത്തയപ്പാനാണു ന്യായം. (3:291–94)	The infernal hollow of darkness with Apollyon.
തീക്കടലാകുമതിൻ നിത്യമാം വൃഥ സഹി-	Fire's lake it is, of torment unceasing,
ച്ചൂക്കനാം സേറ്റനോടും ബേത്സെബൂബാദിയായ	As condemned beings, your portion sharing
മുഷ്കന്മാരോടുംകൂടി നിർഭാഗ്യജീവികളായ്	With spirits offensive—Satan, Beelzebub and their kind,
പാർക്കയെന്നുള്ളതെത്ര സങ്കടം നിങ്ങൾക്കോർത്താൽ. (3:295–98)	Woe unthinkable, mitigation never to find.

The Son, the Logos, to Assume the Guilt

ആയതുകൊണ്ടു നിങ്ങൾ സഹിക്ക വേണ്ടും ശിക്ഷ	Therefore, the penalty to you imputable
മായമില്ലാത്ത മമ പുത്രൻ കയ്യേറ്റുകൊൾവാൻ	For Himself My Son makes assumable:
നിശ്ചയം ചെയ്തിട്ടുണ്ടൂ നിങ്ങളെ വിടുവിപ്പാൻ	Except this peaceable way,
സ്വച്ഛമാമീ മാർഗ്ഗത്തെ കവിയും വഴിയില്ല.	None exists to free thee, I say.
വിശുദ്ധ ലോഗോസാകു മവന്നാലെന്റെനീതി	The Sacred Logos is He, whose righteous ways
പ്രസിദ്ധമായിത്തീരും, സ്നേഹവുമതുപോലെ. (3:299–304)	Shall witness growing fame, His love too, likewise.

ദുഷ്കൃതശിക്ഷയാകും മൃത്യുവിലാഴുമവൻ	Death, that iniquitous power, he shall tackle in person,
സൽകൃതനാകുമെന്നാൽ മൂന്നാം നാളുയർപ്പിനാൽ	Yet rise as the righteous One on the third day's morn;
നീതിക്കുപരിഹാരം വന്നീടുമീ മൃത്യുവാൽ	His return to life shall all demands meet
നീതിഹീനരാം നിങ്ങൾ നീതിമൽകൃതരാകും. (3:305–08)	Of restored righteousness of forgiven guilt.
ഈദൃശ്യം പാപശിക്ഷയാകുന്ന കാർമേഘത്തെ	In this way, the dark cloud of the reign of sin
നോദനം ചെയ്തീടുമ്പോൾ തെളിയും ഭാഗ്യസൂര്യൻ.	When removed, shall dawn the righteous sun.
അതി ന്റെ കിരണത്താൽ പാപാന്ധകാരമെല്ലാം	The thick pall of Hades' night his rays erase,
പവിയാൽ പർവതം പോൽ ധ്വസ്തമായ് ഭവിച്ചിടും.[13] (3:309–12)	Say, as may the Pavi the mountain pulverize.

Promise of Paradise Restored

മരണം കുടികൊണ്ട മാലിന്യ ദേഹം നീക്കി-	From death shall God thy corrupt frame free
ത്തരുമീശ്വരൻ നാശമേലാത്ത ശരീരത്തെ.	And with the incorruptible endow thee;
കഷ്ടവും സങ്കടവും വ്യാധിയും മരണവും	Impervious to pain, plague, and peril
പ്ലുഷ്ടമായ് വീണ്ടും നിങ്ങൾ പറുദീസയിലെത്തും. (3:313–16)	Ye shall return to Paradise to dwell.
ഈവിധം സ്ത്രീസന്താനം സർപ്പശീർഷത്തെ തകർ-	Thus shall by the provident Word, in time determined,
ത്തീടുമെന്നുള്ള വാക്യം സംസിദ്ധമാകും ധ്രുവം	The Seed of Promise crush the serpent's cunning head:
ദേവനീ വിധം ചൊല്ലീ ലോഗോസിൻ യാഗാർപ്പണം	Herein to Adam the Lord unveiled the far-seen saga
ഭാവനാർത്ഥമാ യാദത്തിനുപദേശിച്ചിതു. (3:317–20)	Of the movements prescient in the Logos-*yaga*.
ശുദ്ധമാം മൃഗത്തിനെ നിഹനിച്ചിട്ടുയാഗം	Creatures of purity, figures of life-gift,
തത്രൈവ നടത്തിനാ നാദമാദേശം പോലെ.	Adam offered, for God his guilt to lift;
യജ്ഞാവസാനത്തിങ്കൽ യജ്ഞീയമൃഗത്തോലാൽ	The victim's hide at the *yajna* severed
വിജയിയായ ദൈവം മർത്യരെയുടുപ്പിച്ചു. (3:321–24)	God their bodies in comfort covered.
നഗ്നത്വമപകരിച്ചീടുവാൻ മർത്യൻ കണ്ട	For to shield from nakedness man could find
ഭഗ്നമാം വാദപത്രവസ്ത്രമീ വിധം നീക്കി.	Only sorry means like the woven leaves he donned.
അതിഗംഭീരമാമിത്തത്വത്തെ തെളിക്കുന്ന	None too small is our need to be robed—
പ്രതിപാദനമെത്ര യജ്ഞകർമോപാഖ്യാനം. (3:325–28)	A truth observed in all *yajnas* performed.

---

[13] *Pavi* is the thunderbolt from Indra, the god of war and natural forces, including thunder, in Indian mythology. Apparently, the power in *Pavi* suffices to pulverize the *parvata* or the mountain, if it needs to be removed.

ഏദനിലാരംഭിച്ച ദിവ്യമാമിക്കർമ്മത്തെ	This holy rite, commenced in Eden,
മേദിനി വാസിവർഗം നെടുകെത്തുടർന്നത്രേ.	Humans of all lands saw as bounden.
ഏതുദിക്കിലുമുണ്ടു യജ്ഞവേദികളേവ-	Look out anywhere, see altars reared,
മേതുദിക്കിലുമുണ്ടു യാഗാർത്ഥം മൃഗങ്ങളും. (3:329–32)	And likewise watch, stock for slaughters raised.
ലോഗോസുപ്രജാപതിയെന്നുള്ളപേരുകളെ	Epochal names, *Prajapati* and Logos,
യാതൊരാൾ വഹിച്ചുവോ ദിവ്യനാമപ്പുരുഷൻ	Also as *Purusha*[14] and the Pure Man proclaimed,
സ്വശരീരത്തെ യാഗസാധനമാക്കിയെന്ന	Himself on the altar a sacrifice made
കുശലാധായി തത്വമാണിതിൻ നിഷ്കൃഷ്ടാർഥം. (3:344–48)	That blissful truth is its numinous essence.
ഏതർത്ഥത്തെ പുരസ്കരിച്ചാണല്ലോ ഭൂവിൽ	The Aryans grasping its inspired intent,
പൂതമാം യജ്ഞകർമ്മം ചെയ്യുന്നതാര്യവംശർ	At their altars did *yajnas* present;
ക്രൈസ്തവമതം യൂദമതത്തിൻ സത്താകയാൽ	Since Christian precepts are in substance Judaic,
നിസ്ത്രപമുരച്ചിടാം യജ്നീയ മതമിതി. (3:341–48)	One could name it *yajna* Semitic.

Expulsion from the Garden

പശ്ചാദി ദൃശ്യം ചൊന്നാനീശ്വരൻ ഗുണദോഷ	God then said: Adam now can tell
നിശ്ചയം ലഭിച്ചാദാം നമ്മിലേകനെപ്പോലെ	Between good and evil, like one of us; as well,
ഭവിച്ചു; തൽക്കാരണാൽ പതിവിൻപടിയവൻ	He may in driven risk, reach out for another fruit
സ്വഹസ്തം നീട്ടി ജ്ജീവവൃക്ഷത്തിൽ നിന്നുഫലം	This time of the tree of life, and thus suit
പറിച്ചുഭക്ഷിച്ചിട്ടു മരണരഹിതനായ്	Himself to the tragic eternity of personal sin.
തിരിയാതിരിപ്പാൻ നാം കരുതീടുക വേണം. (3:349–54)	
എന്നുരച്ചാദാമിനെ സഭാര്യനായുദ്യാനം	Quick action ensued: out came the man and his mate
തന്നിൽ നിന്നപസരിച്ചിട്ടതിൻ പൂർവദ്വാരി	From the garden, expelled, and at the eastern gate
ഘൂർണ്ണായമാന ജ്വല ചന്ദ്രഹാസങ്ങളേന്തും	Appeared the angelic hosts of armed charge
വിണ്ണവപ്പരിഷയെ സ്ഥാപിച്ചാൻ സർവേശ്വരൻ.	Bearing lightning's swords against powers large.
പ്രസ്തുത വൃത്താന്തത്തിന്നംശങ്ങൾ പോലും നമ്മെ	Mere bits of this tale, even less than bits,
നിസ്തുല ദുഃഖാഗ്നിക്കു വിറകായെരിക്കുന്നു. (3:355–60)	Will ignite the woe in us of the wailing pits.

[14] The supreme Creator in the Vedic pantheon, but also identified as other mythical figures of divinity. *Prajapati* has the offices of the creation and preservation of life. His name means "the Lord of Creatures" or "the Ruler of Men," and is deeply benevolent to humans. Comparative literary readings widely describe him as a Christ figure.

Purusha, according to Vedic writings, is the cosmic Man or Self, who manifests the entire universe. The sacrifice of *Purusha* by the gods was necessary to bring life into the world, according to the Vedas. Here again, the cosmic Man who is the source of all life, is a figure Simon presents as the one to restore the fallen man.

ആനന്ദഭൂമിയായാകുമുദ്യാനം വിട്ടെഴ്വിധ-	From shalom's garden, O God, where could Adam
മാദമൻ ഹവ്വായോടുമിറങ്ങിപ്പോന്നു കഷ്ടം!	With his better half retire, both homeless become?
ഉന്നതസ്ഥാനത്തു നിന്നധസ്താൽ പതിപ്പതി -	Is there a fall sadder than the one
ലുന്നതമായനഷ്ടം വേറെയൊന്നുണ്ടോ കേൾപ്പൂ. (3:363–64)	From the highest of places so blissfully won?
രാജകീയമാം സർവമഹിമാവോടും കൂടി	The emperor enthroned in splendor one day
ഭ്രാജിതാസനത്തിങ്കലിരിക്കും മണ്ഡലേശൻ	Fortune had him to beggary convey!
ഹാ! ജവം നിജൈശ്വര്യ നിലയിൽനിന്നുനീങ്ങി	Dreadfully move unseen the summoned hands
നീചയാചകനായി അതീരുവതോർക്കാവതോ? (3:365–68)	To plunge or raise men by speedy errands.
പുറത്തുപോവിനെന്ന ശബ്ദത്തെ നിയോജ്യന്മാ-	Enforcers thundered their command, "Depart!"
രുരച്ച പോതിലെല്ലാ ദൈവികസ്വാന്തനവും	All solace divine thereat did them desert
മറന്നിട്ടിടിയേറ്റ തേൻ മാവു പോലെ ദുഃഖ-	Like the deep honey giant[15] by lightning struck,
സരിത്തിൽ വീണൊഴുകിപ്പോയിതു ചൈതന്യവും. (3:369–72)	Sap dried and vigor-rid, in bone-shaking shock.
ആ ജന്മം പരിചയിച്ചുള്ളൊരു വാസസ്ഥലം	Eden was their native domicile
നീചന്മാരുടെ പാദ വിക്ഷേപമേൽക്കാ സ്ഥലം	Which evil footprints would never defile—
ആധിവ്യാധികളുടെ വിത്തുകൾ മുളയ്ക്കാത്ത	For pangs and plagues an unbudding space
മേദിനീഭാഗം മധു ക്ഷീരങ്ങളോലുന്നിടം. (3:373–76)	Where honey and milk flowed in surging race.
ആഹാര പദാർത്ഥങ്ങൾക്കുചൃത മഹാനസം,	For food a fare of viands served aplenty,
മോഹനസമ്പത്തുകൾക്കന്നൂത ഭണ്ഡാകാരം,	For treasures prized, a growing plenitude.
ആനന്ദപരിമള കാറ്റുകൾവീശുംദേശ-	Winds and breezes of effects salutary,
മാനന്ദാമൃതവർഷമേകുന്നമേഘദ്വാരം,	Showers ambrosial from clouds in canopy;
ദൈഹികക്ലമത്തെയുമാത്മിക മാന്ദ്യത്തെയും	Ills of the body or spirit inert none,
വൈകാതെനീക്കും ജീവഭൂരുഹംനിൽക്കുന്നിടം	Stands nigh Life's Tree of healing renown
സ്വർഗമാംസരസ്സിലെ സുവർണപദങ്ങളാം	In the florid vistas meet the angelic concord
സ്വർഗ്ഗസത്തുകൾ സമ്മേളിപ്പോരുസഭാസ്ഥാനം	At harmony's capital of ruling accord—
ലോകൈകസാമ്രാജ്യത്തിനേകമാം തലസ്ഥാനം	The only door for celestial ascension.
നാകലോകത്തിലേക്കുള്ളേകമാരോഹണം. (3:377–86)	
നക്ഷത്രതുല്യമായ പൂക്കളെകൊണ്ടു മന്ത—	Flowers that pass for stars and earth's green
രീക്ഷത്തിൻ കാന്തിചിന്നും പച്ചപ്പുൽത്തറയാലും,	Below that image the glories of worlds unseen,

---

[15] Simon speaks of the giant mango tree, laden with sweet and fragrant fruit. It is not uncommon to see such huge trees utterly destroyed by tropical lightning strikes.

സന്തതം വിചരിക്കും ദേവന്മാരാലും മായാ—	Angels crisscrossing in cordial converse,
ബന്ധനം തകർക്കുന്ന ദൈവസന്നിധിയാലും	God's Presence that *maya*'s[16] chain shatters,
ഭൂവിലേ ദ്യോവെന്നപോൽ ശോഭിക്കുമുപവനം	Heaven to earth come, the great concurrence
ഭാവനാതീതം ഭവ്യനിചയം ഭാസാംപദം. (3:388–92)	Of perfections measureless in confluence:
ഇങ്ങനെയുള്ളനിജവാസ ഭൂമിയെവിട്ടു	The travailing mortals must but abandon
തിങ്ങിന ദുഃഖംപൂണ്ടു മർത്യരെങ്ങനെ പോരും?	The place of benevolence and high provision?
അങ്ങുമിങ്ങുമായ് നോക്കിയെന്തിതെന്നറിയാഞ്ഞു	Aghast, their eyes run in panic flits
ചിന്താമഗ്നരായ് നിന്നു സംഗതിയറിഞ്ഞപ്പോൾ	Of bewilderment; a fresh pang of grief hits
തകർന്ന മനസ്സോടും നിറഞ്ഞകണ്ണീരോടും	Them every minute, each heavier than the one prior;
കരഞ്ഞുപറഞ്ഞേറെ സങ്കടമാദിമർത്യർ.	They bemoaned their deed, yet God deemed it fair,
എങ്കിലും ദൈവത്തിന്റെ ശാശ്വതനീതിക്കൊരു	To let stand the effects of choices made,
ഭംഗമേശായ്‌വാനീശനവയെ ഗണിച്ചില്ല. (3:393–400)	Lest God's order of justice in any manner fade.
ആകയാൽ ബാഷ്പപപൂർണ്ണ നേത്രയുഗങ്ങളോടും	Anguished over the future just acquired
ഭീകരമായ ഭാവിയോർത്തു വൻതാപത്തോടും	And the life strings fond so quickly severed,
ഉദ്യാനത്തിങ്കലനു ബദ്ധമാം ജീവിതന്തു	From the bonds of Paradise starkly shunned,
സദ്യോദാതമാമ്മാറു ഹൃദയാഘാതത്തോടും	They paced on, heavy of foot, turning around
പ്രാണനിർവിശേഷമായ് നിരന്തം സ്നേഹിച്ചതൻ	Still, again and again, for one more glance
ഫ്രാൻസു രാജ്യത്തോടന്ത്യമാകിയ വിടവാങ്ങി	Of their lost home. At his dismal leave of France
നിത്യമായ് പിരിഞ്ഞൊരു നെപ്പോളിയന്റെ മർമ്മ—	For which he would trade his heroic soul,
സ്പൃക്കായ വിയോഗത്തേ നിസ്സാരമാക്കും വിധം	The great Napoleon saw sorrow, in immense whole—
ഇടയ്ക്കു പലവുരു തിരിഞ്ഞുനോക്കിപ്പാരം	A mere passing loss that, were we to compare
തുടുത്ത മുഖം വിളർത്തസ്ത ചേതനരായും	The griefs of the hero and of our ancestral pair.
എന്നേക്കുമായിപ്പറു ദീസയ്ക്കു യാത്രചൊല്ലി-	All vigor drained, tear-soaked and pale, once for all,
പ്പോന്നയ്യോ പടിവാതിൽകടന്നു, കഷ്ടം! കഷ്ടം! (3:401–12)	Alas! alas! they to Paradise bade dire farewell.

Cain and Abel: The First Fratricide

സുതന്മാരിരുവരും സഗർഭ്യരെന്നാകിലും	The sons twain, though of womb selfsame,
നിതാന്ത ഭേദം കാണായ്‌വന്നിതായവർ തമ്മിൽ.	Stood one clear apart from the other.

---

[16] Illusory appearance of the sensory world.

ഏകരാം പിതാക്കളിൽ നിന്നുളവാകുന്നൊരു
ദേഹികൾക്കെതുല്യത വരികിൽ ചിത്രമല്ല.
ഏകമേഘത്തിൽ നിന്നു കൊടുതാമിടിത്തീയും
മോഹനതരമായ മഴയും വീഴുന്നില്ലേ? (4:107–12)

Granted, the progeny might in attributes differ
Even of parentage single, none curious a claim.
Lo, from the lone cloud proceed, do they not,
Refreshing downpours and the lightning bolt?

സത്തമമായുള്ളൊരു പുഷ്പാംപോലെയുംകിളി
പോയ്ക്കളഞ്ഞുള്ള കൂടുപോലെയുമിരിക്കിലും
പുത്രാ! നിൻ ദേഹമെന്തൊ കാന്തിയാൽ ലസിക്കുന്നു.
സത്യമാം മതത്തിന്റെ സംസ്ഥാപനാർത്ഥമത്രേ
പുത്ര! നിൻമൃതി; അതു മൃതിയല്ലൊരിക്കലും.
നിത്യജീവനെ പ്രാപിച്ചീടുന്ന കോടാകോടി
രക്തസാക്ഷികളിൽ നീ മുമ്പനായ് ഭവിച്ചാലും. (4:208–16)

At once the loveliest flower in its fulsome powers
Or sanctity's nest bereft of its winged tenant,
Thy body lies, a halo hovering over its lay of rest.
Nay, Death this is not, nor loss by ill fate, my son,
But the core cord of all true religion.
Forerunner thou art to the marching crores
Of pilgrims in martyrial robes
On their journey to the unfading city.

Excerpt from Noah's Sermon

വിഷയ ഭോഗങ്ങളാലില്ലൊരു തൃപ്തി, യവ
സുഷിരമുള്ള പാത്രം പോലെയാണതിൽ പകർ-
ന്നൊഴിക്കും ഭോഗ നീരാനിമിഷം കൊണ്ടു ചോർന്നു
കഴിയും കഥ, പിന്നെ പാത്രവുമുടഞ്ഞീടും.
ചങ്ങലയിലുമാശ ചങ്ങല ഭയങ്കരം
ചങ്ങലത്തളയ്പ്പിങ്കൽ നിൽക്കുമേകത്ര ബദ്ധൻ.
ആശച്ചങ്ങല കൊണ്ടു ബന്ധിക്കിൽ അലർകം പോ-
ലാശകൾ തോറും ഓടി നടക്കും നിലയെന്യേ. (6:125–32)

Sensual hunts but lure and tease: They,
Like the sieved cask, receive the frothing juices
Of concupiscence, yet void them anon, and to pieces
Dash, and with its drain, the whole vessel.
Fierce is desire's chain, besting the clamping steel.
Chains of lust pin the strong to the captive post;
Worse does passion, which, with built up lust,
Turns the mind rabid, in its fitful onward thrust.

Noah Mocked about His Ship

തോടില്ലാസ്ഥലത്തിങ്കലെന്തിനു പാലം?പാർപ്പാൻ
നാടില്ലാസ്ഥലത്താരു തൊഴുത്തുവച്ചീടുന്നു?
കൂടില്ലാതിരിക്കുകിലെന്തിനു കിളി? മാറ-
ചൂടില്ലാത്തവനെന്തു സംഗതിക്കരുവയർ? (6:89–92)

Why build a bridge where runs no creek sate,
Or erect a stall where no livestock roams,
Or for tidings tarry where no pigeon homes?
Worse yet, why match a maid with an effete mate?

The House of Abraham

Abraham's Grief

പുത്രനില്ലാത്ത ഭവനം വനമേവ
മാത്ര ചൊല്ലുന്നഭിജ്ഞന്മാർ അശങ്കിതം;
സത്രമില്ലാഞ്ഞാൽ പഥികർ അഗതികൾ;
പത്രമില്ലാഞ്ഞാൽ അസുന്ദരം ശാഖകൾ;
മിത്രമില്ലാഞ്ഞാൽ മുഴുക്കും ഭയം പതി—
പുത്രരില്ലാഞ്ഞാൽ ഗൃഹം നിഷ്പ്രകാശകം. (15:40–46)

Sans its seed, the home is a heath,
Maxims hold this smarting truth.
Innless towns men vagrants make,
Leafless limbs a barren brake.
A friendless face shows its fear run free.
A childless home a shelter sombre.

Abraham's Covenant Sacrifice

ഓട്ടിനാനബ്റാ മവയേ ത്തദന്തരേ
പെട്ടവന തൃന്തബാഢമാം നിദ്രയിൽ.
അന്ധകാരം മഹാ ഭീതിയു മബ്രാമി-
നന്തരംഗത്തിൽ ഭവിച്ചു; പരമേശ്വരൻ
ചൊല്ലിനാന ബ്രാമോടന്യ ദിക്കിൽ തവ
നല്ലരാം സന്തതി നാനൂറു വത്സരം
പാർത്തു തദ്ദേശ്യരെ സേവിക്കുമായവ
രാർത്തി ചേർക്കും ഭവത്സന്തതിക്കെങ്കിലും
ശിക്ഷിച്ചു പീഡകന്മാരെ ദയാന്വിതം
രക്ഷിച്ചു കൊൾവവൻ ഭവദീയരെ ദ്രുതം. (15:127–36)

Abram chased the ravenous raptors
Back, over and over, keeping the presents
Pure for the Lord's flaming torch path.
His limbs failing, all strength spent
A sleep of leaden lull closed his eyes,
Great fear too, him at once gripping;
Said the Lord, then: "Thy goodly seed
That thou seest not today, behold,
In privation shall pass centuries four
Serving harsh aliens; take heart, though,
They shall to this land entitled return,
Due judgment on the foe served in full."

Sarah and Hagar: Domestic Jealousies

സാറായ് കടുതര വാക്ശരം ഹാഗറിൻ
മാറത്തു ചെന്നു തറയ്ക്കും പടിക്കഹോ
പേമാരി പോലെ ചൊരിഞ്ഞു പലവുരു
വാമാമണിയെ നിരാഹാരിയാക്കിയാൾ.
ചെയ്യുന്നതൊന്നുമേ ബോധിച്ചിടാത്തതി-
നയ്യായിരം കുറവുച്ചരിക്കും ജവാൽ. (16:45–50)

വയ്യാതൊരിടത്തൊന്നിരുന്നു പോയാലതു
കയ്യുണ്ട കുറ്റമായി ലക്ഷീകരിച്ചീടും.
എന്തെങ്കിലുമെതിർ ചൊന്നാലുലക്കയാൽ

Sarai's harsh tongue sped arrows into the heart of Hagar,
Though a slave, of no mean degree a sensuous figure,
The charming object of her mistress' ample ire
Times none too few went she without a meal.
Nothing Hagar did pleased her mistress, the litany
Of her faults ran in unending refrains.

If she sat to rest to catch her breath,
Sarai would charge it as capital crime.
One word heard in defense would drive

'മോന്ത'യ്ക്കു കുത്താനരികത്തണഞ്ഞിടിലും.	The mistress for a pestle bash.
ഭർത്തൃസമീപത്തു ശയ്യ വിരിക്കുകിൽ	Were Hagar to make her master's bed
ചത്വരത്തിങ്കലെറിഞ്ഞു കളഞ്ഞിടിലും. (16:51–56)	Out to the yard will the covers fly.

കോണിലെങ്ങാനും മറഞ്ഞുനിന്നാഗറെ	If Abram in a romantic moment though rare
പ്രീണനം ചെയ്വാൻ ധവനൊരുങ്ങുന്നതായ്	Was espied with Hagar in some corner,
കാണുകിൽ കാണിയും സങ്കോചമില്ലാതെ	The mistress spins in with frenetic rage: out flow
നാണമിളകുന്ന വാണികൾ ചൊന്നിടും.	Words so welting smart that no mercy show.
മന്ദസ്മിതം തൂകിയെന്നു കേസുണ്ടാക്കി-	A mere smile from Abram a high risk runs
യന്നുപാത്രങ്ങൾ തകർക്കും പരാക്രമി. (16:57–62)	Of Sarah smashing piles of pots and pans.

വസ്ത്രം വെളുപ്പിച്ചുടുക്കുകിൽ "നോക്കവൾ	If the maid's clothes are fresh, she goes,
ക്കുർത്തിങ്ങിടും ഡംഭ" മെന്നു ജല്പിച്ചിടും.	"Look, how haughty her moves!" Folks,
കൂട്ടരേ! കേൾക്കുവിൻ വീട്ടുകാരൻ പുരാ	This old man brought home a young vixen:
ചേട്ടയാകും ചെറുപെണ്ണിനെ കൊണ്ടന്നു	Her wishes his way, overnight the henhussy,
പാട്ടിൽനിറുത്തിയ കാരണത്താൽ മമ	So biddable. She today is my home's queen,
വീട്ടിന്നധികാരിയായി വന്നവളിതാ	With his full assent; boundless his pleasure in her;
തട്ടിയെടുത്തു മനസ്സു മറിക്കയാ-	Now with child too, on top of the world, and why,
ലിഷ്ടമയാൾക്കു ജനിച്ചവളിൽ തുലോം.	Up for a fresh fight, hey, just for the kick of it.
കുട്ടിയുമായെന്നഹങ്കരിച്ചു മമ	
തട്ടുകേടുണ്ടാക്കുവാനൊരുങ്ങുന്നിതാ. (16:63–72)	

ദുഷ്ടയിവളുടെ വാക്കുവിട്ടൊന്നുമേ	He holds the line by this harpy's word
ചേഷ്ടയില്ലാ നരനെന്നു ബോധിക്കണം.	He has lost his mind, be it said;
ഹാഗാർ കരഞ്ഞാലയാളും കരഞ്ഞിടും,	Hagar's eyes tear up? So do his;
ഹാഗാർ ചിരിച്ചാലയാളും ചിരിച്ചിടും;	A smile breaks on Hagar's lips? So does on his;
ഹാഗാറെ ഞാനൊന്നു ശാസിക്കിലെന്നുടെ	Were I to check or stop her somewhere,
ഹാ! ഗളം ഞെക്കാനൊരുങ്ങും നിരങ്കുശം. (16:73–78)	My neck is in his grip, for sure.

പെണ്ണിന്നടിമയായ് ത്തീർന്നുള്ള മർത്യനു	"A henpecked man shall have a hellish home,
തിണ്ണന്നകപ്പെടും ദണ്ഡങ്ങളെന്നുള്ള	I swear," yowled Sarai her normal nag line.
നിർണ്ണയവാക്കു ശരിയായ് ധരിക്കുവാൻ	"Love-blind the elder waltzes with the shapely slave,"
കണ്ണറിവില്ലാ ഗ്രഹപതിക്കൊട്ടുമേ.	Shouts Sarah, with fresh fodder for the village gossips.
ഇത്ഥമയലത്തു കേൾക്കുംവിധം വിളി-	A teeth-gnashing ogress, in fits of jealousy,
ച്ചുതൃധി കോച്ചമായ് ഘോഷിച്ചു തന്നുടെ	And assault force, Sarah comes at Egypt's poor daughter
പല്ലും കടിച്ചെരു രാക്ഷസിക്കൊപ്പമായ്	Charging in and out, unchallenged, each time
കൊല്ലാകൊല ചെയ്തു സാറായി മേവിനാൾ. (16:79–86)	Leaving Hagar just alive for the next thrashing.

An Angel Appears to Hagar on Her Desert Flight

ഇക്കോര ക്രിയ സഹ്യമല്ലാതെയാ—
മുഗ്ദവിലോചന വീടുവിട്ടോടവേ
യാഹ്‌വെയിൻ ദൂതനവൾക്കു പ്രത്യക്ഷനാ—
യാഹ്വയം ചൊല്ലി വിളിച്ചു തദ്ധാർത്തക—
ളാകർണ്ണനം ചെയ്ത ശേഷം വദിച്ചിതു:
ശോകംകളക നിൻസന്താന വല്ലരി
പൂത്തുഫലിച്ചതിൻ കായ്കൾ പരിണതാ-

വസ്ഥയിലെത്തിപ്പൊഴിയും വിധമഹോ!
സംഖ്യേയമല്ലാത്ത മട്ടിലഭിവൃദ്ധി
തങ്കുന്നതാക്കി സ്ഥിരീകരിക്കും; തവ
ഗർഭസ്ഥനാം ശിശു പുത്രസന്താനമാ-
ണർഭനാമ വന്നിഷ്മയേലെന്നു പേർ
തജ്ജന്മശേഷം കൊടുക്ക, യഹോവ നി-

ന്നുച്ചരുദിതം ശ്രവിക്കുക കാരണം. (16:88–100)

കാട്ടുകഴുതയ്ക്കു തുല്യനാകുമവൻ
നീട്ടും കരം സമസ്തർക്കും വിരുദ്ധമായ്
നീട്ടുമവരുമവന്നെതിരായ് കരം
പാർക്കുമവൻ സോദരർക്കെതിരാം ദിശി.
ആകയാൽ ഹാഗറേ! സ്വാമിനിതന്നരി-
കാമയമന്യേ ഗമിച്ചുവശംവദ-
യായിരിക്കായവൾ ക്കെന്നുചൊന്നാനന്ദ-
ദായിയാം ദൂതകൻ മാറിമറഞ്ഞിതു. (16:101–08)

സുപ്രസന്നോദയനാകിയ ദേവനേ
വിഭ്രമവേളയിൽ കണ്ടാശ്വസിക്കയാൽ
ഉൾകമലം തെളിഞ്ഞു ബുദ്ധചിത്തയായ്

നിഷ്കളങ്കാദരമോതിനാൾ ഹാഗറും: (16:109–12)

മദ് ദർശകനാകുമീശ്വര നത്രാപി
മദ്ദൃഷ്ടികൾക്കു വിഷയമായതദ്ഭുതം!
തത്കാരണാദ് വിഭോ മാം പശ്യസീ തി, ദി-
വ്യാഖ്യ നൽകീടിനാൾ യാവിന്നുപാവനീ.

തേനൈവ ബീയർലഹൈറോയ് തൃഭി-
ധാനം ലഭിച്ചാ മരുവിൻകിണറ്റിനും. (16:113–18)

Undefended in torment daily
Distraught she fled, but ran squarely
Into Yahweh's angel in the wilderness,
Who, greeting Hagar in celestials' manner,
Said to her thus: "Mind not your hurts, Hagar,
The fruit of your womb in due season
Shall bring you progeny of enduring numbers;

A male child you bear; name him Ishmael
For all to know how the Lord has heard
Your great cry of agony in these blazing sands."

"Like unto the onager his way and his will
His arms against the nations raised
And theirs against him, duly for battle.
In ranges against his brethren's tents
Shall he pitch his own. Heed then my word,
Hagar, return to thy mistress, free of fear,
And with her stay amenable," said bearer fair
Of tidings and from sight forthwith vanished. (16:101–08)

For this moment past of distress privy
Was for Heaven on her to image its mercy;
Her wisdom unclouded, in divine wonderment,
Spoke Hagar this word in spirit reverent:

Seen of me is He who alone as God sees me
To my eyes the marvel, He. Wherefore she,
"Beer-lahai-roi," named the gurgling spring,
And the self-caused Jah in the same term's ring.

Abraham Hosts Angels

Chapter 18 of Genesis is a watershed moment in the book's narrative. The childless Abraham has received the promise of a natural heir, but the fulfillment of it is yet to take place. Abraham is ninety-nine years old and still holding on to the assurance that he has received from God. He has a son through his Egyptian maid Hagar. Neither Hagar nor his son is in the good graces of Sarah. Their future in Abraham's household is short. The place is called the Oaks of Mamre. One day, while seated in front of his tent, Abraham notices three strangers coming toward his dwelling. He invites them to dine and to rest in the shade. They oblige. Before they leave, the prominent one among them tells Abraham that "next year this time" Sarah would bear her own son. As they leave, the same distinguished personage tells Abraham about the imminent judgment that is coming upon Sodom and Gomorrah, the two great cities of sin that would soon burn.

ലോകനമയ്ക്കു നിയുക്തരായുള്ളവർ	Like those very ones charged to bless the world
ലോകപീഡയ്ക്കൊരുങ്ങീടുന്നതു പോലെ	Design its torment instead, why does the sun,
ലോകചക്ഷുസ്സാം ദിനകരനെന്തഹോ!	The eye to watch the earth, dispense for it
ലോഹിതാശ്വനു സമനായ് ചരിപ്പതും!	Such furnace fire? So wonders the firmament
ഇത്ഥം നിരൂപിച്ചു തന്മുഖം നീലിമ	And elects to don itself in soothing blue.
കൈകൊണ്ടു നിൽക്കുവതല്ലേ വിഹായസം?	Therefore, make no haste, but be pleased to rest
ആകായലങ്ങു കടന്നുപോകാതിവി-	Thyselves under the tree shade, hither, I pray.
ടാനഗച്ഛായയിൽ വിശ്രമിച്ചീടുവിൻ. (18:61–68)	

അല്പമാം തോയമെടുത്തുടൻ നിങ്ങടെ	Allow me, my Lords, to give quick ablutions
നൽപ്പൂഴും പാദം കഴുകാനരുളണം.	For thy feet of solely sacred motions;
പൂപശകലമിങ്ങാനയിക്കാമതു-	I shall then serve a bread's morsel
മൂലം പ്രശാന്തമാക്കേണം വിശപ്പിനെ. (18:69–72)	To relieve thy hunger from the desert trail.

പിന്നീടു വേണമെന്നാകിൽ ഭവാന്മാർക്കു	As it suits, my Lords, thy pleasure,
നന്ദ്യാ തുടരാം വഴിയാത്ര പൂർവവൽ	Resume thence thy journey as before.
എന്നുപറഞ്ഞൊരു നേരമവരുടൻ	The visiting trio answered, "Proceed
ചൊന്നാർ: ഭവന്മതംപോലെചെയ്തിടുക. (18:73–76)	As you are moved, in this cast of thy mind."

ആതിഥേയന്മാരിലഗ്രഗണ്യനാകിയ	Abraham, of all men most hospitable,
നീതിമാനബ്രഹാം ദിവ്യപഥികരെ	Seated the celestials at the tree's foot
വൃക്ഷമൂലത്തിൽ സുഖമായിരുത്തിയി-	In good comfort and dashed to Sarah:
ട്ടക്ഷണം സാറായ്ക്കരികിലേക്കോടിനാൻ. (18:77–80)	

Simon's Verse: Selected Pieces

ആയവളോടു പറഞ്ഞാൻ ത്രിശേടക	To her said he: Three measures of flour take
മാവെടുത്തു കുഴച്ചപ്പമുണ്ടാക്കുവാൻ	Knead it fast and with it fresh bread bake;
ഗോവത്സമേകം പിടിച്ചു ഭൃത്യൻ വശം	To a speedy servant the duke his order gave:
പാകപ്പെടുത്തുവാനേല്പിച്ചു ധാർമികൻ. (18:82–85)	A youngling calf prepare as fine dish to serve.
പക്തി ചെയ്തുള്ളൊരീ മാംസവു മപ്പവും	The meat and bread with creams and curds
ദുഗ്ദ്ധം നവനീതമെന്നിവ സാദരം	So swiftly readied for the etreated lords.
അദ്ധ്വനീനാഗ്രേ വിളമ്പിവച്ചബ്രഹാ-	Abraham stood by, humble and reverent,
മിദ്ധാദരം നിന്നു ശുശ്രൂഷണത്തിനായ്. (18:85–88)	Host and servitor, eager for their words.
അന്തർഹൃദയത്തിലുൽഭൂതമായൊരു	From stirrings within of deep respect
ബന്ധുരഭക്തിയാം പാണികൾ മൂലമാ-	Moved his hands in flowing acts of devotion;
ഗന്തുകർക്കേകിയ ഭോജനമായവ-	The stately guests, sat pleased and honored
രത്തമില്ലാപ്രീതിയോടശിക്കും വിധൗ	By the served meal. The chief among them
ചോദിച്ചതിഥിപ്രവരൻ: കുടുംബിനി-	Asked the devout host: Where is thy lady?
യേതിടത്തിങ്കലിരിക്കുന്നു? വസ്ത്യത്തി-	"Nigh by in the house, my Lord," said her man,
ലാണവളെന്നു പ്രത്യൂക്തി ചൊന്നീടവേ-	And the Great One went on thereat to say:
യോതിനാൻ പാന്ഥപ്രമുഖൻ കൃപാകുലൻ: (18:89–96)	
"ആണ്ടൊന്നതീതമാകുമ്പോൾ വരുമഹം	"This time next year I shall come again
വീണ്ടുമിവിടെയപ്പോതു സാറയ്ക്കൊരു	When Sarah shall mother her scion":
പുത്രനുണ്ടാകു" മീവാണി കേട്ടിട്ടവ-	In tickling disbelief a demure protest
ളുദാഹസിച്ചതസാദ്ധ്യമെന്നോതിനാൾ.	Uttered Sarah, resisting the Great Guest
ആഗന്തുകൻ പ്രതിവാകൃമുരച്ചിദം:	Who in dense brevity said in calm command:
യാഹവ്യയ്ക്കുസാദ്ധ്യമല്ലാത്തതില്ലൊന്നുമേ	"Not a thing prevents Yahweh's hand."
തത്വമിതുധരിക്കാതെ സാറാ ചിരി-	This Law yet on her to take hold,
ച്ചുത്തമവാണിയവിശ്വസിച്ചീടിനാൾ. (18:97–104)	Sarah giggled, the perfect divine word,
	Always firm, to her seemed only fancied.
എങ്കിലും വത്സരമൊന്നു കഴിഞ്ഞുഞാൻ	"Yet shall I be seen again after another year's run.
മംഗളധാമമാം നിൻ നികടേ വരും.	At my return to refresh to thee this moment's import
അപ്പോൾ തനയനൊന്നുണ്ടായിരിക്കുമീ-	When behold, Abram, thy wife shall rock an infant son
ത്വത് പത്നിയാൾക്കെന്നു ചൊന്ന പോതായവൾ-	In her bosom, for her maternal joys' famed report."
"നാഹമഹാസിഷ" മെന്നുരച്ചു ഭയാൽ.	Blushing red, chaste fear, Sarah exclaimed,
"മോഹാ ദഹാ സീസ്ത്വ" മെന്നാൻ പഥികനും. (18:105–10)	"I did not laugh" hearing of her own childbearing;
	"Laugh you did," said the traveler, the Man unerring.

Judgment of Sodom

വിഷയവിഷസർപ്പമേ! നിന്നെ വിട്ടോടിടിലും
വിദ്രുതം നീ പാഞ്ഞു ദംശിപ്പൂ മർത്യരേ.
മഹിളയുടെ മനതളിരിലമിത വിഷയാശ താൻ
മാരണഹേതുവായ് മങ്ങിക്കിടക്കുന്നതും.
പ്രിുദയമതിലണുവളവു ലിവ്യുണ്ടെങ്കിലോ
സംയമി താനും സ്ഖലിക്കും സ്വനിഷ്ഠ്രായിൽ.
മുനിയുടെ മനം കരണ്ടൂർധ്വമാക്കീടുന്ന
മൂഷികനത്രേ വിഷയാശ നിർണ്ണയം.
ദഹനനെയശിച്ചിടാം വിസ്താരമേറീടുന്ന
ജലനിധി കുടിച്ചീടാം ക്ഷോണീധരത്തിനെ
ക്കരമതിലെടുത്തിടാം മാനസത്തിൻ യമം
പെരുതുപണി സാധിച്ചു കൊൾവാനസംശയം.
മണലഖിലമെണ്ണിടാം ചണ്ഡവാതങ്ങളെ -
ക്കയറതിൽ നിയന്ത്രിച്ചുകെട്ടിനിർത്തീടലാം,
ഹൃദയ വിഷഭത്തിനെ സ്ംയമിക്കുന്നതിൽ
പെരിയ പണിയെന്തിഹോ! മാനുഷർക്കിബ്ഭുവി.
(19:583–598)

Vishaya's[17] beast, all venom's spring!
Victims flee your speed and sting:
Minds you load with lecherous forms,
And warp their ways by manic norms.
Musings on a maid's mind's move
Welled in, when roused, may killers prove.
Seeping lust, in trace though slight,
May flail and fell ev'n the grave by it.
Vishaya's mouse, in a *muni*'s mind,
A cavern carves by constant grind.
Work enough and one well may
Quench a blaze or the oceans dry;
Roll the globe to a palm-size sphere;
All sea-sands number, or the great gales bind;
The mind takes more, in ways its own,
And humans war with its venom unwon.

നഗരിയതിലതി കുതുക മാർജിച്ചസ്വത്തുക്കൾ
നാരീമതല്ലികയോർത്തനേരം തൃഷാ
പരവശതപെരുകിയവൾ പിന്നോട്ടുനോക്കിനാൾ
പാപഹന്താവിൻ നിദേശമോർക്കാതവൾ.
മനുജരിതുവിധ മഖില ജഗദധിപവാക്കിനു
മാറുപാടായ് പ്രവർത്തിച്ചു നശിക്കുന്നു. (19:599–604)

The wealth amassed in the storied city
From its lure Lot's wife still unfree,
Onward her foot, but fireward her head
The chasing flames she takes in disregard,
As mortals do with what heaven does decree.

Blindness and Chaos over the Cities

അതിഥി ജനഹേളനം ചെയ്വാനൊരുമ്പെട്ട
ചതിയ രമരാഗ്യരിൻ സാധുവാം ശിക്ഷയാൽ

അനുപതി വലഞ്ഞുപോയ് വീട്ടിലെത്താനുള്ള

വഴിയുമറിയാതെയായ് വൈവശ്യമാർന്നിതു.

അഭിലഷിതമണുവളവുമൊത്തതില്ലെങ്കിലും

അദൃവേശ്മ പ്രാപ്തി മാത്രം കൊതിച്ചിതാ
പലവഴി നടക്കുന്നു പാത വിട്ടോടയിൽ. (19:463–69)

The riffraff out to heckle the divines
Earned the dues proper for their smarty schemes.
Direly lost, they bump along where anywhere is nowhere.
The Sodomic night's plans of orgies shunned,
Any help homeward seemed a good enough goal.

---

[17] Libidinal desire or concupiscence.

പലരഥ പതിക്കുന്നു കണ്ണുകാണായ്കയാൽ.	Some, stumbling, fall hither and thither
നിജസരണിയെന്നുറച്ചന്യ ദിക്കിന്നുള്ള	In their blinded shuffling course. Northward heads
പദവിയിൽ നടക്കുന്നിതേ താനുമാളുകൾ.	The southside man, of his purpose cocksure.
ഭവനമതു തെക്കിലാണേകനെന്നാകിലും	One sees his door, but his very next step
തിടമൊടുവടക്കോട്ടു പോകുന്നു ഭോഷനായ്.	Headlong pitches him into the lightless well.
മനമതിലൊരൂഹമുണ്ടെന്നുറച്ചന്യനോ	Another dares the thick, dark night
വസതിയോടടുക്കവേ ചാടിനാനന്ധുവിൽ.	And bumps his face on post and pillar.
അപരനഭിമാനിയാ യാസ്ധ്യ മെന്തെന്നോതി	A deluded churl gets rough-handled
മുഖമതു തകർക്കുന്നൊരത്താണിമേലുടൻ.	For his witless visit in tipsy trespassing.
നിജഭവനമെന്നോർ ത്തൊരന്യവീട്ടിൽ ചെന്ന	
കുരുടനു കിടച്ചേറെ മർദനം നിർദയം. (19:470–80)	
അകിഴുമര മത്താണിയെന്നിവയ്ക്കുള്ളൂക്കു	Beams and barriers took the most bangs
സ്വകമവയവങ്ങളിൽ തട്ടിച്ചു നോക്കിയും	From fisted threats of ranting rogues;
സദനമത്തിലെത്തുവാൻ സാധിച്ചിടാതെയും	Listless they spun, unhomed and lost,
വഴിയിൽ ഗതി ഹീനരായ് നിന്നുപോയേവരും. (19:481–84)	Though not by intent in the least.
ദിവിചരരോടതിവികൃതി ചെയ്‌വാനൊരുമ്പെട്ടു	The foul deeds done to the sons of light
ദൈവ ശിക്ഷക്കു വശംവദരാകയാൽ	Brought them speedy judgment's fright;
വിഗതസുഖസുഹൃദയരവർ വല്ലപാടും ചെന്നു	Wits impaired, like doddering ghosts,
വീട്ടിലെത്തീടുകിൽ ഭാഗ്യമെന്നോർത്തുതേ. (19:485–88)	Sodom's blinded men were blown around.
നിശവളരെയാകവേ നാഥരെക്കാണാഞ്ഞു	The night far spent and their men still out,
നിതുവനരസജ്ഞമാർ നേരേ പുറപ്പെട്ടു	The restive women had their edgy fits;
ഗതനയനരായ് വെറും കുറ്റി പോൽ നിന്നിടും	Out they came, like hustling scouts,
മനുജരെ ഗ്രഹത്തിലേക്കാനയിച്ചാർ ദ്രുതം. (19:489–92)	And dragged home the zombie louts.
ശരണഗത രതിസുഖദ ശയ്യയേറീടിലും	Pleasures indulged as were wont, their beds
ശാന്തമായില്ല മനഃക്ഷോഭമപ്പഴും.	Gave little ease to them; fury raging within
സ്വപ്നമതു കൂടെയും മാറിനിന്നിക്‌ ഖലർ	Repelled all their rest. Sleep seemed to refrain
സ്പൃശ്യരല്ലെന്നുള്ള ചിന്തയാലെന്നപോൽ. (19:493–96)	From Sodom, whose men stood immune to its touch.

Fire and Brimstone over Sodom

ഭയജനകരജനിയിതു വിധമവർ കഴിച്ചിട്ടു	An eerie night of horror thus past,
ഭാനൂദയത്തിലുണർന്നുകൊള്ളുംവിധൗ	At dawn they rose, and lo, torrents
ദുരിത ചയദഹനനുടെ കീലായാൽ ഭൂതലം	Of flames from the sky descend
ചുട്ടുപൊരിച്ചൊരാസോദോംപുരിക്കുമേൽ	With sulphuric powers in relaying charge,
ഗതകരുണ മഖില ജഗധിപതി നഭസ്സിന്നു	Scorching the grounds of Sodom
ഗന്ധകമഗ്നിയും വർഷിച്ചു ഘോരമായ്. (19:497–502)	To a sterile chemical crust of foul stench.

ഗഗനപഥമിതിനുടയ നാന്ദി യായിട്ടഹോ!	Heavens boomed their portending thunder
ഗംഭീര ശബ്ദം മുഴക്കി ഭൂവെങ്ങുമേ.	Of dooming wrath on rankness to render.
ജ്വലനഘന ഘടകളുടെ നടുവിലിടിവാളുകൾ	Fireclouds housing unearthly lightnings
ജാതരോഷംപരന്നാകാശവീഥിയിൽ	Cleave the sky in fiery archings.
പ്രളയമതി ലുയരുന്നൊരു ചണ്ഡവാതങ്ങളും	Storms of fire, like ranges of mounts emerge
പ്രത്യുൽക്രമിച്ചു നിഷ്പ്രത്യൂഹമാം വിധം. (19:503-08)	In doomsday's contest of rage and charge.
നിമിഷസമയം കൊണ്ടു ദിവ്യാശു ശുക്ഷണി	A mere instant is all it took for the vaults
നിർഗളിച്ചംബര ദിക്കിൽ നിന്നക്ഷണം.	Of fire from the sky to break forth, no halts.
വലിയനിലയങ്ങളും വൻമാളികകളും	Great halls, mansions, the estates
വൻപരാം പൗരരിൻ തുംഗനിവാസവും	Of the ruling elite, places of magistrates,
വിപണികളിലതിനിബിഡ മുയരുമുരു ശാലകൾ	Towers of trade as high as Vindhya's peaks,
വിന്ധ്യാദ്രിയോളം കിളർന്നവൻമേടകൾ	Gardens, colonnades, houses of religion, temples,
പ്രപകളൊടു മാനികര മട്ടഭേദങ്ങളും	Palaces, offices of ministers of Kashyapa's school,
പ്രാസാദ സൗധങ്ങൾ വേശ്യാഗൃഹങ്ങളും	Men of knowledge of ancient scrolls
കനകമണിമയനിലയനി ചയനിബിരീസമാം	Distinguished in service, their residences
കാശ്യപീന്ദ്രൻതന്റെ കാന്തോപകര്യയും	In the city's prime sectors and secure enclaves,
വിഷയപരവിഷയശത മതിനിശിതബുദ്ധിയാം	Places privileged, but of wanton ways,
വിജ്ഞാനമുശയിൽ വച്ചുരുക്കിസദാ	And even brothels.
വിഹിതനിജകൃത്യരായ് മന്ത്രികൾപാർക്കുന്ന	
വിസ്താരമേറും വിനോദഹർമ്യങ്ങളും. (19:509-22)	
സ്ഥപതിഗണ മയസിപണി ചെയ്യുവോർ താമ്രികർ	Wood crafters, metalsmiths, braziers, artists, poets,
സ്വർണകാരന്മാർ കുലാലവൃന്ദങ്ങളും	Goldsmiths, shellcrafters, washermen, potters,
രജതനഥ ശാംഖികൻ തന്തുവായൻ ക്ഷുരി	The barber, weaver, violinist, sycophant, magician,
രസിക ജന രത്നമാം ചിത്രകാരൻ കവി	All such guildsmen, and of the intellect, learning's man,
വിരുതുടയ വൈണികൻ മാലികൻ സൗചികൻ	Too many for count or telling, the descended fire consumed.
വിദ്യോപാജീവിയുമായി കുശീലവൻ	
ഇതി ബഹുലതൊഴിലുകളിലേർപ്പെ ട്ടിരുന്നിടു-	
മീദൃക്കുകൾക്കുള്ള ധിഷ്ണ്യോൽ ക്കരങ്ങളും	
പണി പൊരുതുപറയുവതി നഖിലനിലയങ്ങളും	
പാവകൻ ഭസ്മീകരിച്ചുവീഴ്ഞ്ഞിടിനാൻ. (19:523-32)	

The Casting out of Ishmael

The birth of Isaac makes the faultline of mistress–slave power struggle increasingly deeper and permanent. Sarah demands that the Egyptian Hagar and her son Ishmael be sent away from the home. Abraham caves in. The section below is the agonizing conversation between Hagar and her son on their way into the wilderness.

അമ്മേ! എവിടെ നാം പോകുന്നുവെന്നുള്ള	"Mother, where are we going?" Hagar's son
നിർമായമാം പുത്രചോദ്യപത്രം	In innocence queries, a poignant question
യാത്രയാമൃഗപരീക്ഷണ ശാലയിൽ	In earth's harsh school, for ages to ponder:
ലബ്ധമായെങ്കിലും കണ്ണുനീരാൽ	Grief drowned out her verbal answer;
പ്രത്യുക്തി രേഖപ്പെടുത്തുകയാൽ ജയ-	The lad pressed on, when, in choked voice
ലിസ്റ്റിലവൾ പേരുകണ്ടതില്ല.	Said she to him: My child, your other mother and I
വീണ്ടുമനുയോഗിച്ചിടുന്ന ബാലനു	Only have had a home of discord to share, whereby
തൊണ്ടയിടറി ബദൽ കൊടുത്തു:	Much aggrieved, your father reckoned we should fare
കുഞ്ഞേ വിമാതാവും ഞാനും പരസ്പരം	Much better, at places one away from the other;
രഞ്ജനയില്ലാതെ പാർത്തു നിത്യം	Therefore, to that place is our journey on this dawn.
ശണ്ഠ പിണയ്ക്കുന്ന കാഴ്ചയാലോത്യന്ത	Asked the lad again: So, in peace to live, in the space our own,
കുണ്ഠത യുണ്ടായിട്ടച്ഛനിന്നാൾ.	My father will have a dwelling for us two built?
രണ്ടാളും പിരിഞ്ഞു പാർക്കേണമെ-	Hagar answered: The all-worlds' Lord, has a promise spelt
ന്നിങ്ങളോടോതി വിഷണ്ണചിത്തൻ	That He, your father's God, will, have all such cares met.
ആയതു മൂലമകന്നു പാർത്തീടുവാ-	
നാണുനാം പോകുന്നതീയുഷസ്സിൽ.	
ബാലകൻ ചോദ്യമായ്: നമ്മൾക്കു പാർക്കുവാ-	
നാലയം താതനൊരുക്കുമെന്നോ?	
ഹാഗർ പ്രതിവചി: ച്ചങ്ങനെയല്ല സ്വർ-	
ലോകേശനാം നിൻ പിതാവിൻ ദൈവം	
സാനുകമ്പം നമുക്കാലയം നൽകുമെ-	
ന്നാണു പറഞ്ഞതെന്നോടു താതൻ. (21:453–74)	

Isaac's Sacrifice

Abraham is severely tested at many a turn in his life. As he was living happily with his wife and the son of her miraculous birth, God asks Abraham to travel a three-day distance from Beer-sheba[18] to Mt. Moriah and to sacrifice Isaac. This episode is understood as a typological event that foreshadows the voluntary, redemptive, and sacrificial act of Jesus surrendering his life in obedience to the Father in heaven:

ആരോഹണ മവരോഹമിവ മൂലം	Ascents and descents frazzle the comely youth
പാരം തളരുന്ന ചാരുരൂപൻ	As did they, years thousand-twice past,
രണ്ടായിരാമാണ്ടു പിൽപാടു യൂദരിൻ	When the Greater Man, who, bound by Jewish ill will,
ശുണ്ഠി നിമിത്തം നിബദ്ധനായി	Bore the fatal weight of the beams of the wood,
കെണ്ടൻ കുരിശു തൻ തോളിൽ ചുമന്നുകൊ-	On his shoulders, under the scalding sun,
ണ്ടെണ്ടീശ ഭസ്മമാക്കും വെയിലിൽ,	Over the scorched earth: A sweat denser
പണ്ടില്ലാമട്ടിൽ വിയർത്തു വലഞ്ഞതി-	Than any ever before from human pores
കുണ്ഠത തിങ്ങുമുടമ്പിനോടും	Sprang from his body, too minced for godly eyes:
ഇണ്ടലാൽ തൊണ്ടയിടറി മുറയിടും	The holy women witnessing, wail, their throats
വണ്ടാർകുഴലിമാർ കൂട്ടമോടും	Wound-sore, as the Son of the Most High climbing
കണ്ടകൻമാരുടെ മദ്ധ്യേ കൊലമല	The steep heights of the killer's hill,
മണ്ടയിലേക്കു നടന്നുപോകും	Criminals flanking Him along the way,
വിണ്ടലനായകപുത്രനെ, യെന്മന-	The Lord of Life, whose figure, etched on
തണ്ടിലമർന്നിടും തമ്പുരാനെ,	My heart, I see within, refreshed over and over,
വേണ്ടവിധത്തിലനുസ്മരിപ്പിച്ചിടു-ന്നുണ്ടു നിരന്തരദു:ഖദമായ്. (22:173–88)	A grief indelible.
സ്വർലോക ജീവന പീയൂഷ പായികൾ-	To them who drink of the springs of God
ക്കല്ലലുള വാകിലൊന്നിനാലും.	Fear of harm is of concern none.
വാളുകൾക്കൊന്നുമേ ഛേദിപ്പാൻ മേലല്ലോ	Them the sword will sever not,
കാളുന്ന തീയ്ക്കും ദഹിച്ചുകൂടാ.	Nor the raging flame consume;
വെള്ളത്തിനൊട്ടും നനയ്പ്പാൻ കഴിവില്ല	Nor can the tidal depths them contain;
തെല്ലുലർത്തീടില്ല ശുഷ്കവാതം.	And the dry wind's touch is of effect vain.
അച്ഛേദ്യമായു മദാഹ്യമായും പര-	Unseverable, unburnable, unharmable,
മക്ലേദ്യമായു മശോഷ്യമായും	Unwasting, unwithering;
നിത്യമായ് സർവ്വഗതമായ് സ്ഥിരമായി	Eternal, omnipresent, constant,

[18] The southernmost boundary of Israel in biblical times, Beer-sheba is fifty miles south of Jerusalem, which makes Abraham's three-day journey to Mt. Moriah being a justifiable length of time.

വ്യത്യയമന്യേ യചാല്യമായും	Unchanging, unshaken, secure existent—
സംസ്ഥിതി ചെയ്യുന്ന ജീവനാണാത്മിക-	Such is the life the elect of God enjoy.[19]
സത്യവത്തുക്കൾക്കു ലബ്ധമിപ്പോൾ. (22:495–506)	
ഇപ്പാരിതോഷിക ലബ്ധിയാൽ ധന്യനാ-	A child given of such signal favor
മിസ്സഹൻ തന്റെ ബലിമരണം	Isaac, though slain, shall not go counted lost;
നിശ്ശേഷനാശമല്ലെന്നും പുനർജ്ജീവ-	Rather, shall he rise to live anew,
നസ്ഥലായ് പുത്രന്നുകിട്ടുമെന്നും	So resolved, faith's hero, Terah's son,
വിശ്വാസമുള്ളിൽ ലഭിച്ചു തെളികയാൽ	Bound fast his own son as sacred offering
വിശ്വാസവീരൻ തിരഹപുത്രൻ	On the altar and raised the knife whereupon
സ്വയശരീരമുപാകൃതമാക്കീടു—	Came a jolting command from the still horizon:
മേകസുതനെ വരിഞ്ഞുകെട്ടി	
അധ്വരവേദിയിൽ വച്ചിട്ടറുക്കുവാൻ	
കത്തിയെടുത്തു പിടിച്ചുടനേ	
ഉച്ചൈസ്രമായ ശബ്ദമൊന്നുണ്ടായി	
സ്വച്ഛ വിഹായ പഥത്തിലപ്പോൾ. (22:507–18)	
അബ്രഹാം കേട്ടു തിരിഞ്ഞോരു വേളയിൽ	Abraham turned around, startled, behold,
ശുഭ്രാംഗനാമൊരുദൂതനോതി:	Bright clad appeared an angel with this word:
പുത്രനെ യാതൊന്നും ചെയ്യരുതിത്രയും	"Stay the knife! Spare the lad! The bidden deed
മാത്രമേ വേണ്ടു; ഭവമനസ്സിൽ	Is deemed done, for thy heart and its devout thought
ശ്രദ്ധയും ഭക്തിയും വ്യക്തമായിട്ടു ഞാ-	Are by this thy deed made full evident."
നിത്തവ്വിൽ ബോധ്യപ്പെടും വിധമായ്. (22:519–24)	
സന്താന ശൂന്യത ലേശം ഗണിക്കാതെ-	"At my word, thy sole child's loss
യെൻ തോഷമാത്രസ്പൃഹ നിമിത്തം	Was to thee sheer faith's repose,
നീകഴിപ്പാനായ് തുടങ്ങിയൊരിബ്ബലി	As bespeaks this deed. Blood willed,
സാകൂതമംഗീകരിച്ചുകൊണ്ടേൻ. (22:525–28)	Blessing bestowed, I accept as blood spilled."
ഭക്താഗ്രഗണ്യനും കൃത്യനിരതനും	Foremost as faithful and duteous in conduct,
ത്യക്ത വിഷയ സ്പൃഹനുമായ	Abraham, of all sensual lures renunciant,
അബ്രഹാമിശബ്ദം പുത്രവിമോക്ഷത്താ-	Received the voice heard, with greater delight
ലുൾപ്രമോദപ്രദ മെന്നതേക്കാൾ	Than with his son's recall; though sweet, that gift

---

[19] These attributes in serial parallelism will yield greater rhythmic impact if the original words of the poem are used in the translation. Words like *ashcedya* (unseverable), *adahya* (inconsumable), *akledya* (unhurtable), *ashoshya* (imperishable), *nitya* (eternal), *sarva-gatha* (omnipresent), *achalya* (immovable), *avyatyaya* (unchanging), or *stira* (permanent) are frequently used for their high functional value in Indian philosophy or poetry. The prefix "*a*" that marks most of the terms here are widely employed both in Sanskrit and the other Indian languages, just as they appear in Greek usage.

യാഹ്‌വയിൻ സമർപ്പണത്തിന്നു പ്ര-	Was only an obstacle to the assumed measure
ത്യൂഹമായത്രേ ഗണിച്ചതുള്ളിൽ. (22:529–34)	Of the fulness of worship for Yahweh pleasure.
ഏവം നിരുദ്ധമനാകുമബ്രഹാം	Under a command of such severe wonder
കൈവന്ന വാഞ്‌ഛരാ വിഹതി മൂലം	Abraham stood in dread with hardly the power
താപമനസ്സോടു പിന്നിൽ നോക്കീടവേ	To move; then, a quick crackle in the nigh thicket
മേഷമൊന്നുണ്ടൊരു വള്ളിതന്നിൽ	Drew him instantly to the struggling sight
കൊമ്പു കുരുങ്ങിക്കിടക്കുന്നു സന്തോഷ-	Of a lamb, of all things a lamb, caught
സംഭ്രമത്തോടവിടെത്തിയബ്രാം	In the tangling bush: swiftly he freed
ആടിനെ മോചിച്ചു കൊണ്ടുവന്നദ്ധ്വര-	The squiggling animal, and in grateful surprise
വേദിയിൽ വച്ചു ബലികഴിച്ചു. (22:538–44)	Sacrificed it, on Isaac's altar, and in his place.
കുത്രാസ്തി മേഷമെന്നോമൽ കുമാരക-	For his son's curious but credulous mind,
ന്നുധ്യാവിൽ വച്ചനുയോഗിക്കുമ്പോൾ	Abraham's word was of the sufficing kind.
അസ്മൽകുലദൈവം സന്നദ്ധമാക്കുമെ-	"Father, where is the sheep for the altar?" asked the son.
ന്നസ്മയമോതിയ നൈജവാക്യം	Replied the parent: "Our God will provide one."
സാഫല്യവത്തായി അത്തിരുകമൂലമാ-	That word, inspired, and forthwith fulfilled
യാശിഖരിക്കവൻ "യാ" ധരത്തിൽ	On the hallowed ground, Abraham named
കാണപ്പെടു മിദമർത്ഥമിയലുന്ന	"Yahweh Jireh," for the "Provider Lord" thence famed.
"യാഹ്‌വെയിരേ"യെന്നു പേർകൊടുത്തു. (22:545–52)	

Jacob's Years in Paddan Aram

Love's Labors Lost—and Won

Jacob the son of Isaac travels to Paddan Aram in Mesopotamia where his maternal uncle Laban lives. The purpose of his long journey of possibly a month is for him to find a bride from his own people. Laban has two daughters, Leah and Rachel. Leah lacks beauty and is not desired. Rachel is lively and attractive. Jacob falls in love with Rachel right at first sight. Laban is happy to give Jacob his daughter, but not without a bride price assessed in terms of seven years of labor. Jacob agrees. When seven years pass, Jacob is tricked into taking Leah as the bride with the cultural excuse that the younger daughter can be given in marriage only after the older one has been. Jacob is now given the sour incentive of another seven-year term of service for Rachel, which he still willingly does. Genesis 29–31 narrates Jacob's life of twenty years in Laban's household. Here is Laban's initial conversation with Jacob on the terms of service:

മാമക ഭാഗിനേയാ! നിന്നുടെ ചര്യ മൂലം	My nephew, mine own blood, your service
കേമമാം സന്തോഷമുണ്ടെനിക്കു മനക്കാമ്പിൽ	Gives me reason plenty to rejoice:
എങ്കിലും നിർവേതന സേവനം ധനികനാ-	Nonetheless, to serve a man of no small wealth,
മെങ്കലൊട്ടപഹർഷഹേതുവായ് തീരുന്നില്ലേ? (29:89–92)	Hush about wages, wouldn't hearers it loathe?
ആയതു നിമിത്തം നീ വ്യർത്ഥമായ് സേവിക്കേണ്ട	Therefore, think not your work goes void of pay;
മായമെന്നിയേ വേണ്ട വേതനമുരച്ചാലും.	Name your price, dawdle not, nor say nay.
നിഷ്പ്രതിഫലകർമ്മംചെയ്യിക്കും പുരുഷനെ	Usurping one's worker's sweat, a revolting thought,
യിപ്പൃഥ്വി തന്നിലാരും നിന്ദിക്കുമെന്നംശയം. (29:89–96)	Draws contempt from all the world over, no doubt.
എന്നതുകേട്ട നേരമിസ്സഹാത്മജനുള്ളിൽ	Hearing this, the son of Isaac, began to gloat
ധന്യോഽഹ മിതി നിനച്ചീവിധമാലോചിച്ചു:	Over the good turn of his course in the foreign lot:
എന്നുടെ വരവിപ്പോൾ ഫലിച്ചു മാമാത്രുക്തിയാൽ	My mother was right on the mark, see now,
കന്നൽനേർ മിഴിയാളാമൊരുത്തി തന്നെ വേൾപ്പാൻ	A bride of my dreams does this sojourn bestow;
തന്നെയാണല്ലോ പണിപ്പെട്ടു വന്നതിദ്ദിക്കിൽ	All else pales, vying in Rachel's glow.
പിന്നെയുള്ളൊരു കാര്യമതിന്നു താഴെയല്ലോ. (29:97–102)	
അതിനാൽ രൂപവതിയായ രാഹേലിനെ	Therefore, fairest be my wages, forget silver or gold,
വേതനമാക്കിസ്സേവ ചെയ്തിടാമിവനിഹ	The lone gem of Aram, Rachel, mine own to hold;
ജേഷ്യായാം ലേയാവെന്ന കന്യക വൈരൂപ്യത്തിൽ	Leah, the older, by looks less desired,
ജേഷ്ഠ്റായ്ക്കു സമാനയായ് കാണുന്നൂ തന്നിമിത്തം. (29:103–06)	Be as older kin, and only so, esteemed.
ക്ലിന്നാക്ഷിയാകുമവൾ തന്നെ ഞാൻ സ്വീകരിക്കി-	I repeat, said Jacob: I shall by no means take Leah
ല്ലബ് ജലോചനയായ രാഹില മാത്രം പോരും.	The watery-eyed; give me the lotus-eyed Rahila!
മാനസതാരിലേവം ചിന്തിച്ചു രസജ്ഞനാം	Said he, musing within himself. Have me labor-bound,
മാനവൻ യാക്കോബിത്ഥമുരച്ചു ലാബാനോടേ:	For flock or fields, O kinsman, seven years round,
നിന്നുടെ മകളായ രാഹിലക്കായി നിന്നേ	In servitude, for your younger daughter
ചിന്തയന്യേയേഴു സംവത്സരം സേവിക്കാം ഞാൻ. (29:107–12)	For whose sprightly self, no price is burden's matter.

ചൊന്നുടൻ ലാബാൻ, നന്നു! കുഞ്ഞേ! മറ്റൊരുവന-	And Laban said: What more would I want, my child!
കന്യയെ കൊടുപ്പതിൽ നല്ലതായതു തന്നെ.	Much rather I that you take my virgin daughter
ഇത്രയും കേട്ട പോതു ശ്രവണാമൃതത്താൽ	Than some stranger. Laban's words, fell like nectar drops
ദിഗ്ദ്ദമായ് തീർന്നു, ഭംഗ്യാ സേവയുമാരംഭിച്ചു. (29:113–16)	On Jacob's ears and thus began the service of romance.
എന്തുവേണമെങ്കിലും ചെയ്യുമായവൻ മടി	Give him any task, no displeasure shows;
ചിന്തയിൽ പോലുമില്ല സേവനചികീർഷയാൽ.	The harder the work, the merrier he goes.
രാവിലെയെഴുന്നീറ്റാൽ സന്ധ്യായാവോളം ജോലി-	From dawn to dusk, ran bone-crushing chores
യാവതിലധികമായി ചെയ്തീടുമത്രയല്ല	Of the homestead or further outdoors.
രാവിലും വല്ല കൃത്യമേകുകിലതുനിജ	Sunset or night was not the day's end
ഭാവുകനിതാനമായ് ഗണിച്ചു നിർവഹിക്കും. (29:117–22)	Nor of his on-call labor, errand on errand.
വിശപ്പു ദാഹങ്ങളെ സഹിച്ചും മധുരിമ	To pangs of hunger and to parching palate
കശപ്പു ശീതമുഷ്ണ മിത്യാദി വിഗണിച്ചും	He said, hold on; sweet or bitter, so be it;
അരയിൽ പഴന്തുണി നിയതം ചാർത്തിക്കൊണ്ടും	A rag for his waist was his field attire;
ദുരയിൻ വിളനിലമായ തൻ സ്വാമിയുടെ	A rogue his master, whose undying desire
കരകാണാതെയുള്ള കാമിത സമുദ്രത്തേ-	For the shoreless sea of riches this obliging servant
അരണം ചെയ്താൻ നിത്യം കൃത്യമാമുഡുപത്താൽ. (29:123–28)	Was the acquirer, to his commands compliant.
രാഹില തന്റെ കാര്യമോർക്കുമ്പോൾ ലാബാന്റെ	A mere thought or glimpse of Rahila
ദാസദാസനാകിലും ഭാഗ്യമെന്നുരച്ചവൻ	Made the term of toil a mere note in love's law
മാതുലഭാര്യതന്റെ ശിരസ്സിൽ ചൊരിയുന്ന	Should it make him even Laban's servant's servant.
പൂതിഗന്ധിയുള്ള കടുവാക്കുകളെല്ലാം	The horrid tongue of his wife and its stench of no relent,
സ്വർലോകത്തിൽനിന്നു ചൊരിയും പൂമഴയ്ക്കു	Again, took he in rather for floral showers
തുല്യമായെണ്ണിത്തന്നെ നയിച്ചാൻ ദിവസങ്ങൾ. (29:129–34)	From heaven against Aram's bondage powers.
ഇങ്ങനെയേഴു കൊല്ലം കഴിച്ചു ബഹുദുഃഖം	Thus spent he all seven years, affliction
തിങ്ങിയാദൃശ്യവൃത്തി സന്തോഷമായിത്തന്നെ.	Not abating, but in maturing affection.
അല്കാലമായ് തോന്നീ യാക്കൂബന്നാക്കൊല്ലങ്ങ-	Like a pleasant dream time's course spanned
ളുൽപ്പലാക്ഷിതൻ പാണി ഗ്രഹണ പ്രലോഭനാൽ. (29:135–38)	For its winning end was the promised bridal hand.
പ്രേമമേ നിന്നുടയ വശ്യശക്തിയിൽപ്പെടാ-	Oh Love, lives there a giant of wisdom or wit,
ബ്ദ്ധീ മഹാബുദ്ധികളാരാണുള്ളതു ചിന്തിക്കുകിൽ!	Your spell or sway anywhere to discomfit?
നിൻമൂലം കഠിനമാം കഷ്ടവും സൗഖ്യമായി	You make travail seem bliss, and truly so;
ട്ടുൺമയി തോന്നും; ദീർഘവർഷങ്ങൾ ദിനങ്ങളാം. (29:139–42)	The long trail of years, but mere days, free of woe.

Jacob's Departure from Paddan Aram

Laban continues to shortchange Jacob while his family with two wives and two concubines grows with many childbirths. Taking advantage of Laban's absence from home, Jacob leaves Aram with his wives, maids, and children.

എങ്ങു ഭർത്താവിന്റെപാദം ചരിക്കുന്നി-	Whither falls the man's foot on his course
തങ്ങുതന്നെ ഭരണീയമാർക്കും ഗതി.	Thither goes the woman's too, in polite pace.
ചന്ദ്രനെവിട്ടു പിരികില്ല ചന്ദ്രികാ;	No way is her lent light shunned by the moon
ചന്ദനത്തെയുപേക്ഷിക്കാ സുഗന്ധവും. (31:123–26)	Nor is the fragrance from the *chandan* gone.
ലാബനീ വാക്കുകൾ കേട്ടൊരു മാത്രയി-	Like the outplayed charmer whose prized snake
ലാവിലചിത്തനായ് കർത്തവ്യമൂഢനായ്	Made off in one slick slithering act,
പാമ്പു പോയൊരു പാമ്പാട്ടി പോൽബഹു-	Laban stood dazed, told of the jolting fact,
സംഭ്രമം പൂണ്ടങ്ങുഴന്നു തുടങ്ങിനാൻ. (31:207–10)	Beaten at his own game, the Aramean rake!.

Jacob's Wrestle with the Angel at Jabbok[20]

Though dubious in his conduct, Jacob's life shows many private scenes of profound spirituality. At Jabbok, Jacob sends his large family and livestock across the ford, wary about this powerful brother's announced approach toward him. He is left alone in the dark when an unknown person, later recognized as an angel, takes him on in a wrestle. Amazingly, the angel is in the grip of Jacob who would not release him except by granting him a blessing. The angel does bless him, but also changes his name from Jacob to Israel. Genesis 32 provides the full account of the encounter.

രജനി മുക്കാലുമിവ്വണ്ണം പോയിട്ടും	Most of the night in such tussle spent,
വിജിതനായില്ല നരൻ സുരാഗ്രനാൽ	The frail man prevailed, and wouldn't relent;
ജയമസാധ്യമെന്നൊടുവിൽ കണ്ടുതൻ	In the perplexing bout of wrestlers unequal,
ഭുജാഹതികൊണ്ടു യകൂബവങ്ക്ഷണം	A blow in the dark came from the celestial,
അവശമാക്കിയ നിമിഷം യാകുബൻ	A "touch" that struck Jacob's thigh's sinew,
വിബുധനെച്ചുറ്റി പ്പിടിച്ചു കൈകളാൽ.	Too quick and strong for a defensive swerve.
അടവിമധ്യത്തിൽ കൊടുലതകളാൽ	Strength-sapp'd slid he, the underdog,
ജടിലമായുള്ള നിബന്ധനം തന്നിൽ	Yet not of strength void to keep in hold

---

[20] One of the streams east of Jordan which originates in the mountains of Gilead and flows into the Jordan. Of the multiple meanings of the term "Jabbok," an important one is "wrestling."

ഇറങ്ങിമാറുവാൻ കഴിവുതെല്ലന്യേ	The *asura*,[21] and to his feet tearfully clinging,
കുഴങ്ങി നിൽക്കുന്നോ രജപോതം പോലെ	Hemming him in the woodsy foliage
യകുബക ഭുജാലതാ വലയത്തിൽ	Like a lamb caught within a crevice.
വികുണ്ഠിതാശനായ് നിലകൊണ്ടാൻ സുരൻ. (32:265–76)	
ഉഷസ്സുദിക്കുന്നു വിടുകനീയെന്നെ	"It's daybreak: let me leave, O, man upright
ദ്വിഷദ്ഗണ വന്ദഹന്ദാവ! നീ.	And foe to evil!" the Lord, of Isaac's son did entreat,
സുപർവാവീവണ്ണ മുരച്ചനേരത്തു	Who, without taking the least umbrage
വിഗർവമോതിനാ നിസഹകാത്മജൻ:	At the roughing from the greater hands' usage,
പ്രകൃത്യതീതമാം കരാവമർദത്താൽ	Answered: "O, Lord, thou, the essence of effulgence,
വികർത്തനാഭനാം ഭവാ നിദ്ദാസനെ	By thy disabling touch of my limbs' defense,
മമോരുസന്ധിയിൽ പ്രതിഹനിക്കയാ-	Without doubt, have hurt into wholeness thy servant,
ലമായമാളറിഞ്ഞ ഭിവന്ദിക്കുന്നേൻ. (32:277–84)	He sees thee now as he must, in wonderment."
അമോഘമാകിയ നിജവചനത്താൽ	Thou who by thy Word of good effect
തമോഘടയുടെ നിരസനം പുരാ	The fortress of darkness demolished
നിവൃത്തിച്ചെങ്ങുമേ വെളിച്ചമേകിയ	And brought the reign of light in place,
സുവൃത്തനാം ജഗത് പ്രഭോ! നമസ്കാരം.	Oh, World-ruler, receive my praise.
പ്രളയ വെള്ളത്തിൻ നടുവിലെത്രയും	In the midst of the original waters
ലളിതമായൊരു വിതാനവിസ്തൃതി	Thou, who spread a firmament vast
യുളവാക്കിട്ടതു സുവാതപൂരിത	And filled it with all beneficent airs,
നിലയമാക്കിയ വിഭോ! നമസ്കാരം. (32:285–92)	Of such splendor's author, receive my praise.
നയനമോഹനപദാർഥ ജാലത്താ—	Of those that journey in the distant lands
ലയനം ചെയ്യുവോർക്കമന്ദ സമ്മദം	Of exceeding visual feasts of exuberance
അരുളിടും സ്ഥലം ജലമിവ പുരാ	Over regions of waters and shores,
പിരിച്ചതിർവച്ച വിഭോ! നമസ്കാരം.	Maker Mighty, of borders to them, receive my praise.
കറുത്ത പട്ടൊന്നു വിരിച്ചതിൻ മീതേ	Eye-filling spread of the nightly silk
നറും വെണ്മുത്തുകൾ നിരത്തിയ മട്ടിൽ	Where the twinklers display a path of milk
ഭഗണ ജാലത്താൽ തിളങ്ങി ശോഭിക്കും	Of lavish vastness for each one's race:
ഗഗനം സൃഷ്ടിച്ച വിഭോ! നമസ്കാരം. (32:293–300)	Their Maker Thou, receive my praise.
മകരമത്സ്യാദി ജലചരങ്ങളും	The whale, the fish, and hosts of the deep,
ഗരുഡ പക്ഷ്യാദി നഭചരങ്ങളും	The eagle and the lovers of the airy leap,

---

[21] A divine being. "Sura" becomes "asura" with the prefix "a," meaning, a mortal.

നിയതം നിർമ്മിച്ചു നഭസ്സുമബ്ധിയും	Each in order in the sky and the sea,
പ്രിയതമാക്കിയ വിഭോ! നമസ്കാരം.	All pleasant, their Maker mighty, my praise receive.
മൃഗത്തെ നിർമൃതി കഴിച്ചതിൻ പിൻപൂ	Before the days of the blood-shed altar,
ജഗത്ര്യധിപരായ് മനുഷ്യവർഗത്തെ	Thou who made humans a ruling race,
അഗണ്യതേജസ്സാ വിരചിച്ചുള്ളോരു	Grantees of a better world's grace:
ഖഗ നിഷേവിത! വിഭോ! നമസ്കാരം.	O Thou, of the celestials served! Receive my praise.
അടിയനജ്ഞത നിമിത്തമങ്ങയോ-	A cloddish head prompted my scuffle
ടടർക്കു ഭാവിച്ചേൻ, പൊറുക്കതു ഭവാൻ;	With thee, my Lord, forgive my folly.
ഇരുളിലങ്ങിങ്ങു ചരിച്ചിടും മർത്യൻ	Who by habit takes the night cover route,
ഗുരുവിൻ കാലിലും ചവിട്ടും മൂഢനായ്. (32:301–12)	Well might he trample even the guru's foot.
ഇതര പാപങ്ങൾ ബഹുലമായെന്നെ	Great are my sins of distressing count,
വിതത ദുഃഖത്തിലമഴ്ത്തുന്നിപ്പോഴും.	In drowning grief they immerse me still;
അതുസകലവും ക്ഷമിച്ചു കാക്കണേ	Erase them I pray, by thine amnesty kill
വിദൂരണമെന്നേ ദയാപയോനിധേ! (32:313–16)	All their springs, thou of mercy's full font.
മമഭുജം വിട്ടു വിമുക്തനാകുവാ-	To be free of my grappling hold,
നമരവര്യാ! നീയഭിലഷിക്കുന്നു.	O Immortal One, I'm by thy plea told.
ശരി, യതെങ്കിലു മടിയനിലാശി-	Fair though this call, I make bold to say
സ്സരുളിടാതങ്ങേ വിടുകയില്ല ഞാൻ. (32:317–20)	Bless me first, or as my hostage stay.
ഇതുപറഞ്ഞ പോതമര ബന്ധനം	Barely let he his lips this resolve sound,
പുതുകി വർദ്ധിച്ച വിധത്തിലായിതു.	The angelic hold all the stronger seemed.
മുറുകി ചുറ്റിലു മയോവലയം പോ-	Wound all around like an iron bond
ലിരുകിലേഖനുമതിൻ നടുവിലായ്. (32:321–24)	The Divine One stood in the circle bound.
പദാപഹാരി തൻ ഭുജാനിബന്ധത്തേ	This supplanter's hold is not undone
വൃഥാവിലാക്കുവാ നമരനും കൂടാ.	Even by immortals. All the same,
മനുഷ്യക്കൈകളും മഹേശവിശ്വാസാൽ	Mortal arms by faith in the Great name
മനുഷ്യദുർല്ലഭ ബലം ലഭിക്കുന്നു. (32:325–28)	Can power gain, power in the flesh not common.
അനുഗ്രഹിക്കുവനതിന്നു മുൻപൊരു	Blessed shall you be as sought, first though
സുനാമധേയം ഞാൻതരുന്നുപുത്തനായ്.	To thee a new name must I bestow
യകൂബനെന്നുള്ള പഴയ പേരിനി	And discard the Jacob of old: for on earth
വിഗളിതമായി ബ്ഭവിക്കേണം ഭുവി	Have you with heaven wrestled and prevailed
സുരനരനൊടു ജയിച്ചു കൊൾകയാൽ	Over the divine One. Go now, henceforth hailed,
തരുന്നുഞാനിസ്രലീതി തവാഭിധ്യാ. (32:333–38)	A prince, Israel, the chosen of God.

Rape and Revenge at Shechem

When Jacob had settled in Shechem, his only daughter Dinah went about the city, socializing, and attracted the attention of the prince of Shechem. He wanted her to be his own, then and there. Shechem violated her, but was ready to make up for the offense by marrying her with his father's blessing. The sons of Jacob, however, were too incensed at the disgrace their sister suffered, and slaughtered all the men of that city. Genesis 34 describes the violent episode.

ശോണാധരമവൻ കണ്ടൊരുമാത്രയിൽ	The instant glimpse of her crimson lips
തൂണുപോൽ നിന്നു പോയ് വിസ്മയത്താൽ.	Dazed him, and stood he like a pilaster.
ഉത്തുംഗമാം കുജയുഗ്മം നിമിത്തമാ-	The virgin's high, heaving breasts, did the rest,
മത്തൻ വിചിത്രതയാർന്നനല്പം	Adding fresh frenzy to his wonder. Passion, powered,
കാറൊളി കൂന്തൽ വനത്തിലൊളിക്കുവാൻ	All sentience and reason left the hot blooded youth,
കുറുവളരെ വളർന്നു ഹൃത്തിൽ.	Except for the beastly musth to hide himself
പൊൻ നിറമാണ്ടുള്ള മേനിയിൽ തന്നുട-	In the dense forest of her dark tresses.
ലൊന്നുരസ്സീടുകിൽ ഭാഗ്യമെന്നു	No greater bliss than for her golden skin
തന്നുള്ളിൽ നിശ്ചയം ചെയ്തു ബലാൽ കന്യ	On his own was there to seek: in a lightning spin,
തന്നെയണച്ചു പുണർന്നു ശേഖോം. (34:85–94)	Dinah stood, captive, in Shechem's amorous hold.
അത്ഭുതമത്ഭുതം കാമലോഭങ്ങളേ!	Heavens above! Wealth and women folk!
സ്വല്പമല്ലാതവ ശക്തി ഭൂമൗ.	Powers none too small in you evoke.
ഇശ്ശ്വാസനിവൃത്തിക്കു വേണ്ടി സ്വകാംഗത്തെ	Too ready you stand to serve a lust,
വിഛേദിപ്പാനും മടിക്കാ നിങ്ങൾ. (34:165–68)	Even severing a member, if you must.

Joseph's Prayer in the Pit

Vedaviharam has many prayers in it—some by the omniscient narrator and the others by the characters in the epic. Joseph, the favorite child of Jacob, is a deeply spiritual person, endowed with the gift of prophetic dreams and the ability to interpret them. He gains the largest narrative portion in the book, running from chapters 37 to 50. Below is a small portion of his heart-rending prayer as a destitute cast into a dry well with no hope of rescue.

ദീനസന്ത്രാണയ്ക്കാർത്ഥ നിരതനാകും മമ	O kindly heart, on thy grieving ones for ever intent
മാനസവേദി മീതേ വിളങ്ങും സർവ്വേശ്വരാ!	The Almighty who my mind illumes, in my soul effulgent,

സോദരപരിത്യക്തനായി മറ്റൊരു സാഹ്യ-	Of kin betrayed and of all earth's comfort bereft
മീധരണിയിലില്ലാതുള്ളോരീ സാധുവിൻമേൽ	I lie, in piteous state, unremembered and unsought left,
കാരുണ്യാംബുധേ! തവകടാക്ഷം പതിപ്പിക്ക;	Unclaimed by any memory; in thy tidal mercy
ചാരുവാം നിന്റെ ദിവ്യ വെളിച്ചം ശോഭിപ്പിക്ക.	Cast a glance and rest thine eye on me fondly;
ഘോരമാമാപത്തിന്റെ വഴുതൽ പ്രദേശത്തും	Thou art to me, Oh, sole love, the staying pole,
സാരമാമൂന്നുകോലായ് നിൽക്കുന്നുചിൽകാതൽനീ	On the perilous grounds of slippery steps, the control,
അന്ധകാരത്തിൽ വിദ്യുത്പ്രദീപം; പുഷ്ടിനൽകു-	The guiding light in the dark, nourisher in hunger;
മന്തസ്സുദാരിദ്ര്യത്തിൻ പരയാംകോടിതന്നിൽ.	Wisdom in my folly; honor in the direst of penury,
സുജ്ഞാനമജ്ഞാനത്തിൽ; ജീവാതുമരണത്തിൽ;	The substance of *prajnan*,[22] what would thou NOT for me be?
പ്രജ്ഞാനസ്വരൂപീ നീയെന്തിനിക്കല്ലാതുള്ളൂ! (37:259-70)	

Here is a verbal snapshot of Joseph in the Egyptian prison before the pharaoh commands his release for presentation before him:

ദീർഘ നിശ്വാസ ഹേതുവാൽചുണ്ടുകൾ	Sigh blown years have dried up his lips;
പാക്കുണക്കി നറുക്കിയമട്ടിലായ്.	Seasoned seem they like arecnut chips
നെഞ്ചുകഷ്ഠമേ കൂടുകുത്തീട്ടതി-	That tropical people chew. The youthful chest
ലഞ്ചിടങ്ങഴിവെള്ളം പകർന്നിടാം.	Once of rounded mounds, is now a bony nest
കുക്ഷിയാകവേയൊട്ടി ക്ഷുധാധ്യയാം	In parched cover. Withered muscles, too shrunk
ഭിക്ഷുകി തന്റെ ഭിക്ഷാവപനം പോൽ	For the skin to hold, into the hollows sunk,
ഏറ്റവും കുഴഞ്ഞല്ലോ വിളങ്ങുന്നു	Five-quart deep. Hunger regular in the prison hole
പാറ്റിടുന്നുണ്ടതു മുപവാസത്താൽ. (41:95-102)	Depressed his stomach into a begging bowl.

Patriarch Jacob Meets with the Pharaoh

With the interpretation of a set of dreams, prisoner Joseph rises from the status of Hebrew slave to the premier of Egypt. A famine is raging all over Egypt and the surrounding countries. Joseph's entire, extended household, also victims of the raging famine across nations, arrives in Egypt. Jacob, their father, is one hundred and thirty years old. The pharaoh accords him an audience upon arrival. The two great men converse. Jacob's life of vastly tested experience shows him as a wise man worthy of a king's attention.

---

[22] Sans, for the purest form of wisdom.

ശുക്ലശിരോഹശ്മശ്രു-വാകും	Jacob the hoary haired patriarch,
യാക്കോബു മപ്പറവോനും	And Pharaoh, Egypt's exalted monarch
ആരോഹണം ചെയ്തിരുന്ന മഹാ-	Assumed their grand seats, face to face
കാരമാംപീഠങ്ങൾ രണ്ടും	In majesty exceeding and grace:
പുണ്യഫലസ്ഥാനഭൂവിൻ വട-	Like the two towering mounts
ക്കന്ന്യാദൃശ ഭംഗിചിന്തി	Of Anti-Lebanon, Hermon and Nebo,
രാജിക്കു മാൻറിലബനാ-ദ്രിയിൽ	In God-given glory's glow
ഭ്രാജിക്കും ശൃംഗങ്ങളാകും	Poised to converse:
ഹെർമ്മണും നെബോയുംപോലേ—ദൃശി	
ശർമദമായി വിളങ്ങി. (47:97–106)	

ഏതാൻക്ഷണം നിലനിന്ന—മൗന	A few moments passed solemnly quiet,
ഭാവമാം ഗൗരവമുദ്ര	An unhasting gesture of accented respect;
ഭഞ്ജിച്ചു വൃദ്ധനോടേവം—നൃപൻ	And the sovereign in gracious voice
മഞ്ജുവാം വാക്കിലുരച്ചാൻ:	Thus spoke first:
ലോകേശ്വരൻ തന്റെ യാശി-	By your blissful birth this earth
സ്സങ്ങേക്കേറെയുണ്ടാകയാലല്ലോ	Has become space of hallowed worth:
ഭ്രാഘീയസ്സായൊരീയായു-സ്ത്രീനാൽ	Years how many, if ask I may,
ശ്ലാഘിതനായതു പാർത്താൽ.	Has it been, if it pleases you to say?
ഭാവത്കമായ ജനനം—കൊണ്ടു	
ഭൂവിനെപ്പിവനമാക്കി	
എത്രവർഷങ്ങളായിപ്പോ—ഒന്ന	
ങ്ങുക്തിചെയ്വാൻ കൊതിക്കുന്നേൻ. (47:107–18)	

യാക്കോബുരച്ചു: "നെടുതാമായു—	Jacob said: length of days fares
സ്സേറ്റം കുറുതെന്നപോലെ	None better than its reverse
ശ്യാഘ്യമായ് തോന്നുവാനില്ല—അതു	Little differ the two—for aches
ദുഃഖാഭിഭൂതമാണോർക്കിൽ. (47:119–22)	Come with both, whichever one takes.

ജാതമാകും സമയത്തേ—ക്രന്ദം	The yowl of the moment of birth
ഭീതിദമാകും മൃതിയോളം	Grows and prevails only till death,
ബാധിച്ചിടുന്നു മനുഷ്യാ—യുസ്സി-	Like an ailment bound only to grow
ങ്ങാതുരമാക്കിടും മട്ടിൽ. (47:123–25)	Until any further it can't go.

ആഹാരം നേടുവാൻതന്നേ—നര	Just to find his food alone, suffers
നൂഹാതിഗമായ ദുഃഖം	One, a toil beyond telling;
രാപകലങ്ങുസഹിച്ചീ—ടുന്നു	Day and night it persists
ശാപപരിഗ്രസ്തർ പോലേ. (47:127–30)	As by curses binding.

അമ്മ തൻപാലും കുടിച്ചീ—ടുവാ	Even against the suckling infant,
നമ്പോ! ശിശുവിനുംകൂടി	Dear me, prevails a law hard-set

തൻവാ പിളർന്നുകരഞ്ഞീ—ടുക	That his pangs must first precede
ധർമ്മായ് ക്കാണുന്നു ഭൂവിൽ. (47:131–34)	Before served is the nourishment.
ദേഹസംരക്ഷണം ചെയ്വാൻ-പര	Strive to fortify the body—
മീഹയോടുദ്യുമിച്ചാലും	And at it duly earnest be,
രോഗമാകും പെരുംകാറ്റാ—	Gales of distemper
ലതു ഭീകരമാം വിധംവീഴും. (47:135–38)	Shall fell it sooner or later.
അല്ലെങ്കിൽ ജർജ്ജരമായി—ട്ടുടൽ	If not, the wasting crawl of age
പുല്ലെന്നപോൽ ഭ്രവിച്ചിടും	The body's withering will upstage;
എല്ലാവിധത്തിലും ദുഃഖം—നരർ	Sorrows pervade wherever sojourn
ക്കുള്ളോരു ജീവിതം രാജൻ! (47:139–42)	On earth, mortals, Oh, Sovereign!
ആശകളോരോന്നക്കക്കാ—മ്പതിൽ	When desire drives us by its dictates
പേശലമായ് മുളയ്ക്കുമ്പോൾ	We strive to meet them one by one;
ആയതിൽ സിദ്ധിവരുത്തി—സ്സുഖം	Never does it cease nor lets us rest
മായമന്യേ ലഭിച്ചീടാൻ	Though we think our dues were met.
കായവാങ്മാനസം മൂന്നി—നാലു	Rather, we learn that it behooves us well
മായപോലുദ്യമിക്കുന്നോർ	That a new trial lurks around the bend
ഇച്ഛാനിവൃത്തിയാലുള്ള—സുഖ	With scarce any chance of settled comfort.
സ്വച്ഛതമാർജനം ചെയ്വാൻ	
തക്കതാംമട്ടിൽ ഞെരുക്കം—വിഷ	
ഹിക്കേണ്ടതായ് വരുമല്ലോ. (47:143–52)	
ചണ്ഡമരുത്തിനാലോടും—മേഘ	As in gale the cumulus clouds
പിണ്ഡമെന്നോണം പറന്നു	Flee from sight in withering shreds
മാഞ്ഞു മറഞ്ഞു പോകുന്നു—മന—	So go dreams that us besiege,
മാഞ്ഞതും വൃർത്ഥമാകുന്നു. (47:167–70)	Ill set hopes on things futile.
ഈവിധം നോക്കിടുന്നേരം—നരർ—	Seen this way is mortal's lot
ക്കീഹയാൽ മാത്രമല്ലമ്പോ!	Sorrow's lore of loss and laments:
നൈരാശ്യം മൂലവും ദുഃഖം—ഭൂവിൽ—	Despair breeds a growing grief—on earth
തീരാത്ത വണ്ണം ഭവിപ്പൂ. (47:171–174)	Unceasing is its course.
ജന്മമതിതരാം ദുഃഖം—ദേഹ	Birth itself is sorrow's bed;
ധർമ്മപ്രയത്നവും ദുഃഖം	Body's deeds too are sorrow's seed.
കർമ്മസമുദായം ദുഃഖം—കാല	Added deeds bring proportional pains;
ധർമ്മപദം ബഹുദുഃഖം. (47:175–78)	Even *Dharma*'s[23] path has certain strains.

---

[23] Sans. The law of cosmic order.

സമ്പന്നനാവതുദുഃഖം—ഭിക്ഷ	Riches come with griefs in tow;
യമ്പുന്നതും അതിദുഃഖം	Beg, instead? Far worse a show.
മാനാഭികാംക്ഷയും ദുഃഖം	Pursue glow? Sorrows row;
മാനാഭിഭൂതിയും ദുഃഖം (47:179–82)	Fear we shame? Is anyone secure from its blow?
നീതിമാനാവതു മപ്പോ—ലവ	Upright seem the paths you carve?
നീതിമാനാവതും ദുഃഖം	Crafty men none sadder live.
മൂഢത യെന്നപോൽ വിദ്യാ—ധനം	Sized up grief from learning's wealth
നേടുവതും അതിദുഃഖം. (47:183–86)	Matches folly's unletter'd girth.
എന്നു വേണ്ടിങ്ങു നാം കാണും	Why say more? Through trails of woe,
ഭോഗ[24] വൃന്ദമൊന്നാകവേ പാർത്താൽ	*Bhoga*-bent,[25] we mortals go;
ദുഃഖാനുഭൂതിക്കുതന്നേ —ജാത	For aches alone
രിക്കുവിൽ മാനുഷരെല്ലാം. (47:187–90)	Seem humans born.

Jacob's Deathbed Blessings for the Tribes

Chapter 49 of Genesis describes the deathbed of Jacob the patriarch. His twelve sons who will become the heads of the twelve tribes of Israel are all standing around Jacob's bed. Jacob speaks sitting up in his bed, leaning on his staff, using his last ounce of strength to speak to them. Jacob confers his blessings on each man, which the future will unfold. Judah, for instance, will bear the scepter; Levi will bear the Urim and the Thummim, the symbols of truth and revelation invested in the priestly office. Jacob predicts a time when "the True Swamin" [the Venerable One, the divine Christ] is born in the tribe of Judah as the rightful heir from whom the scepter of Israel shall never be separated.

യഹൂദേ! ഭവദ് ഭ്രാതൃഗണത്താൽ സ്തുത്യൻ ഭവാൻ;	Judah! Above your kindred, exalted, tower:
മഹാരിഗണത്തിന്നു ചെയ്യും നീ ഗളഹസ്താ.	Your foe's neck shall be in your grip's power
ത്വത് പിതൃ സന്താനങ്ങൾ നിന്നതിപ്രതാപത്താൽ	The sons of your father, in constant deference
ത്വത്പുരോഭുവി വീണു സമസ്യചെയ്യും ധ്രുവം. (49:27–30)	Shall bow to the dust, to you in obeisance.
ആരുതാൻ യഹൂദാഖ്യൻ ബാലകേസരിയല്ലോ	Judah, young my lion, the fearless whelp,
ധീരനായിരപിടിച്ചേറിയൊരെൻമകനെ! നീ	His prey any day is of his own help;
പതുങ്ങി സിംഹീസിംഹ സമാനം കിടക്കുന്ന	Of his crouching posture, make no mistake;
മതംഗ പരിപന്ഥിൻ! നിന്നെയാരുത്ഥാപിക്കും? (49:31–34)	Who sports with him then, for vanity's sake?

---

[24] Sans, for sensual pleasure.
[25] Given to sensual desire.

യഥാർത്ഥ സ്വാമിയായോൻ വന്നീടുംവരെ ചെങ്കോൽ	Till such time as the True *Swamin*[26] emanates
യഹൂദാചരണങ്ങൾ വിട്ടുമാറുകയില്ല.	The scepter from Judah's foothold none separates;
സമസ്തജാതികളുമവ ന്റെ മാഹാത്മ്യത്തെ	Nations His great day in keen hope await
സ്മീക്ഷ്യവിധേയരാമിവനാൽ കൃഷ്ണമാകും. (49:35–38)	As He their hope perfects in fulfilled state.
അർദനപടുക്കളായ് മർദനമാർന്നു കാറ്റിൽ	Grapevine tossing in the welcome sways
കുർദനം ചെയ്തുജന ഹാർദ്ദത്തെ വളർത്തുന്ന	Of playful breeze, endear the tending eyes;
ദുർദശാ രഹിതമാമുദ്യാന മൃദവീകകൾ	Thick and lush are the hill slopes nether
ഗർദ്ദഭ ബന്ധക്ഷമ നിലയിൽ ശോഭിക്കുന്നു. (49:39–42)	Where Judah rests his colts in tether.
ശോണവർണമാം ദ്രാക്ഷാരസത്തിൻകണം പറ്റി—	Awash in abundant wine his garment
ച്ചേണിയന്നിലങ്ങുന്നു തദ്വസ്ത്രമുദ്ദേലമായ്.	And thus blood-red his normal raiment;
അന്തിമേഘംപോൽ കാണ്മൂ വീഞ്ഞിനാൽ തന്നേത്രങ്ങൾ	His wine-dark eyes, like the late dusk clouds,
ദന്തങ്ങൾ ക്ഷീരപാന ശുഭ്രമായ് തിളങ്ങുന്നു. (49:43–46)	And the milk-white teeth, are his plenty's lauds.

Wit and Wisdom from *Vedaviharam*

Simon's *Vedaviharam* has abundant lines of wit and wisdom, which stand on their own or as part of the larger narrative. They range from single lines to larger stanzas or extended passages. Here is a small set, all from *Vedaviharam*:

I

ഏകമേഘത്തിൽ നിന്നു കൊടുതാമിടിത്തീയും	Does not the selfsame cloud bring the lightning bolt
മോഹനതരമായ മഴയും വീഴുന്നില്ലേ? (4:111–12)	And the soothing showers for the sower's sod?

II

ശോഭ കണ്ടു തിന്നുമോ തീക്കട്ടയെ? (3:110)	The live coal glows, but will the lips love its kiss?

III

ടങ്കദളന വിമുഖമാം കല്ലിന്നു	Could the rock untouch'd by the chipping tool,
തങ്കുവാൻ സാദ്ധ്യമോ ഭിത്തിയിങ്കൽ?	Help at all on the sculpted wall? (22:107–108)

---

[26] The Venerable one.

IV

വൻപുലി വായിലിരിപ്പവനങ്ങൊരു
പമ്പരം വേണോ കളിപ്പതിന്നു? (22:369-70)

Stuck in the tiger's jaws, does one
Spin a top for tickling fun?

V

... കഛപം കെട്ടീടിലും
കെട്ടുപോകയില്ലോട്ടിയെന്നതു സിദ്ധമല്ലോ. (23:33-34)

Dead in the dust the tortoise fell,
Not so fast its hardy shell.

VI

ഗുണമേറും വസ്തുവും കണ്ടിടായ്കിൽ
തൃണമെന്നു തള്ളിടും മാനുഷന്മാർ. (24:41-42)

Precious gifts of unseen worth
Men will weigh as less than waste.
OR
Guna and *thrina*, alike to the crass mind.

VII

വേലിയടയാത്ത കേദാര സസ്യങ്ങൾ
കാലികൾ തിന്മതു വിസ്മയമോ? (34:95-96)

Little onder if cedar's seedlings,
Unfenc'd, make the kine's free nibblings.

VIII

ഈശിതാക്കൾ നമ്മളീപ്പാരിടത്തിനു
പേശുകിലീശ്വരൻ പേരിനു മാത്രമാം. (11:71-72)

As lords we rule the vast wide world;
In mere name God His place may hold.

IX

കോരാനൊരാളുമില്ലെങ്കിൽ കിണറ്റിലെ
നീര സമൃദ്ധി കൊണ്ടെന്തു ഫലം? വിഭോ? (15:75-76)

Rippling full be the homely well—
If none to draw, to what avail?

X

വധുവി ന്റെ ചിത്തമറിഞ്ഞിടാതെ
ബുധനോടുമാകാ വിവാഹബന്ധം. (24:589-90)

Though seeks a god himself the nuptial bind,
Let the bride alone her own espousal mind.

XI

മത്സ്യമിരയെ കൊതിക്കകൊണ്ടല്ലയോ
ചിത്സുഖം പൂണ്ടു ബലിശത്തിലാവതും? (25:129-30)

Is not the fish's craving flight
That hooks it on to the fatal bait?

XII

ശതം കോടി സ്വർലോകർ നമ്മോടു കൂടി
സ്ഥിതന്മാരിതിൻ സത്യമോരില്ല നമ്മൾ. (28:143–44)

Heedless ply we of deploy'd hosts,
The heavenlies, a million million around our posts.

XIII

ഭിത്തിയുണ്ടെങ്കിൽ അതിന്മേലൊരു മഹാ
ചിത്രമെഴുതുന്നതതുങ്ങുതമല്ലഹോ! (31:35–36)

Lo, free stands the wall, so why then wonder,
If some artsy hand does a picture render?

XIV

മങ്ങൽ സമയത്തു ഭാര്യയായ് തീർന്നവൾ
മങ്ങൽ സമയത്തു പോക ഞായം. (21:429–30)

She who at dusk came as presumed bride
At like hour may leave as maid unmade.

XV

രഞ്ജന കുറയുന്നു ഡംഭിയിൽ മനുഷ്യർക്കു;
കജ്ജളം പിടിപെട്ടാൽ സ്വർണവും നിഷ്പ്രകാശം. (37:101–02)

Favor fails with the biggity air;
The gleam of gold its stains impair.

XVI

വലുമയെഴുമധിപതികൾ സവിധമതു പൂകുവോർ
വല്ലതും കാഴ്ചയായ് കൊണ്ടുപോയീടേണം.
പരപുരുഷ ഗുരുജരാ പിതൃരഹിത സന്നിധൗ
പോയിടൊല്ലാ വെറും കൈയാലൊരുത്തരും. (43:51–54)

When appearing before a person of state,
Go with a gift of his honor's dictate.
Unseemly the hands empty before the aged,
The guru, and the orphan, the God-imaged.

XVII

ഇരുളിലങ്ങിങ്ങുചരിച്ചിടും മർത്യൻ
ഗുരുവിൻകാലിലും ചവിട്ടിടും മൂഢനായ്. (32:311–12)

Who by habit takes the night cover route,
Well might trample his guru's own foot.

XVIII

... നിശാമുഖേ
വഴിയിലൊരു കയറുമുറി കാണ് കിലും പാമ്പെന്നു
വാദിച്ചുപോകും വലിയവിജ്ഞാനിയും. (43:82–84)

A cut piece rope on the nightly trail
A serpent seems, should judgment fail.

And here are the closing lines of *Vedaviharam*:

... മനുഷ്യ	This truth lies plain to the observing eye:
മാന്യജീവിതം പോലുംചിലന്തിനൂലിന്മേലും	Human life, even of the noble and the high,
പുകത്തൂണുകൾമേലും സ്ഥാപിതമായ സൗധ—	Fares none more than castles of pipe dreams
പ്രഖ്യാണ്ഡമെന്നു കാണാമേതൊരു നേത്രത്തിനും.	Built on cobwebs or smoke in airy columns.
(50:96–98)	

Note: Some of the lines provided here may appear in other portions of this book as they serve the context.

4

K. V. Simon and John Milton: Epic Stars of the East and of the West

K. V. Simon has too many striking biographical and vocational parallels with John Milton for a perceptive reader to overlook. Both men were precocious as child learners and persons of enormous powers of intellect as young adults. Both composed solid verse from their pre-teen years onwards. As Alexander Pope said of himself with regard to his poetic career, both Milton and Simon grew up "lisping in numbers." Both were born in musical families and were passionate about poetry and music. Edward Phillips, Milton's nephew, speaks of his uncle's "excellent ear" for music and his ability to bear a part in both vocal and instrumental performance.[1] Exceptional tutors taught both prodigies in their childhood. Milton was well to do, and so his father, in good judgment, made provision for his education that would prepare him for future greatness. Simon was not wealthy, but his parents and his older brother and mentor K. V. Cherian set him on course for advanced reading and writing without much need for assistance at all. From early days on, Simon had proved himself to be an autodidact [self-learner]. Neither Milton nor Simon cared much for the old scholastic method of learning, presumably because their intellectual capacities kept them ahead of their peers. Both were schoolmasters in their earlier days; Milton taught two of his nephews and a few other children selectively from families of means. Simon's home was a school day and night, as we have seen, and scholars ranged from school grades to advanced professional tracks. In particular, his two nephews, K. M. Varghese and K. M. Daniel, two future stars in Malayalam literature, enjoyed privileged instruction from Simon. K. M. Varghese lived with Simon, assisting in his uncle's daily writings and ongoing publications. Even after his marriage, Varghese and his young bride lived in the Simon household, which was not all that strange in a century of joint-family

---

[1] Helen Darbishire, ed., *The Early Lives of Milton* (London: Constable, 1932), p. 3.

culture. In their boyhood itself, both Milton and Simon wrote original verse in classical languages and translated verse from other tongues; both rendered twenty-three Psalms each in metrical verse; both wrote the majority of their shorter poems in their twenties and the larger works in their latter days. Milton's three great epics—*Paradise Lost, Paradise Regained*, and *Samson Agonistes*—came out in his latter days, with publishing dates that set his age at fifty-nine and sixty-three. Simon's *Vedaviharam* came out when he turned forty-eight. Both poets had their epics making bold departures from the established tradition: whereas mythical or legendary themes were the presumed material for epics, Milton settled on the biblical theme of the fall of man, out of a hundred topics he had mulled over. The same is true of Simon, who was very ready to render all sixty-six books of the Protestant Bible into verse, but had to settle for a lower reach. Both men were already in their positions of high public visibility as writers, reformists, or apologists among their people, although Simon, unlike Milton in this regard, steered clear of the politics of church and state altogether.

Milton and Simon were separated by two centuries historically, and geographically by the great seas. Milton's birth year coincided with the arrival of the British East India Company, the commercial face of England in India. The "company" declared that its goals were trade and commerce, but the whole subcontinent found itself transformed into a colony of the empire with hundreds of its rajahs reduced to the level of feudal vassals to the British throne. This status continued for two full centuries until 1947, three years after the death of Simon. It could be said that Simon lived his entire life in colonial India, technically as a subject of Queen Victoria and her successors through George VI.

India in *Paradise Lost*

Incidental as it might seem, India does appear in Milton's writings. In *Paradise Lost*, Book II, Milton uses the wealth of Ormus and of "Ind"—"Where the gorgeous East with richest hand/Showers on her kings, Barbaric pearl and gold."[2] Milton cites the great example of peace and prosperity of India's northwest region with the fields of "lambs or yeaning kids ... towards the springs of Ganges or Hydaspes, Indian streams" (PL 3.434–36). Ganges is India's mythical river with attributes of

---

[2] John Milton, *Paradise Lost* 2.2–4. All quotations of *Paradise Lost*, hereafter identified as "PL" and in modern spelling, with book and line numbers from http://knarf.english.upenn.edu/Milton.

divinity. Hydaspes is the ancient name for today's Jhelum River. Now, those are places, though in the colonial Indian mainland, many days' journey away from Simon's home. Milton comes down south to Simon's own land of "Malabar" to describe the highly tragic scene of human fall: in Book IX of *Paradise Lost*, after their fall and when God calls out Adam, he and Eve do some hurried tailoring—with fig leaves to make their first suit. That "fig," notes Milton, is

> … not that kind for fruit renown'd;
> But such as at this day, to Indians known,
> In Malabar or Deccan spreads her arms
> Branching so broad and long, that in the ground
> The bended twigs take root, and daughters grow
> About the mother-tree, a pillar'd shade
> High over-arch'd, and echoing walks between. (PL 8.1099–105)

"Malabar," as we have seen already, is the name for the greater coastland of Southwestern India, the most prominent part of which would be Kerala, Simon's homeland. This region is very lush in vegetation. Deccan is slightly up north, which cartographers mark as Southcentral India. Both regions, even all of India, have the abundant presence of the huge shade trees called the banyan, which has the ability to "plant" itself, meaning, sending forth aerial roots and expanding its upper branches into the open spaces. A single banyan tree spreading itself over two or three acres and growing for hundreds of years is only a normal phenomenon. Under its shade many public activities such as business, entertainment, or socializing may be going on. Milton may or may not have had a botanical confusion with the fig and the banyan, however. There are fig leaves large enough to cover a person's whole face or chest, but banyan leaves may not be larger than palm size. There is hardly any need for doubt, however, that Simon has passed by, and perhaps even rested, under a banyan shade or two.

While we are touching trees of fruit and shade, I might also add that Milton was believed to have been a vegetarian, and Simon certainly was one. Both men were light eaters. In his Elegy VI, Milton recommends a simple diet of herbs, eating "a bloodless banquet" and drinking "in beechen goblets" the sober wine of the crystal waters, living like "him of Samos" [Pythagoras]. This recommendation makes many think that Milton personally might have been a vegetarian. In his description of Adam and Eve given charge of Eden, Simon unambiguously avoids any hint of meat-eating: in chapter 1, after the creation week is concluded, thus comes God's blessing to them:

Figure 4.1 Banyan Tree. Photography by Delonix, courtesy of Wikimedia Commons, Creative Commons Attribution-Share Alike 3.0 Unported License. Image reproduced without modification. https://commons.wikimedia.org/wiki/File:Banyan_Tree_at_ The_Valley_School_,_Bangalore.JPG

Milton's alluded fig tree, with the botanical name of ficus benghalensis, is known in India as the "banyan tree." It grows and branches out quite rapidly, developing "pillared" shades that can fill up large areas. Its leaves make heavy foliage, but the single leaves are not large enough for Milton's comparison of them with the "Amazonian targes." However, another species of fig known as the "fiddle fig" (*ficus auriculata*) found in tropical regions, including India, has large leaves that favor the Amazonian comparison.

സ്ത്രീപുമാന്മാരാം നിങ്ങൾ സന്താനപുഷ്ടിയോടു	Bless this earth, you, the prime human spring;
ഭൂമിയിൽ പെരുകിയിട്ടംബുധി ചരത്തെയും	To this earth your number's increase bring;
ഭൂചരകേചരങ്ങളാകിയ സർവ്വത്തെയും	Rule the seas, the soil and the sky by power benign,
നീചത കൂടാതെന്നുമടക്കി ഭരിക്കുവിൻ.[3] (VV 1:257–62)	Fed of facile fields, man and beast, as I assign.

This ordinance is voiced again in "Enjoy the fruit, of any tree to your fill,/ Save of knowledge, good and ill" (VV 2:121–23). Milton was also rather light of frame, reportedly suffering from continual headaches lifelong. Simon indeed was of Spartan living habits, short of stature, and a victim of chronic colds and headaches. Both men had weak eyesight: Milton's failing eyesight brought him to total blindness by age forty-two, and Simon, who was never seen without a book in hand or within quick reach of one, even in his bed, was so shortsighted that he had to hold a book within inches from his eyes. We have verse portraits

---

[3] Citations from Simon's *Vedaviharam* will appear with the abbreviation "VV," followed by chapter and line numbers.

of both men by their exuberant admirers: first, here are four lines from "The Neapolitan, Giovanni Battista Manso, Marquis of Villa, to the Englishman, John Milton":

> What features, form, mien, manners, with a mind
> Oh how intelligent, and how refined!
> Were but thy piety from fault as free,
> Thou wouldst no Angle, but an Angel be.[4]

The overtones of Pope Gregory the Great's quip at seeing the young slave Angles not to be missed, let this also be noted that the slaves were seen in an Italian market, and Manso's praise also comes from Italy where Milton was the guest of nobles and prelates, including a cardinal at the Vatican. Now let us turn to Simon, whom his adoring mentor and poet-friend Mooloor presents as follows:

ഹ്രസ്വത്വം പൂണ്ട ഗാത്രം വലിയ തല, വിശാ–	Stature smallish, pate pronounced, forehead lofty,
ലാഭമാകും ലലാടം	Speech sparkling, full pleasing; visage bright; bearing
വശ്യോക്തിത്വം, സ്വപക്ഷ പ്രകടന പടിമാ–	Noble, honor's scion, this Simon, of dazzling
വക്ഷര പ്രസ്ഫുടത്വം	Oratory, the pristine rapids of mysteries weighty.
അസ്വാർത്ഥപ്രീതി തേജസ്ഫൂരിത മുഖ, മിതേ	
മട്ടി ലൗൽകൃഷ്യവാനാ–	
മിസൈമൺ, കൊച്ചുമർത്യൻ, സുമതി പൊടി –	
പൊടിപ്പൂ പ്രസംഗ പ്രവാഹം.[5]	

The oratory of Simon that Mooloor praises was employed primarily in his mission of religious reform as was the case with Milton too. Both Milton and Simon were "church-outed," so to speak; Milton who was intended for ministry in the Anglican Church decided against it by the time he exited Cambridge. Simon was excommunicated, as we have already seen, by the Mar Thoma Church for introducing the teaching on "believer's baptism," himself being baptized after his personal study of the scriptures and the history of reformation. This experience also helped, which, among other things, brought about the context of the first ever book in Malayalam on "believer's baptism." Milton was in agreement with the reformist thinking concerning baptism too, among other doctrinal matters, thus favoring the Anabaptist and independent movements regarding the teaching. However, the two men continued lifelong as ministers within the church on a much larger scale, armed with multiple gifts to inspire

---

[4] https://ivu.org/history/renaissance/milton_poemata.htm. Accessed June 16, 2022.
[5] Mooloor S. Padmanabha Panicker, "Verse Portrait of K. V. Simon" in *VV*, p. 10.

reform. Milton saw feasible alternatives to episcopal "tyranny" in the Calvinistic model of church governance in the Presbyterian Church and aggressively urged the Anglican society to adopt it, although he moved on to Congregationalism and finally to the Independents. Simon, on the other hand, had no alternative place to "join," and so had to create his own church and model of governance in it. He moved on from the Mar Thoma to go on as an independent believer, gradually gathering like-minded people of faith into a worship body called the "Viyojithas" or "Separatists." Eventually the Viyojithas merged with the totally egalitarian evangelical community called the "Brethren."

Both Milton and Simon were also prolific authors of pamphlets and polemical literature aimed at radical reformation in their respective lands. Both also wrote works of history, treatises, in-depth works of theology, and mainstream literature. Their letters, translation titles, and output in learned journalism add further to their corpus of writings. Both were the "go to" men in their societies for their people for intellectual and spiritual leadership. Both could churn out tracts and treatises of high impact in record time. This was an age of tracts modeled after the Marprelate tracts and the polemical writings of Luther and Wycliffe.[6] Milton committed himself to pamphleteering for twenty years as a public figure because he thought that it mattered as part of his civic vocation. Simon countered controversy even longer through hundreds of his topical and journalistic articles. Both were laymen with unequaled learning to whom their adversaries were no threat at all.

The Times and Home Grounds of Simon and Milton

Religion and civic life were inseparable in English history, and they were certainly so in Milton's England. The Reformation that swept through Europe was only making sluggish or halting progress in England as Milton saw it. The king, the church, and Parliament were beholden to each other. The king as the titular head of the church and its "supreme governor," appointed the senior clergy of the church as advised. In the two decades following Luther's parting ways with Catholicism, the Protestant following that he inspired emerged as Lutheranism, spreading all over Germany. Its neighbor Geneva became a Protestant theocracy of sorts under the French Reformer John Calvin. Reinforcing the spreading new

---

[6] Barbara Lewalski, *The Life of Milton: A Critical Biography* (Hoboken, NJ: Wiley & Sons, 2008), 138.

movement were waves of acceptance of Protestantism in France, the Netherlands, Scandinavia, and Scotland. England, though now severed officially from Roman Catholicism, still maintained its episcopacy and liturgy, which became issues of resistance among the reform-minded people. The "Reformation" started by Henry VIII differed in spirit from the Reformation of Luther, Calvin, or Knox because the king left it where his immediate personal agenda ended. Episcopal power and liturgical worship with "Romish" leanings appeared to be getting reinforced through Archbishop Thomas Cranmer's liturgical work, *The Common Book of Prayer* (1549) and Archbishop William Laud's affirmation of it. Revisions of the *Common Book* occurred in ensuing years, but during the Civil War and Cromwell's Commonwealth years it was suspended, until a new edition appeared in 1662.

William Laud as Archbishop of Canterbury was firm on the role of the Anglican Church through liturgy and a strong episcopacy, with bishops holding even secular offices supporting the monarchy. The people of Scotland resisted the Prayer Book and it resulted in the clergy and gentry meeting at Edinburgh to sign a National Covenant to defend the Scottish Church from any move by King Charles I to introduce the English Prayer Book into the Scottish Church. Milton disapproved of the control of personal faith as a matter subject to laws of the government. By the time he was just past thirty, Milton was firmly anti-prelatical even as he was anti-royalist.

Milton saw "pernicious effects" in both episcopacy and the existing monarchy, both of which he believed had to go. The Presbyterian vision of government would, in his view, bring about a church free from hierarchies and a commonwealth over which an "untutored king" advised by the "godliest, the wisest, and the learnedst ministers" as a "holy and equal aristocracy"[7] would perform their duties. In his tract "On Prelatical Episcopacy," Milton demands that the nation be purged of the old "popish" appendages of liturgy, canons, courts, privileges, and all possible means of private acquisition of wealth. There was to be no expectation of claimed rights of succession to bishoprics either by entitlement of some kind or by laying on of hands because the scriptures provided support for neither. In *Of Reformation*, Milton rejects the claim of "antiquarians" who support episcopacy with their appeal to tradition, showing

---

[7] John M. Wolfe, et al., eds., *The Complete Prose Works of Milton*, Vol. 1 (New Haven, CT: Yale University Press, 1953), 600. Subsequent references go by the abbreviated title, CPW.

how the bishops and elders of the ancient times were elected by popular voice, "unrevenu'd and unlorded."[8] Any patristic text contrary to this conclusion, Milton argues, is heretical because the church Fathers themselves made the scriptures the only guide for Christians. "Custom without truth," warns Milton, "is but agedness of error."[9] In "The Reason for Church Government," Milton argues that episcopacy was developed over time rather than anything modeled from the Aaronic priesthood of the Old Testament.

Simon's preparation for public life in the Eastern world was along the same tracks that Milton took. Like Milton, even Simon was, at least technically, an English subject, but once-removed, so to speak. The British did bring their own church to India, but as is commonly misunderstood, it was not intended to help, hurt, or to compete with the native religious establishments. Any British church service on the Indian soil was solely for British citizenry resident in India. Religious work by British subjects among the natives was prohibited by the company until the nineteenth century when the small but highly effective evangelical teams of CMS missionaries brought printing, education, journalism, social services, human rights affirmation, and campaigns against racism, caste, and bonded labor. It was this connection of the Anglicans with the St. Thomas Church that introduced the ideas of reform to the native church in Kerala. As stated already, Simon's own denomination of Marthomites came into being as an Indian affiliate body of the Anglican Communion in the late nineteenth century. This formally connected Simon with the Church of England, for what it was worth. Like the Anglicans in England, the Marthomites removed some of the traditional rituals, liturgy, feasts and Lents, but not all of them. Reformation on a scale that took place in Europe was yet to happen in India. It would be Simon who would have to bring it to his people, with his learning, writings, teaching, and public life of four decades of popular evangelical oratory.

The term "Reform" could stir a storm anywhere in Europe in Milton's day. It would have meant nothing in Simon's secular Kerala, but would raise pandemonium in the strongholds of the Syrian Christian orthodoxy and episcopacy at that time. Any suggestion of departure from their inherited doctrines also was perceived as a threat to their status in the racial matrix. After all, they had been a people under their own archdeacon who had the powers of an ecclesiastic and a prince of his people, with an army of 30,000 soldiers, according to the native records.

[8] CPW, I 549.
[9] Ibid., 561.

The European Reformation stripped the continental church of its many rites and rituals. Milton was wholly in support of the natural language of the heart for prayer, where even groanings, if they did not distract the decorum, would be acceptable. In Milton's world, the reformed faith groups trimmed down the ancient list of sacraments from seven to two, those being baptism and the Eucharist in the Protestant Anglican Church. The Puritans, who insisted on scriptural precedent for everything in their belief or practice, demanded that even those two sacraments themselves be re-examined. In doing so, they argued that the baptism given to an infant is a proxy act rather than a voluntary act by the person receiving the sacrament. An infant brought to the church after a few weeks or even months of its birth was to have some designated person to stand in for the child and to declare the words required. The reformists taught that the child should attain the age of understanding before being presented for baptism and make a proper, personal confession of faith. The so-called "Anabaptist" groups that were emerging all over Europe reinforced this perspective. Milton, as Barbara Lewalski notes, was on the side of the dissenters and the Anabaptists about baptism. The term "Anabaptists" simply means "rebaptizers." Simon, like Milton and the Anabaptists, upheld the belief that in the first century, baptism was given in the manner John the Baptist and the disciples of Christ did, giving it only to persons of independent understanding who could see the significance of it as symbolic identification with the death, burial, and resurrection of Christ. In *Paradise Lost*, Archangel Michael provides Adam a vision of Christ's followers baptizing new believers in "the profluent stream," indicating Milton's own pleasure in the kind of water used for that purpose (PL 12.442).

To no one's surprise, this mode of baptism by immersion as a new practice was enough to rock the whole traditional Syrian community, which had neither the interest to deviate from tradition nor to examine the scriptural teachings or patterns of the act. Simon wrote a book on the subject showing the full justification for the individual taking baptism only after voluntarily confessing their personal faith in Christ. The next was the removal of all ancient symbols considered sacred: the altar, the incense, the ornate sanctuaries, the steeples, the shrines and all the apperati, and of course, even the prelacy that sustained it all. The church was no more than a building that took shape from mere human labor; the human body was to be the dwelling place of God, Simon contended, as did the Europeans of kindred spirit a few centuries earlier.

Milton lived dangerously as a public figure and appeared fearless of the consequences that lay ahead. As a "wanted" man hiding for his safety, Milton was betting on the fulfillment of his career. There was a real likelihood of him being slain before the three great classics were written, under the shroud of permanent blindness. In a country where established traditional thinking agreed with James I's dictum, "No bishop, no king," Milton called for the removal of kings and to have a general council of ablest men in their place. Milton wrote his incendiary tract on the "Tenure of Kings and Magistrates," justifying the execution of Charles I, written during the king's trial and published within two weeks of his execution. Equally risky was "The Ready and Easy Way to Establish a Commonwealth," a subsequent tract against the restoration of Charles II. Furthermore, in *Of Reformation*, he calls for the execution of bishops and condemns them to their eternity in hell. William Laud, the archbishop who had championed episcopacy under Charles I, had ruled that "anyone who did not worship according to the prescribed ritual was a Separatist, no matter how small the deviation."[10] Bishop James Ussher and Bishop Joseph Hall, whom other ministers, by Milton's own admission, were unable to withstand in public arguments, were his personal opponents in the pamphlet wars.

There need be little argument that Milton's fame rose as he employed his enormous intellectual and communicative powers through the tracts. The king, Parliament, the church, and the reform groups heard him and lacked the power to stop him if they disagreed with his reasoning. There were direct answers given in the case of attacks of which there was no scarcity. The strategy of message delivery varied according to the occasion. His tract, *Of Reformation* in two books, was addressed to an anonymous friend. *Of Prelatical Episcopacy* was addressed to Bishop Ussher, and the *Reason for Church Government* to Bishop Hall. By doing so, says he, "I brought succor to the ministers, as it was said, scarcely able to withstand the eloquence of this bishop, and from then onward, if the bishops made any response, I took a hand."[11]

In his own world, Simon was serving Kerala in the manner Milton served England, but always as an irenic man of letters and as a prophet. There were quite a few subsets within the Syrian population that did not see eye to eye on matters of doctrine. While they kept each other at bay, the community overall spurned the zealous reformist orientation of Simon. Yet when they faced a common adversary like Nambiathiri and passions ran high on both sides, Simon was the sole defender against the onslaught, as already shown. Simon's

---

[10] Michaelbryson.net, accessed June 29, 2022.
[11] CPW IV, 622–23.

in-depth knowledge of Vedic literature, religions, and philosophy helped quiet the conflict, demonstrating how objective critical reasoning with patience can help ensure agreeable community life.

Prose of the "Left Hand" and Prose of the Equal Hand

A large portion of Simon's prose is purpose-driven and polemical, like Milton's. At least half a dozen of his prose titles read like live debates, sometimes even with dramatized illustrations. In *Nicolavya Matham* or [*Nicolaite Religion or Episcopacy*] (1936), like Milton he argues that the ancient church had no order of exalted clergy to govern it, nor a sacerdotal system operating in ritualism. The words "bishop" and "presbyter" were merely synonyms in apostolic language for elders elected from within the local congregation. Any practice of investing a bishop by laying on of hands, then, is therefore a vain exercise, he contended. In *Roma Sabha* [The Church of Rome and Its Use of the Word of God] (1939), translation of a work by W. P. Harris into Malayalam, Simon refutes the claims of two Catholic clergymen that the church Fathers formulated or endorsed an ecclesiastical hierarchy. Simon states that the contrary is the truth as one can see from the writings of post-apostolic figures like Jerome, Basil, Chrysostom, or Eusebius, who taught people "to rest on what is written," and to "seek nothing but the scriptures to establish the truth." Simon's *Satya Veda Mukuram* [The Mirror of the Word] is a polemical response to a tract by Fr. Thomas Menachery who argues that the Bible by itself as a source of authority in matters of faith is insufficient; the church alone, not individuals, should interpret the scriptures; the church and its clergy are protected from error in interpretation; the Bible with tradition alone is the foundation of the Christian faith. Simon refutes these assertions with abundant evidentiary data from various eras of history. Here is a sound bite from one of its pages in a question on doctrinal disagreements within the Catholic Church itself:

> Would you like some examples of doctrinal discord in historical Catholicism? The Son has no beginning, says one venerable father; He has, says another; pray to the angels, instructs one; no need to pray to them, says another; the communion bread transforms, teaches one; no, it does not, says another; baptism is for regeneration, declares one; no, it is only a sign of rebirth, says another; the purgatory exists, asserts one, no, there is no purgatory, assures another; hell is for ever, says one father; no, it's only temporary, says another; the Word is the foundation, says one father; yes, but not without tradition as the foundation,

says another. The teaching of Origles [could have different spelling] is lunacy, says Theophilos; Jerome is inconsistent and erroneous, says Augustine, and so on. One could go on with more of such, all of them heard from the Catholic Babel a thousand years before the first Protestant was spotted.[12]

A name like Menachery is hardly mentioned in Simon discussions today, but the background of *Satyaveda Mukuram* shows that the tract wars between the priest and Simon ran through many issues of *Nazrani Deepika*, a major daily of the times, in the late 1920s.

Simon's treatise *Thritwa Bodhini* [Concerning the Trinity] is a work like St Augustine's *De Trinitate*, the whole book built up as a debate with two Russellites, K. C. Oommen and Cherukara C. V. Mathai. In the book, Simon, who generally only grants qualified approval of the church Fathers as sources of interpretive authority, respectfully upholds St. Athanasius as "learning's star from the school of Clement and Origen," showing how formative his singlehanded labors had been in harmonizing the scriptures on the Trinity. Although it might be a matter mostly for academic discussion today, in the fourth century CE, the theological controversies over the Trinitarian and Arian definitions of the godhead of Christian theology were issues of life and death, one might say. Simon delves into the topic historically and theologically, with support for the concept of the Trinity being universally present in all major religions and schools of philosophy. The biblical prophets, the gospel writers, and the Nicene Fathers are examined thoroughly; widely revered Hindu sages like Swami Vivekananda, Sankaracharya, and Swami Vidyaranya are also cited for their teachings on how the Trinity was part of the ancient knowledge of India.

Simon and Milton dismiss episcopal acts of installing clergy by the symbolic act of laying on of hands as a sign of power invested. Simon challenges his opponents to look at unordained men of great fame such as D. L. Moody, Charles Spurgeon, Andrew Muller, F. B. Meyers, and others. Equally dismissible is to him the ruling on license being enjoined for publishing and reading of books to prevent questions from the laity.

Pashandta Mardanam [Thrashing Heresy, 1924] is a collection of 22 pamphlets responding to C. V. Mathai, a former member of Simon's then-nascent Brethren group. The questions raised provide Simon the opportunity to explain why "the toxic heresies of higher criticism, high churchism, universalism,

---

[12] K. V. Simon, *Satyaveda Mukuram*, 119, http://www.bethanyaroma.com/bookspage.php?chapter_id=168#page/8

evolutionism, and sacerdotalism"[13] deserve total rejection. Simon also rejects the traditionalist argument that episcopacy deters schisms in the church: in proof, he points out the rivalries among medieval religious orders like the Franciscans, the Dominicans, the Carmelites, the Jesuits and the like, and worse yet, the great schism of 1054, where the Christendom of the East and the West broke apart. Simon also points to the Great Western Schism (1378–1417) in which three popes were simultaneously in office at three locations, each with his own following, denouncing and excommunicating his rivals.

These five prose works of Simon not only fit the genre of Milton's polemical prose, but they have also had the same efficacious missional purpose of passionately involving their audiences in reform. Both Milton and Simon are thought of as poets primarily by the general audiences; they are prose writers too, of no less power. Milton slights his prose as the work of his "left hand" despite his epic success with it. Simon was happy with prose and verse alike. Simon's prose was the work of his facile hand, equally effectual at any task that occasion demanded, which we shall see in a few random examples.

The variety of genres in both Milton and Simon offers many parallels from the elegy to the epic in verse and from letters to treatises in prose. In verse, the most prominent works of the two will be *Paradise Lost* and *Vedaviharam*. Simon wrote during the Neoclassical era in Malayalam. As noted earlier, a spate of *mahakavyas* had filled the literary scene in Kerala during this period, clearing the way for its emerging Romantic movement in the new century. According to the norms of Indian Rhetoric or *Alanakara Sastra*, particularly those set by the seventh-century Sanskrit grammarian Dandin, a *mahakavya* is a court epic of exalted subject matter, with an accomplished hero of noble pedigree and a true event as its story; it begins with a happy opening, progresses through conflicts, adorned with eighteen kinds of descriptions which include cities, mountains, oceans, pleasure parks, the joys of love, weddings, wars, and campaigns; the whole work must have *rasa* pervade it; the narrative must have metrical variety; it must be beautifully ornamented, and must end in triumph: a work of such beauty and variety will be immortal.[14]

It would take only a few pages of *Vedaviharam* to see that Simon has no problem meeting and surpassing these criteria, with the additional value of

---

[13] K. V. Simon, *Pashandta Mardanam*, http://www.bethanyaroma.com/bookspage.php?chapter_id=168#page/8, accessed July 2, 2022.
[14] Pankaj L. Jani, https://www.wisdomlib.org/hinduism/book/jarasandhavadha-mahakavyam/d/doc419449.html

introducing the Semitic tale of the creation of the universe and the first human family. The work maintains full fidelity to the complete fifty-chapter body of the source book, yet at the same time provides captivating, imaginative expansion of the numerous episodes of the Mosaic account. Simon wrote *Vedaviharam* at record speed—within a single year—in the midst of his constantly pressing public ministries. His goal in the poem is to provide a singable *gadha* like Ezhuthachan's *Adhyathma Ramayana* and Cerusseri's *Krishnagatha*. Traditionally, Hindu homes in Kerala would have the regular devotional reading or recital of Ezhuthachan's rendition of the Rama story. Simon praises the Hindu culture that inspires active taste in poetry through their religious works of great literary merit. "Is it any wonder at all," Simon asks, "that a Hindu, growing up soaked in the ambrosial sweetness of inspirational poetry, becomes a poet, or at least becomes an aesthete?" "Christians are not created without the abilities of their Hindu brethren in this regard," adds Simon, "but they only need to allow the God-given but dormant seed to sprout."[15] Simon reminds his readers that of all literary works in the world, the *Rg Veda* and the Mosaic books of the Old Testament would suffice to show that *Easwar bhakti* or devotion to God is the unexcelled subject matter for poetry and that its musical reading is both inspirational and instructive.

Simon's epic challenges the traditional belief that the *itihasa* (the core story) of an epic should be a native myth with its familiar color and content. *Vedaviharam* as a Semitic story was foreign to the conventional Indian ear. So were the names of the characters that fill the various stories within the epic. Simon indigenizes them for the Malayalam audience: *Adaman* for Adam, *Abram* for Abraham, *Terasuthan* for son of Terah or Abraham, *Lottan* for Lot, *Issahan* for Isaac, *Rahela* for Rachel, *Yakooban* for Jacob, *Parron* for pharaoh, *Daveedan* for David, *Hadriyaan* for Hadrian, *Keturakha* for Keturah, *Kuscunthain* for Constantine, *Sidom, Sidumam,* or *Sudamam* for "Sodom." The wording of the opening lines of Simon's invocation is done with such *bhakti* sentiment that "even the most orthodox Hindu would bow in obeisance," says Balakrishnan, who then invites the reader to take a look at the long string of synonyms that Simon summons to speak of or to address God: *veetharoopan, vimalabhan, aadi karanan, ahara pradan, vanditha padambujan, paramananda moorti, vishudhaathman, jagadipa, janimarana rahita, sharmada, thampuran, sarvashaktan, jagannivasan,*

---

[15] K. V. Simon, *Vedaviharam*, Preface (Tiruvalla: Mahakavi K. V. Simon Foundation, 1989), 19.

parameshti, amaravaryan, and so many more.[16] These words are of Sanskrit roots and inflections, which are evident traits of literary Malayalam. Simon's learning and knowledge, at least until his time, surpassed what his peers had. Most of them were working essentially with old repertoire of legendary native myths or tales. As a result, they were generally only the retellings of old predictable plotlines with a slight personal slant where possible.

Vedaviharam opens a Hebraic–Christian vision of history, where time and eternity touch each other through orders of creation, represented in the temporal and the celestial. In the "beginning," which is before undetermined ages or aeons in the boundless past, God creates the heavens and the earth, entirely in glory. The "treacherous host" of the inhabitants of that world (these are not of the Adamic race), by their abuse of it, had made the earth desolate and unlivable. Primeval floods turned the planet into a watery waste, drowning it in disuse for as long as it has existed since. The Omniscient God then enters the scene, light appears as the first redemptive resource in a new order of creation, and darkness departs. Within the massive body of waters, there was an embryonic space, a vacuum, which by God's command, becomes the sphere of mixed airs of indiscernible proportions, resulting in earth's eventual atmosphere. By divine command the waters move away for dry land to appear, vegetation covers the ground, and the sun, moon, and constellations light up the firmament. Fish, fowls, and animals by species populate their new home, God himself being the Cause, the Creator, and the Initiator of all that is seen and known.

Vedaviharam and *Paradise Lost:* Concordant Contents

Numerous passages in *Paradise Lost* or even in *Paradise Regained* correspond in content likeness and descriptive particulars with Simon's *Vedaviharam*. I choose a short range of specimen texts from *Paradise Lost* for quick side by side readings with portions in *Vedaviharam*. Let us start with Milton's universally familiar invocation of Book I. Milton follows the formulaic practice of seeking the aid of the muse in composing his heroic work, but as William B. Hunter has noted, in Books I and III the muse has only a vague identity; in Book VII and

---

[16] B. C. Balakrishnan, "Padakuberanaya Mahakavi" in *Satabdi*, 123–24.

IX she appears as Urania,[17] not as a deity that dwells on Mt. Olympus, but as the divine Spirit "heavenly born before the hills appeared," Olympus included. Like the Holy Spirit that speaks to prophets in visions and dreams, she is "the celestial patroness who deigns her nightly visitation," enabling the poet to be a transmitter of what she "in eternal wisdom did converse." Milton's firmness in his departure from tradition comes in this bold statement of the opening invocation:

> Or if Sion hill
> Delight thee more, and Siloa's brook that flowed
> Fast by the oracle of God; I thence
> Invoke thy aid to my adventurous song,
> That with no middle flight intends to soar
> Above the Aonian mount, while it pursues
> Things unattempted yet in prose or rhyme. (PL 1.10–16)

The aid he seeks must come from Sinai or Sion Hill. Both were places of divine revelation to humanity. At Sinai the great shepherd–prophet Moses was inspired with many signs of divine favor. From Sion Hill, which is another name for Jerusalem, Jesus sends a blind man with mud paste applied over his eyes, instructed to wash it away in the spring of Siloam; when done, the man miraculously gains his eyesight. Biographically, the lines have a lyrical echo from the burden of Milton's own personal blindness. Also, with his knowledge of the scriptures, Milton would have thought of the many places in the Old Testament where a prophet would be asked, "What do you see?" (Jer. 1:11; Amos 7:8; Zech. 4:2) or told, "Write what you see in a book" (Rev. 1:11, 1:19). Milton definitely wants, "with no middle flight," to soar past the shrines or mounts of the Canaanite deities in his ambitious pursuit of things yet unattempted in prose or verse.

Simon opens the *Vedaviharam* beseeching inspired knowledge from the "Most High God," the Hebraic "Yah" of the Old Testament. Written out in Malayalam, "Yah" ["യാ"] linguistically is a single character, still a word, with a double meaning:

യാതൊന്നിൽ നിന്നു സർവമുൽപ്പന്നമായിടുന്നു	That from which all beings source
യാതൊന്നിൻ സാഹായ്യത്താൽ നിലനിൽക്കുന്നു സർവം	That by which all feel one force
യാതൊന്നിലെല്ലാമന്തേ വിലയിക്കുന്നാ ദിവ്യ	That which indwelt radiates all
"യാ" തന്റെ പാദാവിന്ദങ്ങളേ മമാലംബം. (VV 1:35–38)	That Yah's footstool, my strength I call.

---

[17] Stevie Davies and William B. Hunter, "Milton's Urania: The Meaning, Not the Name, I Call," *Studies in English Literature 1500–1900*, Vol. 28, No. 1, *The English Renaissance* (Winter 1988), pp. 95–111, p. 95.

The word *yathonnil* in the first three lines is a pronoun referent, meaning "that which" in each instance. In the fourth line, the term *Yah* stands for the poetic synonym of the name of Jehovah, the word play giving us an epiphanic moment, rather than the giggle of a quick pun. The invocation continues, addressing *Yah* directly:

നിന്തിരുവടിയുടെ മാഹാത്മ്യമുരയ്ക്കുവാൻ	Where lives a rhetor, declaim-set,
അന്തരാ ചിന്തിച്ചൊരുങ്ങിടുന്ന വാഗ്മിയുണ്ടോ?	With inspired words of eloquence fetch'd?
എന്നിരിക്കവേ വെറും മന്ദനാമിവൻ ജ്യോതിർ	How then would I, a slow wit wight,
മന്ദിരാ നിൻചരിത്രമെങ്ങിനെ വർണ്ണിച്ചീടും? (VV 1:43–46)	Oh, Glory's Castle, of thee indite?

ഊഴിക്കു നിർമ്മാതാവേ! ദൈവനിർണ്ണയമാകും	Maker to this dusty orb, through depths unplumb'd
ആഴവും ബഹുവിധ വ്യാഖ്യാനഭംഗങ്ങളും	Does thy counsel run; senses veiled and substance sealed,
ചുഴുറ്റ ഗഹനാർത്ഥ ശബ്ദാം തിമികളു-	How may one dare the tides traverse–
മേഴുന്ന വേദമാകുമാഴിയി ലാറിങ്ങും? (VV 1:67–70)	Those Vedic springs that birth thy seas?[18]

എങ്കിലും അവിടുത്തെ സാഹ്യമായിടുന്നൊരു	Nevertheless, secure in thy deep sea ship
തുംഗമാം പ്ലവയന്ത്രം തന്നിൽ ഞാനിരിക്കുകിൽ	A voyage done as thou wouldst equip
വൻകടലിതിൻ ചില ഭാഗങ്ങൾ വീക്ഷിക്കുവാൻ	Through tides unbound of thy Word's waves,
സങ്കടമന്യേ സാധിച്ചിടുമില്ലൊരു തർക്കം. (1:71–74)	Shall marvels unveil, my heart raves.

Not to be missed is Milton's petition in his "address to Light" in Book III, lamenting, yet celebrating his blindness: "Irradiate, there plant eyes, all mist from thence/Purge and disperse, that I may see and tell/Of things invisible to mortal sight" (PL 3.51–55). A reader familiar with the book of Ezekiel would recall God transporting, in visions, the prophet to multiple instructive sites, and the prophet vividly recalling all of those movements. Where Milton has a thesis of justifying the ways of God to man to execute in Book I, Simon is asking that he be justified in seeking an unveiled view of Jehovah's *Vedic* world of the shoreless sea of transcendent knowledge. The prayer leads the poet forthwith to his task of narrating what existed prior to any conceivable era of earthly history:

ആദിയിലാദി ദൈവമാകാശഭൂമികളെ	In the beginning of beginnings, planets and space
മേദുരഭാഗങ്ങളായി സൃഷ്ടി ചെയ്തനന്തരം	Emerged as realms of God's manifest grace.

---

[18] Religious texts of ancient India, written in Sanskrit. Although referring primarily to Hindu religious and philosophical writings, the term *veda* is used as a synonym for the scriptures of other religions as well.

മേദിനീതലവാസമാർന്നുള്ളോരക്കാലത്തെ	Earth stood pristine, until the wasting touch
പാതകപ്പരിഷയിൻ ദണ്ഡനദ്യാരാ ലോകം	Of the treacherous host, rid this haunted patch—
നിർജ്ജനമായിത്തീർന്നു; പ്രളയതോയം കേറി	This world—of all its dwellers. Ground and elements
മജ്ജനം ചെയ്യിച്ചെല്ലാദിശയും നശിപ്പിച്ചു	Lay dead; floods filled the earth in deluge depth,
വായുവിൽ ചരിക്കുവാൻ പക്ഷികളില്ലാതായി	But with fishes none, and the air, void of fowls of mirth.
തോയത്തിൽ മത്സ്യങ്ങളെങ്ങുമേ കാണ്മാനില്ല. (VV 1:75–82)	
മഹത്താമന്ധകാരം വെള്ളത്തെ മുഴുവനും	Great was the darkness that overlay the water
മറച്ചു വ്യാപിച്ചിതു കണ്ടിക്കാർനിര പോലെ.	Like mountainous ranges of lightless matter.
ഇങ്ങനെ നൈമിത്തിക പ്രളയവെള്ളങ്ങളിൽ	Causes obscure and effects untraced
തുംഗമാം ശിഥിലത പൂണ്ടലക്ഷണമായും	Besieged the world for ages ahead,
അവ്യപദേശ്യമായുമജ്ഞേയമായും ലോക–	So it seemed, God-ordained.
മവ്യയ നിയോഗത്താൽ കിടന്നു ബഹുകാലം. (VV 1:83–88)	
എത്ര നാളിപ്രകാരമിരുണ്ട വെള്ളങ്ങളിൽ	How long lay the earth submerged in this state
പ്രിഥ്വി നിർലീനമായിക്കിടന്നെന്നറിവില്ല.	Also remains unknown. All the same, at its end
തദ്യുഗാന്ത്യത്തിലീശൻ പ്രളയോഗദകമധ്യ	The Lord's spirit by desire stirred, moved to create
ത്തുദൃത്താം സിസൃക്ഷയോടവരോഹിച്ചു സ്വയം. (VV 1.89–92)	An order afresh, Himself solely, Himself sufficient.

And here is a glimpse of how Milton presents the world at the point of creation:

> On heavenly ground they stood; and from the shore
> They viewed the vast immeasurable abyss
> Outrageous as a sea, dark, wasteful, wild,
> Up from the bottom turned by furious winds
> And surging waves, as mountains, to assault
> Heaven's height, and with the center mix the pole. (PL 7.210–215)

Both Milton and Simon agree in their science of the pre-creation earth, except that Simon sees the biblical earth having been laid waste in an earlier period of inhabitation by the "treacherous" host who so ruined it as to make it unlivable. The latter earth is found emerging from, in Milton's description, the "immeasurable abyss, outrageous as a sea, dark, wasteful, wide/Up from the bottom turned by furious winds and surging waves" (PL 7.211–13), yet the "Omnific word" commands silence to end their discord, and Chaos hears His voice. Earth becomes part of the universal order, "self-balanced on her center hung" (PL 7:242).

The creation of light and the creation of the sun in the Genesis narrative have raised the logical question as to where the pre-solar light came from. Both Milton and Simon appear to have considered that likely question, and so the narrative offers this report from Milton:

> Let there be light, said God; and forthwith Light
> Ethereal, first of things, quintessence pure,
> Sprung from the deep; and from her native east
> To journey through the aery gloom began,
> Sphered in a radiant cloud, for yet the sun
> Was not; she in a cloudy tabernacle
> Sojourned the while. (PL 7.243–48)

The creation of Milton's sun does take place as one of "two lights," one for day and the other for night. Among the questions Simon answers in his apologetic work, *Is the Bible Believable?* he seems to resolve the issue without much concern for conflict, using the very scientific principle assumed in Milton, i.e., light is an ethereal phenomenon, not a material object like the sun (Question 12). Whether Simon knew it or not, he happens to have Milton's textual support for this point. Milton's choice of the word "ethereal" could not have been accidental. Simon sees "the sun, moon and the stars" appear as the result of a single command, which caused all of them to appear as a heavenly cluster (VV 1.123–26), thus separating the pre-solar light from the solar.

Similar is a key creation word that both poets use: embryo. "The earth was formed, but in the womb as yet/Of waters embryon immature, involved (PL 7:276–77), according to Milton. Simon sees the tiny embryo in the midst of the primeval waters, a vacuum nearly imperceptible, evolving into the atmosphere of finely proportioned gasses that must sustain life on the planet (VV 1.105–08).

Now let us see how the two poets introduce scenes of creation from the first ever human family. Here is Simon's description of Eve as Adam is awestruck at her mesmerizing loveliness:

ഉറക്കമുണർന്നവൻ കണ്ണുകൾ മന്ദം മന്ദം	In softly blinks his leaden eyes from repose freed
തുറക്കുന്ന നേരമൊരു ദിവ്യയാം നാരീരത്നം	When an angel-form before him stood; his senses seized,
തനിക്കുമുന്നിലായ് നിൽക്കുന്നു വിഭാതത്തിൽ	Like the dawning sun seemed she, on a clear morn,
കനൽക്കുനേരായ് കിഴക്കുദിച്ച ഭാനു പോലെ. (VV 1:191–94)	In glory's glow, as fresh in the orient it shone.
എന്തു ഞാൻ കാണുന്നതീ ചന്തമേറിയ കാഴ്ച്ച!	Ravishing sight! So comely a form!

ഹന്ത! മിന്നലീ ഭൂവിൽ പിണ്ഡിതാകൃതിയായോ?	What? Is lightning bodied for an earthen home?
ചന്ദ്രനെ വെടിഞ്ഞിങ്ങു ചന്ദ്രിക വരാവതോ?	Or, from the moon its goodly glow, does sever'd flow?
സാന്ദ്രസൗഭാഗ്യ മൂർത്തി യെന്തൊരു നവസൃഷ്ടി? (VV 1:197–200)	Or, Delight dense, imaged as new creation show!
കിടപ്പാനെനിക്കൊട്ടും കഴിവില്ലെഴുന്നേറ്റു	Hold still in gaze? No, how must I? Rather, dash
പൊടുക്കെന്നവളുടെ യടുക്കലോടിച്ചെന്നു	Would I, o'er to her celestial self, and have awash
തുടുത്ത കാന്തിചിന്നുമവൾ തന്നുടലിന്മേൽ	Her exuding loveliness in affection's showers
വെടുപ്പായ് പ്രേമമാല ചാർത്തണമാശ്ളേഷത്താൽ. (VV 1:219–22)	And embraces like garbs of unearthly flowers.

Now, here is Milton presenting his version of Eve, right from "under the forming hand" of God:

> On she came,
> Led by her heavenly Maker, though unseen,
> And guided by his voice; nor uninformed
> Of nuptial sanctity, and marriage rites:
> Grace was in all her steps, Heaven in her eye,
> In every gesture dignity and love.
> I, overjoyed, could not forbear aloud.
> This turn hath made amends; thou hast fulfilled
> Thy words, Creator bounteous and benign,
> Giver of all things fair! but fairest this
> Of all thy gifts! nor enviest. I now see
> Bone of my bone, flesh of my flesh, myself
> Before me: Woman is her name; of Man
> Extracted: for this cause he shall forego
> Father and mother, and to his wife adhere;
> And they shall be one flesh, one heart, one soul. (PL 8.484–99)

Milton dramatizes the creation scenes of Adam and Eve through their earliest memories with God, their dreams and their first mutual sightings, the instant force of mutual attraction, and the desire to belong to each other. Simon describes it in Moses' perspective. He shows Adam naming every animal in the garden just once, and that one name suffices and is correct, but he names his helpmate twice, first as "woman" as the latest member in the order of creation, and then as "Eve," the mother of all living beings. Biblical commentator Adam

Clarke points out that the "second" name has the literal meaning of "life" in the Hebrew language.[19]

The Temptation and the Fall

Eden is a place of knowledge. Adam's unerring knowledge is demonstrated in his naming of all living beings entirely by himself. In order to name something correctly, one must have absolute knowledge of its internal and external natures. Created in the image of God and moving about in a world untainted by sin, that ability in Adam was natural. In the garden stands the tree of the knowledge of good and evil, of which we have no detailed description. Yet, even before Adam's fall, Raphael warns Adam that knowledge works under levels of restraint and applicability. He is advised to be lowly wise and to think of only what concerns him and his being. A while later Satan enters the scene with the proposal that exploits the value of knowledge and gives false knowledge to his curious human victims. He tells Eve that they cannot go wrong with the pursuit of knowledge and his reasoning in support of it is forcefully persuasive. See how Simon reports it:

ജ്ഞാനത്തെ കവിഞ്ഞു നാം കാമിപ്പാനെന്തൊന്നുള്ളൂ?	What more to seek than the power of knowledge?
ജ്ഞാനിയായ് തീരുമ്പൊഴു തീശ്വരനായീ, ഭദ്രേ!	It exalts us as God's own equals, Beloved!
നിഷ്പ്രയാസേന ദൈവ നിലയിലെത്താമെന്നു-	Leap up to God's very state! The Great Mother
ള്ളത്ഭുതവാർത്ത കാതിൽ തട്ടവേ ജഗന്മാതാ	Of all took the bait, and felt raptured to the gates
സ്വർഗ്ഗത്തിൻവാതിൽ കണ്ട മട്ടിലങ്ങാനന്ദിച്ചാൾ. (VV 3:37–41)	Of heaven, gloating in joy beyond all measure.
ഭർഗ്ഗനാം സർപ്പത്തിന്നു സ്വാഗതം ചൊല്ലീടിനാൾ	The deceiver received his designed welcome
തർക്കമൊന്നുണ്ടതിനും ച്രത്യുക്തി ലഭിക്കുകിൽ.	Though not without unease in Eve, some.
തർക്കം വേണ്ടിതു നല്ല മാർഗമെന്നുറച്ചവൾ	The queries went well, she thought, and answers sway;
ചോദിച്ചു: സഖേ! ഭവദ്ഗീരു പോൽ ച്രവർത്തിച്ചാൽ	She then asked: "Friend, will this the good I own betray
ഭൂതവുമുദർക്കവു മില്ലെന്നായ് വന്നേക്കുമോ? (VV 3:42–46)	And forfeit our future's promises withal?
വാഗ്മിയാം ഭുജംഗേന്ദ്രൻ ചൊന്നു: ഞാനൊരു സർപ്പം	The fawning *Bhujanga* [serpent king] continued: A mute

---

[19] *Clarke's Commentary: The Song of Songs*. https://www.studylight.org/commentaries/eng/acc.html, accessed June 30, 2022.

വാഗ്മിതയെന്നല്ലറിയാട്ടവും ഞങ്ങൾക്കില്ല.	Reptile merely am I, of no gift of sound or speech.
എന്നുടെ സംഭാഷണശക്തിക്കു നിദാനമീ	The voice thou hearest of me is solely from the fruit
സുന്ദരദൃമഫലഭോജനമൊന്നു മാത്രം. (VV 3:47–50)	Of charming power thou fearest even within touching reach.

Satan is a liar and the father of lies, and has been so from the beginning, says Jesus. Satan tells Eve that he was a reptile, which he was not. He was an archangel, but a fallen one. He adds that he was gifted with the power of speech from the eating of the forbidden fruit, which is falsehood, stated intentionally. Further persuasion goes on with steely logic:

തിര്യക്കാം എനിക്കിത്ര വൈശിഷ്ട്യം വരുത്തിയ	To me, a lowly crawler, has this celestial fruit
വീര്യവൽഫലം വ്യർത്ഥമാവില്ല നിങ്ങൾക്കൊട്ടും	Such excellence lent. No cause have I to dispute,
അതിനാൽ ഭയപ്പെടാതെടുത്തു ഭക്ഷിക്കുവിൻ	And therewith to ponder. Come, to the welcome relish;
മൃതിയുണ്ടാകയില്ലീ സൽഫല സമാസ്വാദാൽ. (VV 3:51–54)	In no wise shall one by such great gifts perish.
ഹൗവ്വാ ചൊന്നതിനേവ: മീഹലമശ്യമെങ്കിൽ	Howwah [Eve] then answered thus: so goodly
സർവപാലകനതു തടയാനിടയില്ല.	If this fruit, the Great Ruler's forbidding seems unlikely.
ക്ഷുദ്ര ജീവിയിൽ പോലും കൃപയുള്ളവൻതന്റെ	Would He that in mercy pities the meanest pest
പുത്രരാം ഞങ്ങൾക്കിതു നൽകാതെയിരിക്കുമോ? (VV 3:21–24)	Withhold for us His children His garden's best?

Anticipating Eve's hesitation or even possible refusal to explore forbidden knowledge, Satan plays up the power of reason. Both Milton and Simon capture the design of Satan's temptation plan. His questions are of the caliber and rhetorical planning as might be expected of the classical Greek and Roman orators, as Milton notes.

Once the temptation has worked out fully as designed, and Eve has tasted the fruit and has shared it with her husband, the consequences are cosmic. "At the evil hour of the bite," the earth feels the wound and Nature gives out signs of woe that "all is lost." The sky weeps. Planetary motions affect the earth. Poles of the earth are shifted by angelic labor at God's command. In the description of disasters Milton says,

> Thus began
> Outrage from lifeless things; but Discord first
> Daughter of Sin among the irrational

Death introduced, through fierce antipathy.
Beast now with beast 'gan war and fowl with fowl
And fish with fish; to graze the herb all leaving
Devoured each other; nor stood much in awe
Of man, but fled him, or with countenance grim
Glared on him passing. (PL 10.708–16)

Simon catches the same fatal hour, with expanding accounts of internal fear and dread in Eve. As she took the bite, "A tremor convulsive, and smarting pains/Flashing from head to foot were her immediate gains/And changes of alarm filling all of nature" (VV 3:88–90).[20] Simon shows the alteration in animal behavior in a period slightly later in history for an agreeable reason. He lets the animal kingdom survive the Noahic deluge during which they lived in the big ship, but when they entered the new world, they showed selfishness and discord. The hitherto pastoral herds become merely a live food chain that we now see:

The lizard on the little emmet preys,
While behind it the vile snake strays;
The snake with the lizard clawed in shock,
Makes a sumptuous seize for the hovering hawk.
Flies feed the frog, the frog the serpent,
Serpents the peafowl, and to man the pheasant:
So run the hunts that cut their count
And undo the life bonds of their deluge shelter;
Creatures thus their conduct alter,
Humans topping the predaceous chain. (VV 9:119–28)

Man in the post-deluge era is stripped of the power of dominion he had in Eden, having become a target of predatory creatures of all elements. Any superiority he seems to have is largely because of the use of force or fear inspired. Human behavior also has changed ever since, says Simon.

There still are many more portions in their epics where Milton and Simon echo mutually. Simon has Adam and Eve offering their morning prayers to God in the Garden (VV 2:184–222). Milton has the couple singing a hymn unto God in PL V 105–208. While Adam and Eve have their nuptials in PL 4.710–15

---

[20] The Malayalam lines say:
വൈദ്യുതമായ ശക്തിയാപാദശിഖം വ്യാപി-
ചുദ്ദാമഭയം ഭ്രമംവേദനയാദിയായ
ഭവിഷ്യത്ഫലങ്ങളെ യുദ്ദീപിച്ചപോലെ
യവൾക്കുതോന്നീ, മാറ്റമുണ്ടായി പ്രകൃതിക്കും. (VV 3:87–90)

and in lines 740–52 of the same book, their "rites mysterious of connubial love" are matched in Simon's lines in VV 1:215–28. The demons celebrate man's fall in PL 10.460–520 and in Simon's VV 3.161–76 where he directly uses Milton's coinage of "Pandemonium" as the infernal capital. These are only examples of other parallel portions rather than a complete list.

Two Exit Escorts

Milton's story closes with Archangel Michael's prophetic revelation of Adam and Eve's post-Edenic life, showing the destruction of the old world through the Noahic deluge and a new human order starting in Noah as its "second source." Sin and death still continue in the new world until the end of the church age, but the promise of the "seed of the woman" God made to Adam and Eve in Eden will be manifest in the fullness of time. The understanding about that Seed as of the lineage of Abraham and of King David uplifts the mind of Adam who, in the place of the lost Paradise has been promised "a Paradise within." Milton gives the departure scene of Adam with his wife, hand in hand, thus:

> In either hand the hastening Angel caught
> Our lingering parents, and to the eastern gate
> Led them direct, and down the cliff as fast
> To the subjected plain; then disappeared.
> They, looking back, all the eastern side beheld
> Of Paradise, so late their happy seat,
> Waved over by that flaming brand; the gate
> With dreadful faces thronged, and fiery arms:
> Some natural tears they dropped, but wiped them soon;
> The world was all before them, where to choose
> Their place of rest, and Providence their guide:
> They, hand in hand, with wandering steps and slow,
> Through Eden took their solitary way. (PL 12. 637–49)

Simon also brings his narrative to a close in a manner similar to Milton's, but adds an allusion to the tragic fall of a political hero of modern history, Napoleon Bonaparte:

ആകയാൽ ബാഷ്പപപൂർണ്ണ നേത്രയുഗങ്ങളോടും	Anguished over the future just acquired
ഭീകരമായ ഭാവിയോർത്തു വൻതാപത്തോടും	And the life strings fond so quickly severed,
ഉദ്യാനത്തിങ്കലന്നു ബദ്ധമാം ജീവതന്തു	From the bonds of Paradise starkly shunned,

സദ്യോദാത മാമ്മാറു ഹൃദയാഘലാതത്തോടും	They paced on, heavy of foot, turning around
പ്രാണനിർവിശേഷമായ് നിരന്തം സ്നേഹിച്ചതൻ	Still, again and again, for one more glance
ഫ്രാൻസു രാജ്യത്തോടന്ത്യമാകിയ വിടവാങ്ങി	Of their lost home. At his dismal leave of France
നിത്യമായ് പിരിഞ്ഞൊരു നെപ്പോളിയന്റെ മർമ്മ—	For which he would trade his heroic soul,
സ്പൃക്കായ വിയോഗത്തേ നിസ്സാരമാക്കും വിധം	The great Napoleon saw sorrow, in immense whole–
ഇടയ്ക്കു പലവുരു തിരിഞ്ഞുനോക്കിപ്പാരം	A mere passing loss that, were we to compare
തുടുത്ത മുഖം വിളർത്തസ് ചേതനരായും	The griefs of the hero and of our ancestral pair.
എന്നേക്കുമായിപ്പറുദീസയ്ക്കു യാത്രചൊല്ലി-	All vigor drained, tear-soaked and pale, once for all,
പ്പോന്നയ്യോ പടിവാതിൽകടന്നു, കഷ്ടം! കഷ്ടം! (VV 3.401–12)	Alas! alas! they to Paradise bade dire farewell.

Milton has Archangel Michael on a mission of high dignity to escort the fallen first parents of humanity out of Paradise. In Simon's version God himself comes down to remove them from Eden. God sends them out with comfort, telling them that His Son, also to be known as the Logos, or Prajapati of the Indian mythology, has offered to redeem them by his own substitutionary sacrifice. As a result, suffering, pain, plagues and even death itself will all be undone, and humans shall be brought back to Paradise. Simon also underscores God's greater concern that the fallen humans, if allowed to remain in Paradise, may run the risk of reaching out for the fruit of the tree of life too and eat of it, thus perpetuating their fall and its consequences.

The Seed of the Woman

Eve's reach for Satan's bait brought about a cosmic tragedy, punished by a triple set of curses from the Creator, first to the serpent, second to Adam, and the third to Eve. The Serpent, who embodied Satan, will hereafter crawl in the dust, its head to be crushed by the seed of the woman, whose heels he would bruise. Adam would find the ground cursed with thorns and thistles and must eat his bread by the sweat of his brow, and he must, as a body made of dust, ultimately return to dust. Eve would have the pain of childbearing and shall be subject to her husband. Simon renders those utterances of divine displeasure in Sanskrit for the aura it has as the language of the Vedas, appropriate for the speech of divine beings, starting with these words to the Serpent:

കർമ്മേദ മകരോസ്ത്വാ; തസ്മാദ് ഗാർഹിക വന്യ —	This deed thou hast done; see thyself therefore found

പശൂനാം വൃന്ദാദ്ഭൂശം ശാപാപി ഗ്രസ്തോ ഭൂത്വാ	Of creatures all, of the wild and the common ground
വക്ഷസാ ഗമിഷ്യസി; കിഞ്ച ത്വം യാവജ്ജീവം	Most curse-lain, on thy belly crawling,
ഭൂതലോ പരിസ്ഥിത ധൂളീ: സംഖാ ദിഷ്യസി	Eating the dust for thy meat, and groveling
യോഷിത സ്ത വാപി ച യുവയോർ വംശ്യാനാം ച	In disgrace. Between thine and the woman's progeny
വൈരിതാം പരസ്പരം ജനയിഷ്യാമി നൂനം.	Shalt exist, hear this, perpetual enmity;
ത്വച്ഛീർഷം തസ്യാപത്യ മാഹനിഷ്യതി; തദ്വ—	From her seed thy kind shalt crush'd heads take
ദാഹ നിഷ്യസി തസ്യ പാദമൂലിപി ത്വജ്ഞഃ (VV 3.233–40)	Though on their heels thou might lesions make

While the penal import of these utterances is severe and certain, they still bear redemptive comfort to Adam and Eve, but not to Satan. The serpent will provoke enduring hatred between itself and the seed of the woman. "The seed of the woman" is an overarching symbol, type, or metaphor that will control all of scriptural history. It journeys prophetically from Genesis through Revelation, goes past this present age and even the millennium when the ultimate judgment on Satan is carried out. Simon says that Eve possibly thought that what God said would happen immediately, making her very first child that seed, which would take vengeance on the devil. She at this moment is the sole biological birth source of the human race. The term "seed" is a prophetic metaphor for "progeny." The promise of the seed crushing the Serpent's head in Genesis 3:15 is traditionally understood as *proto evangelium*, or, the first ever declaration of the gospel, already set in motion.

Milton devises a narrative framework for the fallen Adam to grasp how the seed of the woman will journey through a chosen bloodline. God would not let Adam and Eve exit Eden "disconsolate" (PL 11.112), which is why Archangel Michael provides Adam a panoramic vision of future history. Michael leads Adam to the highest peak in Eden from where all of earth's great places in all directions are viewable. Eve is temporarily at a nearby spot, but both Adam and his wife are in a realm above the sensory world from which alone can revelatory knowledge be grasped. Adam, as we understand from his earlier dialogue with Raphael, is already familiar with the deep sleep state brought on him by God. Michael's chronology of the vision of the first parents' generations begins only after they exit Paradise into the sin-marred soil of the earth. In the vision Adam sees two young men, one violent and the other gentle and innocent, the former killing the latter. Adam is shocked when told that they are his own sons of whom the older one is going to be the author of the first ever murder. The succeeding visions go on to other people, places, and events good and bad such as Enoch who walks with God, Noah the preacher of righteousness and "the second source" of humanity (XII 7, 13), Nimrod the tyrant and the first hunter, the Tower of Babel, the patriarchs, kings and nations, until the Son of God joins "manhood to Godhead" (PL XII 389).

Israel, yet to be formed and known as the chosen people or nation per Archangel Michael's timeline, devoutly preserves the prophetic texts that touch this theme. The seed of the woman manifests itself in their scriptures through foreshadowing types and symbols through a very slow course of precise but ponderous movements until it reaches its own prophetic "fullness of time," as Apostle Paul points out (Gal. 4:4). Moses, who writes about the matter first, has the "high office" to introduce the "One greater, of whose day he shall foretell/ And all the prophets in their age, the times/Of great Messiah shall sing" (12. 241–44), says Archangel Michael. Patriarchs like Abraham, Isaac, Jacob, Joseph, Moses, David, and other such figures in Israel's genealogies (Mt. 1 or Lk. 3, for example) exist as witnesses of the supernatural, speaking either directly about the seed of the woman, or foreshadowing it. In the family of Abraham, "the Seed" begins to take titular names. Abraham was a pagan Chaldean called by God to migrate with his whole family to Canaan. He then was a childless man and the husband of the beautiful but barren Sarai, who was well past childbearing age. Yet God promises him a son in whom all the world would be blessed. The childless Abraham is shown the stars of the sky and told that his progeny will be in such multitudinous numbers like the stars of heaven or the sands of the seashore. Despite the promise of God, everything within human reason persuades Abraham to think that he will go the way of all flesh, leaving behind a childless barren woman. He gathers enough courage to ask God if he will see anything more than a technical succession through his Syrian steward Eleazer. God assures Abraham that his own natural seed, the seed of his loins, will be his heir. To confirm this promise, God cuts a private covenant with Abraham in the setting of a large sacrifice with a prescribed set of clean animals and birds. The severed bodies of the animals attract wild birds which Abraham chases away for as long as he could, but soon a deep sleep from God comes upon Abraham wherein he sees visions of the future filled with the history of his "Seed," which in the next four hundred years becomes prolific enough to be a nation. However, they will also be suffering in captivity in Egypt during the said period, after which they will return to take possession of the land promised to Abraham and his generations. Joseph H. Summers expresses regret that Milton omits many of the visions and narratives, including the sacrifice of Isaac,[21] but Simon closes that gap, with the full accounts of all of them taken from Moses. Abraham's own seed will proliferate largely enough to become the chosen nation of Israel, birthed, formed, and returning to Canaan. Here is Simon's description of Abraham's dream-vision:

ഓട്ടിനാനബ്റാ മവയെത്തദന്തരേ	Abram chased the ravenous raptors
പെട്ടവനതൃന്ത ബാഢമാം നിദ്രയിൽ.	Fearing their unclean descent on his presents
അന്ധകാരം മഹാ ഭീതിയു മബ്രാമി-	Pure for the Lord's flaming torch path.
നന്തരംഗത്തിൽ ഭവിച്ചു; പരമേശ്വരൻ	All strength spent, his aged limbs fail,
ചൊല്ലിനാന ബ്രാമോടന്യ ദിക്കിൽ തവ	Lead-heavy sleep his eyes assail,
നല്ലരാം സന്തതി നാനൂറു വത്സരം	Great fear gripping his soul likewise:
പാർത്തു തദ്ദേശ്യരെ സേവിക്കുമായവ	Then heard he the Lord: "Thy goodly seed
രാർത്തി ചേർക്കും ഭവത്സന്തതിക്കെങ്കിലും	That thou seest not yet this day
ശിക്ഷിച്ചു പീഡകന്മാരെ ദയാന്വിതം	Shall in privation pass centuries four
രക്ഷിച്ചു കൊൾവവൻ ഭവദീയരെ ദ്രുതം. (VV 15.127–36)	Serving harsh aliens; take heart, though,
	They shall to this land entitled return,
	The judgment on foes full blown."

The vision of the future given to Abraham and the manner of it parallels Adam's, evidently. A biblical prophecy may have both immediate context and distant contexts. The original context which might be local may be the immediate reason for the prophecy, but its latter day application assumes much wider relevance. The person who prophesies is often unaware of the future scope of what is said because it is yet to be fully revealed. For instance, Jeremiah prophesied about Rachel mourning for her children (Israel) when the Babylonians took them into captivity. The date of that prophecy would be around 586 BCE, a time of national calamity. However, Rachel's cry was first heard ages earlier, in the 1800s BCE, while she was dying in the agony of childbirth with Benjamin. Rachel is eponymously the mother to Israel said to be crying again when Herod slaughters the innocent infants at the time of the birth of Christ in Bethlehem. Between the Babylonian captivity and Christ's birth is almost six centuries when Matthew's Gospel says: "A voice is heard in Ramah, lamentation, weeping and great mourning, Rachel weeping for her children, refusing to be comforted, because they were no more" (Mt. 2:17–18).

---

[21] Joseph H. Summers, *The Muse's Method: An Introduction to Paradise Lost* (Binghamton, NY: Center for Medieval and Early Renaissance Studies, 1981), 191.

One little strand of the story of Christ's nativity in the Gospel of Matthew provides another illustration of the multi-point fulfillment of biblical prophecy. The parents of Jesus flee with the infant Jesus to Egypt for protection from Herod. This flight is apt to be fraught with perils, even though such a miraculous birth was declared over so many centuries. Once Herod or those who sought the infant's life are dead, the parents return with Jesus, who is still only a child, to Israel. Matthew is quick to note that Hosea 11:1 says, "Out of Egypt have I called my Son." The statement in Hosea is a repeat of Exodus 4:22 where God is heard commanding Moses to demand of the pharaoh that Israel "His firstborn son" must be let go to worship him. Matthew sees greater relevance in these texts than the men themselves who spoke or wrote them down.

Let us return to Abraham's trance in which he has seen his progeny. He is still childless, however. When he is eighty-six, he gets a son called Ishmael through his Egyptian slave, but that is not the child of promise. The legal "Seed" must be the one through Sarah, and the wait continues. Another thirteen years later, Isaac is born, when Abraham is a hundred years old. Many happy years later, as divine commands go, God tells Abraham to sacrifice that very Isaac on Mount Moriah. True to the nature of his steadfast faith, Abraham goes with his son and his servants to Mount Moriah. The servants stay back near the foot of the mountain, and the father and son ascend the hill. Isaac is carrying the firewood, so, not seeing a lamb among the required items, he asks his father where the lamb for the sacrifice is. The father assures him that God will provide them with one. At the mountaintop where the altar is built, to his shock, Isaac finds himself bound up. As Abraham raises his knife to slay his son, he hears the command of God forbidding the act. A lamb, as Abraham told his son would be found, appears caught in the nearby thicket, which is readily sacrificed in Isaac's stead. Abraham and Isaac return to the servants who assumed that this was just another spiritual exercise of their master. Here is Simon's account of this incident:

ആരോഹണ മവരോഹമിവ മൂലം	Ascents and descents weary the comely youth
പാരം തളരുന്ന ചാരുരൂപൻ	As did they years thousand-twice past,
രണ്ടായിരാമാണ്ടു പിൽപാടു യൂദരിൻ	The Greater Man, who, bound by Jewish ill will,
ശുണ്ഠി നിമിത്തം നിബദ്ധനായി	Bore the fatal weight of the beams of the rood,
കെണ്ടൻ കുരിശു തൻതോളിൽ ചുമന്നുകൊ-	On his shoulders, under the consuming sun,
ണ്ടെണ്ടിശ ഭസ്മമാക്കും വെയിലിൽ,	Over the scorched earth: A sweat, denser
പണ്ടില്ലാമട്ടിൽ വിയർത്തു വലഞ്ഞതി-	Than any ever before from human pores,
കുണ്ഠത തിങ്ങുമുടമ്പിനോടും	Sprang from this body, too minced for sensory view:
ഇങ്ങളാൽ തൊണ്ടയിടറി മുറയിടും	The holy women witnessing, wail, their throats sore,

വണ്ടാർകുഴലിമാർ കൂട്ടമോടും	As the Son of the Most High, climbing the steep heights
കണ്ടകൻമാരുടെ മദ്ധ്യേ കൊലമല	Of the killer's hill, criminals flanking Him along the way,
മണ്ടയിലേക്കു നടന്നുപോകും	The Lord of Life, whose figure, etched on
വിണ്ടലനായകപുത്രനെ, യെന്മന-	My heart, I see within, refreshed over and over,
തണ്ടിലമർന്നിടും തമ്പുരാനെ,	A grief indelible.
വേണ്ടവിധത്തിലെനുസ്മരിപ്പിച്ചിടു-	
ന്നുണ്ടു നിരന്തരദുഃഖമായ്. (VV 22:173–88)	

The messianic typology in this event is self-evident. In the wood-bearing, the obedient son Isaac who is ascending the hill to do the will of the father, foreshadows Jesus Christ on the way to Calvary with his cross nearly two thousand years later. Mount Moriah where Abraham built the altar for his son is within sight of Calvary. Let it be noted John the Baptist, the prophetic herald of Jesus, introduces the Messiah to the first-century public of Judea as the Lamb of God that bears the sins of the world.

The genetic progress of the Seed is through Abraham and Isaac, henceforth as a royal bloodline. Jacob, the son of Isaac, dies in Egypt where his son Joseph was prime minister. Before his death, Jacob blesses each of his twelve sons with prophetic words. Each son henceforth becomes a tribe. Of them, the tribe of Judah would be a royal line. Jacob sees many kings of his future generations living out their days, until one identified as "Shiloh" comes, until which time the scepter shall not depart from Judah (Gen. 49:10). Here is Simon's rendition of that part of Jacob's blessing to Judah:

യഥാർത്ഥ സ്വാമിയായോൻ വന്നീടുംവരെ ചെങ്കോൽ	Until the day the True *Swamin*[22] emanates
യഹൂദാചരണങ്ങൾ വിട്ടുമാറുകയില്ല.	Judah's sceptered foothold none violates;
സമസ്തജാതികളുമവന്റെ മാഹാത്മ്യത്തെ	Nations His great day in keen hope await,
സ്മീക്ഷ്യവിധേയരാ മിവനാൽ കൃഷ്ണമാകും. (VV: 49:35–38)	As He their hope perfects in fulfilled state.

Ancient Israel was a nomadic nation, living primarily by farming and livestock. They had no tradition of royalty in civic life. After their entry into the Promised Land, a succession of folk heroes known as "judges" ruled the land before they adopted monarchy. The very first king, Saul, as Milton mentions in Michael's vision, started out well, but ended his career violently. Then follows another one after God's own heart, the second,

---

[22] *Swamin* is a Sanskrit term used in reverently addressing a venerable figure, especially in religion, in India. It has numerous possible meanings such as master, prophet, teacher of the sacred doctrine, or someone of holy living.

> ... both for piety renown'd
> And puissant deeds, a promise shall receive
> Irrevocable, that his Regal throne
> For ever shall endure; the like shall sing
> All prophecy, that of the royal stock
> Of David (so I name this King) shall rise
> A Son, the Woman's Seed, to thee foretold,
> Foretold to Abraham, as in whom shall trust
> All nations, and to Kings foretold, of Kings
> The last, for of his Reign shall be no end. (PL 12.321–30)

So now we see that the "seed" is a person, a Son, and the Son of David, to be a king in the royal line of David. David is in the lineage of Abraham; he is the "Son" or descendant of Judah, one of the twelve tribes of Jacob. As David's "Son," the same seed is also the ultimate heir to the throne of David. King David himself becomes the source of many prophetic utterances and writings about the seed. Of the 150 Psalms in the Old Testament, David is the author of at least seventy-three. Psalm 2 speaks of "the Son," begotten, heard as the voice of God; Psalm 8 speaks of that Son as the ruler of the nations of the earth; Psalm 16 speaks of his uncorrupted body rising from the grave; Psalm 22 gives the graphic details of the torment of crucifixion, "hands and feet" being pierced, recalling the Edenic curse of "the bruised *heels*," rather than just one heel; "lots cast for his clothes" and the New Testament scene of the soldiers at the foot of the cross, dividing Jesus's stripped clothes among themselves and the casting of lots for his seamless robe so that it would not be cut up, thus not serving the desired value in owning it; Psalm 34 declares that none of his bones will be broken in spite of the extreme violence and injury inflicted on him on the way to the crucifixion and after it; an attending soldier spears the crucified body's torso to be certain that life has left the body and therefore it is approvable for removal from the cross; the soldier's lance does not fracture any of the bones of Christ, as reported by Apostle John in his Gospel, 19:36; and that the act of piercing would happen was also a prophecy from Zechariah 12:10. In one of his post-resurrection appearances narrated in Luke 24, Jesus himself explains how the many prophecies found in Moses and all of the prophets had to be fulfilled in him.

Robert L. Deffinbaugh points out that the profile of the seed of the woman who should destroy the ancient serpent and its works is so specific in its diverse prophetic particulars that no human effort could orchestrate it.[23] The Messiah that Israel was expecting had to be a suffering servant, a prophet, the great high priest and king, specifically of David's lineage. Just a little pace down the prophetic timeline from David is seen the prophecy of a virgin conceiving a child who shall be called "Emmanuel," meaning, "God with us" (Isa. 7:14). However, as the archangel tells Adam, when the Son was born to the virgin (the emphasis on the virgin mother, with no reference to the male "seed" in Christ's birth scriptures), "a stranger" (Herod) will have seized the scepter from the sons of David, and the anointed King had to be born "barred of his sight." Nonetheless, the Eastern sages (the magi) come with their offerings for the Christ Child, the seed of the woman, "A virgin is his mother, but his Sire/The Power of the Most High" (PL 12.368–69). The virgin's child Jesus, as is written of him, "accursed and nailed to the cross/By his own nation slain for bringing life," (ibid., 413–15) dies, but soon revives, death having no power over him. This "godlike act/Annuls thy doom, the death thou should have died/In sin for ever lost from life; this act / shall bruise the head of Satan, crush his strength, defeating Sin and Death" (ibid., 427–30). Here is one stanza out of the many from Simon on the same theme of the sacrifice of the Incarnate Son:

ഈവിധം സ്ത്രീസന്താനം സർപശീർഷത്തെ തകർ-	Thus shall by the provident Word, in time determined
ത്തീടുമെന്നുള്ള വാക്യം സംസിദ്ധമാകും ധ്രുവം	The Seed of Promise crush the serpent's cunning head:
ദേവനീ വിധം ചൊല്ലി ലോഗോസിൻ യാഗാർപ്പണം	Herein to Adam the Lord unveiled the far-ranging saga
ഭാവനാർത്ഥമാ യാദത്തിനുപദേശിച്ചിതു. (VV 3:317–20)	Of the movements prescient in the Logos-*yaga*.

The "education" that Adam receives from Archangel Michael brings him into the heart of the scriptural mysteries that the "great expectation" of all ages is embodied in. Mary, the seed of the woman, who makes that title possible, is "high in the love of Heav'n, yet from my loins," and the Son thus born, shall be the Son of the Most High, who unites "God with man," (PL 12.378–80) learns Adam, to his delight.

Milton's allusions to the Serpent make straight connections to the language Christ himself uses. While sending his disciples for a practicum, as it were, in the application of spiritual authority, Jesus gives them power and authority over

---

[23] Robert Deffinbaugh, "The Story of the "Seed"—The Coming of the Promised Messiah," https://bible.org/article/story-seed-coming-promised-messiah, accessed July 2, 2022.

all demons (Lk. 9:1). Upon their return they report that even the demons yield to them in his name (Lk. 10:17). Jesus responds: "I saw Satan fall like lightning from heaven. Behold, I give you authority to trample on serpents and scorpions and over all the power of the enemy and nothing shall by any means hurt you" (Lk. 10:18–19). The language at the close of the Gospel of Mark is more specific: "They will take up serpents, and if they drink anything deadly, it will by no means hurt them; they will lay hands on the sick, and they will recover" (Mk 16:18).

The Songs of Simon

In 1925 when Simon was forty-two years old, his collected songs appeared under the title *Sangeetha Ratnavali* as a volume of 210 poems. Nearly six decades later, the Mylapra Gospel Society brought forth its sequel with the same title, but with 259 songs, which still had excluded the longer poems like *Nalla Samaryan* [The Good Samaritan], *Nishakalam* [Seasons of the Night], or *Ente Grandhasala* [My Library]. Other collections with large numbers of Simon's hymns have come out in between, in some of which Simon is a bulk contributor or editor. His songs had already been popular across the Malayalam country for at least two decades prior to the first publication date. No definite count of Simon's hymns and songs exists. Professor K. M. Daniel, a nephew of the poet who also had direct knowledge of his writings, sets the number at 300 at the very least, cautioning that a well-driven retrieval initiative could bring out scores more of Simon's individual poems from the archives of contemporary publications, which have always pursued Simon contributions whenever possible. Like Milton, Simon also wrote his shorter poems in the first half of his short life.

The scripture is the primary inspirational source of Simon's verse. The inner certainty that he experienced about his faith as a precocious eleven-year-old had only deepened in his growing years with his expanding learning. The songs show a great variety of themes: the sovereignty and the immutability of the Word of God; Christ in the great variety of his manifestations, pre-incarnate, incarnate, resurrected, and returning; the call to turn to Christ and his gospel; conduct of life in the pursuit of wisdom; the flight from sin; the typological motifs of the person and work of Christ; visions of earth's millennial age; devotions and meditations; didactic and mystical poems; rendition of scripture portions and chapters into new songs; odes and orisons; celebratory songs, and even children's verse, and translations.

Let us take a handful of Simon's songs for a quick review of how they sound and what they say. Song 49 "പാടും നിനക്കു നിത്യവും" ["I will sing unto thee all my days"] in *Sangeetha Ratnavali* [identified as "SR" hereafter] is a good start. Here Simon dedicates himself to the courtly charge of composing inspired verse for an enthroned sovereign, echoing the opening verses of Psalm 45:

പാടവമുള്ള സ്തുതി പാഠകനെന്ന പോൽ	Like the scribe of courtly mandate
തേടും ഞാൻ നല്ല വാക്കുകൾ–പരമേശാ!	Seek I words that suit thy state, Paramesh!.[24]

He asks that his tongue be "a speedy pen of a skilled scribe" when he carries out his bidden duty. It is a similar prayer that he offers in the invocation of his epic where he asks for divine inspiration. Another song, SR 33 "പരമ കരുണാ രസരാശേ!" ["God, the king and fount of mercy utmost"], confesses how he has experienced inspirational fulfillment in composition:

നാഥാ നിന്നാവിയെൻ നാവിൽ വന്നാകയാൽ	Lord, my tongue thy spirit quicken;
നവമായുദിക്കും കൃപകൾ പൊഴിക്കും	Praises raise, their echoes thicken;
നലമൊടഹമുര ചെയ്തിടും മമ ചെയ്തിടും നിൻകൃപാ	In pleasure rich I'll proclaim, yea, thy mercy's moves,
കലിതസുഖമിഹമരുവിടും സ്തവമുരുവിടും ദയ പെരുകിടുന്നൊരു–	In lays inspir'd measure thy lenity's flows.
പരമ കരുണാ രസരാശേ!	

Primacy of the Divine Word

As he tells us in the opening of *Vedaviharam*, Simon believes that the universe came into being from the spoken Word of God. That Word continues to speak as it did in the creation story and in every ensuing age and event. The Gospel of John declares the God-spoken Word as a person, seen and heard as Christ, also identified as the "Wisdom of God," speaking in first person in Proverbs 8:30–31. Simon addresses Him in the praise hymn "സ്തോത്രം ശ്രീ മനുവേലനേ" [SR 17, "Adoration of Immanuel"] thus:

ആദി പിതാ വോതിയതാ–	[Aadi-pitav-othiyathaa–
മാദി വേദ നാദമേ– മമ ജീവനേ!	maadi veda nadameh–mama jeevaneh!]

These eight words in two lines condense the many theologies about the godhead and a stream of the philosophies of origins in the East and the West. *Aadi* means the primeval beginning; *Pita* means the Father or life-giver; *Veda* is the

---

[24] *Paramesh* is the Sanskrit term for the "Lord of Lords" or "the Most High God."

divine Word, and *nada* is the sound of the voice of God. These are simple but elegant Sanskrit terms of endearing devotion to the Indian ear. *Veda* and the "Word" in Simon mean and mediate the same truth as interlingual synonyms. So now the two lines run roughly thus in meaning: "The spoken Word of the Father of the beginning of all beginnings, Oh, my being's sole spring!" Neither Moses nor the sages of the East in Simon's home culture disagree with the poet's understanding of the divine Word in the manner it is phrased.

A large number of Simon's poems come as meditative hymns on the *Veda* or the Word. The statements the poet makes in them are of universal appeal, causing no dissent to people of faiths other than his. See a few lines in SR 114 "തേനിലും മധുരം" ["Sweeter than honey"], a lyric on "the sweetness of the Veda":

തേനിലും മധുരം വേദമല്ലാതി-	Besting the tastes of nectars rare
ന്നേതുണ്ടു ചൊൽ തോഴാ!	If not *Veda*'s word, aught else, my peer?
നീ സശ്രദ്ധമതിലെ സത്യങ്ങൾ വായിച്ചു	Search and own its sacred spell
ധ്യാനിക്കുകെൻ തോഴാ!	And on its sounds you constant dwell.
മഞ്ഞു പോൽ ലോക മഹിമകൾ മുഴുവൻ	Like melting snow, world's glitters all
മാഞ്ഞിടുമെൻ തോഴാ! -ദിവ്യ	Shall give way, my peer!—the celestial
രഞ്ജിത വചനം ഭഞ്ജിതമാകാ	Word that quenches not, but conciliates-
ഫലം പൊഴിക്കും തോഴാ-തേനി	Its bounteous fruit none abates, my peer!
പൊന്നും വസ്ത്രങ്ങളും മിന്നും രഥങ്ങളു-	Gold and garbs and glowing gear-
മിതിനു സമമോ തോഴാ!-എന്നും	Dare they match its claims, my peer!—
പുതുബലമരുളും അതിശോഭ കലരും	New strength ordains, fresh light fetches,
ഗതിതരുമന്യൂനം	And steadfast this your course prospers.
തേനോടു തേൻ കൂടതിലെ നൽതെളിതേ-	Not finer drips nor purer drops
നിതിനു സമമോ തോഴാ! ദിവ്യ	Of pristine combs of honey, my peer!-this
തിരുവചനം നിൻ ദുരിതമകറ്റാൻ	Wisdom has your scourges purged,
വഴിപറയും തോഴാ!	Oh, hear my kin—see new paths forged!
ജീവനുണ്ടാക്കും ജഗതിയിൽ ജനങ്ങൾ	Life it yields for earth's mortals,
ക്കതിശുഭമരുളീടും—നിത്യ	And added goodness day by day—Grants them
ജീവാത്മ സൗഖ്യം ദേവാത്മാവരുളും	Weal, everlasting weal of the holy One;
വഴിയിതുതാൻ നൂനം.	The path to keep is this alone.
കാനനമതിൽ വച്ചാനന്ദരൂപൻ	The Fallen One in arid waste
വീണവനോടെതിർക്കേ-ഇതിൻ	Stood to test the Lord of Hosts—His Word

ജ്ഞാനത്തിൻ മൂർച്ച സ്ഥാനത്താലവനെ	Of Wisdom him repell'd,
ക്ഷീണിപ്പിച്ചതെന്നോർക്ക—	Its judging edge by none withheld.
പാർത്തലമതിലെ ഭാഗ്യങ്ങളഖിലം	The gains of th' earth evolve and pass
പരിണമിച്ചൊഴിഞ്ഞീടിലും—നിത്യ	In turns and courses their entire mass—the Word Eternal-
പരമേശവചനം പാപിക്കു ശരണം	Secure refuge for sinners still:
പരിചയിച്ചാൽ നൂനം.	Own it to see it by tractable will.

The poem is the counsel of a sage who desires to see his hearer exalted by its message. The knowledge it offers has the power to reconcile heaven and earth. The lure of "gold and garbs" should be dispelled by the *sruti*[25] or the hearing of the voice of the Supreme Lord. Simon's knowledge of the Vedic understanding of *sruti* as the whole body of sacred utterances "heard" and transmitted shows that he himself has received that *sruti*. Notice, especially, the stanza on the "Fallen One in arid waste": the allusion is to the well-known portion in the Gospels of Matthew and Luke in which Satan, as shown also in Milton's *Paradise Regained*, is overcome by the divine Word.

A pair poem, SR 115 "മധുരതരം തിരു വേദം" ["The Sweetness of the Sacred Veda"] delivers a similar message derived from experience:

മധുരതരം തിരുവേദം	Of sweet allure is *Veda*'s script,
മനസമോദ വികാസം	Vistas vast of ecstasy!
തരുമിതു നിത്യം പരിചയിച്ചീടിൽ	Love it, live it, and in its keep
നിരവധി നന്മകളുണ്ടാം	Stately favors are thine to heap
പരമ ധനമിതിൽകണ്ടാൽ	From its immense jewel troves.
വാനൊളി നീങ്ങിയിരുളുമന്നേരം	When fades the day and night assails thy space
ഭാനുവിൻ ദീപ്തിപോൽ നിന്നു	Lost is not thy light; thy Greater Sun will efface
ഭാസ്സുരുളീടുമിതെന്നും	The nighting pall, and thy skies by light to dazzle.
ബഹുവിധ കഷ്ടമാം കൈപ്പുകൾ മൂലം	Tested much through the wormwood trail,
മധുരമശേഷവും പോകെ	If the savor known is of no avail,
മധുവിതു നൽകിടും ചാലേ!	Comes anew a nectar grail!
നിസ്വത്ര നിന്നെ നികൃതനാക്കുമ്പോൾ	When want strips you of your substance,

---

[25] Sanskrit word for the sacred script, the scriptures that the sages have received by their own inner "hearing," contrasted with "smriti" that denotes what is remembered as inherited or acquired knowledge.

രത്നവ്യാപാരിത തന്നെ	The word brings you the treasure stones
പ്രത്ധനിയാക്കും നിന്നെ	Of its gems of ancient store.
അജ്ഞനു ജ്ഞാനം അന്ധനു നയനം	Light to the lost and sight to the blind,
നല്കിടുമീശ്വര വചനം	Boons are these of *Easwar's*[26] Word:
പുൽകിടുന്നു വിജ്ഞരിതിനെ	Embraces these the lofty mind.

The song SR 117 "കരുണാനിധിയാം താതനേ!" ["Father of all mercies"] extols the greatness of the Word, the scope of its study, and the necessity of it. Here is a snippet (I leave the beautiful Sanskrit terms unchanged):

സുരലോക രേഖകളിതു-സർവ്വനേരവും	*Rekhas*, these of the high *loka*,
മമ മോദമായിരിക്കേണം	Make them wholly my *moda*;
ദിനവും പുതിയ ഭംഗി വളരും വെളിച്ചമിവ	Newer its light, with beauty twinned,
ഇതിൽ നിന്നു കണ്ടിടുവാൻ തുണ ചെയ്ക പരമാത്മൻ-	Daily birthed, help me behold, Most high Lord.

Rekha means a record, a document, or proof of high value, a ray of light, or a drawn line. *Loka* means world or universe. *Moda* means bliss or joy. "Mine eyes have seen the salvation of the Lord," says Simeon the venerable elderly man who came to the temple at the hour the Christ Child was brought by his parents for his dedication. Simeon's recognition of Christ was by inner revelation. Similar was the received "sight" or understanding of the Samaritan woman who meets Christ in John 4, or the two men of Luke 24 walking toward the village of Emmaus on the night of the resurrection as the risen Jesus himself joined them, seemingly like a stranger. Christ in all his timeless manifestations, before the creation of this world, through it, and following it, as understood from the Old and New Testaments, is the hero in Simon's verse. "നിന്റെ പേശലമാം ചരിതമെന്തതി വിപുലം!" ["How hugely vast thy beauteous lore!"], exclaims Simon in SR 61 "മാനുവൽ മനുജസുതാ"! ["Manuvel, ManSon"]. A flashing summary of the "lore," for someone new to it, comes in two companion poems, the first of which is SR 131 "വെള്ളങ്ങളിൻ മീതിൽ" ["Hovering over the Waters"], a two-minute version of the creation story—from the earth of the primeval waters to the habitable, pleasant world of the humans in Eden. The second poem balancing the creation tale is the Christ story from birth to crucifixion and resurrection in SR 141, "കീർത്തിക്കുവിൻ പാടി കീർത്തിക്കുവിൻ" ["Glorify, in a Song of Praise"] in thirteen stanzas. Because it bears retelling, that story is told again in another longer poem, SR 69

---

[26] *Easwar* is another Sanskrit synonym for God.

"കേൾക്കാതാരിനി?" ["Is There One Yet to Hear?"] with the Edenic theme of the seed of the woman crushing the head of the serpent.

The experience of time with its division of the past, present, and future is the result of human fall, says Amy Boesky in her study of Milton's narrative chronology.[27] Someone with Boesky's thinking could find Simon's distress and weariness with the nature of time working as a heavy conditioning factor in his poems. Time is mute and unchangeable, making of itself an existential burden to all living beings. In the SR 216 "Song of Moses and of the Lamb," Simon speaks of the slow, barely perceptible progress of the Word or the *Veda* through the ages until it culminates in the slain Lamb of God:

എത്രനൂറ്റാണ്ടുകൾ തന്തിയിഴന്നൊരു	How many centuries slow in slug-foot
ദൈവത്തിൻ വീണയാം വേദമിതാ!	Has moved this veena, the Lord's very *Veda!*
കമ്പിമുറുക്കിയേ മേളംശരിയാക്കി	Wind the strings and prepare the orchestra–
ഏകസ്വരം മുഴക്കീടുന്നിതാ!	That sound of oneness in nations throughout!

Time in its potent stillness serves divine decrees, containing within itself the massive settlement of millennia past and the ages of the future which also will fade into their own past. Simon shows himself as a conscious participant in the cosmic motion of time under divine control. His songs connect the music of the morning stars at creation (Job 38:7) with the song of Moses (Ex. 15:1–18) and the Song of the Lamb (Rev. 15:2–4). In between, "A thousand years, in thy sight, is but a day just past," says Simon in his own version of Psalm 90.

The Prophetic Call in Simon's Poems

Simon reminds the reader that an appointed season, however weary that might seem to us, is given to all humanity to embrace the divine Word. The scriptures periodically show a righteous voice addressing a generation or a whole culture of rebellious people as found in the days of Noah, Elijah, or Jeremiah. Milton touches on this phenomenon in Michael's vision of the antediluvian world where the righteous Noah was seen as nothing more than a laughingstock in his culture. Not a stranger to mockery and rejection, Simon also sees continual occasion to offer exhortations and appeals for heeding good counsel. SR 71, "പാപീ, നീവേഗം വന്നേശുവേ കുമ്പിടുക" ["Haste to Yeshu, and to Him bow"] is

---

[27] Amy Boesky, "Paradise Lost and the Multiplicity of Time," in *A New Companion to Milton* (Chichester: John Wiley & Sons, 2016), 408–20, 416.

the call to an indifferent world not to disregard "the acceptable time." SR 73 "അരികിലത്രേ നിൻ ചാവറിക" ["Nigh by thee see death's shadow"] reminds the reader of the power of death to surprise the living, anywhere, anytime. SR 77 "കളിയാമോ കനലോടെതിർത്തീടിൽ?" ["Sporting with Live Coal?"] cautions against habitual resistance to the call of God:

കളിയാമോ? കനലോടെതിർത്തീടിൽ?	Sporting?—a mere mole—
കളിയാമോ? പരനോടെതിർത്തീടിൽ?	With the Almighty, the live coal?

SR 78 with the title "തിരയേണ്ടയോ" ["Shouldn't we be seeking?"] carries on the didactic reasoning with the reader, but does not hide the awaiting judgment of the sinful earth by fervent fires:

നിഴലെന്ന പോൽ നീങ്ങിടുന്നിതു കാലമെന്നതോർക്ക നീ	Time shall fade, and like the shadow wane;
തഴൽപവും താണിടാതതു ശക്തിയായ് കത്തുമേ	Yet judgment's fire stores its furious bane.

The didactic poems may be considered verse homilies against humans pridefully overestimating the power of the flesh or the material world that will sooner or later crumble and fade. Poems of this category open with an apostrophe, an invitation, or a hortative call for a well examined life anchored in God.

Simon has unwavering certainty about the millennial future of this earth under an eternal king. Without the promise of a redemptive future under a righteous king who will remove all evil to its deserved place of foretold judgment, the flawed life of this present age would not make sense, he believes. SR 101 "വരുന്നിതാ നാഥൻ, വാഴുവാൻ ഭൂമൗ!" ["Here comes the Lord"] foresees a prophetic timeline at the final point of which the Father's promised throne shall be given to the Son, the lawful ruler:

പിതൃഭരണാസനമവനു ദേവൻ നൽകു-	The Father's throne in accord bold,
മധിപനാമിവനെന്ന പ്രവചനമുണ്ടു്-	For His rule ensues, as seers foretold.

Before he assumes that power, the corrupt world governments have to go. The Messiah, the greatly anticipated ruler, will bring his righteous rule to this earth with the New Jerusalem as the royal capital:

ജരിച്ച ഭരണങ്ങൾ മറിച്ചു നീക്കിത്തന്റെ	Crumbling kingdoms cast down he must,
വരിച്ച സതിയോടൊത്തു ഭരിച്ചിരുന്നീടാൻ-	With his bride, to sit enthroned, just.

SR 136 "കാണുന്നിതാ വാനിലൊരു മാനിനി!" ["Behold a Bride Readied!"] and SR 137 "പുത്തൻ യെരുശലേമേ!" ["Oh, New Jerusalem"], two companion poems, run their full length to describe the New Jerusalem, in entirely different constructs and details. In SR 256, "സീയോൻ മല മീതിൽ" [On Mount Zion], the pacifist Simon visualizes that day with personal pleasure:

യുദ്ധ കലഹങ്ങളെല്ലാമൊഴിഞ്ഞിടും	Of wars and quarrels none need fear;
സർവ മർത്യരിലും സത്യദൈവ ഭക്തി മുളയ്ക്കും	Mortals shall all sprouts of piety bear.

The temporal sorrows give way to healing, recompense, and gratitude. Falsehood and divisions that ruined the earth cannot even exist in the new world because their feeding sources cannot exist in the new world's environment of purity.

Types and Tropes in Simon Verse

Figurative devices of startling instructive power appear everywhere in Simon's verse. They also prepare us for pleasant, epiphanic moments of inspiration. Let us consider SR 175 "വാഞ്ഛിതമരുളിടും വാനവർക്കധിപ! നീ" ["Grant us blessings desired"] a *bhajan*, very Keralite in its melody and meter, and universally relevant in its meaning. It is a prayer song; the prayer is not for bounties of the world, but for the riches of the Word. The famous theophanic event that Moses witnesses in Exodus 3 inspires the whole poem. Here is its background: the eighty-year-old Moses, a Hebrew fugitive from Egypt, is tending his father-in-law's sheep in the land of Midian in the Sinai desert. All of a sudden, he catches sight of large flames of fire covering an acacia bush in the blazing desert sun, but the bush is unconsumed. Out of the flames God speaks to Moses, calling him to go down to Egypt to set his people free from slavery. Early church Fathers interpret the burning but unconsumed bush foreshadowing St. Mary's virginity: the bush was wrapped up in flames, but the nature of the bush stays as it was. The Holy Spirit's power overshadows Mary, and the virgin bears the Christ Child, the divine Word. Her virginity stays unimpaired.

The instructive focus of SR 36 "ദേവജന സമാജമേ!" ["The Gathered Elect"] is the stone-writ law of the Old Covenant being fulfilled by Christ who thereby creates a "new-heart people" of the Spirit. It is a hymn of doctrine, touching the baptism of one spirit, making all human family partakers of one same bread and one single cup; the high priest of its symbolic tabernacle is once for all replaced by the greater High Priest Christ as the mediator of the new covenant. SR 255 "എൻ വാസമിതുതന്നെ ധന്യൻ" ["This my place of dwelling"] offers a close up study of the tabernacle, the portable iconic structure that served as site of God's presence and the sacerdotal services of the Levitical priests. Simon has written an entire book with the exhaustive analysis of every part of it. He says that the whole Old Testament is a compendium of "types" or figurative images foreshadowing the particulars in Christ's ministry to the world. The "types" housed in and around the tabernacle are the altar, the sacrificial offerings, the door, the curtains, the shewbread, wine, incense, the lamp, the tablets of the Law, the Mercy Seat, the pillars, the hovering cloud and all of the rest. The tent stood in the geometrical center of the desert camp of Israel. On each side of it are pitched the tents of three of Israel's twelve tribes. Its position and the manner of its move are a visual lesson to all that the Presence of God was central in their lives. The New Testament teaches that the tabernacle serves as a type of Jesus himself, as priest, high priest, the slain lamb, the bread of life, and the express image of God in the Holy of Holies, who also said, "where two or three are gathered together in my name, I will be in their midst" (Mt. 18:20).

Closely related to the theme of the tabernacle is the poem "യഥാർത്ഥ മന്ന" [SR 254 "The True Manna]," which Simon opens an extended metaphoric meditation. The manna fell on the camp of Israel every morning as their daily provision. While it is the very means of sustaining life, it typifies humility, found covering the desert ground every morning, over a bed of dew, in such thick plenty for each family to gather right from its doorstep. It will melt away as the sun rises. Each day it is to be gathered, but not to be stored up for the following day. Each new day brings its own provision without fail. The "type" in the manna finds its fulfillment in the great "I am" statement of Christ who declared "I am the bread of life," and "I am the living bread that came down from heaven" (John 6:35, 51).

Around one half of Simon's songs are *bhajans* with charming simplicity, but of startling effectiveness. Others belong to a wide range of study levels for their full richness to be grasped. The Sanskrit poem "Manavendra" that he composed when sixteen years old has a dense three-page glossary and is challenging for the average scholar. We therefore might find that song limited in its audience. Hymns like "ശ്രീമനുവേലം ഭജേ" ["Worship Sree Manuvel"], and "പാപി! കേൾനീ" [SR 65 "Sinner, pay heed"] are also Sanskrit-dense, but they reward the reader with their inspired weight of wisdom and hortatory content. SR 152 "സച്ചിതാനന്ദഭജനിൻ" is a longer poem of thirty-two couplets of parabolic utterances, again, definitely didactic. SR 162 "അഞ്ചാം രാജിതമുണ്ടാം" ["There shall rise a fifth empire"] is a poem that harmonizes the prophetical portions of the books of Daniel and of the book of Revelation. It is certainly accessible, but perhaps not for a reader hurrying through the lines.

Critics have noted some of Simon's poems to be of high challenge levels for common readers. B. C. Balakrishnan is quite straightforward in asking readers not to hold Simon's learning against him. He says thus in his study of Simon's *Vedaviharam* and the songs: "*Vedaviharam* is a poetic gem. Its author is a poet of exceedingly vast learning. Few poets own the kind of word-wealth he possesses. Even the most well read of readers might find it at times difficult to follow his word choice and usages."[28] In prosody, Simon never needed to pause for a rhyming sound or word. Even as he went on, say many of his admiring readers, the words seem to have been standing ready to serve. Whereas many of his contemporaries, even the learned ones, often had to close the gaps by inelegant devices, Simon never had any such struggle. According to Balakrishnan's count, *Vedaviharam* has over 100,000 words, of which 60 percent are Sanskrit-derived. Thirty-eight thousand of them are pure Malayalam words. He lists a large number of words from Simon's usage which are yet to make their way into the dictionaries of Malayalam. Here are some of his examples: *krameedham*: bridge; *samsthyayam*: house; *bhittam*: small portion; *vighasam*: food; *drushyath*: rock; *alarkkam*: mad dog; *bharmam*: rule; *lundtanam*: loot; *hidtanam*: departure. *kulaya*: stream; *dhuni*: river; *ikshu*: sugar cane; *kumbhiram*: crocodile; *barhinam*: peacock; *pracheeram*: wall; *ruja*: sorrow; *saithakam*: desert; and *yoshith*: woman. Balakrishnan calls him *pada-kubera*, meaning the "Kubera" of diction. Kubera is the name of the mythical deity of wealth, so by extension, for Simon as a master of letters, it is a suitable appellation.

The Dravidian languages, like Sanskrit their parent, are also diction-rich. A poet would find great pleasure in the abundant supply of synonyms that most terms have in them. Consider a simple word like the "sun" and its synonyms, each with its own attractive nuances: *Aditya, ansu, arka, arun, bhanu, bhaskar, dinakar, dinesh, divakar, kapil, kiran, kathiravan, prabhakar, ravi, rohit, sanu, savita, sunoj, tapan, uday, ushapati*, and still many more. And now for another common word like "water": *amritam, neer, jalam, panyeeam, pushkaram, thanneer, thanni, vellam, thoyam, salilam, kamalam, vaanam*, and more. Now look for synonyms of these words or any other word in another language. The variety could be much smaller. Translations from languages with choice limits will unavoidably show the constraints of expression. Let us see how this resourcefulness of the language manifests in Simon's writing. Here is one of his simpler songs:

മംഗളം ദേവദേവനു –	Blessings to the God of gods
പ്രതിദിനവും മംഗളം ദേവദേവനു	And lauds fresh to him each new day.

---

[28] B. C. Balakrishnan, "Padakuberanaya Mahakavi" in *Smaranika*,121.

ഭംഗമില്ലാതെ പരമോന്നതനായുലകി-	To Him that all space in power does fill
ലെങ്ങും നിറഞ്ഞു മരുവും പരാപരന്നു	And acts likewise, the Supreme One.
ജീവനില്ലാതിരുന്നോ രാദിജലമതിന്മേ-	Hovering, who, over the primeval floods
ലാവസിച്ചുയിർ കൊടുത്ത പിതാ മഹന്നു	Gave them life-stirring breath, the Great Father.
ഏകജാതനാം തിരു സൂനുവേ ദയയോടു-	To the giver of the Holy Child to the world
ലോകരക്ഷയ്ക്കു നൽകിയ സുരാധിപന്നു	The gift of mercy in salvation's mould, the Ruler of *Suras*.
നീതിയോടിഹ ലോക ജീവിതം കഴിപ്പതി-	To him that with His Spirit grants
ന്നാവിതന്നനുഗ്രഹിക്കും അഖിലേശന്നു	Days on earth and life lawful, Master to all!.
ദേവനിവാസമാക്കി ബ്ഭൂവിനെ ശരിയാക്കി	To him who ordains grace to turn
മേവുവാൻ കൃപയരുളും സദാ തനന്നു	This dreary earth into the home of God, God Eternal.

Each couplet addresses God, but the term of address is new in each case. The song starts with *deva devan* [God of all gods], moves on to *para paran* [the Supreme One"], then to *pita mahan* [the Great Father], and to *suradhipan* [the Lord of the suras or angels], on to *akhileshan* [Lord or Master of all], and closing with *sada thanan* [God Eternal]. In the source language these are all names tastefully created with thoughtful connotations. Simon's use of Malayalam in this manner marks the introduction of a fresh, native flavor in Christian verse with which orthodox Christianity of the nation had only marginal familiarity.

Texts Other than of Genesis Versified

Simon has many poems that serve as verse renditions of scripture texts, from both the Old and the New Testaments. Let us not forget that his original plan was to produce the complete Bible in singable meters. The work he has done in that direction shows how easily the complete project could have been accomplished, if only he had a tiny measure more of time. SR 150 "വനവും തനിനിലവും" [The wilderness and the dry land shall rejoice] is technically an individual poem, but also a high fidelity translation of Isaiah 35, which describes the millennial earth. The Psalms in their original are songs to begin with, but Simon's translations bring them out in sonorous Malayalam, lending the feeling that the source texts themselves were in Malayalam. Psalms 15, 23, 45, 72, 73, 84, 122, 125, 127, 131, 133, 136, or 145 would suffice as examples. Moving on to the New Testament, Simon offers many gospel episodes in verse. The parable of the foolish virgins in Matthew 25 stands alone as its own verse tale. SR 149 "ചിത്തം കലങ്ങിടൊല്ല" ["Let not your heart be troubled"], a song in the melody of a lullaby, gives the comforting words of Christ from the Gospel of John 14 where Jesus is coming to the final hours preceding his arrest and crucifixion. Simon's ten-couplet poem SR 146 "ഇടുക്കുവാതിൽ" [Through the strait gate"] narrating othy 13:24–30 is one of these. The parable of the wedding banquet in othy 14:15-24 combined with Matthew 22:1-4 gets a brisk and witty retelling in SR 124 "രാജാത്മജ വിരുന്നതിൻ വിവരം." othy 15:25–35 is given a parallel narrative in another poem, SR 98 "കേൾപ്പാൻ ചെവികളുള്ളവൻ" [He that has ears to hear]. SR 136 "കാണുന്നിതാ വാനിലൊരു മാനിനി" [Behold a bride descend] narrates Revelation 21 entirely, describing the descent of New Jerusalem from heaven.

Didactic and Mystical Poems

Simon's readings of the poetical books of the Bible (Job, Psalms, Song of Songs, Proverbs, and Ecclesiastes) have in turn produced his own works of verse and prose. Proverbs, Ecclesiastes, and the Song of Songs are the works of Solomon that show the imprint of the monarch's famed wisdom. Ecclesiastes shows the sheer vanity of life on the one hand, and the possible triumph over vanity on the other, through the observance of "the whole duty of man" (Eccl. 12:13–14). Simon's theme selections from Solomonic writings are numerous, whole chapters and parts. His interpretive work *Sha-Labdaya*, a Hebrew phrase meaning "the Flame of Jah," is a full-length commentary on the Song of Songs. The anatomy of Solomon's Song has been puzzling scholars of every age with its sketchy plotline, though it has been part of the Jewish canon from the Septuagint onward. Commentator Andrew R. Fausset points out that the Jews compared the book of Proverbs to the outer court of Solomon's temple, Ecclesiastes to the Holy Place and the Canticles [Song of Songs] to the Holy of Holies.[29] The story of the Song is of mainly three characters, which would be King Solomon, an attractive shepherdess identified as the "Shulemite," and an anonymous shepherd. Both the king and the shepherd have passionate interest in the shepherdess, as interpretations vying for endorsement go. Her name, Fausset reminds us, means "the Daughter of Peace," also the feminine form of Solomon, meaning, the "Peaceful One." Christian mystical readings, conventionally allude to the Shulemite as a type of the Bride of Christ, the Shepherd as her hero, and Solomon as an unwelcome rival to the Shepherd. Here is a moment of a dialogue

---

[29] Adam Clarke, *Commentary on the Song of Songs*, Studylight.org., retrieved July 2, 2022.

between the Shepherd and the Shulemite found in SR 122, "ശാലോമിയേ വരികെന്റെ പ്രിയേ" [Salome, Come away, my Beloved]:

ലോകവെയിലാറി തീർന്നിടുമ്പോൾ	The scorching sun now fades and sets;
മൂറിൻമലമേൽ ഞാൻ വിശ്രമിപ്പാൻ	The hills of myrrh our slopes of rest;
സിംഹഗുഹകളും പുള്ളിപ്പുലികളിൻ	Come away, beloved, free from fears,
പർവ്വതവും വിട്ടു പോരിക, നീ ശുഭേ!	Of dens of lions and leopard's lairs.

And the maiden responds:

എൻപ്രിയനെ വരിക ഗന്ധമലകളിലെ	Like a gazelle on the fragrant hills
മാനിന്നു സമനായി നീ–മണവറയിൽ	Of spices, come running, in leaps of thrills,
ഓടി വരിക ജവമായ്!	To my chambers sprint, in ravishing power!.

Other stanzas show how deep her love for her beloved is and how the apparent attempts by a third party to lure her away would be futile:

ഏറിയ വെള്ളങ്ങൾക്കു പ്രേമം കെടുത്തുകൂടാ	Waters deep can't quench love's fire
ഹാ നദി മുക്കുകില്ല സർവ്വസമ്പത്തും	Nor will it floods drown, nor lucre
നൽകുകിൽ മൂല്യമാകില്ല.	Stand as its equal, though traded.

And then come the unflattering lines on Solomon himself, showing how his offers of wealth and other royal promises utterly fail to impress her:

ആയിരം പണം തരാമെന്നുരച്ച ശലോമോൻ	A thousand *panams*, your proffered gift,
രാജ! നിൻ ധനമെനിക്കു വേണ്ട നീയതു	Rajah Solomon, could be suitably fit
ലോകർക്കായി കൊടുത്തുകൊൾക.	For worldlings lost in your excesses.

A thousand "pieces of money" or *panams* could be either in silver or gold. *Panam* is a synonym for money in general or the pre-modern nomenclature for a certain denomination of Indian coins. Simon's use of the words *panam* and *Rajah* produce a subtle narrative effect: they give Solomon an Indian style of direct address that makes the Hebraic king adequately Indian, and gives to his money the status of a native coin of Kerala. The *panam* could be silver, gold, or any of the other forms of money in use. His offer being rebuffed, Solomon allows the chaste resolve of the young maiden to win the praise of the reader.

Through his poems of Solomonic themes, Simon popularized the phrase "the fairest of ten thousand" as a title of adoration for Christ. They also appear as a theme thread for Simon's poems on Solomon's romance themes. The poem SR 99 "മഞ്ഞുകാലം കഴിഞ്ഞിപ്പോൾ" ["The winter is past"], which falls under that theme (Songs 2:10–14), again describes the narrator's passionate pursuit of a lovely maiden. The focus is entirely on her, though she still is unseen: "Come away, my dove, hidden in the rock's clefts and cliff's coverts," he implores, having reminded her earlier not to miss the ripe figs and the refreshing grapes of the season (SR 99). Poem SR 100, "മേലിലുള്ളൊരുശലേമേ" [O Jerusalem Above!] uses the same scripture text of the Song of Solomon 2:10–14 to address another bride for whom also the Shulemite serves as a type. This latter one is figuratively the spotless Church of Christ who awaits his promised return. She would soon traverse constellations and galaxies as she is raptured away by Christ, her spouse, whose courtly and worshipful attendants are now keenly awaiting her arrival. Meanwhile, in her devout reflections, she describes her spouse, the mystical Christ figure, thus in SR 213:

ലിബന തുല്യം മുഖസ്വരൂപം	Libana's equal in face's form,
ദ്രുമമതു ദാരുകമിതിനു സമം	Tree Cedar, in looks wholesome.

The lines of Malayalam provided here in pyrrhic feet stirs music in anything that moves. The word meanings go deeper than do the sounds. *Swaroopam* signifies a sacred image in religion; in philosophy it means "own-form" as we speak of divinity. Politically in India, the kingdoms of Malabar identified themselves with the entity title of *swaroopam* added to their dynastic names such as the *Venad Swaroopam, Perumpadappu swaroopam*, or *Kolathu swaroopam*. *Libana* is Simon's coinage for Lebanon. The perfect male figure (the type of Christ) exalted in the poem is matched with the *druma*, or a choice tree, the *darukam*, a variant of *devadaru*, the poetic Malayalam name for cedar. The significance will be complete only with the full phrase, the proverbial "Cedar of Lebanon," found in the Song of Songs, the book of Psalms, and in the prophetical books.

Occasional Poems

Some of Simon's best-known songs were written at the request of friends or at the most unexpected moments of inspiration. Edayaranmula writes about Mammen Bhagavatar, a national gold medalist and honoree many times over, a traditionalist Syrian Christian, invited frequently to Hindu temples for performance. Edayaranmula himself was present at one of the performances (a cutcherry, the typical, stage-floor concert, no furniture for performers) which, for the Bhagavatar, had a discouraging start. The great maestro tried one or two numbers, but then switched to a new song, "യേശുനായക ശ്രീശാ നമോ" [SR 55, Lord Jesus, Glorious One, Hail]. As he picked up the second stanza, the entire grounds seemed lifted up.[30] This was one of the three or four songs

---

[30] Edayaranmula K. M. Varghese in *Smaranika*, 296–97.

Simon wrote for the Bhagavatar around that time. "ആദ്യന്തമില്ലാത്ത നിത്യന്റെ കാന്ത്യാ" [SR 202] is a wedding hymn that Simon dictated while pacing back and forth in the courtyard of a friend's home with his disciples. The song was his personal benediction and wedding gift to the friend's daughter. "നോക്കിലാർക്കും മതിവരാ മന്ദിരം" [SR244] is a kind of "river song," very popular in Simon's native regions of the Pampa. Between short distances along the river, people would wait for the ferry boat, non-mechanized, directed by a simple pole if it is for the crossing of the river; for larger sailing parties or row teams, the song would be sung to the rhythm of the oars. Simon was waiting at the landing when a boat and its singing party of rowers drew ashore. With no time lost, Simon had the rendition of Psalm 122 in the same meter, describing the serenity and beauty of Jerusalem, closing it with the final stanza as a doxology. Likewise, while he once was in the capital city of the state, he witnessed a ceremonial police parade. Instantly he composed "ക്രിസ്തു നാമത്തിന്നനന്ത മംഗളം ദിവസ്ഥരേ" [SR 54 Christ's name in torrents hail], the content of which is the festive praise of Christ the King:

ക്രിസ്തുനാമത്തിന്നനന്ത മംഗളം ദിവസ്ഥരേ	Christ's name hail in torrent-praise, ye godly folk,
നിസ്ത്രപം ശിരസ്സുണച്ചു സന്നമിപ്പിൻ തത് പദേ!	Unabash'd, at his feet, worship due evoke!.

The rhyme and the rhythm of this song give out a ready military beat. In comparative hymnology, this would be a Malayalam parallel or companion to Edward Perronet's "All Hail the Power of Jesus' Name," which according to Professor C. Michael Hawn, has a "stately tune in Duple meter … [with] the character of a coronation march."[31] Similar is Simon's own version of the victory song of Israel in Exodus 15 as they cross the Red Sea with the pharaoh and his forces pursuing them into the dry land between the parted waters. The waters close in as soon as Israel clears the passage. Once on the other shore, they erupt into a song of triumph, which is titled "പാടും പരമനു പരിചൊടു ഞാൻ" [SR 51 "The Song of Moses"]. Simon has his own rendition of the song in eleven stanzas of epic description. Here is one of them:

യുദ്ധ മനുഷ്യനവൻ യാഹെന്നവന്റെ നാമം	Man of War is He, Yah is His name
സത്വരം ഫറവോനിൻ സൈന്യം രഥങ്ങളെയും	An instant sea sweep was His move of fame
അബ്ധിയിൽ തള്ളിയിട്ടു യുദ്ധ നേതാക്കൾ മുങ്ങി	To the nether go the pharaoh's troops and horses
ഗുപ്തരായ് ചെങ്കടലി ലത്തലോടവർ താണു.	In the sea-jaw ride of his proud concourse.

---

[31] C. Michael Hawn, "History of Hymns: All Hail the Power of Jesus' Name," www.umcdiscipleship.org/ accessed June 28, 2022.

The lines are full of speedy action, with the sure-footed pace of the divine movements which the poet transmits to the reader.

Millennial Songs

The setting of time in Simon's poems ranges from the local and temporal to the unknown *aadi* or the beginning of beginnings to the prophetically envisioned millennial and the eternal. SR 151 "ശോഭനമാം ശ്രീനഗരം" [The radiant city] describes a vision of the descent of Jerusalem from heaven, figuratively like a comely bride, the Bride of the Lamb, imaging perfection in every limb; her brightness is like the star ruby's (*yespi-kal* or *Suryakantam*); her foundations have the names of the twelve apostles; all of her gates are open. The song mentions several attractive "negations" to the city that are otherworldly positives, all of which underscore its glory: the Son of God himself being present there, no temple is necessary; there is neither the sun nor the moon appearing in its firmament because the Lamb is its whole and sufficient source of light; the gates of the city will not be shut, day or night; night is not a concern because this is a city of no sunset. SR 137, "പുത്തൻ യെരുശലേമേ!" [Oh, New Jerusalem!] is the prayer of the longing of a universal family that sees the New Jerusalem as their sacred mother under whose shadow they will have a secure home. The poet is deeply conscious of the stark difference between where he is and where he will be. He describes the divine design of that place like an eyewitness in direct sight of it. SR 136 "കാണുന്നിതാ വാനിലൊരു മാനിനി!" is a full verse version of Revelation chapter 21, presenting "Salem," an endearing appellation for the lovers of Jerusalem among her people as the church, which also is spoken of as the Bride of the Lamb. Simon's great classic "അംബ യെരുശലേം അംബരിൻ കാഴ്ചയിൽ" [Amba Yerusalem] shows the imminent appearance of the heavenly city, like the bride all adorned for presentation to her groom; she is attired in robes of righteousness; here her sun and moon will never leave their places and her own brightness is never lost. She muses in songs of abounding *rasa*, and by herself she sings, in continual pleasure. And then there is a fleeting mention of something that is *not* on her:

കനകവും മുത്തു രത്നാ ഇവയണികില്ലെങ്കിലും	Shuns she though gems and gold of glittery beam,
സുമുഖിയാമിവൾ കണ്ഠം ബഹുരമണീയമാം—	Comely-fac'd, does her neck, so carven seem.

She wears no jewelry! The holiness movements of Simon's day, his own included, taught their believers to forgo jewelry, even a wedding ring. It was all the more startling in the largely conservative Indian society where, at least for women, some quantity of gold is part of normal attire. Simon's mention of New Jerusalem being unadorned with gold is a bantering jest, commending Kerala's Viyojithas and the Pentecostals who had shunned jewelry, and still do, as a mark of spiritual discipline. The practice has since gained the power of a doctrine in the Keralite holiness subculture, for which the defense offered is a couple of Bible verses, one from 1 Peter 3:3–4 and the other from 1 Timothy 2:9–10, where both Peter and Paul respectively urge women to love simplicity rather than showy luxury. However, we have no lack of Simon's own verse passages elsewhere, where he would describe the attraction of ornaments in figures of loveliness in his epic, in the Psalms, or in the book of Revelation.

Simon reconciles the prophetic future of this earth eschatologically and scientifically. The present earth and firmament, says he, will give way to the prophesied "new heaven and new earth." The removal of the present earth will be by fire, as mentioned in 2 Peter 3:10. In his commentary on the book of Revelation, Simon states that a complete destruction of this earth is not necessary for a new heaven and earth to come to be. The earth was not created for outright elimination, but redemption.[32] It is also unreasonable to think that God would create the starry vistas and planetary ranges merely for us to see as remote decorations of our planetary neighborhood, he comments. Simon believes that as the redeemed humanity grows and multiplies, the outer planetary bodies will need to be inhabited.

Music and Metrics in Simon's Verse

Simon's verse is to be *read* and *heard*. While Milton brought the unconventional iambic blank verse from the stage into the epic and maintained it throughout his work, Simon had his *Vedaviharam* written in fourteen various Dravidian meters, each determined by the content and mood of the movement. Here are their names: *keka, kakali, misra kakali, makanda manjari, sheelavati, Kalyani, parayanthullal, bhujangaprayatham, annanada, pancacamaram, induvadana, drutakakakali, kalakanci,* and *mohini*. Of these fourteen, the weighty-footed and solemn *keka* appears to be the lead meter. All of the Dravidian meters have strong musical orientation, as A. R. Rajaraja Varma has stated.[33]

---

[32] K. V. Simon, *Commentary on the Book Revelation*, 2nd ed. (Tiruvalla: Satyam Publications, 1936), ch. 21.
[33] K. M. George, *A. R. Rajaraja Varma* (New Delhi: Sahitya Akademi, 1979), p. 63.

Likewise, Simon has used over seventy *ragas* and ten *talas* (the metrical framework for the structure of musical beats) in his songs. Neither the *raga* nor the *tala* has an equivalent in Western music. As the meter is to prosody, the *raga* in Indian classical music is to its melody. The melodic structure, based on a scale of notes, creates a mood or *bhava* that is unique to the *raga*. Hundreds of *ragas* are in use, and theoretically, thousands of them exist or can be created. *Ragas* are set to specific times of the day or night, seasons, or occasions: *Gandhara, Dhanasi, Sudha Bhairava, Bhupala, and Saurashtreya*, for instance, are morning *ragas*; *Sankarabharana, Valahamsa, Saveri*, and *Khamboji* are noonday ragas; *Gauri* is for the evening; *Kalyna* for the beginning of the night; *Kedara* for late night; *Megha raga* is the proper melody for the rainy season; *Vasanta* for the spring, and *Hindola* for the festive occasion. A well composed Carnatic or Hindustani song has the rapturous power to transport the soul to the great realms of *rasa*, which also would mean that the mere reading of a lyric, even the most consummate one, without the auditory complement, leaves the engagement of that composition incomplete.

Edayaranmula K. M. Varghese states that among Christian poets who compose Bhakti hymns that meet all of the *lakshanas* (the criteria or attributes) of the perfect hymns or *kirtans*, Vidwankutty and Simon are the most accomplished. Some of their poems have such closeness that their affinity might make one think that it is the other's work. Comparing their hymns, it is difficult to determine who surpasses the other in melody and sensory appeal. Where the grandeur of classical music, the *gravitas* of the subject matter with its depth and variety, the power of *bhavas* or moods, and the architectonics of the lyric are critical considerations, Simon is a safe bet as a model. The rhyming patterns of Simon are profuse and effortless; the diction of pure *manipravala* and the rhetorical devices used also go the same way. Simon's era was also a time in Malayalam literature where the tastes and talents of the likes of "Thunchan, Kunchan, Unnai, Irayimman Thampi and Valiakoi Thampuran were held as absolute models," says Edayaranmula. Critics of the age respected only the merits of the levels of such men, by and large.[34]

The rhyme schemes in Simon's poems come in abundant variety. Metrical units vary from couplets to units of eight lines or more. Prosodic integrity is a basic, but effortless strength of all of his poems. Patterns of rhyme vary according to the meaning and mood, line by line or foot by foot, or even in

---

[34] Edayaranmula, *Satabdi*, 304–05.

alternating syllables, in beats of startling speed and regularity. Any of Simon's verse portions will illustrate his spontaneity and metrical mastery, but "സദനേ മാമകമേ വാഴും കദനേ" [SR 198 "Holy One who in me abides"], മനതാർ മുകുരത്തിൻ [SR126 The Mind Mirrored] "പരമകരുണാ രസരാഗേ" [SR 33 O, Font of Mercy!], and "നീതിയാം യഹോവയേ!" ["Jehovah! The Righteous One!"] will suffice to cite as examples for a quick glance. Tradition expects the *sahitya* (lyric or text) of a Carnatic performance *kriti* to be written by a singer–poet. Simon was always providing it as an instant value to his work.

Among Simon's companion poems and sequence poems one can see the poet's easy facility with creative variety. He writes more than one poem on a particular text or theme in a good many of his compositions: "The Lord's Prayer" is given in two versions (SR 211 and 212); Psalm 23 is written as pair lyrics (SR 223 and 224); so are Israel's lamentation psalms of their Babylonian captivity (SR 219 and 229) and the vision of the messianic reign in Jerusalem (SR 256 and 257). It would seem that as soon as Simon is done narrating a scripture text or while yet doing it, he sees a competing poem in formation, awaiting his approval. The new one arrives without any redundancy in content or melody to dampen a reader's interest.

Among his sequence poems, a tight-knit cluster of seven, written as verse epistles to the seven churches of Asia Minor, is vintage Simon. Individually, they would be superb Carnatic performance *kritis* [lyrics]. Their text source is in the book of Revelation, chapters 2–3. We know that the entire book of Revelation is written as a visionary report of Apostle John from his exile on the barren Isle of Patmos in Asia Minor, which would be the Western region of Turkey. There the apostle receives Christ's command to write individual epistles to the churches of the cities of Ephesus, Smyrna, Pergamos, Thyatira, Sardis, Philadelphia, and Laodicea. When viewed in a map, these locations show somewhat of the outline of a garland, around a courier route of the first century. Saturated with symbols, allusions, metaphors, imagery, and the sights and sounds in it, the book presupposes helpful familiarity with the entire scriptures, especially the books of prophecy as background knowledge. Each church in the cluster receives an admonishing assessment of its spiritual status from Christ. Simon would have enjoyed bringing forth these lofty compositions as also the author of a learned commentary on the book of Revelation. A parallel reading of Simon's Revelation Letters with John Donne's

La Corona, a sequence of seven meditative sonnets on Christ, would be an edifying experience. The language of the lyrics that Christ speaks in Simon's letters is of high elegance, regal in tone and mood, and the sentiments evoked are of reverential awe.

Simon, a Lover of Peace

Simon engages the reader quite vigorously and pleasantly in his poems, yet he maintains a self-effacing persona in all of them. In the prose works, debates, and discourses, his intellect and learning do their service for the task at hand without any desire for personal attention. Any reference to his own self in the poems only shows him as an anonymous servant of Christ. Attempts to construct a personal profile of Simon the man from his songs or even his longer poetical works might lead us to some random hints, but little more. Offenses he has suffered are readily forgotten. In a series of poems called the "Anniversaries" ["വാർഷിക സ്തവങ്ങൾ"] Simon has occasion for joy and grief alike, but he chooses to show only his magnanimity, so that there would be no occasion for conflict. In the song "രാജസുതാ! സമയൊന്നിന്നായിതാ" [SR37 "For yet another year, Oh, royal Son!], he says:

| വേലകൾ വിഭിന്നമാകാൻ കാലമ ണഞ്ഞുള്ള പല | Forces not a few wished to see us scatter; |
| വേളയിലും നിൻ കൈയ്യന്യേ വേറെയൊന്നും തുണച്ചില്ലേ– | Foresight of mercy thine held us together. |

Sometimes it is the brethren themselves that bring disaffection, very much like a house infecting itself. Verse 7 speaks, in very broad terms, about the infightings and dissonance that run continually:

| വാർഷിക സംരക്ഷണത്താൽ ഈർഷ്യ കലർന്നിടാതിന്നീ - | Yearlong stood thy peaceable care |
| വാർഷികമാമുത്സവത്താൽ. കർഷിതരാമെങ്ങൾ നിന്നിൽ | From petulant ire, for this festive fair. |

"ശോഭിത ദൃക്കുകളാം" [SR 40, "Ye of Angelic Sights"] is a ten-year anniversary song of Simon's then-nascent Viyojitha Samaj. Parochial hostilities and intolerance were rife all around. Without listing people or problems, Simon recalls the adversarial powers of the traditional churches taking aim at his organization, and God aborting their plans. However, with any offense past or present, Simon has no vitriol against his opponents.

We have seen that Simon is a pacifist. Samuel Chandanapally notes how fortunate Simon was to have NOT become a witness of the great destruction of Hiroshima and Nagasaki which took place within a year of his passing. The song "മന്നവനാം മിശിഹായെ" [SR 106 "Restless for the Messiah-King"] is a prayer lyric and a lamentation over a war-torn world. The poem cries out for the promised return of the Messiah to establish peace on earth. He is distraught to see that Christians who should oppose war are instead the very agents of them:

യുദ്ധസന്നദ്ധരായയ്യോ ക്രിസ്ത്യ- ന്മാർ-ഘോര	War-geared stand, even Christian men—
യുദ്ധമതിന്നിറങ്ങുന്നു ദയനീയം;	For combats bloody, scarce for thanks:
ബോംബുകളും ടാങ്കുകളും ഭുവനത്തെ തീരെ	Earth lies in mantling dust, coated ashen
ചാമ്പലാക്കി ക്കളയുന്നു പാർത്തായോ	From fuming bombs and ground-tearing tanks.

Other stanzas of the poem lament the power of the gospel betrayed by those to whom the stewardship of this earth has been committed. The good that science was meant to do for the world is now reset to ruin it, instead, he regrets. He closes the song with a prayer for the cleansing of the firmament from the foul odor of military fires and to fill it with the aroma of the flowers of a new order of life.

Among Simon's translations is one entitled "The Golden Age of the Earth," with a sub title, "Translation of a Milton Poem." Stanzas IV, XV, and XVI of Milton's "Nativity Ode" are clearly identifiable in its body. The theme is very millennial, describing the messianic reign of this world in which all war weapons shall be turned into farm tools, and strong morality will make security patrols for civic life needless. Wars and conflicts shall be unheard of, and "Death shall be in futile wait, without a prey to seize." "മേലിലുള്ളെരുശലേമേ" [SR 100, "Jerusalem Above"], "വരുന്നിതാ നാഥൻ" [SR 101, "Here comes the Lord"], "പുത്തൻ യെരുശലേമേ!" [SR 137, "Oh, New Jerusalem"] "അംബയെരുശലേം" [SR 220, "Jerusalem, Noble Mother"], "വന്നിടുവിൻ സോദരരേ!" [SR 245 "To the Summit of Pisgah"], "സീയോൻ മല മീതിൽ മമ" [SR 256, "Over Zion's crest"], "വിശുദ്ധ സീയോൻ" [SR 257 The Lamb leading Zion's host], and "യേശുരാജൻ ആയിരമാണ്ടു" [SR 258 "Christ's royal reign"] are among other poems that are thematically unified, sequence poems that resound Simon's unflagging certainty of the establishment of the thousand-year reign of Christ on earth.

A Sage of Letters

Intellectually and spiritually, Simon is a free citizen of the world and a poet–prophet to the wide world with his Malayalee voice. He is happy and content in his place as the inhabitant of a world that is under restoration through the redemptive work of Christ. Simon sees the entire history of the universe merely as the wrappings of what is moving through the center of it—the *Veda* of Christ, journeying to its culmination in his eternal reign. He wants to have everyone he has seen and known in this world to be with him in the coming City of God. In SR 245 "വന്നീടുവിൻ സോദരരേ" ["Come, Brethren!"] he invites all of his fellow sojourners to the top of the symbolic Pisgah, from where they can gain a view of the Promised Land of eternity. In his signature manner of typological teaching, he offers the exodus journey of Israel as a paradigm of human life on earth. For Israel that journey starts with the liberation from Egyptian slavery, led through the parting Red Sea signifying baptism, shepherded by the lawgiver Moses under the protective canopy of the cloud in the desert sun and guided by the pillar of fire at night, both of which are the express signs of divine presence. At the end of the journey is the Jordan which signifies death, but it is only the door to a believer's future in the millennial kingdom ruled by Christ. A river that proceeds from beneath the throne of God will provide healing and wellbeing to the whole world, says the poem. In SR 244, "നോക്കിലാർക്കും മതിവരാ മന്ദിരം" ["The Look Never Enough"], the poet envisions Salem, the City of Peace, where his brethren and friends will share eternal dwellings of peace with him. SR 227, "മംഗളമായി നാം വാഴും" ["We shall reign in bliss"], a widely sung millennial song, gives a radiant vision of the age ahead, the greatest joy of which will be the poet's eternal reunion with all the souls he had the privilege of loving.

As with Milton, poetics and piety meet as twin powers in Simon, one reinforcing the other, with oracular utterance that forced his people to think and act. Hundreds of his songs fill the published verse volumes across denominations, many of which even have die-hard doctrinal differences with each other. The corpus of writings by Simon spreads across disciplines and offers abundant scope of study and research. While some of his known works have been presumed lost, there are helpful tracers to locate many of his undiscovered writings. Kandathil Mammen Mathew, the late chief editor of *Malayala Manorama*, urged the literary leaders of Malayalam to initiate projects to unearth Simon's still unpublished works, to bring forth updated editions of books that are now out of print, to produce a critical study series of Simon's works, and to build a museum library of Simon literature, both primary and secondary, and memorabilia. A venture of this kind, though multipronged, would not be difficult at all for Simon's followers today. Every Brethren home tends to have a library, which Simon himself modeled for them; compared with other denominations, the Brethren have a high ratio of writers, composers, and publishers, thanks primarily to their Simon legacy; his community overall is well resourced to implement the program that Mammen Mathew recommends.

When *Vedaviharam* was released, celebratory events were held in many cities of the Malabar coast. Cambridge scholar, scientist, Sanskrit poet, and Simon's contemporary I. C. Chacko said in his approbatory message nearly a century ago: "Without anyone's cheering, your verse will be established in Malayalam literature, sooner or later. When many of today's poets have faded into the recesses of time, our progeny shall speak of you as a revered bard like Homer, Virgil, and Milton."[35]

---

[35] I. C. Chacko, Message of Commendation in *Vedaviharam*, February 28, 1931.

Appendix

എന്റെ ഗ്രന്ഥശാല
[My Library]

Simon wrote this poem on request for the Malayala Manorama Special Edition of 1931. The poet tells us how all of life's high reaches exist within anyone's reach through discriminate reading, himself being a grateful discoverer of that truth. Great minds of all ages and cultures have become his close kindred through the written word that surrounds him. One might say that the poem is also a brief intellectual autobiography of Simon, in verse. Please see Chapter I, pp. 88–90 for a portion of this narrative in translation.

സംഭവസംപൂർണ്ണമായ് ജീവിതാംബരമാകെ–
ജ്ജ്റുംഭിത ശബള മേഘങ്ങളാൽ വ്യാകീർണ്ണമായ്
നനാനുഭവതുംഗതരംഗവിചാലന–
മാനദണ്ഡമായ്ഞീരുന്ന നാൽപ്പതിൽപരം കൊല്ലം
എന്നുടെ സർവസ്വവുമായിരുന്നുള്ള സദ്ഗ്ര–
ന്ഥാന്വയനികരമേ! നിങ്ങൾക്കുനമസ്കാരം.
പഞ്ചമവയസ്സിലെൻ കണ്ണുകൾക്കാകർഷണ–
മഞ്ചമായ് ഭവിച്ചിതു "ശിക്ഷാമഞ്ജരി" ദ്വയം.
പദ്മരാഗവും പച്ചക്കല്ലുമെന്നതു പോലെ
നൽപൊടു വിളങ്ങുമീ പുസ്തകങ്ങളിലൊന്നു
കിട്ടുവാൻ കരഞ്ഞു ഞാൻ നിർഭരമപ്പൊളെസ്റെ
ജ്യേഷ്ഠനാം ഗുരുവരൻ പ്രേമപൂർവകമെന്നെ
നോക്കിയിട്ടുടൻ വാങ്ങിത്തന്നിതു ഹരിദുർണ്ണ
പക്ഷമാം ഗ്രന്ഥം പച്ചക്കിളിയെയെത്തുരും മട്ടിൽ.
ആയതു വാങ്ങിച്ചു ഞാനൂണിലുമുറക്കിലു–
മായാതമോദം താഴെ വയ്ക്കാതെ കൈത്തലത്തിൽ
പിടിച്ചു മത്സ്യസാക്കൾ ചൊല്ലിത്തന്നതു കേട്ടു
പഠിച്ചേനെഴുതിനേനൊക്കെയുമോർക്കിൽ ചിത്രം!
അക്കാലംമുതൽ ഗ്രന്ഥവർഗത്തിലേതാകിലു–
മിക്കിശോരാന്തികത്തിലില്ലെന്നുവന്നാകിൽ
ഉൾക്കളമസന്തോഷവഹ്നിയാൽ തപിച്ചിടും
മക്കൾക്കുമാതൃ വിപ്രവാസത്താലെന്നപോലെ.
നിങ്ങളോടുള്ള നിത്യ സംസർഗ്ഗനിരതിയാ–

ലന്നിവൻ ബാലസാധാരണമാം കളികളും
അവശ്യം വേണ്ടതാകും വ്യായാമവിധി താനും
വിവർത്തിപ്പിച്ചേൻ ഗ്രന്ഥവാചനസ്വരൂപമായ്.
വിബുധ മോഹനമാം ഭാവത്ക പത്രാസൃങ്ങൾ
ദിവസം തോറും കുനിഞ്ഞിരുന്നു വീക്ഷിക്കയാൽ
എന്നുടെ പൃഷ്ഠാന്ഥിക്കു ഭവിച്ച വളവിനെ
"ഭംഗി" യെന്നുരക്കുന്നേൻ സംസ്കൃത ഭാഷയിൽ ഞാൻ.
പ്രേമഭാജനങ്ങളേ! നിങ്ങടെ മാഹാത്മ്യത്തെ-
ത്തൂമയിലറിയാത്ത ബാലിശവിദ്യാർത്ഥികൾ
ഭാവത്കപത്രങ്ങളെക്കീറിയും യുഷ്മത് പൃഷ്ഠ-
ത്താവിലാംഗുഷ്ഠ മുഭ്രപതിച്ചും കാണും വിധൗ
എന്നുടലിന്മേലേവം ചെയ്യുവാതാണെനിക്കു
നിർണ്ണയം സഹ്യതരമായതു വിചാരിച്ചാൽ.
നിങ്ങടെ സ്വാമിത്വത്തെക്കാമിക്കുമൂലമെന്റെ
തുംഗമാം സമ്പാദ്യങ്ങളാകവേ തുലഞ്ഞിട്ടും
ലേശവുമനുശയമേശുന്നില്ലിവനഹോ!
നാശമില്ലാത്തയുഷ്മന്മുഖ ദർശനം പോരും.
സുവർണ്ണ പ്രഭതിങ്ങിവിളങ്ങും യുഷ്മന്മൂല-
ലിപികൾ ദൗർഭാഗ്യത്തിൻ സൂചകമായിട്ടല്ല
വിപുലാതലം തീറു വാങ്ങിയ കരണമായ്
വിശയസ്പർശമെന്യേ കാണുന്നു നീണാളിവൻ.
യഥാർത്ഥമിത്രങ്ങളാം നിങ്ങളെന്നരികിൽ വ-
ന്നുദാരതരമായ വാഗ്വിലാസങ്ങൾ മൂലം
ചിലപ്പോൾ പ്രഭുതുല്യം ശാസിച്ചുമപ്രകാരം
ചിലപ്പോൾ ചങ്ങാതിപോൽ ഹിതങ്ങളൂർ ചെയ്തും
ചിലപ്പോൾ കാന്താസമം മാധുര്യവാക്കുരച്ചും
മലപ്പു മനസ്സിനു മാറുമാറാക്കീടുന്നു.
ചൂരലിൻ പ്രയോഗവും കോപവും കൂടാതത്രേ
പൂരണം ചെയ്വതെ ന്റെ ജിജ്ഞാസ നിത്യം നിങ്ങൾ.
നിശ്ശബ്ദതരമായ നിങ്ങൾ തന്നദ്ധ്യാപനം
നിശ്ശേഷമനുകാര്യമല്ലൊരു ഗുരുവിന്നും.

ശരസമ്പൂർണ്ണമാകും ശരധിപേറീടുന്ന
വിരുതനായുള്ളോരു ധാനുഷ്കെന്റയുമേപ്പാൾ
ഉത്തമപുത്രപൗത്രപൂർണമാം കുടുംബത്താ-
ലുദ്വേലം ശോഭിക്കുന്ന ഭവനാധിപന്റെയും
നിർഭരാഭിമാനമാണെന്നുടെ ഗ്രന്ഥങ്ങളേ!

നിഷ്പ്രതിബന്ധം നിങ്ങൾ നിർഭാസ്യമാനങ്ങളായ്
മാമക ഗ്രന്ഥ പേടി തന്നിലധ്യാസിപ്പതു
സാമോദം കാണുമ്പൊഴുതെന്നിലുണ്ടാവതിന്നും.
കാലദേശാദിഭേദമെന്നിയേ വിശ്വാസ്യത
കോലുന്ന സഖാക്കളാം സാഹിത്യപുടങ്ങളേ!
ദുഃഖിയായെന്നേ നിങ്ങളെപ്പോൾ കണ്ടുരുദയ–
വുൾക്കമലത്തിലാർന്നു ഹിമശീതളമായ
വാക്കുകളുച്ചരിച്ചു മാമകസന്താപത്തെ
നീക്കിയതില്ല? ദാഹം വിശപ്പെന്നിവയ്ക്കുള്ളോ–
രൂക്ഖിലവും മറന്നീടുവാൻ പോരും വണ്ണം
സത്കവിതാമൃതത്തിൻ മഞ്ജുലവർഷണത്താൽ
എത്രഘട്ടങ്ങളെന്നെയാനന്ദ നൃത്തം ചെയ്യി–
ട്ടുത്തര ലോകവാസസൗഖ്യമേകിയതില്ല?

    എത്ര നൂറ്റാണ്ടു പിന്നോട്ടിവനെ കൊണ്ടുപോയി
    വിത്രുതവിജ്ഞാനികൾ, യുദ്ധവീരന്മാർ, ഭൂപർ,
    അത്ഭുതതരത്യാഗമിയന്ന യോഗീന്ദ്രന്മാ–
    രത്യർത്ഥം സുകുമാരകലയിൽ പ്രവീണന്മാർ
    എന്നിവർ തങ്ങളുമായ് കൂട്ടിമുട്ടിച്ചു തദീ–
    യോന്നതിക്കുള്ള മർമ്മമറിയും വിധമിവൻ.
    വിഖ്യാതനീത്യാ വിശ്വമടക്കി വാണുള്ളൊരു
    വിക്ടോറിയാഖ്യയാർന്ന രാജ്ഞി തൻ സൗധം മുതൽ
    ബുക്കർ ടി വാഷിങ്ടൻ്റെ കുടിലോളവുമെന്നെ
    വാക്കെന്ന രഥത്തൂടെ നയിച്ചു ചിരം നിങ്ങൾ.
    ചിലപ്പോൾ നിങ്ങളെന്നെ സമുദ്രം കടത്തീട്ടു
    വലിപ്പമേറുമമേരിക്ക തൻ പ്രസിദ്ധമാം
    ഷിക്കാഗോ, ഫിലാദൽഫ്യാ, ന്യൂയോർക്കന്നുള്ള ലോക–
    വിഖ്യാത നഗരങ്ങൾ കാണിക്കുന്നനായാസം.

കാളിദാസനും ഭവഭൂതിയും ഷേക്സ്പീയറും
കോളെഴും മിൽട്ടൺ നവ്യരവീന്ദ്രൻ മുതലായ
ചൂളിടാക്കവിപ്രൗഢർ നിങ്ങടെ വൈഭവത്താൽ
മേളിച്ചു നിന്നുനിന്നീടുന്നെൻ ഫലകത്തിൽ.
തത്ത്വശാസ്ത്രാഭിഖ്യമാം കപ്പലിൽ കർണ്ണധാര–
വൃത്തിക്കു പേർകേട്ടുള്ള സോക്രട്ടീസ്, പ്ലേറ്റോ, ന്യൂട്ടൺ
സ്പെൻസറും ക്യാന്റും ബേക്കൺ തുടങ്ങിയുള്ളവരെല്ലാ–
മെൻ സഭമ്മത്ഥിതികൾ ദിനവും ചിത്രം! ചിത്രം!
എന്തുവിസ്മയമിതെൻ ചിത്തദൗർബല്യത്തിന്നു
ബന്ധുര പരിഹാരം ചെയ്‌വതിന്നായും തദ്വദ്
സന്തതം മമ കൃത്യോൽസാഹനത്തിനും നിൽപ്പു

ചിന്താതിഗാഭ ചിന്തും ഭഗവത്ഗീതാ രത്നം.
പുസ്തകത്തട്ടിലിന്നരികേ കാണുന്നുഞാൻ
പുസ്തകങ്ങളിൽ സർവോൽകൃഷ്ടമാം ബൈബിൾ ഗ്രന്ഥം.
ഇദ്ധരാതലത്തിങ്കലൊരുവനുണ്ടാകയി–
ല്ലിദ്ധമാമിതിനുള്ള ദീപ്തിയെ വർണിക്കുവാൻ.
യാതൊന്നു രണ്ടായിരം കൊല്ലം മുൻപവനിയിൽ
സ്ഫീതമായ് പരന്നിരുന്നുള്ളൊരു മൗഢ്യധ്വാന്തം
നോദനം ചെയ്തു സാക്ഷാൽ വെളിച്ചം നൽകീ തത്വ
ബോധമീ ലോകത്തിന്നു കരസ്ഥമാകും വണ്ണം;
അമൃതമൊഴുകുന്ന യാതൊന്നിൻ വചസ്സിനാ–
ലമരതുല്യരായോർ ബ്രിട്ടാന്യാ കിരാതന്മാർ;
അതുപോൽ മനുഷ്യരായ് ത്തീർന്നിതു ദ്വീപാന്തര–
സ്ഥിതരാം നരമാംസ ഭോക്താക്കൾ യാതൊന്നിനാൽ;
പ്രകൃതി ശാസ്ത്രം ജ്യോതിശാസ്ത്രവും രസതത്രം
സുകൃതി നിഷേവ്യമാമിതര ശാസ്ത്രങ്ങളും
യാതൊന്നിൻ പ്രഭാവത്താലുണ്ടായിപ്പരിഷ്കൃത–
ഭൂതലമാക്കി തീർത്തിബ് ഭൂഖണ്ഡമഞ്ചിനേയും,
രാജ്യതന്ത്രാഭിജ്ഞന്മാർ, ചക്രവർത്തികളാത്മ
രാജ്യത്തെ കയ്യടക്കി വാഴുന്ന യതീന്ദ്രന്മാർ,
സാഹിത്യാംബുജി യേഴും കുടിച്ചു വറ്റിച്ചുള്ള
സൗഹിത്യപരിപൂർണ്ണചിത്തരാം കുംഭോദ്ഭവർ,
ഈദൃശ്യ മഹത്തുക്കൾ സന്തതം തല താഴ്ത്തി–
പ്പാദസീമനി വീണു നമസ്യ ചെയ്തീടുന്ന
ശ്രീദനാം യേശുക്രിസ്തു തന്നുടെ പരിശുദ്ധ
ചേതസ്സിൻ പ്രതിമയായ് യാതൊന്നു വിളങ്ങുന്നു,
ആ ദിവ്യമർമ്മോക്തികൾക്കുള്ളൊരു കേളീരംഗം
മദ് ദുഃഖ പരിഹൃതിക്കേറ്റൊരു സ്വാന്താലാപം,
സദ് ദർശനാനന്ദത്തെത്തരുന്ന ദിവ്യാലേഖ്യം
ഭദ്രമായ് വിജയിപ്പൂ ബിണ്ണിയ യാചാഗ്രാന്മാർക്കം.
ജാതിയാം പുക തട്ടീട്ടസ്ഫടമായ് ത്തീർന്നുള്ളൊരു
മേദിനീ ദേവനേയുമവ്വണ്ണം തേവനേയും
ഏതുമേ ഭേദം കൂടാതൊന്നിച്ചു പേറിടുന്ന
തീവണ്ടി പോലാം ഗ്രന്ഥ ഫലകങ്ങളേ! നിങ്ങൾ.
നിങ്ങളോടനുയോജിച്ചീടുന്ന നേരമതു–
തുംഗ വിദ്വേഷികളും മിത്രങ്ങളായീടുന്നു.
പറയൻ ദ്വിജനായി ത്തീരുന്ന ദിവ്യവഴി
പറയുന്നുച്ചത്തിലെൻ ഗ്രന്ഥപേടിക നിത്യം;
തിരുവള്ളുവരുടെ കുറളിനടുത്തല്ലോ
മരുവുന്നാദികവി തന്നുടെ രാമായണം;

ബൈബിളിൻ സമീപത്തു ഖുർആനുംറുഗ്വേദവും
വൈപരീത്യത്തിൻ കണം പോലുമില്ലാതെ കാൺമൂ.
ഗാന്ധിയാം മഹാരഥനുച്ചയ്സ്സായ് നിഷേധിക്കു-
മന്ധമായിത്തഞ്ഞെ യെത്രയോ മുൻപേ തന്നെ
പുല്ലുപോൽ ഗണിച്ചുള്ള സദ്ഗ്രന്ഥ സന്ദോഹമേ!
കല്ചിച്ച മനം പോലുമുരുക്കാൻ ശക്തർ നിങ്ങൾ.
കർത്തവ്യമൂഢനായിരുന്നോരെനിക്കേറ്റ
കർതവ്യമുപദേശിച്ചെന്നതു മാത്രമല്ല,
ക്ഷീണിതനായിരുന്നോരെൻ മനസ്സിൽ വിനോദാർത്ഥം
ചേണുറ്റ വാണി സന്ദർഭോചിതമോതിക്കൊണ്ടും
വാഗ്വാദ യുദ്ധങ്ങളിലപരിത്യാജ്യമായ
യോഗ്യമാമായുധങ്ങൾ തുടരെ തന്നുകൊണ്ടും
വർത്തിച്ച മാമകീന ഗ്രന്ഥാഖ്യസഖാക്കളേ!
വർത്തിപ്പേൻ നിരന്തരം നിങ്ങളുമൊന്നിച്ചഹം.

Bibliography

Baylor, Michael G., ed. *The Radical Reformation: Cambridge Texts in the History of Political Thought*. Cambridge: Cambridge University Press, 1991.
Boesky, Amy. "*Paradise Lost* and the Multiplicity of Time." In *A New Companion to Milton*, ed. Thomas Corns. Hoboken, NJ: John Wiley & Sons, 2016, 408–20.
Chandanapally, Samuel. *Mahakavi K. V. Simon: A Study*. Pathanamthitta, Kerala: Anaswara Publishers, 1983. https://www.studylight.org/commentaries/eng/bcc.
Clarke, Adam. *Clarke's Commentary: The Song of Songs*. https://www.studylight.org/commentaries/eng/acc/song-of-solomon.html. Last accessed October 15, 2022.
Coffman, James Burton. *Genesis: Coffman's Commentaries on the Bible*. https://www.studylight.org/commentaries/eng/bcc.html.
Corns, Thomas N., ed. *A Companion to Milton*. Oxford: Blackwell Publishing, 2003.
Cowper, William, Trans. *Poemata: Latin, Greek and Italian Poems by John Milton* (2004). https://ivu.org/history/renaissance/milton_poemata.htm. Accessed June 16, 2022.
Darbishire, Helen, ed. *The Early Lives of Milton*. London: Constable, 1932.
Das, Kamala. *My Story*. New Delhi: Sterling Publishers, 1976. https://archive.org/stream/in.ernet.dli.2015.220167/2015.220167.My-Story_djvu.txt. Accessed June 14, 2022.
Deffinbaugh, Robert. "The Story of the 'Seed'—The Coming of the Promised Messiah." https://bible.org/article/story-seed-coming-promised-messiah.
Donne, John. "Sermon LXXII." In *Eighty Sermons Preached by that Learned and Reverend Divine John Donne*, ed. Evelyn Simpson and Reuben Potter. https://contentdm.lib.byu.edu/digital/collection/JohnDonne/id/3493/rec/2, 11–12. Accessed June 14, 2022.
Echoes of Service: A Record of Labor in the Lord's Name in Many Lands. London and Bath: 1899–1935.
George, K. M., Gen. ed. *Adhunika Malayala Sahitya Charitram Prasthanangaliloode* [Modern Malayalam Literature through Literary Movements]. 4th ed. Kottayam, Kerala: DC Books, 2011.
George, K. M. *A. R. Rajaraja Varma*. New Delhi: Sahitya Akademi, 1979.
Hawn, Michael C. "History of Hymns: All Hail the Power of Jesus' Name." https://www.umcdiscipleship.org/.
Hunter, Stevie and William B. Hunter. "Milton's Urania: The Meaning, Not the Name, I Call." *Studies in English Literature 1500–1900*, Vol. 28, No. 1, *The English Renaissance* (Winter 1988), pp. 95–111.

Jamieson, Robert, Andrew R. Fausset, and David Brown. *Commentary Critical and Explanatory of the Whole Bible.* https://www.blueletterbible.org/commentaries/jfb/. Accessed October 15, 2022.

Jani, Pankaj L. https://www.wisdomlib.org/hinduism/book/jarasandhavadha-mahakavyam/d/doc419449.html.

Kurien, T. A. *K. V. Simon: A Biography.* 2nd ed. Angamally, Kerala: Premier Printers, 1990.

Levi, Peter. *Eden Renewed: The Public and Private Life of John Milton.* New York: St. Martin's Press, 1997.

Lewalski, Barbara K. *The Life of Milton: A Critical Biography.* Hoboken, NJ: Wiley & Sons, 2008.

Luxon, Thomas H., Gen. ed. *The John Milton Reading Room: The Complete Poetry and Selected Prose of John Milton,* 1997–2022. Hanover, NH: Dartmouth College. https://milton.host.dartmouth.edu/reading_room/contents/text.shtml.

Malekandathil, Pius. "A Commonwealth of Christians in the Indian Ocean: A Study on the Christians of St.Thomas Tradition in South-West India." In *Early Christian Communities of the St. Thomas Tradition in India,* ed. Peter Kannampuzha. Kochi, India: Syro-Malabar Liturgical Research Center, 2017, 88–137. https://www.nasrani.net/. Accessed June 13, 2022.

Manavalan, Paul. *Kerala Samskaravum Christhava Missionarimarum* [The Culture of Kerala and Christion Missionaries]. Kottayam, Kerala: DC Books, 1990.

Mathai, K. T. *Kalathinte Spandanam* [The Beats of Time]. Compiled by K. M. John and K. M. Philippose. Mumbai: Ebenezer Printers, 2004.

Mathai, Varghese. *The Malabar Mandate.* 2nd ed. Zurich: ICHE, 2015.

Menon, Sridhara, A. *Kerala Samskaram* [The Cultural Heritage of Kerala]. 5th ed. Kottayam: DC Books, 2012.

Michaelbryson.net. Accessed June 29, 2022.

Milton, John. *Paradise Lost.* http://knarf.english.upenn.edu/Milton. Accessed October 15, 2022.

Narayanan, M. G. S. "Gundert Was the Foster-father of Malayalam, says MGS." *The Hindu,* February 3, 2006. https://www.thehindu.com/news/cities/kozhikode/gundert-was-foster-father-of-malayalam-says-mgs/article8186281.ece.

Panicker, Ayyappa. *A Short History of Malayalam Literature.* 6th ed. Thiruvananthapuram: Information and Public Relations Department, 2006. Retrieved from Archive.org, August 22, 2022.

Philip, K. A. "A Short Biography of K. V. Simon." In *Sangeetha Ratnavali,* ed. P. M. Daniel. Mylapra, Kerala: Gospel Tract Society, 1983, xvi–xxii.

Pillai, Govinda, P. *Theranjedutha Prabandangal* [Selected Treatises]. Trichur: Kerala Sahitya Akademi, 2012.

Pillai, Krishna N. *Kairaliyude Katha* [The Story of Malayalam]. 3rd ed. Kottayam: DC Books, 2018.

Simon, Kunnumpurathu Varghese. *Bible Viswasikkamo?* [Can the Bible be Believed?] http://www.bethanyaroma.com/bookspage.php?chapter_id=345#page/20. Accessed October 16, 2022.

Simon, Kunnumpurathu Varghese. *A Commentary on the Book Revelation.* 6th ed. Vennikulam, Kerala: K. V. Simon Foundation, 1987.

Simon, Kunnumpurathu Varghese. "Ente Grandhasala" [My Library]. *Malayala Manorama* Special Edition, 1931.

Simon, Kunnumpurathu Varghese. *Malankara Viyojithan: A Bimonthly 1919–1935* [paper and digitally available, but not entirely]. http://www.bethanyaroma.com/bethanyaroma_articlesdes.php?articles_id=MTc=.

Simon, Kunnumpurathu Varghese. *Nikalovya Matham* [Nicoloite Religion or Priesthood]. Angamally, Kerala: Premier Printers, 1936. Rpt. by C. K. Sam, Edayaranmula, Kerala, 1988.

Simon, Kunnumpurathu Varghese. *Pashandta Mardanam.* Kottayam, Kerala: Malayala Manorama Press, 1924.

Simon, Kunnumpurathu Varghese. *Sangeetha Ratnavali* [with glossary], ed. P. M. Daniel. Mylapra: Gospel Tract Society, 1983.

Simon, Kunnumpurathu Varghese. *Satyaprakashini: A Response to Three Speeches of P. Krishnan Nambiathiri.* 2nd ed. Angamally: Satyaprakashini Depot, 1927.

Simon, Kunnumpurathu Varghese. *Satyaveda Mukuram:* [The Mirror of the Word]*: A Refutation of Thomas Menachery's Bible and the Protestant Religion*]. Edayaranmula, Kerala, np., 1929. http://www.bethanyaroma.com/bookspage.php?chapter_id=168#page/8leandProtestantism.

Simon, Kunnumpurathu Varghese. *Shaa Laptaya* or *Utthama Geetha Vyakhyanam* [An Interpretation of the Song of Songs]. Rpt. Edayaranmula: Emmaus Books, 1983.

Simon, Kunnumpurathu Varghese. *Thritwa Prabhodika* [On the Trinity]. Edayaranmula, Kerala, 1941. Digital edition. http://www.bethanyaroma.com/BethanyAroma_booksdetails.php?books_id=OQ==.

Simon, Kunnumpurathu Varghese. *Vedaviharam.* 4th ed. Kottayam: CMS Press, 1984.

Simon, Kunnumpurathu Varghese. *Verpadu Sabhakalude Charitram* [A History of the Brethren Churches]. Tiruvalla, Kerala: Sathyam Publications, 1999.

Summers, Joseph H. *The Muse's Method: An Introduction to Paradise Lost.* Binghamton, NY: Center for Medieval and Early Renaissance Studies, 1981.

Sunil, V. T. *Sangeetha Nikhandu* [A Dictionary of Indian Music]. Kottayam, Kerala: DC Books, 2012.

"The Venerable Bede." https://celticsaints.org/2014/0526a.html. Accessed June 14, 2022.

Valayil, Stanley John. "The Rise of New Generation Churches in Kerala Christianity." In *World Christianity*, ed. Martha Fredericks and Dorottya Naggy. Leiden: Brill, 2020, 273.

Varghese, Edayaranmula K. M., ed. *Mahakavi K. V. Simon: Janma Satabdi Smaranika* [Centenary Essays]. Kottayam: National Book Stall, 1984.

Viswanathan, Susan. *The Christians of Kerala: History, Belief and Ritual among the Yakoba*. 2nd ed. Delhi: Oxford University Press, 1999, 2001.

Wariboko, Nimi and L. William Oliveri. "Society for Pentecostal Studies at 50 Years." *Pneuma*, Vol. 42 (December 9, 2020), pp. 327–33. Pdf, p. 2. https://brill.com/view/journals/pneu/42/3-4/article-p327_1.xml?language=en.

Wolfe, John M. et al., ed. *Complete Prose Works of John Milton*. 5 vols. New Haven, CT: Yale University Press, 1953.

Index of Key Names and Terms

Abraham, K. E. (early disciple of Simon and the eventual founder of the million-strong Indian Pentecostal Church) 66, 85

Achuten, Itty (Ezhava physician, a distinguished resource person who helped with the compilation of *Hortus Malabaricus*) 102, 104–5

Addai, Mar 32

Ajamedham (goat sacrifice in Vedic times) 60–1

Anabaptist 183, 187

Anglican grammars and dictionaries 102

Arattupuzha (riverside town near Simon's home, the site of Simon's conventions and his public farewell) 67, 72, 96

Arnos Patiri/Ernestus Hanxleden (early European missionary master of Malayalam) 102

Artasastra of Kautilya (influential treatise of economic and statecraft believed to have been created in 2nd century CE or earlier) 102

Arulappan, John C. (associate of Anthony Groves and founder of native missions of Christianpetta, center of a widespread revival in the 1850's in Tirunalveli, South India) 36, 78

Athanasius, St. 90

Augustine, St. 55
  his power of logic in *The City of God* 63

Bailey, Benjamin (translator of the Bible) 12, 23, 34, 106
  among the first major dictionary-makers of Malayalam 103
  creator of the first Malayalam printing press 21, 22–3, 34

Baker, Henry, Sr. (19th century CMS missionary and pioneering European educator in Kerala) 21

Banyan tree 181–2

Baptism, questions on 52–3, 69, 73, 92–3, 183
  Simon's own book on 187, 189, 218, 232

Basel Mission 15

*Bhajan*s/devotional hymns (composed according to Indian musicology) 32, 111
  examples from Simon's compositions 203–18

Bhakti movement/Pietism
  Simon on par in *bhakti* with Ezhuthachan 10
  bhajans and *bhakti* 32
  bhakti in the earlier periods 11–12
  Kochukunju Updeshi (*bhakti* poet) 42
  literary movement against *champoo* sensuality 100
  language of *bhakti* in Simon's verse 192
  best *lakshanas* (attributes) of, in Vidwankutty and Simon 228

Bhashaposhini/Bhasha Poshini (the earliest literary magazine of Kerala founded by Kandathil Varghese Mappilai) 81, 108

Brethren Church (started by missionary Anthony Groves) 67
  non-clerical presbytery model like the Baptists 73
  strictly non-violent conduct and easy victimization 74–8, 86–7
  higher levels of literacy 190, 233
  Viyojitha merger with 184

Buchanan, Claudius (1766–1815, author of *Asian Researches,* organized the translation of the Bible with Patriarch Dionysius I and his native clergy; presented with the lone copy of the Peshitta Bible; translation of the gospels and the Peshitta) 20–3

Calvin, John 184–5
Caste as social order 18
Cerusseri, devotional poet of Malayalam 32
Champoo (poetic kin of *Sandesha kavya* or message poems) 100
Channar Revolts 16–18
Chinnamma (Simon's only daughter, married to George Kochumuriyil in 1941) 39
Chitramezhuth (aka Artist K. M. Varghese, literary critic) 49, 55–6, 98
"Circular 83", (Mar Thoma bishop's decree of excommunication of Simon) 42
CMS (Church Mission Society) 19, 21
Common Book of Prayer, The 186
Coonan Cross, Oath of 13
Cotym College (the original name of CMS College in Kottayam) 22
Courier Press in Bombay 21

Dalits (slaves or worse) 19
 see also caste
Damodaran, N. (award winning translator; chief editor of *Kerala Kaumudi,* junior resident at Simon's home school) 11
Dandin (7th century South Indian grammarian who set the criteria for the *mahakavya* [epic]) 191
Daniel, K. N. (editor of *Sabha Tharaka,* the Marthomite periodical) 50–2
 aggressive defender of the Mar Thoma Church; hostile polemics and doctrinal attacks on Simon; leaves the Mar Thoma and establishes the St. Thomas Evangelical Church of India 52
 Athmavritta kadhanam, his autobiography 56

Daniel, K. M. literary critic; Simon's nephew 11, 85, 179
 estimate of the number of Simon's hymns 211
Daniel, P. M., Mahopadhyaya 46–7
Das, Kamala, writer 39
Das, R. C. (associate of Krishnan Nambiathiri) 58
de Meneziz, Alexio (Portuguese bishop in Kerala) 21
Dionysius I (patriarch of the Orthodox Church in Kerala) 20–1

Edayaranmula (village adjacent to the temple town of Aranmula) 10, 37, 88
Ephrem, St. 12, 32
Ezhuthachen (Father of modern Malayalam, spelt also as "Ezhuthachan") 10
 Simon placed on a par with; exemplar of Bhakti verse; the "father of modern Malayalam" 32, 101

Franklin, Benjamin 31

Gadha (a poetic meter used in legends in Sanskrit and Indian vernaculars, common also in *Bhakti* literature) 192
George, K. M. (public intellectual, discipled by Simon) 11, 109
Gerard, Father (author of *Alankarasastra/ The Art of Rhetoric*) 107

Hundert, Herman (learned German missionary and educator in Kerala) 23, 98
 "foster father of Malayalam"; gives Malayalam its name; creates the Malayalam dictionary, publishes the first newspapers in Malayalam 106
Gurukula 10, 25
Hall, Bishop Joseph, *Reasons for Church Government* addressed to 188
Hortus Malabaricus (compendium of medical names of plants) the first printed work of native medicine produced by Dutch

governor Hendrik van Rhede; the first published work in Europe with Malayalam content 104–5

Howitzer, The (series of polemical essays in response to the attacks of K.N. Daniel) 48

Indian Pentecostal Church 66, 85

James, D. (Tamil music maestro and briefly a resident in Edayaranmula); Simon's tutor in Carnatic music; inspiration for Simon's early compositions in Tamil 37

Jewish diaspora in Kerala 7

Kariattil, Joseph (author of *Vedatarkam*, a work of apologetics) 103

Kunnumpurathu (Simon's "house name") 24, 25, 97

Ezhuthachan (father of modern Malayalam); stabilized the 51-alphabet body of Malayalam with his great *Bhakti* works such as *Adhyatma Ramayanam, Harinama Keerthanam, Bhagavatam Kilipattu* and others 101

Kannassas (family of Malayalam poets in Niranam) 100–1

Kathakali and *Thullal* (long, narrative dances by trained performers) 37, 101

Knanayites (endogamous Christian sect in Kerala named after Thomas or Thomma of Cana) 13

Kochukunju Upadeshi (Christian *bhakti* poet and spiritual leader; known also as Sadhu Kochukunju, Moothampackal Kochukunju) resident of Edayaranmula, like Simon, faces ecclesiastical trial by the Marthomite hierarchy 6, 11, 42, 69, 72

Kovoor, Abraham (Vicar General of the Mar Thoma Church) presided over the trial of Simon's excommunication 21, 40–4

London Mission Society (LMS) 19

Luther, Martin 9, 33, 34, 43–4, 68, 97, 184–5

Mahabharata (India's ancient epic) 10, 82, 101

Malabar Coast (general name for coastal Kerala) 9
    caste system 13
    tiny principalities or fiefdoms; ecclesial and commercial interests of foreign powers 11–19
    Milton's mention of in *Paradise Lost* 181

Malankara Viyojithan/The Viyojithan (Simon's acclaimed journal, reform-oriented, and alternately titled *The Malabar Separatist*) 48–50

Malayala Manorama (leading daily of India) corporate media group inclusive of print and visual media; widely recognized for its ongoing patronage of arts and letters 56, 81–2, 88

Malpan, Abraham (leader of the Marthomite reform, called "the Wyclif of Kerala") 23–4

Mammen, P. E. (reformist Marthomite priest) publisher of *Suvisesha Deepika* (The Gospel Light) 43

Manipravala 100

Manjari (very popular poetic meter in Malayalam, typically used in *Bhakti* verse) 100

Manso, Giovanni Battista, Marquis of Villa 183

Manu Smriti/The Code of Manu (ancient legal text of Hinduism that provides the model of social order) 61

Mappilai, Mammen K. C. (chief editor of *Malayala Manorama* the leading daily of India; patron of letters) 56, 81
    urged Simon to write *Vedaviharam* 93

Mar Thoma Church (reformist denomination that broke away from the traditional Syrian Church in the late 19th century) 24, 34–6, 38, 42, 44, 50, 52, 95, 97, 184

Maramon Convention (Asia's largest annual gathering of Christians) 29, 31
Margom Kali (communal dance that musically narrates the lore of Apostle Thomas) 14
Mari, Mar (early Persian bishop who arrived in India with Mar Addai) 32
Menachery, Father Thomas (Catholic clergyman); wrote *The Protestant Religion and the Bible*; Simon wrote *Satya Veda Mukuram* in response 51
Menon, Chattoo (native Malayalam expert assisting Benjamin Bailey in the translation of the Bible) 103
Milton, John 32, 43, 50, 68, 77, 89, 97
   Simon-Milton comparison 129–30
   biographical and literary similarities 179–233
   both as orators, polemicists, tract-writers, *Of Prelatical Episcopacy* 186
   Of Reformation 185–6
   The Reason for Church Government 186
   times and home grounds of Simon and Milton 184–7
   Vedaviharam and *Paradise Lost*: concordant contents 193–9
   creation and presentation of Adam and Eve 196–8
   scenes of temptation and fall in Simon and Milton 199–202
   mention of Malabar, Deccan, and Ganges and Hydaspes 180–1
Mithavadi/The Moderate (C. Krishnan's newspaper, hosted events for Simon in Northern Kerala) 51
Mohan, Sanal 18
Moor S. Padmanabha Panicker, Simon's mentor 27–8
   writes the verse portrait of Simon in *Vedaviharam* 183
Moshe/Moses Valsalom (teacher, musician, devotional poet and evangelist with the LMS) 33
Munro, Colonel John (Dewan of Travancore); strong advocacy for the princely state and its people; supports the abolition of the "bare breast law"; brings educators from England; establishes the groundwork of modern education, starting with the "Cotym College" 17, 21–2
Muziris (city, prominent port in Kerala's maritime trade, and according to tradition, the place of the arrival of Apostle Thomas in CE 52, 10, 11, 13

Nagel, Volbrecht (German missionary and early contemporary of Simon and Tamil David) 28–9
   founding leader of Kerala's Brethren movement and composer of over 120 popular Malayalam songs 32
Nambiar, Kunchan (prime name in *Thullal,* a musical dance narrative in Malayalam, entirely satirical) 26
Nambiathiri, Chavara P. Krishnan (aka Swami Agamananda, campaigned against Christianity) 56–5
   organized debates 67, 69, 188
   writes a tract, "Did Christ Die on the Cross" [trans] 57
   Simon responds with the reply tract, "The Crucified Christ" 57
Nangeli (Ezhava woman who sacrificed her life resisting the "bare breast law" of Travancore) 17
Nazrani Deepika (major Malayalam daily in Simon's time) 190
Nazranis (another name for the Syrian Christian community, derivative of "Nazarenes," meaning, "followers of Jesus of Nazareth") 14
Nestorians (8th-century Chaldean or Nestorian group that arrived in Kerala) 12
Nishadananda (founder of Sri Krishna Ashram) 11

Onam (harvest festival of Kerala) 10
Oommen, W. O. (Anglican clergyman and educator, invites Simon to Mallappally and supports his labors in that town) 51

Orthodox Church (ancient Church of Kerala that traces its origin to the one St. Thomas founded) 11–15, 19–20, 21–3, 35, 40, 44, 58, 221

Pampa (major river of Kerala that passes through Simon's hometown); a trade route before road and rail 10, 24
   site of Maramon Convention 31
   renown in literature 45
Panicker, Mooloor S. Padmanabha (poet, legislator, physician and mentor of Simon) 11, 27–8, 82, 183
Paremmakkal, Thoma Kathanar (author of *Vartamanapusthakam*/Journey to Rome, the first travelogue in Malayalam 103
Pattu era 98–100
Peaneus, Clement (author of *Samkshepa Vedartam,* the first book printed in Malayalam) 102
Peshitta (Orthodox Bible written in Aramaic, Dionysius I gifts it to Claudius Buchanan, who donates it to Cambridge University) 15
   also identified as *Estrangelo* 21
Pietist movement 32, 33.
Pietists, German 32
Pillai, Govinda, P. (Marxist scholar and journalist) 42, 57, 90, 108
Pillai, Narayana, T. K. (close friend of Simon and a leader in Simon's *Sahitya Darshini*); Simon's elegy, *Nishakalam,* a tribute to Pillai) 45
Pillai, Sankara (literary enthusiast, plantation owner and Simon's "stager") 26, 27
Plymouth Brethren 10
Poonthanam (bhakti poet) 32
Pope Alexander VII 15, 26
Portuguese 19, 21
   burning of all Syriac libraries and writings 14

Qurbana, The Holy 23, 24, 33

Ragas 9, 32, 82, 228
Ram, Rishi (Krishnan Nambiathiri's debate panelist) 58, 63–4
Ramban Pattu (also known as *Thoma Parvam* or the Song of Thomas (1601), by Thoma Ramban Maliekal) 14

Sabha Tharaka (official magazine of the Mar Thoma Church, ed. K.N. Daniel) 42–3
Sahitya Darshini (Simon's literary academy) 44
Samkshepavedartam (first printed work of Malayalam, but produced and published in Rome) 81, 102
Sammarjini/The Cleanser or "The Job Description of a Marthomite Editor," Simon's response to K. N. Daniel's lampoon, *A Brethren Leader's Competencies* 50, 55
Sangam/Sanghom (name of the pre-modern, South Indian cultural and literary era) 11–12, 99
Sankaracharya (8th-century Vedic scholar and ascetic, exponent of Advaita philosophy, and reformer of Hinduism) 61
Satyaprakashini (print version of Simon's debates with Krishnan Nambiathiri) 64
Seed of the woman 59, 202, 204–5, 209–10, 216
Simon, Kunnumpurathu Varghese (Mahakavi/poet-laureate or poet of the epic)
   precocious child poet of *samasyas* [verse riddles] and on demand poems 26–7
   his family and its influence, teenage schoolmaster 31–2
   impact of Tamil David revival addresses 28–31
   Cherian, Simon's older brother and preceptor 25–6; 29–33
   sudden illness and death 38
   far-sighted tutelage of Simon 179
   Thomas (another older brother) dies 31

Simon composes *bhakti* verse; founds
the Viyojitha-Brethren movement
10, 44
the *Malankara Viyojithan* magazine
48–9, 65
Sangeetha Ratnavali (210 hymns,
published 1925) 111
debates with K. N. Daniel 50–5; and
P. Krishnan Nambiathiri, 56–60, 63
debate with Kesavan Jolsyar 65–6
publishes *Vedaviharam* in 1931;
Lecture circuits along the Malabar
corridor and in Madras 83–4
Mooloor's verse portrait of Simon 183
Simon's opponents 87–8
Simon's library hauled away; theft of
gold medal 91
George Mattackal exposes a plan to
snub Simon; P. Govinda Pillai's
outrage at other injustices done 42,
57, 80
Simon's autobiography disappears 25, 88
Solomon (King), trade relations with
ancient India attributed to 12
Song of Songs (Solomon's work),
allusions and interpretations 120,
222–4
See also *Vedaviharam*
Swamy, K. R. N. 21
Synod of Diamper or Udayamperoor 21
Syriac/Aramaic 9
lingua franca of the early centuries 14
used both in business and religious
life by Syrian Christians until the
arrival of the Portuguese, 15, 21
Syrian Christians (Indian faith community
of 1st century founded by Apostle
Thomas)
socially privileged 14
secure and independent until 1500 CE;
forceful subjection to Portuguese
colonialism and Catholicism; their
repudiation control by the Oath of
the Coonan Cross 14–15

Tamil David (the popular identification of
V. D. David, a SriLankan evangelist
of wide renown at the turn of
the 20th century for igniting the
historic revivals of Travancore)
Simon's praise for David 28–31,
34–6
Taravad (ancestral Hindu homestead in
Kerala) 18
Thoma Pattu/Song of St Thomas
(traditional song among Syrian
Christians that narrates the Acts of
Thomas) 32
Thomas, M. M. (Governor, ecumenical
theologian and writer) 42
Thomas, P. J. of Madras University
(literary historian and economist)
49
Travancore (old name for Simon's native
royal province, now part of the state
of Kerala)
Sahitya Parishad in its capital,
Thiruvananthapuram 9, 82–3
Claude Buchanan's visit to 12, 20–2
practice of slavery in 39
LMS, CMS Missions in 40
Vedaviharam in school readings 84
Translation of European works 106–7

Untouchability 16
See also *savarnas* and *avarnas* 16–17
Ussher, Bishop James, *Of Prelatical
Episcopacy* addressed to 188

Vallam kali/snake boat race 10–11
Varghese, Mahakavi K. M. (poet and
literary critic, Simon's nephew and
personal assistant) 11, 14
Varma, Rajaraja (grammarian and poet)
66, 227
Varapuzha grammars and dictionaries 102
Vedaviharam (Simon's epic poem of
12,000 lines, published in 1931)
Simon laureled "Mahakavi";
its composition encouraged
by Mammen Mappilai and
Chitramezhuth; the entire Book
of Genesis versified, in fourteen
Dravidian meters; Hebraic-
Christian vision of history 193
music and metrics in 14–15, 227, 233

invocation 128, 194
prayers in 170
record speed of composition 192
presentation and meritorious
 recognition of Ch 19; "the Burning of
 Sodom" at the Sahitya Parishad 81–4
P. K. Koshy's gift to clear all publishing
 debts of Simon; theft of the civic
 medal 91
wit and wisdom in 175–8
Simon's innovation in using a Semitic
 core story for a Malayalam epic 192–3
diction-rich work of profound learning
 220
the era of mahakavyas/epics in
 Malayalam 193

Vidwankutty/Yusthus Joseph or Rama
 Iyer, biography 33, 36–7
Viyojitha Movement 50
 merges with the Brethren in
 1929; *The Viyojithan,* short for
 Malankara Viyojithan Magazine,
 runs 1819–1935 under Simon's
 editorship; a model magazine
 48–50, 55, 65, 86, 94

Wesley, Charles 33
Wesley, John 28, 34, 40, 70
Wesleyan Holiness 34
Whitefield, George 10, 28, 70

Zinzendorf, Count Nicholas Ludwig 32